Tourism Management
an introduction

Clare Inkson & Lynn Minnaert

SAGE has been part of the global academic community since 1965, supporting high quality research and learning that transforms society and our understanding of individuals, groups, and cultures. SAGE is the independent, innovative, natural home for authors, editors and societies who share our commitment and passion for the social sciences.

Find out more at: **www.sagepublications.com**

Tourism Management
an introduction

Clare Inkson & **Lynn Minnaert**

SAGE

Los Angeles | London | New Delhi
Singapore | Washington DC

SAGE Publications Ltd
1 Oliver's Yard
55 City Road
London EC1Y 1SP

SAGE Publications Inc.
2455 Teller Road
Thousand Oaks, California 91320

SAGE Publications India Pvt Ltd
B 1/I 1 Mohan Cooperative Industrial Area
Mathura Road
New Delhi 110 044

SAGE Publications Asia-Pacific Pte Ltd
3 Church Street
#10-04 Samsung Hub
Singapore 049483

Library of Congress Control Number: 2011931803

British Library Cataloguing in Publication data

A catalogue record for this book is available from the British Library

ISBN 978-1-84860-869-6
ISBN 978-1-84860-870-2 (pbk)

Typeset by C&M Digital (P) Ltd, Chennai, India
Printed in Great Britain by CPI Group (UK) Ltd, Croydon, CR0 4YY
Printed on paper from sustainable resources

MIX
Paper from responsible sources
FSC® C013604

Summary of Contents

Contents

List of Figures

List of Tables

List of Case Studies

About the Authors

Clare Inkson is a Senior Lecturer in Tourism at the University of Westminster. She has extensive experience of working in tourism in operational and marketing roles in the UK and overseas, for tour operators, wholesalers and travel agencies. Her research interests include tourism distribution channels and destination marketing.

Dr Lynn Minnaert is a Lecturer in Tourism and Events at the University of Surrey. Her research specialism is social inclusion and social sustainability in tourism and events: she has conducted research projects into social tourism, the social impacts of the Olympics and social legacy initiatives in the meetings industry. She has lectured in tourism and events management at undergraduate and postgraduate levels in the UK and in a range of different countries – this international perspective is reflected in this book.

1 Introduction

If our lives are dominated by a search for happiness, then perhaps few activities reveal as much about the dynamics of this quest – in all its ardour and paradoxes – than our travels. (de Botton, 2002: 9)

Banner welcoming tourists to Jaipur, India

Source: Juliette Mauve

About This Book

Tourism is an exciting and dynamic sector that is constantly changing. It can affect people's lives in many different ways: for tourists it can be a source of lifelong memories, joy and fulfilment, and for businesses and destinations it is a source of income and employment. As tourism has grown and become an ever more prominent activity, tourism studies as an academic field has also developed.

When studying tourism, you will find that it is a broad and diverse topic area that encompasses several business sectors, and draws on a range of disciplines.

When one of the authors of this book studied tourism in the late 1980s, tourism textbooks were notable by their absence – the library shelf for tourism consisted of five or six textbooks only. Since then, tourism as an academic study has evolved considerably, and now hundreds, if not thousands, of tourism texts are available that consider tourism in a variety of contexts, and focus on specialist forms of tourism activity. This text is intended to provide a solid starting point to your learning about tourism – to give you a strong understanding of the dimensions of tourism, the industries of which it is comprised, the issues that affect the success of tourism in destinations, and the management of tourism's impacts on destination economies, environments and communities.

This text has been written for students who are starting their tourism studies and require a succinct yet comprehensive introduction to the broad, diverse and complex dimensions of tourism. It consists of 14 chapters, each of which focuses on a discrete tourism topic; the book can be read from start to finish in the conventional order, or you can pick individual chapters to read in any order, as and when you need to. The book has been designed to provide a foundation in tourism in line with the QAA recommendations for the structure of tourism degree programmes, and has been written particularly for first and second year undergraduates, so that they will have a strong overview of tourism before they start to specialise in a particular form of tourism or in a particular tourism issue.

The book is broadly structured along three main themes: the demand for tourism, the supply of tourism, and the impacts of tourism. In the second chapter we explain the concept of tourism, how an understanding of tourism has evolved, and the theoretical framework that underpins its study. In Chapters 3 and 4 we consider the factors that influence the demand for tourism by identifying the conditions within an individual's usual environment that enable them to engage in tourism activities, and the forces that motivate tourists to choose tourism as an activity. Chapters 5, 6 and 7 consider the supply of tourism: the industries that supply tourism products in destinations and their common operating characteristics, the role of intermediaries in making these products available for sale to tourists, and the destination itself and common development patterns. The final chapters of the book consider the impacts of tourism on destination economies (Chapter 9), communities (Chapter 10), and environments (Chapter 11) , and how these impacts can be managed to reduce their negative effects and optimise the benefits that tourism can bring to destinations (Chapter 12). Chapter 13 considers how marketing is applied in tourism, and we end the book with a consideration of the future – the future of tourism in general and your future as a young graduate in the tourism sector.

Tourism in the Twenty-first Century _____

As you develop your knowledge about tourism, you will notice that it is a dynamic sector that is often strongly influenced by changes that take place in society – tourism is very much a part of how we live today. It is important to remember that tourism as an activity, as an economic sector and as an area of study, cannot be separated from the wider external environment within which it operates. Tourism is influenced by external issues that have a significant impact on the nature of its development, on the ability of tourism businesses to operate successfully, and on tourism's potential to benefit or to damage destinations. Throughout this book, we consider tourism in the context of contemporary forces that shape the economy and operating environment in general and to which successful tourism enterprises and destinations must be able to adapt and respond effectively. Three of these forces are of particular importance for tourism, and make their influence felt in every chapter of this book: globalisation, sustainability and developments in information and communications technology (ICT). In the remainder of this chapter, we explain the context of contemporary tourism in regard to these forces.

Globalisation _____

SpongeBob SquarePants advertisement in Iran

Source: Lynn Minnaert

Globalisation, at its simplest, means crossing borders. Globalisation is not new: goods, people and ideas have traversed the globe for millennia. In recent times however, globalisation has increased at a rapid pace: new technologies, like jet planes and the internet, have led to global economics, politics and communications (Economist, 2001: ix). Wahab and Cooper (2001: 4) say globalisation is 'an all-encompassing term that denotes a world which, due to many politico-economic, technological and informational advancements and developments, is on its way to becoming borderless and an interdependent whole'. This means that any occurrence anywhere in the world can, in one way or the other, have an impact somewhere else: in another country, in another continent. If for example the cotton crop in India is devastated by floods or a pest, this could mean that clothing prices may go up in North America. Political conflicts in Russia, a major exporter of natural gas, can lead to higher gas prices in Europe. Globalisation describes the process by which events, decisions and activities in one part of the world come to have significant outcomes for communities and individuals in quite distant parts of the globe.

Because it has become easier for goods, ideas and people to cross borders, certain products and cultural phenomena are now readily available almost everywhere. Brands like Coca-Cola, McDonalds and Nike are sold almost everywhere in the world, and popular music and Hollywood films can reach worldwide audiences via global distribution and the internet. Globalisation has also led to multicultural communities, where a range of cultures co-exist and come together (Micklethwait and Wooldridge, 2004). Even though there are still cultural differences between the regions of the world, there is a growing body of products and phenomena that these regions have in common – Beynon and Dunkerley (2000) argue that this marks the emergence of a new 'world culture'.

Albrow (2004) summarises that globalisation can be seen as a combination of four phenomena:

- The values and daily behaviour of many groups in contemporary society are influenced by the state of other parts of the world, and its inhabitants.

- Images, information and products from any part of the world can be available anywhere and anytime for ever-increasing numbers of people worldwide.

- Information and communication technology make it possible to maintain social relationships and direct communication with people all over the globe, across time and distance.

- International laws and agreements ensure that people can move across national boundaries with the confidence that they can maintain their lifestyles and their life routines wherever they are.

Although there may be benefits attached to globalisation, such as the opportunities for communication between people in different parts of the world and the sharing of information, there are also those who claim that globalisation has a series of disadvantages. Examples are that globalisation reduces the power of national governments; that it reduces cultural differences and fades

Ronald McDonald figure in Bangkok, in typically Thai pose

Source: Lynn Minnaert

national identities; that it is a source of environmental degradation; and that it increases the gap between rich and poor.

Critics of globalisation claim that it is often equal to 'global Westernisation' (Sen, 2004: 16) – they argue that the values and products of the West are spread across the globe, with other cultures having to adopt them because the West controls a large share of global financial resources. Although the sharing of innovations and positive Western values may be beneficial, other aspects, such as a strong emphasis on material possessions and profit making, are not always seen as such.

The most commonly uttered criticisms of globalisation are that it increases the gap between rich and poor and that it leads to inequality. An example would be the production of goods in developing countries: because international corporations benefit from the low labour costs and less strict labour laws in developing countries, they can keep the production costs of products low, thus increasing their profits. Because the producers are often international corporations based in developed countries, this can mean the profits are not shared within the developing country. In this scenario, the gap between the developed and developing countries persists (Oxfam, 2004).

Dollar and Kraay (2004) disagree with this analysis. They argue that the long-term global trend towards greater inequality has existed for at least 200 years, and that it peaked around 1975; but, since then, it has stabilised and possibly even reversed. The chief reason for the change has been the accelerated growth of two large and initially poor countries: China and India. They further defend the role of international business as it brings capital and income to the developing country.

Tourism can be seen as part of the process of globalisation – it is a sector with globalised supply and demand, and it is also a social phenomenon that can influence communities around the world. Many tourism suppliers, such as hotel chains and tour operators, have expanded across borders – tourists can, for example, stay in Hilton hotels in destinations ranging from Japan to Jamaica, confident that the level of service and comfort will be the same across the globe. In developing countries, foreign-owned tourism companies may reap the economic benefits from tourism – many people in the host communities, however, are often excluded from the profits tourism can bring. Globalisation has also resulted in a growth in international tourism demand: cross-border travel is on the increase and continental and intercontinental travel is growing fast (OECD, 2008b: 12). Visitors have an increasing number of destinations to choose from – they can find out about them via 'a globalised world of communications and advertising' (Macleod, 2004) and travel to them via extensive transport routes. This has led to an intense competition between destinations, and pressure on certain destinations as they suffer from an excess of visitors.

The globalisation of tourism affects the different aspects of tourism that are discussed in this book. The characteristics of global tourism demand and supply will be discussed in Chapters 3, 5, 6 and 12. Globalised tourism also has far-reaching economic, socio-cultural and environmental impacts on host communities: these will be discussed in Chapters 8, 9 and 10. Finally, the potential to reach a global market has brought about changes in the way many companies market themselves (Chapter 13).

Sustainability

Sustainability is a term for which many definitions exist. Rogers et al. (2008: 5) describe sustainability as 'the term chosen to bridge the gulf between development and environment'. Dresner (2008: 69) explains that 'the starting point of the concept of sustainable development was the aim to integrate environmental considerations into economic policy. More profoundly, it was conceived as an attempt to bring environmentalist ideas into the central area of policy, which in the modern world is economics'.

Originally the term was applied to forestry, fisheries and groundwater, to answer questions like 'How many trees can we cut down and still have forest growth?' and 'How many fish can we take and still have a fishing industry?' Today, 'sustainability' is applied more widely to a variety of sectors and aspects of development. The problem is that this makes the term hard to define. At its core, sustainability balances environmental concerns with an allowance for economic growth: this means that development and growth are not blocked, but the way in which growth is achieved is considered closely. There is, however, not one particular way in which sustainability needs to be achieved: a wide range of actions can be classed as aiming towards this goal. Because the term can be interpreted in many different ways, one could say it has become rather vague – some even say it has become almost meaningless (Dresner, 2008).

Even if there are many different definitions for sustainability, there is a general consensus that it has three aspects:

- *Economic*: maximising income whilst maintaining a constant or increasing level of capital.
- *Environmental/Ecological*: maintaining and maximising the robustness and resilience of the natural environment.
- *Social/Socio-cultural*: maintaining and maximising the robustness and resilience of social systems and cultures (Rogers et al., 2008).

Sustainability and sustainable development came to prominence in 1987, when the United Nations World Commission on Environment and Development, chaired by Norwegian Prime Minister Gro Harlem Brundtland, published its report 'Our Common Future' (United Nations, 1983). The central recommendation of this document, usually known as the Brundtland report, was to balance the competing demands for environmental protection and economic development through a new approach: *sustainable development*. The Commission defined it as development that 'meets the needs of the present without compromising the ability of future generations to meet their needs' (Dresner, 2008: 1).

Further UN Conferences on Environment and Development included the 'Earth Summit' in Rio de Janeiro in 1992, where Agenda 21 was produced. The 40 chapters of Agenda 21 offer an action plan for sustainable development, integrating environmental with social and economic concerns, and articulating a participatory, community-based approach to a variety of issues, including population control, transparency, partnership working, equity and justice. Local Agenda 21 is not binding but many countries have included it in policy making, with municipal governments often taking a strong lead (Blewitt, 2008: 17).

Another milestone for sustainable development was the 1997 Kyoto Protocol, a UN treaty that was signed by over 140 states. The Kyoto Protocol, like many other climate change agreements however, concentrates almost exclusively on reducing greenhouse gas emissions, largely ignoring the other aspects of sustainable development (Blewitt, 2008: 18).

The three determinants of sustainable development are consumption, production and distribution (Rogers et al., 2008):

- *Consumption*: in sustainable development, it is the aim not to use resources beyond the reasonable limit set by nature through regeneration.
- *Production*: sustainable development recognises the need for new production patterns that take into account not only the economic benefits of production, but also the social and environmental benefits.
- *Distribution*: sustainable development aims to reduce poverty and inequality – the socio-economic aspects of sustainability are particularly important here.

Several authors distinguish between strong and weak sustainability. A strong sustainability approach emphasises that resources need to be used in restrained ways as humankind cannot substitute them, and they must be preserved for future generations (Munier, 2005: 15). This is a more hard-line approach, which advocates using resources at the rate they are produced. For example, we currently consume oil a million times faster than it is produced (Dresner, 2008: 3) – a strong sustainability approach would advocate that we need to reduce our consumption of oil to one millionth of its current level. A weak sustainability approach regards resources as a commodity that supports humankind (Munier, 2005: 15): although humankind needs to use them wisely, it allows for a responsible use of them. A weak sustainability approach would seek to reduce the dependency on oil with gradual reduction targets (Dresner, 2008). Blewitt (2008: 29) refers to these terms as 'deep' and 'shallow' ecology.

One of the biggest challenges of sustainability is the development of reliable benchmarks for sustainable development. Dresner (2008: 175) highlights that measuring if sustainability has been achieved is almost impossible, as you would have to have detailed information about the future and which factors will influence it.

Tourism has not escaped discussions about sustainability: as a transport-intensive sector that has seen dramatic growth over the last decades, tourism has been accused of being inherently unsustainable. Some of the key challenges for tourism are the coordination and cooperation between different stakeholders, the limitations of the efforts of the industry (many being voluntary), and the fact that many small-scale businesses operate in tourism (Harris et al., 2002). The challenge of making tourism more sustainable is a key theme throughout this book. Chapter 7 discusses the extent to which tourism should be allowed to dominate destinations and make changes to it. Chapter 10 specifically examines the environmental impacts of tourism on destinations, and proposes measures that can limit environmental damage. Chapters 8 and 9 consider how the economic and social impacts of tourism for host communities can be optimised.

Information and Communications Technology (ICT)

ICT is the use of computer hardware, software, mobile and fixed telecommunications, internet and satellite technologies, to store, process, retrieve and transmit information. ICT is used by organisations to collect and record data, to process information efficiently and accurately, and to communicate internally within and between departments, and externally with partners and with existing or potential customers.

However, the role of contemporary ICT is much more fundamental than simply managing information and communication. Buhalis (2003: 7) describes ICT as 'the entire range of electronic tools that facilitate the operational and strategic management of organisations by enabling them to manage their information, functions and processes as well as to communicate interactively with their stakeholders, enabling them to achieve their mission and objectives'. This quote suggests that ICT makes an important contribution to an organisation's success. Buhalis also stresses the importance of 'humanware' in ICT – that is the intellect, knowledge, expertise and competence that enables an organisation to 'develop, programme and maintain the equipment' (2003: 6).

The impact of ICT on the commercial environment and the operations of organisations cannot be underestimated. ICT has transformed the way in which businesses operate by improving communications and enabling information to be shared, by allowing reliable and efficient information transfer and retrieval, and by integrating departments to facilitate the achievement of common objectives (Buhalis, 2003). ICT speeds up internal processes to allow quicker decision making, reduces staff costs by automating some functions, and has revolutionised the ways in which consumers research, purchase and communicate about products (Middleton et al., 2009). In tourism, for example, the handling of vast amounts of data relating to availability and reservations, price information, and the production of travel documents, is an extremely complex process, which, until ICT became widely used, was time-consuming, labour intensive and vulnerable to errors.

Buhalis (2003) identifies four stages over which the use of ICT has evolved:

Data processing (DP) – from the 1950s, operational efficiency was increased through the automation of information-based processes using mainframe and mini computers. The costs of hardware and programming excluded all but the largest organisations from using them, and in tourism major airlines began using computers to process reservations data, with systems known as computerised reservations systems or CRS (Inkpen, 1998; Sheldon, 1997).

Management Information Systems (MIS) – from the 1970s, data processing was linked to internal information sources such as accounting or inventory to improve management effectiveness and decision making. In tourism, global distribution systems (GDS) were introduced by the airline industry to provide a platform for travel agencies to access the CRS of several airlines, hotel and car rental companies through one system, for instance Sabre and Apollo (Sheldon, 1997).

Strategic Information Systems (SIS) – from the 1980s, management information systems within an organisation could be integrated into ICT networks. Managers were able to customise information to their own needs to produce their own management reports using personal computers to forecast, budget and plan using past data and simulation models. This development enabled more precise decision making and enhanced an organisation's performance. Buhalis suggests that 'SISs were primarily used to support or shape the competitive strategy of an organisation and their ability to gain and maintain competitive advantage' (2003: 12).

The network era – from the late 1990s, the use of local area networks and wide area networks as well as the internet, intranet and extranets has revolutionised communication, allowing for greater collaboration within and between organisations and between consumers. This era is particularly important because it has reduced the significance of location and size as a competitive advantage. For example, very small and remote tourism organisations can now use ICT to communicate with a large, global audience, and the audience itself is partly connected through membership of social networks. Consumers' access to information about tourism products in any destination is available instantly through search engines. The subsequent development of e-commerce has transformed the global economy into one in which potentially everyone is interconnected and organisations compete on a worldwide scale, regardless of their size or location. The opportunities that this has created for small organisations with limited financial resources, and organisations that are based in remote regions are extremely important, particularly in tourism.

The phenomenal speed of developments in internet and mobile technologies since the beginning of the twenty-first century has far-reaching implications for organisations, particularly those in sectors like tourism that rely on the fast transmission of reliable information. Middleton et al. (2009: 243) state that 'information is the life-blood of tourism'. In order to compete effectively, businesses must adapt quickly to new technology, to changes in the ways in which consumers behave, and to new opportunities to communicate with consumers about their products (Middleton et al., 2009).

Many sources refer to different types of internet development: Web 1.0 and Web 2.0. Web 1.0 refers to websites or internet usage with static content that allows data to be posted, viewed and downloaded; its use is limited to the provision and retrieval of information. Web 2.0 is a commonly-used term to describe advanced internet technology and applications including blogs, wikis, RSS (Really Simple Syndication) and social networking. Web 2.0 also allows web content to be used dynamically through the creation of virtual communities and user-centred design that encourages users to generate content and to connect to other users and content providers (Middleton et al., 2009).

The development of the internet, broadband and mobile technology, and the rapid increase in the speed and scale of internet use since the late twentieth century, have transformed the ability of individuals to access information, to connect with others to share information, and to produce their own content to be published on the web. Businesses must adapt quickly to these changes and incorporate new ICT opportunities into their strategies in order to avoid being left behind. Buhalis (2003: 6) stresses the role of an organisation's ICT capabilities as a key component in its competitiveness – 'constant innovation in applications of hardware, software and network computing means that only dynamic organisations that can assess the requirements of their stakeholders and respond efficiently and effectively will be able to outperform their competition and maintain their long-term prosperity'.

The internet has transformed consumers' ability to access information about products and prices, to compare competitors, and to conduct transactions online. In tourism, for example, consumers with access to broadband either on a computer or a mobile phone can check availability, make and pay for reservations, print off documentation and even check-in, without leaving their homes; mobile technology applications allow tourists' mobility within a destination to be tracked (Shoval and Isaacson, 2010), and attractions, accommodation and restaurants to advertise directly to tourists via their smart mobile phones if they are close by.

Social media have revolutionised the way consumers communicate about products and organisations, and the control that organisations have over information about these has been substantially reduced. Social media are extremely powerful because they allow any user to post any comment about any organisation online that potentially could be read by hundreds, thousands or millions of viewers. These posts may reinforce the positive image that the company seeks to project, or could undermine an organisation's own investment in advertising and branding. For example, YouTube allows users to upload video content which can be viewed by an almost worldwide audience; YouTube is viewed in 25 countries and 2 billion videos a day are viewed, with 24 hours of video uploaded every minute (YouTube, 2011).

The power of social networks is demonstrated by Facebook which has more than 500 million active users, 50 per cent of whom will log in on any given day; the average Facebook user has 130 friends, and is connected to 80 community pages, groups and events, and creates 90 pieces of content each month. Two hundred million Facebook users access the site through mobile devices, and are twice as active as non-mobile users. This means that consumers with mobile internet can post comments wherever they are, in immediate response to a situation, which can then be forwarded by 'friends' through their own networks, spreading information virally on the web. In addition, Facebook content can be translated into 70 languages (Facebook, 2011). Twitter is a real-time information network that allows its 175 million registered users to create content that can be viewed by anyone who follows them; approximately 95 million tweets a day are added to Twitter (Twitter, 2011).

Web 2.0 has caused a major shift in power towards consumers (Middleton et al., 2009). In tourism, customer review sites are particularly important to consumers who can check other consumers' opinions and experiences of a supplier before making a purchase decision, and potentially be deterred from making reservations. Tourism businesses and organisations must understand how their customers are influenced by social networks and thereby incorporate social media into their own marketing, using innovative approaches.

At the time of writing, in 2011, Web 3.0 is in the early stages of development. Web 3.0 is regarded as the next generation of the internet and is known as the 'semantic web' because it is capable of understanding the meaning of words, interpreting past searches, and personalising data retrieval. For example, search engines will analyse key word usage and frequencies to interpret a user's search requests and present relevant information.

Recent ICT developments have revolutionised the way organisations market their products, the way tourists research and purchase tourism products, and the ability of organisations to collaborate. Throughout this book, we highlight how ICT can be used to harness operating, distribution and marketing advantages, and the opportunities it offers to small and medium-sized businesses to communicate with potential consumers and collaborate in partnerships.

How to Use this Book

This book offers you a succinct and clear introduction to the many different aspects of tourism that you will study. It has been designed so that you can read the chapters in the order that is most useful to you and the references between chapters will lead you to other relevant information. Each chapter includes several snapshots and one case study to demonstrate how theory applies in practice, and, where appropriate, we have included definitions of specialist terminology in textboxes in the margin. Each chapter ends with self-test questions to check your understanding and a recommended reading list with references to books and articles that can help you develop your knowledge further. We hope you enjoy studying this fascinating topic area.

2 Understanding Tourism

Contemporary tourism is at the same time one of the most significant yet misunderstood phenomena in the world today. (Cooper and Hall, 2008: 4)

Courchevel 1550, France

Source: Clare Inkson

Learning Outcomes

After reading this chapter you will understand:

- **what tourism is and how it is defined**
- **the diversity of supply elements that comprise tourism**
- **the different forms of tourism**
- **how tourism is changing in response to new market and technological conditions.**

Introduction

Tourism today is a familiar and easily recognised activity that is enjoyed by hundreds of millions of people every year. Interestingly though, our understanding of what tourism is and whether it can be described as a distinct industry in its own right, as well as the criteria by which travellers are classified as tourists, is still evolving.

International tourism: Tourism activity by individuals outside their country of residence

Impressive claims are made about the importance of tourism – 'one of the world's largest industries' (World Travel and Tourism Council, 2010), 'one of the fastest-growing economic sectors in the world' (UNWTO, 2010a) – underlining its significance as an economic force. Certainly since the mid-twentieth century the expansion of tourism has been immense, with the growth rates of **international tourism** averaging 6.5 per cent every year between 1950 and 2005 (UNWTO, 2010a), and despite slower growth rates as a result of the global economic crisis that began in 2007, international tourist arrivals are expected to reach 1.5 billion by 2020 (UNWTO, 2010a). Tourism as an activity is enjoyed by substantial proportions of the populations of industrialised economies, and most countries promote their natural, historic or cultural resources as tourist attractions to earn a share of the US$852 billion industry (UNWTO, 2010a).

Tourism is often described as a 'phenomenon', meaning that it is an observable event or occurrence. The occurrence is most obvious in the destinations that tourists visit because of the infrastructure that it usually requires, and the economic, environmental and social impacts of tourism activities. However, an understanding of tourism requires not just an appreciation of what tourists do and need in destinations, but also of why and how the decision to engage in tourism is taken. Therefore, tourism involves the study of places visited by tourists – that is, where tourism is consumed – and of the factors and conditions in the places where tourists live – where the demand for tourism is created.

In this chapter we consider how tourism is described conceptually, the criteria by which travellers are defined as tourists, and the industries that supply the tourism product. We finish the chapter by discussing the main forms of tourism.

What is Tourism?

The word 'tourism' is derived from the Greek and Latin words meaning to turn or to circle, and in the context of a journey means a trip that ends in the same place that it began; a round trip (Theobald, 2005b). It may be stating the obvious to say that tourism involves travel, but not all travellers are tourists and this leads us to one of the main problems in understanding tourism – identifying the forms of travel, and the types of activities, that are, or are not, tourism.

Tourism as an activity is often located within the broader framework of leisure and recreation because, traditionally, tourism was understood as holidays and therefore involved recreational activities during leisure time (Mathieson and Wall, 1982). However, while holidays represent one specific use of leisure time, not all tourism is for leisure purposes.

It has been suggested that the focus on holidays has created a perception of tourism as a superficial, fun and pleasurable activity and has delayed its recognition as a serious economic sector and subject of academic study. This has not been helped by slow progress in reaching a consensus on definitions of tourism and classifications of tourists. In addition, even tourism itself is variously described as 'the travel industry', 'the hospitality industry', 'the visitor industry' and 'the holiday industry', thus adding further to the confusion.

Academics, practitioners and governments have struggled to define tourism for many decades. Definitions of tourism and classifications of tourists have been proposed and amended since the 1940s, and have evolved as tourism itself has evolved and changed. As recently as 2008, the United Nations World Tourism Organization (UNWTO) refined its classifications of tourism and tourists.

Definitions of tourism have evolved into two broad types – conceptual and technical – each with its own rationale and application (Theobald, 2005b):

- Conceptual definitions describe what tourism is by providing a holistic theoretical framework that identifies all the elements of tourism and reflects its multi-faceted and multi-disciplinary characteristics.

- Technical definitions identify who tourists are and what the tourism industry is, specifying the criteria by which travellers can be classified as tourists and enterprises can be classified as part of the tourism sector, in order to collect data about them, understand their impacts, and make statistical comparisons.

We begin by considering conceptual definitions.

Conceptual Definitions of Tourism

Several definitions have evolved since the 1940s as our understanding of tourism has been refined and tourism itself has changed (Mathieson and Wall, 1982). Conceptual definitions should capture the whole essence of tourism by recognising the role of tourists' routine environment as well as where they travel to and the impacts of tourism. One of the challenges of defining the concept of tourism is to include all its components without generalising so much that the description becomes vague.

The snapshot below demonstrates how conceptual definitions of tourism have evolved since the 1940s.

Snapshot 2.1   Conceptual Definitions of Tourism

Conceptual definitions of tourism have evolved over several decades:

> the sum of the phenomena and relationships arising from the travel and stay of non-residents in so far as they do not lead to permanent residence and are not connected to any earning activity. (Hunziker and Krapf, 1942, quoted in Mathieson and Wall, 1982: 1)

> a study of man away from his usual habitat, of the industry which responds to his needs, and of the impacts that both he and the industry have on the host socio-cultural, economic, and physical environments. (Jafari, 1977, quoted in Theobald, 2005b: 11)

> the temporary movement of people to destinations outside their normal places of work and residence, the activities undertaken during their stay in those destinations, and the facilities created to cater to their needs. (Mathieson and Wall, 1982: 1)

These conceptual definitions stress that tourism arises as a result of decisions by individuals to move temporarily from their usual environments. Tourism occurs when people engage in activities as tourists and includes the provision of facilities and services for tourists, and the consequences of tourist activities in destinations.

In 1993 the United Nations endorsed the World Tourism Organization's (WTO) proposed definition of tourism as 'the activities of a person travelling to a place outside his or her usual environment for less than a specified period of time whose main purpose of travel is other than the exercise of an activity remunerated from within the place visited' (WTO, 1991, in Theobald, 2005b: 16). The specified period of time was defined as one year, and the purposes of tourism travel included leisure, business, visiting friends and relatives (VFR), health treatments, religious pilgrimage and 'other' purposes, specified by the WTO's technical classification of tourists. The definition of business tourism excluded travellers who were directly employed and paid by an employer located in the destination. The 1993 definition of tourism was widely adopted by academics, practitioners and governmental organisations. However, definitions of tourism have evolved again more recently.

In 2008 the UNWTO refined their description of tourism further: 'tourism is a social, cultural and economic phenomenon related to the movement of people to places outside the usual place of residence' (UNWTO, 2008: 1). The usual place of residence is interpreted as the geographical location of an individual's routine work and life activities, and individual states determine the distance that must be travelled for a trip to be described as tourism.

This description reflects a more holistic approach to the concept of tourism, recognising that the effects of tourism are not limited to economic interests. From an economic perspective, tourism is defined as 'the actions and behaviours of people in preparation for and during a trip in their capacity as consumers' (UNWTO, 2008: 106), recognising the significance of tourist spending for tourism within their usual environment, as well as within the destination visited.

The tourism activities for a single trip therefore occur in at least two locations – the tourist's usual environment and the place or places they visit during the trip – and occur over several stages – before departure, during the trip, and on the return home. Additionally of course, in order for tourism to occur, these locations must be connected by transport routes and infrastructure. Tourism therefore involves a number of separate elements.

Mathieson and Wall (1982: 14) illustrate this well by describing tourism as a 'composite phenomenon' comprised of a range of components and relationships that together form a coherent conceptual framework (see Figure 2.1).

Mathieson and Wall's Conceptual Framework of Tourism

Mathieson and Wall (1982) identified three basic elements to tourism:

- *The dynamic element*: representing demand for and forms of tourism, which are fluid and subject to change.
- *The destination element*: originally called the static element, representing the tourist and the characteristics of their behaviour, the characteristics of the destination, and its static capacity and environmental and social threshold.
- *The consequential element*: representing the economic, environmental and social impacts that occur as a result of the interaction of the dynamic and destination elements, and their measurement and control.

These elements are incorporated into a conceptual framework to illustrate the inter-relationships between them (see Figure 2.1).

The framework identifies tourism as the interaction of demand and supply, and shows how each affects the other and creates impacts in the destination. These impacts must be managed and controlled by measures implemented within the destination. The framework illustrates how change in one element influences and changes the other elements. The framework illustrates well that the study of tourism requires an understanding of a broad range of discrete subject areas and issues: marketing is used to manage and influence the dynamic element; economics, sociology, ecology, planning, development processes and business management influence the destination element; while destination, business, and environmental management influence the consequential element.

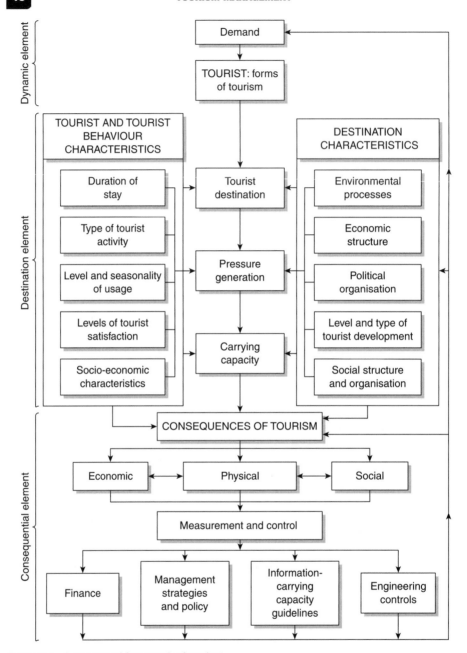

Figure 2.1 A conceptual framework of tourism

Source: after Mathieson and Wall (1982: 15) in Wall and Mathieson (2006: 20). Reprinted with permission from Pearson Education Limited.

Conceptual definitions tell us what tourism is, but they do not specify any technical characteristics such as the distance from the usual place of work or residence that must be travelled in order for a trip to be recognised as tourism.

Technical Definitions of Tourism

Technical definitions specify the criteria by which travellers are recognised as tourists and businesses and organisations are recognised as being part of the tourism sector. This may appear to be an easy task but in reality it has proved to be a difficult and ongoing debate.

Clear and standardised technical definitions are important because:

- They facilitate the collection of statistical data about the size of tourism and its economic value to enable governments to measure tourism and understand its influence on their economies.

- They help tourism suppliers to identify trends and anticipate changes in demand, in order to respond effectively.

- Internationally and nationally standardised definitions of tourists enable countries, regions of countries and individual destinations to compare tourism performance in terms of the number of arrivals and their economic contribution through expenditure in the destination.

These comparisons cannot be achieved unless each destination uses the same definitions to identify the travellers that are tourists, the businesses and organisations that are tourism enterprises, and the forms of expenditure that count as tourism expenditure. The process of standardisation has been slow because a number of organisations have researched and proposed technical definitions independent of each other, and reaching a consensus, particularly internationally, is not straightforward. In the meantime, individual states have defined tourists and tourism enterprises using their own criteria.

The need for clear and standardised criteria to identify tourists and tourism enterprises increased during the 1980s as the economic potential of tourism and its interdependence with other industry sectors was recognised more widely by governments around the world. The ability to compare tourism's contribution with the performance of other industry sectors in a national economy, for example construction or agriculture, required the use of the same measurement criteria and classifications. During the 1980s the WTO and the United Nations Statistics Division began a review of the definitions and classifications used for tourism statistics in order to improve their compatibility and consistency with other national and international statistical systems. At the same time, a number of other international agencies were investigating methods for harmonising classifications of tourism and collection of data. In 1995 the EU initiated legislation to harmonise and improve the tourism statistical data collected by member states, and in 1997 the OECD proposed classifications to be used in its members' national accounts (UN, 2010).

Tourism is often considered from one of two perspectives – the demand side, and the supply side:

- Demand-side perspectives consider tourism consumption and identify the characteristics of tourists and their behaviour and expenditure in destinations. Technical definitions of tourism have traditionally focused on the demand side.

- Supply-side perspectives examine the businesses and organisations that supply tourism products. Many authors claim that the supply-side understanding of tourism has been neglected (Cooper and Hall, 2008; Theobald, 2005b) and the evidence considered later in this chapter seems to support this view. It should be noted, however, that the UNWTO has been taking steps for some time to improve definitions and classifications of tourism supply, but this is a particularly challenging task.

Demand-side Definitions

Demand-side definitions identify the characteristics that distinguish tourists from travellers for other purposes, and specify purpose of visit and duration of stay. Definitions have evolved since the 1930s, but at the time of writing the most recent revisions were proposed in 2008.

In 1937, for statistical purposes the League of Nations defined an international tourist as one who 'visits a country other than that in which he habitually lives for a period of at least 24 hours' (Theobald, 2005b: 12). In 1945 the UN endorsed this definition and added a maximum duration of six months. Note that this definition refers to international tourism and does not recognise travel to another country for less than 24 hours as tourism. Additionally, it does not define the purpose of the visit.

Significant refinements to this definition were proposed in 1963 at the UN Conference on International Travel and Tourism. The conference recommended the use of the term visitor to describe 'any person visiting a country other than that in which he has his usual place of residence, for any reason other than following an occupation remunerated from within the country visited' (Theobald, 2005b: 13). The conference identified two broad purposes of travel for tourism and included activities beyond the traditional understanding of tourism (Leiper, 1979):

- Recreation, holiday, health, study, religion and sport.
- Business, family, mission or meeting.

Visitors would then be classified as either:

- Tourists, if they stayed in the country visited for at least 24 hours, or;
- Excursionists, if they stayed less than 24 hours in the country visited, and not overnight. This was to include cruise ship passengers who stayed overnight on-board ship (IUOTO, 1963, in Mathieson and Wall, 1982: 11).

These definitions were endorsed by the UN Statistical Commission in 1968 and approved in 1976 as the provisional guidelines on statistics of international tourism (UN, 2010). They only referred to international tourism however; the value of **domestic tourism** was recognised in 1980 by the WTO's Manila Declaration that extended the terms visitor, tourist and excursionist to include domestic tourism too. Individual countries' own statistical definitions continued to define the distance from home, purpose of travel and length of stay (Mathieson and Wall, 1982).

> **Domestic tourism:** Tourism activity by individuals within their country of residence

In 1991 the WTO and the Canadian government jointly hosted the International Conference on Travel and Tourism Statistics in Ottawa. The conference recommended a group of statistical definitions of domestic and international tourism which coordinated with other international statistical standards, for example the balance of payments, international migration statistics and the System of National Accounts (UN, 2010).

The recommendations specified the purposes of tourism travel more explicitly as:

- Leisure, recreation and holidays.
- Visiting friends and relatives.
- Business and professional.
- Health treatment.
- Religion/pilgrimage.
- Other.

In 1993 these recommendations were approved by the UN as *The Recommendations on Tourism Statistics*. This was the first international agreement to provide a uniform system for tourism statistics with common interpretations of tourism concepts, definitions and classifications (UN, 2010).

In 2004, the WTO was integrated into the UN as a specialised agency to co-ordinate all the organisations that were involved in proposing how tourism statistics should be compiled. In 2010 the UN's statistical division published new recommendations on technical definitions and classifications of international tourism in order to:

- Make them applicable to developing and developed economies worldwide.
- Make them consistent with definitions and classifications used by other national and international organisations that collected economic, household and migration statistics – for example, the International Labour Organisation (ILO), the International Monetary Fund (IMF), the European Union (EU), the Economic Commission for Latin America and the Caribbean (ECLAC).
- Make them applicable at sub-national as well as national levels.
- Consider destinations at a regional, municipality or other sub-national level.

- Make them conceptually precise.

- Be measurable.

The *International Recommendations for Tourism Statistics 2008* (UN, 2010) confirmed the 1963 interpretation of visitors as either tourists or same-day visitors (excursionists), and revised the purposes by which trips are classified as tourism to two broad types, personal and business/professional, with further sub-classifications as outlined in Table 2.1. Of course, on one trip a visitor may undertake a variety of these activities. To avoid confusion, the classification recommends that trips are classified by their main purpose, without which the trip would not take place.

Table 2.1   The UN's classification of the main purpose of a tourism trip

Classifications of tourism purpose	Examples
Personal Holidays, leisure and recreation	Sightseeing, visiting natural or man-made sites, attending sporting or cultural events, recreational sports activities (skiing, riding, golf, tennis, diving, surfing, sailing, climbing, etc.), using beaches, swimming pools and any recreation and entertainment facilities, cruising, gambling, attending summer camps, resting, honey-mooning, fine dining, well-being & fitness (spas, therapies), staying in a vacation home owned or leased by the tourist
Visiting friends and relatives (VFR)	Visiting friends and relatives, attending weddings, funerals or other family events, short-term caring duties
Education and training	Formal or informal short-term courses or study programmes, professional or other special courses, university sabbatical leaves
Health and medical care	Receiving short-term hospital, clinic, convalescent services, health and social institutions, visiting health resorts for medical treatments
Religion and pilgrimage	Attending religious meetings and events, pilgrimages
Shopping	Purchasing consumer goods, for personal use or as gifts
Transit	Stopping at a place without any specific purpose other than being en route to another destination
Other	Volunteer work, investigative work, temporary unpaid activities not included elsewhere
Business and professional	The activities of self-employed and employees not linked to direct employment in the destination region: attendance at meetings, conferences (congresses), trade fairs and exhibitions, giving lectures, performing concerts, shows and plays, buying and selling goods or services on behalf of non-resident producers, diplomatic, military or international government missions (except when stationed on duty in place visited), NGO missions, scientific and academic research, professional sports, formal or informal on-the-job training courses, crew member on private transport

Source: IRTS, 2008 (2010) © United Nations, reproduced with permission.

It is clear from the conceptual and technical definitions that tourism involves the temporary and voluntary movement of people to places away from their usual environment for personal or business and professional purposes, and the supply of particular products and services before and during their visit. We will now consider tourism from the supply side.

Supply Elements in the Tourism System

The term tourism supply refers to the businesses and organisations that produce the products that tourists consume. Leiper (1979: 400) defines tourism supply as 'the firms, organisations and facilities which are intended to serve the specific needs and wants of tourists'. However, identifying tourism supply is not as simple as it may at first appear because, as Table 2.1 demonstrates, the products that tourists consume are extremely diverse:

- Tourism is often described as heterogenous because it is not a single product, but an amalgam of separate products and services. These products and services are provided by companies and organisations that are part of separate industry sub-sectors, for instance transport and accommodation, which are studied and measured separately.

- The products and services for a single tourism visit may be produced in a number of separate locations, for instance in the tourist's place of residence and in the destination region, and as a result can be described as 'spatially fragmented'.

- Some tourism products and services are used solely by tourists, but in reality many are also used by other types of user too. For example, hotel meeting rooms or restaurant and banqueting facilities may be used by the host community or local businesses, while a transport service may be used by migrants and commuters as well as to transport freight. Therefore, identifying the extent of tourism activities of businesses and organisations can be very difficult.

- The public sector has a significant role in tourism, either directly through the provision or management of attractions for tourists or services to the commercial sector, or indirectly through statutory services such as planning or environmental health, but are often ignored in considerations of tourism supply (Litteljohn and Baxter, 2006).

- Tourists also often consume products which are not part of the traditional tourism sector, for example high street shops and petrol stations that primarily serve the local community. In some destination regions tourism's contribution to their revenue may be substantial.

These problems in identifying tourism supply were recognised by the UN in 2010 which defined tourism supply more broadly as 'a set of productive activities that cater mainly to visitors or for which an important share of their main output is consumed by visitors' (UN, 2010: 2). This recognises that tourists use a range of suppliers, some of whom may not be traditionally tourism related.

This diversity has created great challenges in defining what tourism supply is comprised of, in measuring the value of tourism activities, and in creating a holistic image of what tourism is.

Despite the difficulties in recognising the range of businesses and organisations that form tourism supply, and in identifying the extent to which tourism contributes to their revenue, a supply-side view of tourism is becoming increasingly important because governments need to:

- Analyse the economic value of tourism and understand its links to other economic sectors by measuring its size, its revenue, and the number of jobs it creates.
- Anticipate how policy and planning decisions will affect tourism and the legislative requirements of the sector.
- Consider the effects on tourism of changes in the external environment.

Litteljohn and Baxter (2006) suggest that tourism supply can be considered from either a functional or an income approach.

Functional Approach to Tourism Supply

The functional approach groups tourism supply according its function in tourism; that is, by the type of product it produces or by the nature of its interaction with tourists.

Holloway (1985) identifies the function of tourism supply as either producers, intermediaries, or support services:

- Producers, also known as suppliers, provide the product consumed by tourists and consist of passenger transport operators, accommodation and man-made attractions.
- Intermediaries create links between producers and consumers by selling some or all of the producer's capacity. Intermediaries are travel agencies, tour and MICE operators and wholesalers.
- Support services provide products or services to the businesses and organisations that supply the tourist product, or to tourists. Private sector support services include guiding services, training providers, and travel insurance providers while public sector support services include visa and passport services, and national, regional and local tourism organisations.

Suppliers and intermediaries interact directly with tourists during the decision-making, purchasing or consumption stages. Suppliers and intermediaries can be subdivided by industry, for example the airline, hotel or tour operator industry. We discuss suppliers in detail in Chapter 5 and intermediaries in Chapter 6.

Each category of direct supplier provides a portion of the tourist's experience and is dependent on the other categories for the provision of the remainder. The quality, availability and value of one category will affect demand for the others. For instance, the success of accommodation suppliers in a destination depends on the availability of quality attractions to draw tourists to the destination, and efficient and affordable transport routes to the destination. This interdependence is known as **complementarity** (Middleton et al., 2009) and implies a need for a close working relationship between different types of supplier.

> **Complementarity:**
> Together forming a whole entity

Within a destination, the cooperation and coordination of suppliers is usually facilitated by public sector tourism support services, which also often have a substantial role in providing tourist information, destination promotion, and the commissioning of research to understand visitors to a destination.

The functional approach to tourism supply is useful in simplifying the fragmented nature of tourism and showing how its individual elements are complementary. It also recognises the network of interdependence, relationships and interactions that exist in tourism. The snapshot below illustrates these concepts in relation to an established tourism destination.

 Snapshot 2.2   Tourism in London

View of the Palace of Westminster, London Eye and a River Thames sightseeing cruise

Source: Clare Inkson

(Continued)

(Continued)

In 2008, London attracted over 26 million staying visitors and 130 million day visitors, together spending over £22 billion, and supporting over 250,000 jobs (London Development Agency (LDA), 2009).

London's tourism supply is fragmented across thousands of businesses – five airports, European and UK rail services, 100,000+ hotel rooms, 60,000+ seats for shows, concerts and sporting events, 1,000 exhibitions and conference venues, major galleries, museums and historic attractions, premier shopping districts, 4,000 pubs and 6,000 restaurants (Visit London, 2010).

This supply is mostly static because its fixed capacity can't be increased or reduced if demand changes. Volatile demand can have far-reaching implications for tourism suppliers.

Figure 2.2 (a) and (b) illustrates dynamic demand from overseas visitors to London between 2006 and 2009. Seasonal demand patterns caused by conditions in the tourists' usual environment and within London create annual peaks and troughs, while demand also varies each year because of external economic, political and social influences. The impact of the global financial crisis that began in 2007 can be clearly seen.

Dynamic demand creates employment and financial instability, with much seasonal employment and difficulties in attracting investment to update supply, develop new tourism products, and pay competitive wages.

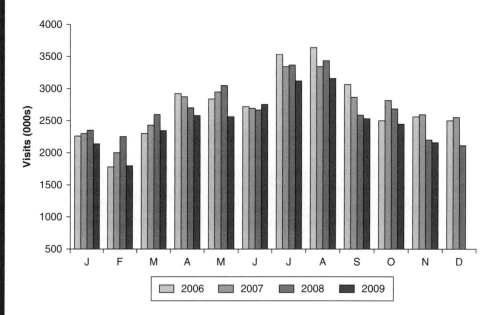

(a) Overseas visits to the UK, monthly, 2006–2009

Source: Office for National Statistics: International Passenger Survey (not seasonally adjusted, provisional results). Crown copyright material licensed under the Open Government Licence.

(Continued)

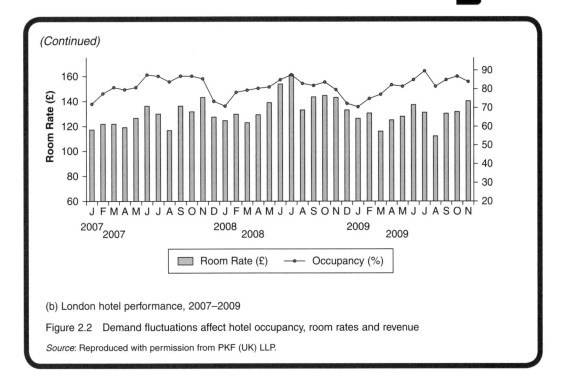

(b) London hotel performance, 2007–2009

Figure 2.2   Demand fluctuations affect hotel occupancy, room rates and revenue

Source: Reproduced with permission from PKF (UK) LLP.

The characteristics of tourism supply vary from one destination to another so it is difficult to generalise about its components. For example, in destinations such as Atlantic City, Las Vegas, Macao or Monte Carlo, casinos form an important element of the tourism supply, whereas in other tourism destinations, they may only be used by the resident community or not exist at all.

In order to identify enterprises that supply tourism products, it is useful to know how significant tourism is to their total income.

Tourism Income Approach

To assess the size and economic contribution of an industry, it is necessary to have a clear understanding of which enterprises form the industry in question. All governments classify enterprises by type and code them to identify their role in the national accounts and to measure employment. To encourage consistency in classification and coding, and comparability between individual countries, the UN introduced international standard industrial classifications (ISIC). However tourism wasn't recognised as a distinct activity in ISIC; instead figures measuring tourism's contribution to an economy were derived from figures on accommodation or catering. This has important implications for the measurement of tourism supply, as it excludes many parts of the tourism sector from statistics on tourism employment and revenue (Cooper and Hall, 2008).

In 1990 the WTO revised ISIC to make it more applicable to tourism and recommended a standard international classification of tourism activities (SICTA). SICTA distinguished between enterprises whose source of revenue was mainly tourism (T), or partially tourism (P), and coded enterprises accordingly.

This approach considers the value of tourism to businesses and organisations, and identifies the extent to which suppliers rely on tourism financially. A tourism income approach enables a more comprehensive understanding of the economic impacts of tourism because it considers all types of businesses and organisations that derive an income from tourism, whether or not they are typical of tourism supply.

The EU used this approach in 1998 to measure tourism employment and identified three types of businesses: core tourism businesses derived 50–100 per cent of their income from tourism; complementary and ancillary services derived 25–50 per cent of their income from tourism, and the remainder derived less than 25 per cent (Litteljohn and Baxter, 2006). However, the reliability of the approach depends on the ability to differentiate between tourism income and other types of income, which is not always possible.

In 2010 the UN recommended describing tourism supply in one of two ways:

- Tourism characteristic products are supply that would be unlikely to exist without tourism, and for which statistical data can be obtained.

- Tourism connected products are supply that would still exist without tourism, or supply that depends on tourism but is not recognised as such globally, for example hospitals, clinics or language schools.

Table 2.2 lists the type of supply that is identified by the UNWTO as tourism characteristic and demonstrates the fragmentation of tourism supply across several industries. This fragmentation has raised doubts about whether tourism can be described as an industry at all.

Tourism as an Industry

A question occupying many academics and economists is whether tourism should be regarded as an industry in its own right. Lobbyists for tourism refer to tourism supply as 'the tourism industry' to highlight its economic value, to compare its value with other industries, and to give credibility to a phenomenon that has struggled to be taken seriously by governments (Davidson, 2005).

There are two definitions of an industry. The traditional economic view of an industry is of a collection of competing enterprises that produce the same product. According to this view, tourism cannot be described as an industry

Table 2.2   Tourism characteristic supply

Products	Activities
Accommodation for visitors	Hotels, resort hotels, pensions, guesthouses, B&Bs, apartments, bungalows, cottages, youth hostels, mountain shelters, cabins, university halls of residence, sleeping cars, boarding houses, campsites, recreational vehicle parks and caravan parks, second homes, timeshare properties
Food and beverage serving services	Restaurants, cafes, food & beverage services in hotels or on ships and trains, self-service & fast-food, mobile food services, bars, nightclubs, bars in hotels, ships and trains, beverage-serving activities
Railway passenger transport	Sightseeing services by rail, interurban railway services
Road passenger transport	Taxis, airport shuttle services, car rental, man or animal drawn vehicles, non-scheduled bus and coach services, cable cars, ski lifts, sightseeing by coach, scheduled bus, coach, trams
Water passenger transport	Rivers, canals, ferries, inland cruises, water taxis, cruises
Air passenger transport	Sightseeing flights by plane or helicopter, scheduled and chartered plane and helicopter services, space transport
Transport equipment rental services	Car and light van hire
Travel agencies and other reservation services	All reservation services for transport, accommodation, cruises, package tours, events, entertainment and recreational services, tour operators, tourist guides, visitor information services
Cultural services	Theatre, dance and music performances, museums, historical sites and buildings, gardens and zoos, nature and wildlife reserves
Sports and recreational services	Stadiums, ice rinks, sports fields, golf courses, bowling alleys, scuba diving, hang-gliding, casinos, horse riding, ballrooms, dance halls, ski hills, beach & park services, fireworks, sound & light performances, amusement parks
Country-specific tourism characteristic goods	Retail trade: duty free shops, specialised retail trade in souvenirs, handicrafts
Country-specific tourism characteristic services	Other country-specific tourism characteristic activities

Source: IRTS, 2008 (2010) © United Nations, reproduced with permission.

because it includes enterprises producing different types of product that complement each other (Davidson, 2005).

Alternatively the standard industrial classification (SIC) regards an industry as a group of establishments with the same primary activity whose size is statistically significant (Davidson, 2005). Tourism as a whole does not fit into this description either, because the primary activities of transport, accommodation and attractions are clearly not the same.

We have seen that tourism results from a combination of the activities of several separate industries producing different but complementary products. Within each individual industry such as the hotel industry or the airline industry, suppliers produce the same product and compete with each other, but it is not possible to identify tourism as a single industry (Davidson, 2005; Leiper, 1990b). Leiper suggests that tourism should be described as a sector that impacts on a diverse range of industries.

In practice though, the term tourism industry is widely used. The UN's 2010 revision of technical definitions recommended using the term 'a tourism industry' to describe a set of enterprises with the same principal activities as are listed in Table 2.2, that collectively are known as 'the tourism industries'.

We have seen so far that tourism is a complex phenomenon that is composed of a variety of elements in different locations and different industries and comes in a variety of forms. Many tourism theorists (Cooper and Hall, 2008; Gunn, 1972; Leiper, 1979; Matley, 1976) suggest that tourism is most easily understood as a system.

Tourism as a System

A system is a collection of individual components that when combined will create a particular phenomenon. In a tourism context the system consists of tourists, geographical regions and the resources required for tourism production and consumption. Each element of the system requires different types of production and consumption, but crucially, these are interrelated and interdependent; change within one element will cause change in the other elements.

Leiper first proposed a systems framework for tourism in 1979 with subsequent amendments in 1990. His model recognises 'how tourism (the behaviour of tourists) gives rise to tourism systems' (Leiper, 1990b: 601) and has made a major contribution to our understanding of tourism (Figure 2.3).

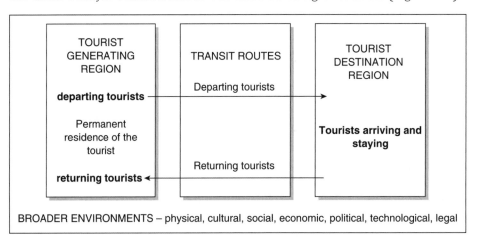

Figure 2.3 Leiper's tourism system

Source: Adapted from Leiper (1979: 404). Reprinted from *Annals of Tourism Research*, 6(4), 1979. Reproduced with permission from Elsevier.

The system identifies how the behaviour of people as tourists creates 'arrangements of people, places and organisations in certain roles' (Leiper, 1990b: 604) with five basic elements: tourists; generating regions; transit routes; destination regions; and the tourism industries. These elements operate within, and are influenced by, broader physical, cultural, social, economic, political and technological environments.

- Tourists are the human elements of the system who temporarily and willingly move beyond their routine environment through the discretionary use of time and money. Leiper (1990) includes business travel if it is not part of the travellers' usual work routine. He describes tourists as the behavioural element of the system.

- Generating regions are the usual place of residence for tourists and the source of demand for tourism. Conditions here, particularly economic and political conditions, influence the ability of residents to engage in tourism, and cause fluctuations in demand levels.

The generating region is the location of the tourism decision-making process and is usually where tourism is planned, booked and paid for, in advance of departure. Subsequently, the generating region is the focus of promotional activities to persuade consumers to engage in tourism and to purchase particular travel products. The travel trade has a major presence in generating regions in the form of travel agencies, wholesalers and tour operators.

- Transit routes are the journey that must be made to reach the destination region. Transit routes determine the destinations that are accessible from the generating region.

The available modes of transport such as air, sea, road or rail, and the necessary infrastructure for their operation, determine the routes available and travel time, while political, economic and technological conditions influence their cost. Transit routes are particularly important in determining the volumes of tourist flows between generating and destination region as it determines a destination's accessibility to potential tourism consumers.

- Destination regions are the location of the resources that attract tourists (Leiper, 1990b). This region is the focus for most tourism studies because the consequences of tourism activities are felt most strongly here and affect the local economy, environment and society in a positive or a negative way. Within the destination, planning and management strategies that influence these impacts are required.

- The tourism industries comprises the businesses and organisations that provide experiences, services and facilities for tourists. Leiper (1979: 401) describes the tourism sector as 'a linked chain' because it is located in the generating, transit route and destination regions, is fragmented across a number of industries, and involves the commercial and the state sector.

Leiper describes tourism as 'partially-industrialised' because tourists' experiences often include non-industrial resources, for example, natural attractions, private homes or private transport (Leiper, 1979), and also often include the consumption of products that are not directly associated with tourism (Leiper, 1990b). The extent of industrialisation of tourism varies between different tourist markets (for example, international tourism is often more industrialised than domestic tourism).

- Broader environments are the conditions outside of tourism that influence the tourism system by affecting conditions in the generating, transit or destination regions. Leiper (1990b) identified a range of broader environments including socio-cultural, economic, technological, political and legal.

The tourism system cannot control the broader environment but must be able to respond to it effectively to ensure that the system continues to function. The first decade of the twenty-first century has been particularly tumultuous for tourism as it has been struck by one catastrophic external event after another – 9/11, wars in Iraq and Afghanistan, the Indian Ocean tsunami, SARS, swine flu, oil price inflation, global economic recession, a shut-down of northern European air space after the 2010 eruption of Iceland's Eyjafjallajökull volcano, and the continuing terrorist threat against Western targets in European cities – with each of these affecting either the ability of residents in some generating regions to engage in tourism, the safety and cost of transit routes, or the appeal of particular destination regions.

The inter-relationship of elements of the tourism system means that the system is dynamic: change in one element is felt across the whole system, creating instability and constant change. This change can be positive or negative. For instance, the 2005 Chinese government's granting of Approved Destination Status to the UK, to allow leisure tourists from China to visit, created a vast new potential consumer market for tourism suppliers within the UK (see Chapter 3 for more detail on this).

The case study below presents an example of influences on the UK tourism system.

CASE STUDY 2.1

THE UK'S TOURISM SYSTEM

The UK is a generating and a receiving region for tourism. In 2009 the UK received 29.9 million visits from overseas tourists (Office for National Statistics (ONS), 2010) and 126 million visits by UK residents (VisitBritain, 2010a), but generated 58.5 million tourist visits to other countries (ONS , 2010).

(Continued)

(Continued)

The top generating countries for UK tourism are France, Ireland, the USA, Germany and Spain, and in 2009 the purposes of all overseas visits to the UK were:

- Holiday: 40 per cent.
- VFR: 29 per cent.
- Business: 21 per cent.
- Study: 2 per cent.
- Other: 8 per cent.

(VisitBritain, 2010b)

Trips by UK residents within the UK were 67 per cent holiday, 19 per cent VFR, and 15 per cent business (VisitBritain, 2010a)

The external environment influences the UK tourism system significantly. UK tourism suppliers need to anticipate the effects of external influences on the demand for their products and take steps to replace falling demand and exploit new opportunities.

Between the end of 2007 and the end of 2009, sterling depreciated by 25 per cent against the US$ and the Euro; this was beneficial for UK tourism as visits to the UK by US and Eurozone visitors became cheaper, and visits by UK residents to the US and Eurozone increased in cost significantly. As a result, the demand for domestic tourism in the UK increased (VisitBritain, 2010a) while outbound tourism fell (ONS, 2010). However, continued recession in the US economy and the subsequent rises in unemployment there are likely to affect the demand for trips to the UK from US tourists, while demand from Ireland is likely to be shaken by the collapse of the Irish economy in November 2010.

In addition, government increases to Air Passenger Duty – a tax levied on all air passengers departing from UK airports – were restructured in 2009 with planned rises in November 2010 increasing the tax on each passenger substantially compared to 2006 levels, depending on the class of travel and distance flown. For example, duty on a business class ticket to Australia was £80 in 2006, rising to £170 in late 2010 (HM Revenue and Customs, 2010). These increases are expected to reduce demand to the UK from long-haul generating regions (VisitBritain, 2010b).

The UK tourism system was again shaken when the US government issued a travel alert to its citizens on 3 October 2010 warning of the likelihood of an Al-Qa'ida terrorist attack against transport systems and tourist infrastructure in the UK and mainland Europe. US tourists were warned to be extra vigilant under these heightened threat conditions.

On 1 January 2010, European Directive 207/58/EC liberalised international passenger rail travel within the EU, allowing European rail operators to compete more freely. This liberalisation affects transit routes to the UK through the Channel Tunnel. At the time of writing, only Eurostar operates through the Tunnel on routes to France and Belgium, however in November 2010, the German rail operator Deutsche Bahn announced that it would begin operating three daily services between London and Amsterdam and Frankfurt from 2013.

(Continued)

(Continued)

Reflective Questions

1 Suggest how tourism suppliers in the UK may be affected by these changes in the external and transit regions.
2 Consider the problems that falls in demand in one generating region may create in destinations.

A systems approach to tourism provides a simple and flexible framework to understand a complex phenomenon:

- It can be applied at a variety of levels, for example nationally to consider tourism flows between two countries, or sub-nationally to identify tourism flows between two regions or two local areas.
- It can be considered in the context of a range of disciplines such as geography, economics, anthropology or marketing.
- It illustrates that tourism is an amalgam of products and experiences that are fragmented across a number of stages and suppliers.

We have seen that tourism occurs when an individual travels temporarily from their routine environment for a range of personal or professional reasons. Tourism includes a variety of separate elements – demand, supply and impacts – and is experienced across three geographical regions – the generating, transit and destination regions. Tourism suppliers are fragmented across these three regions as well as over a number of separate industry sectors. The external environment in the generating, transit and destination regions, over which tourism suppliers have no control, is extremely significant in influencing demand and the impacts of tourism.

We will now complete this chapter by identifying the main forms of tourism.

Forms of Tourism

Tourism can be described in numerous ways to distinguish its many forms. Indeed the term 'adjectival tourism' has developed to demonstrate the ability to add a particular adjective to the word tourism to denote a specific type of tourism destination, activity or market (Ashworth, 2003) The main distinctions between types of tourism are based on:

- The geographical setting of the destination.
- The type of activity engaged in on the trip.
- The location of demand and its relationship to the destination from the national perspective of a country.
- The characteristics of the trip including how it was organised and the number of tourists.

The Geographical Setting of the Destination

Forms of tourism are often characterised by the geographical characteristics of the destination:

- *Urban tourism*: tourism in cities and towns using the resources that are provided primarily for local residents and businesses as attractions for tourists, for example museums, theatres, markets, shops, restaurants, nightclubs, sports and cultural facilities, events and meeting facilities. Transport links to and within urban destinations are usually well developed (Page, 2005).
- *Rural tourism*: tourism in small towns and villages or to remote natural areas. Attractions may be natural, cultural or based on specific physical activities, for example rock climbing, hiking, cycling, and resources may be spread over a wide area. Demand is heavily influenced by the weather. Rural tourism destinations mainly attract holiday, leisure and recreational visitors. Access to and within rural destinations may be limited, and require the use of private vehicles by tourists (Lane, 1994).
- *Resort tourism*: tourism in a place that attracts large volumes of tourists, and where the economy and services are dominated by tourism. Resort tourism may develop in an existing village or town, or be purpose built. Resort tourism is usually located in coastal or mountain regions.

The distinction between tourism types based on the geographical setting of the destination is useful because the type and scale of resources in each type have particular implications for the destination's ability to attract particular types of tourists, the nature of the impacts of tourism, the management of the destination and its ability to market itself effectively.

The Type of Activity Engaged in on the Trip

A further way to describe forms of tourism is by the main type of activity engaged in on the trip. Table 2.3 identifies some of the common types of activity. Descriptions of tourism by type of activity are useful because the latter identifies the main motivation for the tourism trip, the type of destinations and attractions likely to be visited, and the resources required to attract this form of tourism.

Table 2.3   Types of tourism by activity

Heritage tourism	Based on sites of cultural, historical or ecological importance in a destination – monuments, buildings, geographical features.
Eco tourism	Tourism in rural or wilderness environments that actively seeks to educate the tourist about the natural environment and with a focus on enhancing the local environment, economy and host society.
Sun, sea and sand tourism	Coastal tourism for relaxation where climate and beaches are the main attraction.
Cultural tourism	Tourism based specifically on the cultural resources of a destination, for example art galleries, museums, architecture, religion, local lifestyle, language and traditions, and cultural events.
Sport tourism	Tourism for the specific purpose of taking part in a particular sport such as skiing, surfing or golf, or to spectate at a sporting event.
MICE tourism	Tourism for meetings, incentive, conferences and exhibitions. Customers may be companies, associations or individual tourists travelling for business or professional purposes. Incentive travel is a tool used by companies to motivate their workers or representatives and reward them for reaching or exceeding targets.
Event tourism	Tourism to participate in or spectate at a particular organised event which may be cultural or sporting.
Dark tourism	Tourism to visit sites associated with significant sinister events, for example battlefields, prison camps, or murder sites.

Destinations often promote their tourism resources and identify broad market segments by the type of activity. The snapshot below presents the main forms of tourism by activity in South Africa.

 Snapshot 2.3   Tourism in South Africa

Tourists at Howick Falls, KwaZulu-Natal Province

Source: Courtesy of South African Tourism

(Continued)

(Continued)

Tourism has been growing rapidly in South Africa since 1994, the year of the country's first democratic elections. In 1994 3.9 million international visitors arrived, almost doubling by 2004 to 6.7 million. In 2010, domestic and international tourist visits totalled 37.8 million (South African Tourism, 2011).

South African Tourism promotes its resources for tourism as six broad tourism activities:

Forms of tourism	Resources
Business tourism	Over 1,000 conference and exhibition venues of varying sizes from small hotels to large-scale, purpose-built convention centres.
Cultural tourism	Ethnic groups, nomadic tribes, music, rituals, townships and villages, food and wine, plus UNESCO World Heritage Sites including Robben Island.
Eco tourism	Vast wilderness areas, national parks including the Kruger national park, private game reserves, mountain ranges, deserts, vast plains, river systems.
Paleo tourism	Architectural sites of global importance – hominid fossils at the Cradle of Humankind and rock art paintings at Ukhahlamba Drakensberg Park.
Adventure tourism	Climbing, hiking, mountain biking routes and facilities in mountains and natural areas. Surfing and diving facilities on the coast, river rafting facilities.
Sports tourism	Participation or spectating in sports events – rugby, cricket, football, motorsports, horse racing, golf.

Source: http://www.southafrica.info.

In addition to types of activity, descriptions of tourism can be further refined according to the location of demand and its relationship to the destination.

The Location of Demand and its Relationship to the Destination from the National Perspective of a Country _____

From a national perspective types of tourism can be described as domestic, inbound or outbound:

- Domestic tourism is tourism activity by residents within their own country. For example a Thai resident engaging in tourism in Thailand, or a Canadian tourist in Canada.
- Inbound tourism refers to tourism arrivals of residents from other countries. For example in Australia, tourists from Japan, the USA and Europe are inbound tourists.

- Outbound tourism refers to the tourism activity of individuals outside their country of residence. For example Australian residents travelling to Japan, the USA or Europe represent outbound tourism for Australia, but would be inbound tourism for the destination countries (UN, 2010).

Most industrialised economies that do not restrict the mobility of their residents experience domestic, outbound and inbound tourism, although the extent of each varies significantly between individual countries. For example, in 2007 inbound and outbound tourism flows were very different for France and for Japan: France's international tourism consisted of 195.9 million inbound tourist visits and 22.4 outbound tourist visits, while Japan's tourism consisted of 8.3 million inbound tourist visits and 17.2 million outbound tourist visits (UNWTO, 2010b). The implications of inbound and outbound tourist flows are discussed in detail in Chapter 8.

Finally, tourism can be described by the characteristics of the trip.

Table 2.4   Types of tourism by trip characteristics

Independent travel	Tourists not travelling with an organised group. Research, reservations and payments are made by the tourist direct with suppliers, or via a travel agency or wholesaler. Demand for independent travel has increased considerably since internet technology has improved, and as a result of the growth of low-cost airlines.
Inclusive travel (package travel)	A pre-arranged combination of transport, accommodation and/or other travel services, sold at one price, to groups or to individual tourists, and usually organised by a tour operator or travel agency. Usually associated with holidays, leisure and recreation but could also be used for conference and incentive travel.
Group travel	Tourists travelling with an organised group of tourists on the same trip. They may or may not know each other. The trip may be for personal or business/professional purposes. Usually group travel is also an inclusive tour.
Corporate travel	Tourism for business or professional purposes that is organised and paid for by companies. Travel agencies and tour operators may specialise in providing tourism services to corporate customers.
Mass tourism	Large-scale holiday tourism offering standardised products and experiences, requiring major infrastructural development in destinations, and with general appeal to broad tourist markets. Often equated with outbound inclusive travel to coastal resort destinations that have few features distinguishing them from other similar destinations. Often associated with negative environmental and social impacts in the destination, although this is not necessarily true.
Alternative tourism	Often used to describe specialised forms of tourism that attract low volumes of tourists. Often associated with tourism that actively benefits the host economy, environment and society. May also be described as soft tourism, eco tourism, sustainable tourism, responsible tourism or green tourism.

Source: Beaver (2002).

Trip Characteristics

In practice, tourism is often described using certain trip characteristics relating to the composition of the travel party, the method of organisation, or the scale and impacts of the trip. The main distinctions between trip characteristics are outlined in Table 2.4. In reality, there is an overlap between these different ways of describing tourism, for example one tourism trip could be described as outbound, independent, cultural tourism.

Since the 1990s, tourism has changed radically as a result of changes in the external environment. These changes have created a 'new tourism' that was notably researched by Auliana Poon.

Poon's New Tourism

In 1993, Poon published an important text that identified how tourism was being transformed. She argued that the rapid growth of tourism demand and supply between the 1950s and the 1970s had produced a form of tourism that was 'mass, standardised and rigidly inflexible' (Poon, 1993: 4). This mass tourism used the principles of mass production from the manufacturing sector to produce identical holidays in large volumes in the most cost-effective ways. The emphasis on achieving the lowest operating costs led to large-scale development, often in fragile locations, and created a number of negative environmental and social impacts in destinations. Tourists consumed their holidays 'with a lack of consideration for the norms, cultures and environment of the host countries visited' (Poon, 1993: 4). By the 1980s, mass tourism had become the business model for tourism development in many destinations.

Poon argued that mass tourism would not, and should not, survive the four key forces that were beginning to emerge at the end of the twentieth century:

- New consumers.
- New technologies.
- Limits to growth.
- Emergence of a new global best practice.

New Consumers

Poon identified 'new tourists' whose motivations, values and consumer behaviour were fundamentally different to the 'old tourists' of mass tourism. For 'old tourists', tourism was motivated by a break from routine; travel was a novelty and the specific destination was less important. Old tourists were not experienced travellers and felt more comfortable travelling in groups on pre-arranged and pre-paid inclusive tours. They were cautious, and wary of unpredictable situations, preferring consistency of quality throughout one trip; 'if they went first class, they went first class all the way' (Poon, 1993: 10).

In contrast, 'new tourists' are experienced travellers who are independent, flexible and more demanding. They want to be in control of their tourism experiences and use tourism to stand out from the crowd and demonstrate their individuality. They also want to experience something different and are spontaneous, adventurous and flexible. New tourists are happy to research and book their own travel arrangements, and unpredictability may be part of the attraction of the tourism experience. New tourists may combine tourism products from varying price categories on the same trip, for example flying with a low-cost airline and staying in a 5-star hotel.

Poon suggested that the emergence of the new tourist would require tourism suppliers to provide products that were customised to the needs of specific market segments, and that suppliers would have to understand how tourism consumers thought, felt and behaved in order to provide satisfactory experiences.

New Technologies

Poon described tourism as an 'information-intensive industry' for which information technology was an indispensable tool. Poon was writing before the internet was widely used, but even in the early 1990s, she recognised the value of IT in the processing, storing, retrieval and distribution of information. She suggested that IT would be a key tool in transforming mass tourism into new tourism because it would facilitate the provision of high quality, flexible tourism experiences to new tourists. The emergence of the internet demonstrates this clearly; it is now much easier for new tourists to research, book and pay for tourism products. The internet has thus transformed the ability of tourism suppliers to promote to and communicate with potential consumers using digital and mobile technologies.

Emergence of a New Global Best Practice

Poon suggests that developments in IT and the information age that emerged at the end of the twentieth century have created a new understanding – a new paradigm – about ideal patterns of production. In all sectors the emphasis on mass production as a production model is diminishing to make way for flexible production. Mass production generated profits through the production of large volumes of identical products, seeking to reduce the cost of each product through economies of scale, which allowed producers to compete on price. In contrast, flexible production emphasises product quality, the necessity of responding to customer needs and satisfying them through the development of customised products for specific market segments, to enable producers to compete on quality.

Poon suggested that tourism was an ideal candidate for flexible production because of the desire for individuality from new tourists and the information intensity of the sector. New tourism embraces the flexible production paradigm by providing quality tourism experiences that closely match the needs of particular market segments, continuously striving to improve customer satisfaction levels to maintain customer loyalty and innovating in the development of new products. Poon used the term 'holiday-makers' to describe tourism companies that produced quality tourism experiences at prices that compared favourably with mass, standardised and packaged alternatives. She suggested that Disneyland, Club Med, Sandals and the cruise sector were examples of flexible tourism production because their products could be customised to meet the needs of specific market segments while also maintaining low production costs.

Flexible tourism production reduces costs and increases revenue through operational and marketing innovations, rather than purely through economies of scale, for example by working in alliances and partnerships with other tourism or non-tourism related suppliers, using IT to reduce costs through automation, and through innovative pricing techniques.

Limits to Growth

Mass tourism destroys exactly what it seeks – such things as quiet, solace, pristine cultures and landscapes, unpolluted waters, intact reefs, fishes, turtles, mountains, ski slopes, wildlife and virgin forests. (Poon, 1993: 6)

Concerns about sustainability and climate change have questioned the wisdom of unlimited tourism growth. Poon suggested that mass tourism methods of production and consumption that were environmentally intensive could not continue, and that environmentally sound tourism had to be adopted for tourism to survive, and for the negative impacts of tourism to be reduced.

New tourism requires environmentally sound tourism production and consumption, for instance through environmental planning and management in destination development, environmental sensitivity in tourism suppliers' operations, and through changes to consumer behaviour in their choice of suppliers and their activities in destinations. New tourism must be sustainable tourism.

The snapshot below describes the transition from mass to more sustainable tourism in Maasai villages in Kenya's Maasai Mara game reserve.

Snapshot 2.4   Maasai Village Tours, Kenya

Maasai villagers with a visitor

Source: © Tribal Voice Communications, 2010

Maasai village tours are popular with tourists. Until 2006, tourists bought tours for about $20 each from driver-guides who retained 96 per cent of this, forcing villagers to supplement their income by pressurising tourists to buy souvenirs (Times Online, 2007).

In 2006 Tribal Voice Communications, funded by The Travel Foundation, led four villages in a pilot project to end this exploitation and create sustainable tourism experiences to increase tourism's economic benefits and enhance tourists' experience by facilitating a genuine cultural exchange.

The Mara Triangle Maasai Villages Association was established to negotiate collectively and directly with tour operators, to set up a cashless ticketing system and provide training on business practices, customer service, product development and income distribution. Ticket sales direct to tourists through partners in Nairobi and Mombasa and safari lodges prevented driver-guides from charging entry fees. Villages received 100 per cent of the ticket price from

(Continued)

(Continued)

lodges and 75 per cent from tour operator business. Advice to tourists on culturally-sensitive behaviour was printed on each ticket (Travel Foundation, 2007).

Immediately, visits to the four villages dropped because driver-guides stopped visiting. However, revenue increased by 800 per cent from the previous year as a result of the ticketed entry fees. The villages earned $30,000 in the first eight months of operation and visitor surveys showed 100 per cent satisfaction levels (Travel Foundation, 2007). Tourism income was invested in educational and sanitation projects in each village (Tribal Voice Communications, 2010).

Summary

This chapter has considered what tourism is, how it is defined, how tourism suppliers are identified and the ways in which tourism can be described. It is important to remember that our understanding of tourism is still evolving and that some of the conceptual and technical definitions we have discussed have been developed as recently as 2008.

Tourism is a massive sector that consists of a diverse range of purposes of travel, an extensive variety of suppliers and destinations, and numerous forms. It has spawned the development of destinations worldwide and demand continues to grow. Tourism is now studied widely at undergraduate and postgraduate level because of its potential to bring economic, environmental and social benefits to destinations, and to ensure that its impacts are positive rather than negative. The complexity of tourism, its vulnerability to external shocks, its economic significance and its potential detrimental impacts on destination communities and environments have created a need for in-depth understanding of all elements of the tourism system and for professional management to direct the future growth of tourism sustainably.

 ■ **Self-test Questions** ▬▬▬▬▬▬▬▬▬▬▬▬▬▬▬▬

1　Draw Leiper's tourism system and locate within it three examples of the following: types of tourist activity, forms of tourism, types of tourism supply.

2　Consider whether tourism can be described as an industry in its own right.

3　Consider your most recent experience as a tourist – do the characteristics of your trip equate with 'old tourism' or 'new tourism'?

Further Reading

Leiper, N. (1979) 'The framework of tourism: towards a definition of tourism, tourist and the tourist industry', *Annals of Tourism Research*, 6(4): 390–407.

Poon, A. (2003) 'Competitive strategies for a "New Tourism"', in C. Cooper (ed.), *Classic Reviews in Tourism*. Bristol: Channel View Publications. pp. 130–143.

Useful Websites

The Travel Foundation www.thetravelfoundation.org.uk
Tribal Voice www.tribal-voice.co.uk

3 Tourist Generating Regions

Travel and leisure have become an integral part of daily life. These changes in the role of travel and leisure in society as well as changes in the workplace ... all have implications for the travel and tourism industry. (Poon, 1993: 128)

Tourist attraction advertisement on London Underground

Source: Clare Inkson

Learning Outcomes

After reading this chapter you will understand:

- **the conditions that must prevail within a society to enable the development of demand for tourism**
- **why some regions of the world dominate as tourist generating regions**
- **the significance of different purposes of tourist travel in an international context**
- **the main international tourism destination regions.**

Introduction

In Chapter 2 we saw that the study of tourism requires an understanding of all elements of the tourism system (Leiper, 1979) or the tourism framework (Mathieson and Wall, 1982). Leiper (1979) refers to the 'tourist generating region' as an essential part of the tourism system, and Mathieson and Wall (1982) identify the crucial role of the dynamic element – demand – in the tourism framework. In this chapter we consider the conditions that enable the residents of a region to engage in tourist activity.

Levels of demand from tourists in a generating region are a reflection of the economic, social and political conditions that prevail there. Specific **enabling factors** must exist for an individual to engage in tourism. These enabling factors have emerged, or are starting to emerge, in different world regions at different times and therefore there is substantial variation between countries in their ability to generate tourists. This chapter will help you to understand the factors that influence individuals' abilities to engage in tourist activity, and the significance of holidays, VFR, and religious, health and business and professional purposes in international tourism. We end the chapter by considering the world regions that are most popular with international tourists.

Enabling factors: Conditions within a society that make it possible for individuals to engage in particular activities

Conditions that Favour the Development of Demand for Tourism

Despite descriptions of tourism as the fastest growing and largest industry in the world, tourist activity is engaged in by a minority of the world's population. People who do enjoy tourist activity predominantly reside in regions with specific economic, social and political characteristics.

In order for a country, or region within a country, to become a tourist generating area individual residents there must have:

- Leisure time.
- Discretionary income.
- Freedom from political barriers to travel.
- Access to transit routes.
- In some cases, travel intermediaries to buy tourist products from.

These are known as enabling factors that give individuals the option to engage in tourist activity. Countries where these enabling factors are enjoyed by substantial proportions of the population are likely to be major tourist generating regions.

Leisure Time

Leisure time refers to the part of an individual's time that is not committed to work, caring, or any other responsibilities, and can be spent as the individual chooses. The availability of leisure time is a key enabling factor in tourism for personal purposes as defined by the UN (2010) – holidays, leisure, recreation, VFR, education and training, health and medical care, religion and pilgrimage, and shopping. Leisure time is much less significant as an enabling factor for business and professional tourist purposes because this is largely conducted during work hours, during the working week.

The duration and frequency of an individual's participation in tourist activity for personal purposes will depend on the amount of leisure time available. Overall, levels of leisure time have been steadily increasing in industrialised economies since the late nineteenth and throughout the twentieth centuries, aided by the introduction by governments of:

- Public holidays.
- The legal right for employees to receive paid annual leave from work.
- Limits to the working week.

There are significant international differences in leisure time enjoyed by employees; in countries where the other enabling factors for tourism exist but leisure time is relatively low, we would expect the volume of tourist activity generated to also be relatively low. We will now consider the role of national holidays, paid annual leave entitlement and the working week.

Public Holidays

The concept of the public holiday, when most businesses and organisations within a country close down for a day of official holiday, was formalised by the governments of many European countries and in the USA in the mid-nineteenth century. For example, the British government introduced the Bank Holiday Act in 1871 when four specific dates were designated as holidays for banks, and consequently other business sectors that could not operate when banks were closed (Dawson, 2007).

Public holidays celebrate religious and cultural festivals or politically and historically significant events. Inevitably there is much variation between countries in the number of public holidays and the time period that is taken.

Japan and India have the highest number, with 16 a year, whereas the UK, Netherlands and Australia have the lowest with eight (Mercer, 2009). In eastern Asia, workplaces close for one week to celebrate the Lunar New Year, while in countries with a Christian tradition two days of national holiday are usually given at Christmas and at Easter. In Moslem countries three days of national holiday are given to celebrate Eid al-Adha.

In countries where the other enabling factors exist too, public holidays stimulate tourist demand; often there is a surge in movement away from main generating regions as large numbers of residents seek to leave at the same time; for example, during the week of the Spring Festival in 1999, 600,000 residents travelled out of Shanghai (Nyiri, 2006).

Paid Leave Entitlement

Paid leave entitlement stipulates the number of days' leave that an employee is entitled to each year, without sacrificing pay. Most national governments stipulate a minimum statutory entitlement although individual employers may increase this.

The rights of employees to paid leave has been relatively recently won as the snapshot below describes.

 ### Snapshot 3.1   The Development of Paid Leave Entitlement

During the early twentieth century, the pressure to provide formalised paid leave for all employees gained momentum through social and trades union movements internationally. In the years between the World Wars (1919–1939), trade unions in some industry sectors successfully negotiated paid leave for their members. In the UK in 1929, all workers in state-owned industries became entitled to paid leave, and by 1937, annual paid leave for all workers was available in 24 countries including Finland, France, the USSR, Chile, Venezuela and Norway (Dawson, 2007).

In the UK, paid leave for all full-time workers was introduced in 1938, although some salaried, white-collar jobs had already been granted paid leave entitlement for almost 100 years. The UK legislation of 1938 increased the right to paid leave to between 18 and 19 million additional workers, and substantially increased the levels of leisure time enjoyed by UK residents. The level of paid leave entitlement in any country is therefore potentially very significant as an enabling factor for tourist activity.

Research conducted by the International Labour Organisation (ILO, 2010) shows that one-third of countries globally stipulate a minimum paid leave entitlement of 20–30 days per year. However, there is much variation internationally; many Asian countries specify less than 10 days. Half the countries in Latin America stipulate 10 to 14 days annual leave, but the actual range is between six days in Mexico and 30 days in Panama. In Africa, one-third of countries require 20–23 days but the range is wide, with six days in Nigeria and 30 days in Algeria. In developed economies, paid leave entitlement varies from 10 days in Japan to 30 days in Denmark, although interestingly, Australia and the USA have no minimum statutory paid leave requirements at a national level (ILO, 2010).

Paid leave entitlement can directly affect the demand for tourism for personal purposes because it influences the volume of trips that can be taken in one year, the duration of individual trips, and therefore the distance that tourists can travel.

In addition, institutional traditions have a very strong influence on when paid leave can be taken. School holiday periods determine when families with school age children can take holidays, and in some industrial regions it is common for all factories and offices to close at the same time for holidays.

If the maximum statutory paid leave entitlement is added to the number of public holidays, employees in Brazil and Lithuania enjoy the highest number of days off a year (41), which contrasts significantly with employees in Canada (19), China (21), the USA, and Singapore (25) (Mercer, 2009).

In addition to paid leave legislation, most countries also limit the number of hours in a week that an employee can work.

The Working Week

Research by the ILO (2010) shows that on a global scale the average limit to the working week is 40 hours, but again there are significant differences internationally:

- Most developed economies, including the USA, Japan, New Zealand, Canada, and most of Europe, impose a 40-hour working week limit.

- In Asia and the Pacific over 46 per cent of countries that impose a limit have set it at 48 hours per week, and 31 per cent at 40 hours. No universal limit has been set in India and Pakistan.

- In Africa, 40 per cent of countries impose a 40-hour maximum and most of the remainder limit hours to a range between 42 and 45 hours per week.

- In Latin America and the Caribbean, the 48-hour limit to the working week dominates, with 42–45 hours being the next most common (ILO, 2010).

Shorter working weeks increase the levels of leisure time enjoyed by workers, and in areas where the other tourism enabling factors exist, potentially increase demand for short breaks and day trips.

In addition to working hours, typical work days vary internationally. For example, in Israel the typical working week is Sunday to Thursday evening or Friday noon; in Egypt, Syria and United Arab Emirates it is Sunday to Thursday; and in Iran, Saturday to Thursday. In most countries with a Christian heritage, the working week is Monday to Friday. Patterns of demand for business or personal tourist purposes are therefore likely to vary between generating regions.

The factors above indicate that leisure time has a very important role as an enabling factor in the development of demand for leisure tourism activity: it not only determines the amount of time that an individual can potentially use for tourist activities, but also, for some groups, dictates when they can engage in those activities. The variation in levels of leisure time enjoyed by the residents of individual countries suggests that some states are likely to be more significant tourist generating regions than others. However, leisure time alone is not sufficient to generate tourist demand; an individual's ability to pay for tourist activities is a crucial component.

Discretionary Income

Discretionary income refers to any personal or family income that remains after all the basics of life, such as housing, food, utilities, tax and so on, have been paid for. Tourism activity for personal purposes is often described as a discretionary purchase – that is, individuals choose to spend their money on tourist activities: it is not an essential part of life, and spending on tourist activity can be substituted by spending on other discretionary purchases. For example, instead of going on holiday, an individual may buy new furniture, or a new car, or choose to save the money.

Income levels and therefore levels of discretionary income vary between residents within the same region depending on the type of employment and subsequent level of pay that an individual earns. Within the same generating region, there will be large variations between individuals' discretionary income. Where an individual's discretionary income is high, and their levels of leisure time are high too, they may decide to take several tourist trips for personal purposes in a year. In some generating regions where tourist demand is high, for example in the UK, second and even third holidays are not uncommon for a large proportion of the population, along with several short breaks and day trips; research in 2008 showed that UK holidaymakers took more holidays and spent more on them than any other Europeans (Clegg, 2008).

There is an important link between economic development and tourism demand. The process of industrialisation expands opportunities for the business and professional classes who engage in tourism for business and professional purposes, as well as for holidays, leisure and recreation.

Industrialisation stimulates business tourism to source new markets and materials for manufacturing, the need for conferences to share knowledge with other professionals, and the demand for exhibitions to display products and expand markets. It also increases incomes by creating employment opportunities, particularly in professions that require a skilled and educated workforce, such as banking, insurance, shipping and law. Growing demand for tourism in Europe and the USA in the nineteenth century has been partly attributed to the growth of the middle classes within those economies (Weiss, 2004). In emerging economies in the early twenty-first century, the growth of the middle class is stimulating the growth in demand for leisure tourism. India, China, Russia and Brazil are becoming increasingly important as generating regions for international tourism as a result of the increase in urban middle-class consumers, stimulated by rapid economic growth in the final decades of the twentieth century.

Demand that depends on discretionary income is vulnerable to change if an individual's income changes. The snapshot below discusses the impact of the global recession on the UK as a generating region for outbound tourism.

 Snapshot 3.2   The UK as a Generating Region

Airline advertisement on London Underground

Source: Clare Inkson

(Continued)

(Continued)

The UK has been an important generating region for several decades. Many years of economic growth, low unemployment rates and low borrowing rates encouraged UK residents to spend on tourism. In 2005, UK residents were the third highest spending outbound tourist market (Mintel, 2005).

In 2008, UK residents took 69 million trips outside the UK: 45.5 million trips were for holidays and 8.9 million for business and professional purposes (ONS, 2010, cited in Gill, 2010).

The global economic collapse that began in 2007 has had a far-reaching effect on demand for tourism. Figures on outbound tourism from the UK show consistent falls in demand that had not recovered by 2010. In 2009, outbound trips by UK residents fell by 15 per cent compared to 2008, the largest decline since the 1970s. Outbound trips for business and professional purposes saw the highest decline with a 23 per cent drop from 8.9 million to 6.9 million.

Spain and France were the most popular destinations for UK outbound visitors and although they received 21.3 million visits from UK residents in 2009, this was lower than in previous years.

Rises and falls in discretionary income affect tourist demand within a generating region and also influence flows of tourists to destination regions; when incomes fall, individuals seek cheaper destinations, cheaper accommodation and transport and take fewer or shorter trips. In 2009, visits by UK residents to Egypt and Lithuania actually increased as tourists sought more affordable destinations (Gill, 2010). We discuss the impact of this in detail later in the chapter.

Freedom from Political Barriers to Travel

The ability to travel for business or leisure, or indeed any purposes, requires individuals to have the freedom to travel. In some societies, an individual's freedom to travel internationally, and perhaps domestically, is strictly controlled by the government, through the requirement to obtain exit visas or through limited access to passports, for example in China, Cuba and North Korea.

More indirectly, governments may impose currency restrictions limiting the amount of money that can be taken outside of the country, thereby effectively limiting the duration of, and expenditure on, outbound tourism. For example, the UK government imposed exchange controls that prohibited UK residents from taking more than a specified amount as a travel allowance outside of the UK; in 1952 this travel allowance was £25 but had increased to £1,000 by 1979 when the policy was terminated (Holloway, 1985).

In addition, even in countries where outbound travel is not officially regulated and controlled by governments, inbound and outbound tourist flows may be restricted by diplomatic tensions between governments. This attitude is often demonstrated through the existence, or not, of transit routes between two countries. For example, the US trade embargo prevents US passport holders from travelling freely to Cuba and there are no direct transit routes between the USA and Cuba. Similarly, there are no direct transport links between the UK and northern Cyprus, so outbound tourists from the UK must travel via Turkey. Until July 2008, all flights between mainland China and Taiwan had to be routed via Hong Kong or Macao because of diplomatic tensions between the two states.

In addition to visa and currency restrictions, tourist flows between generating and receiving regions are influenced by government attitudes to the economic regulation of transport. Economic regulation describes the controls and restrictions that prevent transport operators from responding freely to market demand and competing with each other. Until the late 1970s most states regulated coach, sea, rail and air services, but since the late 1970s a process of liberalisation, led by the USA, has relaxed government controls of domestic and international transport in many countries. The removal or reduction of economic regulation within the transport sector is often linked to specific benefits for passengers and for tourism. Factors such as the ability of new entrants to operate routes, the ease with which new routes can be set up, demand being allowed to determine the frequency of departures, and operators competing on price can often result in greater choice, more convenience and lower prices for passengers. For tourism, these changes are very significant as they stimulate demand from the generating region.

Arguably the deregulation and liberalisation of civil aviation has had the most significant impact on tourism; according to Forsyth (in Graham et al., 2008: 74), 'for many countries, aviation policy is tourism policy – if they wish to stimulate the growth of tourism, the most effective single measure they can take is to liberalise their international aviation arrangements, if they can', thus liberalising transit routes to major generating regions. We discuss the liberalisation of transport in detail in Chapter 5.

Transit Routes

'Transit routes are paths linking tourist generating regions with tourist destination regions, along which tourists travel and include stopover points' (Leiper, 1979: 397). Transit routes are a fundamental element of tourism, without which, tourism would not be possible. Transit routes create the physical link between generating and receiving regions, determining where, when and how tourists can travel, and the length and cost of their journeys.

Duval (2007) states that the relationship between transport and tourism is determined by a framework consisting of three key components: modes, networks and flows. We will consider each of these in turn.

Modes of Transport in Tourism

The term transport mode refers to the method used. Page (2005) identifies three main modes of transport (water, land and air transport) and within each mode, a range of types has evolved over time, some of them specifically as types of tourism transport:

- *Land*: private and rental cars, campervans, motorbikes, bicycles and taxis; bus and coach services; intercity and local trains.
- *Water*: cruise ships, passenger liners, canal and river boats, ferries, pleasure craft.
- *Air*: scheduled and charter airline services; scenic flights by hot air balloon, helicopter, light aircraft; space flights.

Advances in transport since the sixteenth century have revolutionised personal mobility and the ability of individuals to participate in tourist activity. The growth in demand for tourism is inextricably linked to developments in transport technology that have made each mode of transport faster, safer, and more affordable.

Technological advances that developed new types of transport or invented new engine technologies increased speed and therefore reduced journey times, expanding the range of destinations that could be reached from a generating region within a specific travelling time. For example, the development of the railway in the late nineteenth-century USA transformed travel times between New York and San Francisco from six months to one week in 1869, and between New York and Chicago from three weeks to 72 hours (Weiss, 2004) Those distances can now be travelled in six hours and two hours 20 minutes hours respectively by air. The impact of the railways in England and Wales between 1840 and 1870 was also spectacular: passenger volumes by train increased 20-fold and in the mid-1830s, it was anticipated that on a new route, passenger numbers would be at least double the volume of people who would previously have travelled the same route by road (Bagwell, 1974).

The invention of the jet engine and its application to passenger aviation transformed the speed of flight; for instance, the cruise speed of the Britannia 310, a turbo-prop, which came into service in 1956, was 571km/hour, but was surpassed three years later by the Caravelle VI R, a turbo-jet, whose cruise speed was 816km/hour (Doganis, 1991).

In addition to improvements in speed, technological advances that increase the capacity of vehicles have been particularly important in making some transit routes more affordable.

Capacity increases allow the total cost of operating a service to be divided among more passengers, thereby reducing the unit cost of each seat. A good example of this has been the development of wide-bodied planes since the late 1960s that have provided almost double the capacity of previous planes, as shown in Table 3.1.

The most popular mode of transport in tourism is land, specifically road transport, but this does vary between countries, depending on the level of

Table 3.1   Increases in aircraft capacity since 1968

Make & model	Year of introduction into service	Passenger payload capacity
Douglas DC-8-63	1968	259
Boeing 747	1969	493
Boeing 747–300	1983	660
Airbus A380	2007	882

Source: adapted from Doganis (2009: 9) and reproduced with permission from Routledge.

infrastructure provision, and on the distance tourists travel from their generating region. Aviation's share of international tourism is growing and, as Figure 3.1 illustrates, this is now over 50 per cent.

On some routes, high speed rail travel is becoming particularly important as a mode of transport for tourism. The snapshot below describes the re-emergence of rail travel in the early twenty-first century.

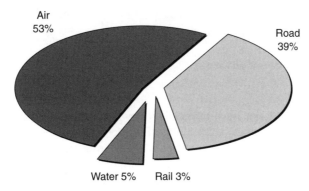

Figure 3.1   International tourism by mode of transport, 2009

Source: UNWTO (2010b: 3) © UNWTO 9284401811.

 Snapshot 3.2   High Speed Rail Travel

Towards the end of the twentieth century interest in rail travel re-emerged with the introduction of high speed train networks connecting major urban centres, which compete favourably in terms of travel time with flights. The first was in Japan in 1964 on the Tokyo–Osaka route, known as the Shinkansen or Bullet Train (Arduin and Ni, 2005), and more countries have subsequently revitalised their railways by investing heavily in rail infrastructure and high speed trains; for instance Trains à Grand Vitesse (TGV) in France, Intercity Express (ICE) in Germany, Pendolino trains in Italy and Alto Velocidad Espana (AVE) in Spain, all travelling at speeds of between 280 and 350kph.

(Continued)

(Continued)

Eurostar trains at St Pancras International London

Source: Clare Inkson

On many routes, high-speed trains have replaced air travel and road transport as the most popular mode of transport. AVE trains on the Madrid–Barcelona route, launched in 2007, can achieve speeds of up to 350kph and have reduced the airlines' share of passengers on the route from 88 per cent to 40 per cent in two years. Indeed, research suggests that rail could capture between 60 and 90 per cent of traffic on journeys of two to three hours, suggesting that rail travel provides a feasible alternative to air travel on such distances (SDG, 2009).

The ability of individuals to engage in tourism, and their choice of destinations to travel to, is determined by the transport networks that link generating and destination regions.

Tourism Transport Networks

Networks are the pattern of transport services that are operated either by a particular mode of transport or by a particular operator.

Geographers refer to networks as the routes operated within a mode or by a type of transport (Duval, 2007), for example a rail, ferry, cruise, road or air network. The development of networks linking generating and destination regions requires the provision of appropriate infrastructure – for instance airports, railway track, port facilities or maintained roads. Often the provision and quality of transport infrastructure are a reflection of economic development. MacKinnon et al. (2008) suggest that wealthy regions and nations enjoy superior transport infrastructure and a greater choice of services than less developed ones: 'modes of transport are better connected, their geographical reach is greater and fewer places are inaccessible' (2008: 10). Involvement in tourist activity is therefore likely to be easier for residents of wealthy countries who enjoy access to a range of well developed transport networks.

Individual transport operators operate networks made up of their own routes, and determine frequency of departure and capacities based on forecasts of demand. Commercial operators constantly evaluate the effectiveness of their networks and make modifications in response to changes in demand. The decision to stop operating a route, or to increase the frequency of departures on a route, will directly affect the volume of tourist flows between a generating and receiving region. For example, British Airways scrapped its route between London Gatwick and JFK in New York in October 2009 because of unacceptable profit levels, but introduced a new route to the Maldives (Business Traveller, 2009).

Transport networks determine the choice of destination regions to which tourists can travel from the generating region and when they can travel. The cost of particular transit routes determines their affordability to different social groups.

Tourism Transport Flows

A transport flow is the volume of demand for a network. Transport flows may be comprised of different types of user who use the transport network at the same or at different times; for example, rail and air services or road networks may be used by commuters, the local community or freight operators, as well as tourists.

Tourism flows themselves may consist of different types of tourist, for example business, leisure and VFR tourists, who will exhibit different seasonal patterns and different purchasing characteristics and abilities to pay. Transport operators will use pricing mechanisms to manage flows of demand to ensure that those tourists who have no choice about when to travel, for instance business tourists travelling during periods of peak business demand and leisure tourists travelling during peak holiday periods, pay the highest fares, while fares for the least popular departures will be deliberately low to stimulate demand. We discuss this in more detail in Chapter 5.

Transit routes create the physical link that enables individuals to move between generating and destination regions. However the distance between generating and destination regions creates difficulties for producers of tourist products in promoting to, and communicating with, potential customers, and has created a role for companies acting as intermediaries.

Travel Intermediaries

Tourists usually need to research, reserve and pay for transport and accommodation, and sometimes attractions too, in advance of their departure; therefore tourism suppliers need to find effective ways to enable this within the generating region. Internet technology has transformed their ability to do this, but before this became possible many suppliers relied on intermediaries to do this on their behalf.

Intermediaries, in the form of tour operators and travel agencies, create a link between producers and tourists and provide a channel by which individuals in generating regions can research, book and pay for tourist products before they leave home. Travel agencies provide points of sale in the generating region for the suppliers of tourist transport, accommodation and attractions, while tour operators sell pre-arranged packages of trips that provide assistance during the trip in the form of a local representative or a tour manager.

Tourism intermediaries have existed since the mid-nineteenth century in generating regions where the development of enabling factors increased tourist demand. The beginning of the Thomas Cook group, one of the world's largest travel brands today, demonstrates the importance of intermediaries in facilitating tourist demand, as the snapshot below describes.

 Snapshot 3.3 Thomas Cook

In 1841 Thomas Cook, a cabinet maker living in the English midlands, began organising day trips by rail for his fellow Temperance Society members. He made no profit from these trips but recognised their commercial potential: by chartering a whole train, he could sell tickets at lower prices than an individual would pay directly to rail companies.

In 1845 he began organising domestic trips by rail commercially and expanded his programme to include outbound group 'Cook's Tours' to Europe in 1855, to America in 1866, and in 1869 to Egypt and Palestine. In 1872, he launched annual round-the-world tours using steam ships across the Atlantic, the new US railway network, ships across to Asia and the newly-opened Suez Canal. These pre-arranged group tours were sold at an inclusive price and led by an experienced tour leader.

Thomas Cook is credited with two major developments:

1 The inclusive tour – removing the complexity and reducing the risk for tourists by organising the whole trip.
2 Two administrative systems that simplified travel:

  • hotel vouchers – that are presented at hotels in lieu of payment
  • the Cook's Circular Note – an early form of travellers cheque so tourists could avoid carrying large amounts of cash.

Source: Thomas Cook Group PLC (2008)

The role of intermediaries in stimulating and facilitating tourism cannot be overlooked. Tour operators have made outbound tourist trips more accessible and affordable for tourists and are often associated with the rapid growth of destinations (sometimes very controversially), particularly on the Spanish Mediterranean coast during the 1960s and 1970s. Travel agencies have provided a convenient source of travel advice, reservations and payment for tourists within their home towns, in advance of their trip. Without intermediaries, the ability to research, organise and reserve tourist products and plan trips would be much more complex.

However, the internet has transformed the ability of suppliers to communicate with potential customers directly, and, as a result, the role of intermediaries has reduced in some generating regions. In the late twentieth century, in generating regions with large numbers of residents who were experienced in buying tourism products and confident travellers, a process of 'disintermediation' occurred, whereby growing numbers of tourists began to research, reserve and pay for tourist trips independent of tour operators and travel agencies. The tourist markets for intermediaries in Europe and the USA matured and stopped growing, and in some cases, shrunk. In response, powerful intermediaries such as Thomas Cook, the TUI Travel group, American Express and Kuoni have expanded into Brazil, Russia, India and China to exploit opportunities in these newly emerging generating regions. We discuss the role and characteristics of intermediaries in detail in Chapter 6.

This section of the chapter has discussed the role of enabling factors in creating tourist generating regions. It is worthwhile remembering that no two generating regions have experienced identical patterns of growth in tourist activity by their residents: some have experienced consistent growth for two centuries, some generating regions emerged in the late twentieth century, whereas others are still experiencing very low levels of demand that show no significant growth. The penetration of tourism demand within a generating region is known as travel propensity.

Travel Propensity

Travel propensity measures the penetration of tourist activity within a generating region's population during a stated period, usually a year, and is measured as either gross or net travel propensity.

Gross travel propensity is calculated by measuring the number of tourist trips that occur from a generating region as a percentage of the population (Bowen and Clarke, 2009).

Data collected in 2005 showed that the generating regions with the highest gross propensities for outbound travel were Sweden (140.2 per cent), the Netherlands (100.9 per cent), and the UK (102.2 per cent); in each of these generating regions, the number of outbound trips exceeded the size of the population. Substantially lower gross outbound travel propensities were seen in the USA (19.4 per cent), Russia (14.2 per cent) and China (1.6 per cent) (Mintel, 2005).

Net travel propensity measures the percentage of the population that takes at least one tourist trip and identifies the proportion of the population in a generating region that participates in tourism. Net travel propensity will never be 100 per cent because there will always be some individuals who do not engage in tourist activity; Cooper et al. (2008) suggest that the maximum net travel propensity in a developed country will be between 70 and 80 per cent. To understand the demand for tourism it is useful to break this down into three basic elements:

- *Effective or actual demand*: describes the number of individuals within a generating region who engage in tourist activity. Tourism statistics measure this form of demand.

- *Suppressed demand*: describes the number of individuals within a generating region who would like to engage in tourist activity but are unable to. Suppressed demand can be further broken down to either potential demand or deferred demand. Potential demand refers to those who are unable to engage in tourism because of their personal circumstances – perhaps they have limited leisure time or disposable income. Deferred demand refers to those who are prevented from travelling by external factors – for example, because of political restrictions on freedom of movement or poor access to transit routes. If the factors that suppress demand are removed, this form of demand will become actual demand.

- *No demand*: within a generating region there will always be individuals who do not wish to engage in tourism.

Changes to an individual's leisure time, income or freedom to travel, or the development of a new transit route, may transform suppressed demand into actual demand. It is not uncommon however for actual demand to fall in a generating region and become suppressed demand in response to external events, for example when economic conditions reduce or threaten the level of individual disposable income available.

Mathieson and Wall (1982) describe tourism demand as dynamic because it is unstable and liable to change in response to changes in personal or external conditions. The extent to which demand changes is described by economists as elasticity of demand.

Elasticity of Demand

Elasticity of demand measures the sensitivity of demand to changes in consumers' income or to price changes.

The relationship between demand and price is usually inverse, that is, the higher the price of a product the lower the demand – and vice versa. Price elasticity varies between tourist markets: for instance business tourists are often described as price inelastic because demand does not increase when prices fall, whereas demand from leisure tourists is often stimulated by lower prices. Research conducted by Durbarry and Sinclair (2002) showed how price changes in one destination could affect demand in a second destination. They conducted research to measure the elasticity of demand for tourism to Malta by forecasting the impact of price changes in Malta, and of price rises in its main competitor destinations. They found that a 1 per cent increase in prices in Malta would cause a 2.9 per cent fall in tourism demand, while a 1 per cent increase in prices in Spain or Cyprus would increase the demand for Malta by approximately 1.5 per cent. Income elasticity describes how changes in personal income affect demand; as we have seen, tourism has a positive income elasticity of demand because as incomes rise, tourist demand often increases too. Durbarry and Sinclair (2002) found that a 1 per cent rise in income in Malta's main generating regions would increase the demand for Malta by about 0.7 per cent.

China is a very interesting example of the development of conditions that will stimulate an increase in the propensity to travel. The case study below explains China's development as a tourist generating region.

CASE STUDY 3.1

CHINA AS A GENERATING REGION

Travel agency in Hong Kong

Source: Suzanne Tan

(Continued)

(Continued)

Until relatively recently, Chinese citizens did not undertake tourism as a leisure activity. Maoist ideology saw leisure tourism as the product of a bourgeois society and did not permit it (Zhang, 2003: 15, cited in Nyiri, 2006: 3). After the early 1980s, outbound tourism from China was permitted for business or VFR purposes but government approval was required for each trip (Nyiri, 2006). Tourism for holidays, recreation or leisure was considered to be an activity that was only undertaken by Westerners, who began visiting China after Mao's death in 1978 (Nyiri, 2006).

When Maoist ideology started to be reformed, government attitudes to tourism changed. In 1985, the National Tourism Administration of the People's Republic of China (CNTA), which had previously focused on attracting inbound tourism, created a domestic travel department. Its first plan relating to the development of domestic tourism was approved in 1993 (Li, 2007).

Around the same time incomes in urban areas were increasing, and in 1995 the working week was reduced to five days. In 1996 the CNTA celebrated the 'Year of Leisure and Vacation', and in 1997, the development of domestic tourism became a policy priority. In 1999, the number of public holidays was increased by the government from eight to 10, creating three 'golden weeks' when businesses would close down: China National Day on 1 October, May Day on 1 May, and the Lunar Festival in Spring.

The emergence of enabling factors in China in the mid to late 1990s created rapid growth in tourist demand amongst the urban consumer class. In 1997 the government officially recognised outbound leisure tourism and introduced the 'Provisional Regulation of the Management of Outbound Travel by Chinese Citizens at their own expense'.

Outbound travel regulations required countries seeking to attract Chinese leisure tourists to enter into bilateral tourism agreements, known as Approved Destination Status (ADS), with the Chinese government (Li, 2007). Within five years, 20 ADS agreements had been established; by the end of 2008, 134 ADS agreements had been set up, including in 2008 the USA. Chinese leisure tourists cannot travel to countries that do not have ADS.

At first, visa regulations required Chinese outbound tourists to travel on organised group tours (with a minimum of five people) operated by approved tour operators and sold through CNTA-approved travel agencies. However, the demand for independent travel is now one of the strongest trends in outbound travel (VisitBritain, 2010c). Chinese outbound tourists are granted visas to travel independently if they can demonstrate that they have financial means, that they will return to China at the end of the trip, and that they are able to maintain themselves during the trip through their adequacy in the destination's language and reservations for accommodation (VisitBritain, 2010c).

China is potentially the largest generating region in the world; the UNWTO predicts three times the global average growth rates in outbound travel. Growth in demand for outbound group tours has been immense – CNTA statistics (in Li, 2007) show that in 2005, 6.79 million Chinese tourists travelled on group tours and in 2006, 8.43 million. In total, in 2006, 34.5 million Chinese tourists travelled outbound, including business, conference, VFR and educational tourists.

(Continued)

(Continued)

Reflective Questions

1 Consider the role of the Chinese government in stimulating the demand for outbound travel. Do other national governments adopt a similar function in international tourism?

2 Why would destination regions be keen to enter into ADS agreements with the Chinese government?

The potential value of China's emerging market is highly significant; if these growth rates are realised, more destination countries will compete for an increased share of the Chinese market and historical patterns of international tourist flows will be transformed.

We will now consider the most significant tourist generating regions for international tourism.

Generating Regions for Outbound Tourist Visits

Demand for international tourism has grown rapidly since the mid twentieth century. UNWTO's numbers, reproduced here as Figure 3.2, demonstrate the rapid speed of this growth in demand since 1950 and its projected continued growth by 2020. The graph shows that international tourist visits grew from about 35 million trips in 1950, to over 600 million in 2000.

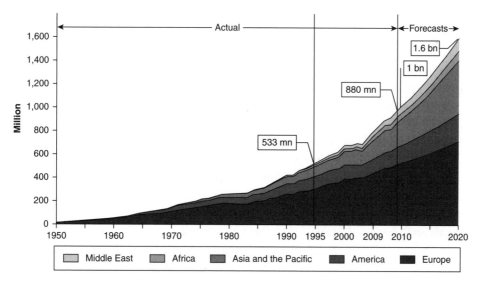

Figure 3.2 The growth in demand for international tourism

Source: UNWTO (2010b: 11) © UNWTO 9284401811.

Historically Europe and North America have dominated as tourist generating regions for international tourism, but at the beginning of the twenty-first century this domination is now being challenged by a very rapid growth in demand from generating regions like China where international tourism is a relatively new activity. The newly emerging tourist generating regions will have a very significant impact on international tourist flows. The importance of these shifts in demand and the emergence of new tourist generating regions cannot be overestimated.

The Main Outbound Generating Regions

Outbound tourism has been dominated by tourists from Europe since the 1950s because the enabling factors for tourism existed there simultaneously first. In addition, international tourism is relatively easy for Europeans because of the proximity of countries and the availability of efficient transport networks between European states. International tourist visits by residents of one country to another country within the same region are defined as 'intraregional tourism'. High levels of demand for intraregional tourism by Europeans explains Europe's dominance both as a generating region and a destination region.

UNWTO (2010b) data show the proportion of demand for international tourism by world region: Europe generates the most international tourists (54.7 per cent) followed by Asia and the Pacific (20.1 per cent), the Americas (16.4 per cent), the Middle East (3.4 per cent) and Africa (3.0 per cent). The three most significant generating regions for outbound tourism – Europe, Asia and the Pacific, and the Americas – are a reflection of the number of industrialised economies within each region. In addition, the large share of outbound tourism in Europe and Asia and the Pacific can be explained by the relative ease of intraregional travel within both regions. Interestingly though, average annual growth rates of demand for international tourism between 2000 and 2009 were highest in the Middle East (8.9 per cent), Africa (6.5 per cent) and Asia Pacific (5.0 per cent) compared to 1.1 per cent and 2.2 per cent in the Americas and Europe respectively (UNWTO, 2010b).

Table 3.2 shows the generating regions that spend the most on international tourism, namely the total spending on outbound tourism for the 10 highest spending countries. However, we should note here that the propensity for travel outbound is relatively low in some countries as a proportion of the total population, for example in China and the Russian Federation. Where this is the case, and where demand is growing at rates higher than the global averages, for example in China and Russia once again, we can expect those countries to become even more significant as generators of demand for, and expenditure on, international tourism in the future.

Table 3.2   International tourism's top spenders

Rank		International Tourism Expenditure (US$ billion)		Market share (%)	Population 2008	Expenditure per capita
		2008	2009	2009	(million)	(US$)
	World	**941**	**852**	**100**	**6,792**	**125**
1	Germany	91.0	81.2	9.5	82	989
2	United States	79.7	73.2	8.6	307	238
3	United Kingdom	68.5	50.3	5.9	62	814
4	China	36.2	43.7	5.1	1,335	33
5	France	41.4	38.5	4.5	63	615
6	Italy	30.8	27.9	3.3	60	467
7	Japan	27.9	25.1	3.0	128	197
8	Canada	27.2	24.2	2.8	34	717
9	Russian Federation	23.8	20.8	2.4	141	147
10	Netherlands	21.7	20.7	2.4	16	1,255

Source: UNWTO (2010b: 10) © UNWTO 9284401811.

Forms of Tourism

Figure 3.3 illustrates the contribution of each form of tourism to total international tourism demand. The figure shows that statistics on VFR, health and religious tourism are combined so identifying the growth of each of these separately over time is not possible on the basis of these data. The figure identifies leisure, recreation and holidays as the main purpose of international tourism.

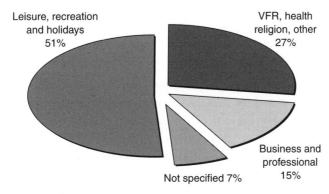

Figure 3.3   Inbound tourism by purpose of visit, 2009

Source: UNWTO (2010b: 3) © UNWTO 9284401811.

So far in this chapter we have considered the factors that must exist in generating regions to enable individuals to engage in tourist activity. The combination of leisure time, disposable income, freedom to travel, transit routes and often the services of travel intermediaries influences the distance that tourists can travel from the generating region and their choice of destination. We have identified the generating regions with the highest propensities of outbound travel, and it is useful now to consider the most significant flows of international tourists by identifying where those tourists travel to.

International Tourist Flows

The most significant destination regions in international tourism are shown in Table 3.3, illustrating the volume of international tourist arrivals within each world region.

Europe's domination of the international tourist market is clear. However, the rate of growth in demand for Europe as a destination region is not as fast as that of other regions. Europe has dominated as a destination for international tourist visits since the 1950s, but this dominance is being eroded by the emergence of new destination regions: the Americas since the 1960s, East Asia and the Pacific since the 1970s, Africa since the 1980s, and the Middle East and South Asia since the 1990s.

Within each destination region, there are significant variations in the volume of international tourist arrivals. This is a result of a number of factors existing within individual national destination areas that affect their attractiveness to inbound visitors. These factors include climate, political stability, exchange rates, the extent and quality of physical tourism development at the local level, transport links, government attitude to inbound tourism, and international image. We consider these issues in more detail in Chapter 7.

Summary

We have seen that tourism demand grows in response to the development of conditions within a society that facilitate increases in disposable income and leisure time. For these conditions to have a significant impact on levels of demand for tourism, they must exist simultaneously with the availability of fast, affordable transit routes and the freedom to travel. Additionally, the involvement of travel intermediaries has played a significant role in making almost all forms of tourism more accessible and affordable.

This chapter has shown that Europe has traditionally dominated as the main generating and receiving region of the world. However, this domination is being slowly eroded with the emergence of new generating and receiving regions in almost each decade since 1950.

In the early twenty-first century, the conditions that stimulate demand for tourism are prevalent in most developed countries. Tourism has become a multi-billion dollar activity, generating millions of trips per year. The projected

Table 3.3 International tourist arrivals

	International Tourist Arrivals (million)							Market share (%)	Change (%)		Average annual growth (%)
	1990	1995	2000	2005	2007	2008	2009*	2009*	08/07	09*/08	'00–'09*
World	**438**	**533**	**663**	**802**	**901**	**919**	**880**	**100**	**2.0**	**-4.2**	**29**
Advanced economies[1]	**300**	**339**	**423**	**451**	**496**	**494**	**470**	**53.4**	**-0.4**	**-4.9**	**1.2**
Emerging economies[1]	**139**	**194**	**260**	**351**	**405**	**425**	**410**	**46.6**	**4.9**	**-3.4**	**5.2**
By UNWTO regions:											
Europe	**265.0**	**309.1**	**392.2**	**441.0**	**485.4**	**487.2**	**459.7**	**52.2**	**0.4**	**-5.7**	**1.8**
Northern Europe	28.6	35.8	43.7	52.8	58.1	56.4	53.1	6.0	-2.9	-5.8	2.2
Western Europe	108.6	112.2	139.7	141.7	153.9	153.2	146.0	16.6	-0.4	-4.7	0.5
Central/Eastern Europe	33.9	58.1	69.3	87.5	96.6	100.0	89.5	10.2	3.5	-10.4	2.9
Southern/Mediter. Eu.	93.9	103.0	139.5	159.1	176.8	177.7	171.1	19.4	0.5	-3.7	2.3
Asia and the Pacific	**55.8**	**82.0**	**110.1**	**153.6**	**182.0**	**184.0**	**181.2**	**20.6**	**1.1**	**-1.6**	**5.7**
North-East Asia	26.4	41.3	58.3	86.0	101.0	101.0	98.1	11.1	0.0	-2.9	5.9
South-East Asia	21.2	28.4	36.1	48.5	59.7	61.7	62.1	7.1	3.4	0.6	6.2
Oceania	5.2	61	9.6	11.0	11.2	11.1	10.9	1.2	-0.9	-1.8	1.4
South Asia	3.2	4.2	6.1	8.1	10.1	10.3	10.1	1.1	1.1	-1.5	5.8
Americas	**92.8**	**109.0**	**128.9**	**134.0**	**143.9**	**147.8**	**140.7**	**15.9**	**2.8**	**-4.8**	**1.0**
North America	71.7	80.7	91.5	89.9	95.3	97.7	92.1	10.5	2.6	-5.7	0.1
Caribbean	11.4	14.0	17.1	18.8	19.8	20.1	19.5	2.2	1.2	-2.9	1.5
Central America	1.9	2.6	4.3	6.3	7.8	8.2	7.6	0.9	6.4	-7.4	6.5
South America	7.7	11.7	15.9	19.0	21.0	21.8	21.4	2.3	3.8	-1.6	3.3
Africa	**14.8**	**18.9**	**26.5**	**35.4**	**43.1**	**44.2**	**45.6**	**5.2**	**2.5**	**3.1**	**6.2**
North Africa	8.4	7.3	10.2	13.9	16.3	17.1	17.6	2.0	4.8	2.5	6.2
Sub-Saharan Africa	6.4	11.6	16.3	21.5	26.9	27.2	28.1	3.2	1.1	3.4	6.3
Middle East	**9.6**	**13.7**	**24.9**	**37.8**	**46.7**	**55.6**	**52.9**	**6.0**	**19.0**	**-4.9**	**8.8**

Source: UNWTO (2010b: 4) © UNWTO 9284401811.

increase in growth of demand suggests that by 2020 participation in tourism will have penetrated further into emerging generating areas, and, consequently, more destination areas will also emerge to satisfy this demand.

 ■ **Self-test Questions**

1   Investigate the levels of outbound tourism from a country of your choice, using UNWTO statistics available at http://unwto.org/. Can you explain this level of demand and suggest how it may change in light of economic and social trends within that region?

2   Consider the domestic and international transport networks that exist within your selected generating country. Can you suggest where residents can travel to most easily as tourists?

3   How has the global economic crisis affected tourist demand from your selected generating region?

Further Reading

Henshall, B. and Roberts, R. (1985) 'Comparative assessment of tourist generating markets for New Zealand', *Annals of Tourism Research*, 12(2): 219–238.
Lim, C. and McALeer, M. (2005) 'Analysing the behavioural trends in tourist arrivals from Japan to Australia', *Journal of Travel Research*, 43(4): 414–421.

Useful Websites

United Nations World Tourism Organization: http://unwto.org/
World Travel and Tourism Council: http://www.wttc.org/

4 Tourism Demand

A child on a farm sees a plane overhead and dreams of a faraway place. A traveller on the plane sees the farmhouse ... and thinks of home. (Burns, 2008: 6)

Tourists gather to watch coverage of the Royal Wedding in Hyde Park

Source: Lynn Minnaert

Learning Outcomes

After reading this chapter you will understand:

- the different motivators that underlie tourists' desire to travel, and understand the main models of tourism motivation
- the uses and limitations of tourist typologies
- the different models of decision-making processes that apply to tourists when they select and buy travel products
- the different methods that can be used to monitor and forecast tourism demand.

Introduction

In the previous chapter we discussed the conditions that enable an individual to participate in leisure tourism. However, the existence of these enabling conditions is not sufficient to explain why an individual chooses to spend their leisure time and discretionary income on tourist activity. The most basic question therefore is this: why do individuals engage in tourism in the first place? Why do they spend their money on tourist trips when there are so many other consumer products to choose from? And once they have decided to spend their money on tourism, why do they go to certain destinations and engage in certain activities, when there are virtually limitless choices on offer? Furthermore, how do they make these decisions, and what can the tourism industry learn from this?

In this chapter we consider a number of issues related to the demand for tourism. We begin by discussing tourist motivations: the underlying psychological drivers that create the decision to travel and influence the decisions tourists make. On the basis of these decisions, tourists are often categorised into different tourist types, and we consider a number of models of tourist typologies, their usefulness and their limitations. We then look more closely at how these travel decisions are made, before discussing how tourism demand can be measured, monitored, and forecasted.

Tourist Motivations

Academics have been interested in the motivations behind tourism behaviour and travel for several decades. Their research has resulted in a wide variety of definitions and models of tourism motivations. This section provides an explanation of the most significant approaches.

Definitions

The motivation for tourism has been defined in different ways by numerous authors. Table 4.1 contains a number of examples of these.

The different definitions show that tourist motivation is a complex concept to describe and research. Pearce and Lee (2005) point out that tourist motivation is not the same as the purpose of travel: it is easy to identify whether an individual travels for leisure or business, for example. The underlying motivations for tourism though may be **covert**: they may be formed within a traveller's psyche and based on their individual needs and wants. A number of models have been developed over the last decades that have

Covert: Hidden, not openly shown or avowed

Table 4.1   Definitions of motivation

A psychological condition in which an individual is oriented towards and tries to achieve a kind of fulfilment. (Bromley, 1990: 264)
It acts as a trigger that sets off all the events involved in travel. (Parrinello, 1993: 234)
A state of need, a condition that serves as a driving force to display different kinds of behaviour toward certain types of activities, developing preferences, arriving at some satisfactory outcome. (Backman et al., 1995: 15)
The cause of human behaviour. (Mook, 1996: 12)
A set of needs, which predispose a person to participate in touristic activity. (Piznam and Mansfield, 1999: 7)
The driving force behind all actions (Pearce and Lee, 2005: 226)

attempted to structure these needs and wants and their relationship to tourist behaviour. The following section discusses a selection of these – it does not refer to all models that are in existence, but introduces the most influential ones.

Tourist Motivation Models

There is no one commonly agreed theoretical approach to understanding tourist motivation (Holden, 2005: 67). Instead, a number of models, each with their own particular focus and emphasis, propose a framework to better understand what motivates tourists. These are usually rooted in social science disciplines such as psychology or sociology. There are similarities and overlaps between some of the models, and, in general, they complement, rather than contradict, each other. The choice of model for use in a particular study or research project often depends on which aspect of motivation is being studied – and it is not uncommon for researchers to draw on different models in the same text. We have distinguished between models using four themes: tourist motivation as a result of needs; tourist motivation in relation to a 'centre'; tourist motivation as a ladder/career; and tourist motivation as a combination of push and pull factors.

Tourism in Relation to Needs

In these models, it is proposed that tourists become involved in tourism to fulfil a need that cannot easily be fulfilled in their own environment. Several tourist motivation models are based on Maslow's (1954) Hierarchy of Needs. Maslow identified five human needs that he then organised into a hierarchy as depicted in Figure 4.1.

On the first level, we find *physiological* needs. These are the most basic needs that have to be met for a human being to survive and function. Examples are food and drink, sleep and sexual activity. If these needs are not met, then

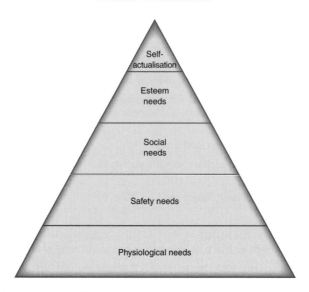

Figure 4.1   Maslow's Hierarchy of Needs (after Maslow, 1954)

human beings start to focus fully on satisfying them, and all other needs disappear into the background.

On a second level, we find *safety* needs. Examples of these are security, stability, freedom from fear and chaos, and the need for law and order. Self-protection is a very basic human need, and Maslow argues it will dominate all others if threatened. In extreme situations, such as wars, practically everything can look less important than keeping safe. In non-extreme situations, this can refer to job security or the need for insurance or a savings account.

On the third level, there are *social* needs, also called *belonging and love* needs, which refer to giving and receiving affection. This can involve a partner, family members, or friends. When these needs are not satisfied, the person feels lonely, rejected and ostracised. This person's behaviour may then become focused on forging relations via joining clubs, networks, or indeed, going on a group holiday.

The fourth level is occupied by *esteem* needs: these refer to the need humans feel to have a stable and high evaluation of themselves. This high evaluation is reached through self-respect, or the respect of others. We achieve this via our achievements and competences, or by accruing fame, glory, prestige and appreciation.

The highest level of needs is *self-actualisation* needs. This level refers to the need humans feel to develop themselves, and to do something they are particularly talented in. Artists feel a deep need to be involved in their art; athletes find themselves in their sport. The form these needs take will vary greatly from person to person: self-actualisation principally refers to whatever it is that makes people feel they are realising their potential and developing their full capabilities: 'However, the common feature of the needs of self-actualisation is that their emergence usually rests upon some prior satisfaction of the physiological, safety, love and esteem needs' (Maslow, 1954: 22). In other words, before people can develop themselves fully, all other needs will usually need to be met first – it is hard to focus on self-realisation when one feels hungry, unsafe, lonely or unappreciated. An individual is therefore motivated to satisfy needs from the bottom level upwards, and progress cannot be made from one level to another unless the lower levels are satisfied.

Tourism can be seen as a way to meet a number of these needs. Although it is not a basic need, such as food, shelter or safety, it can potentially fulfil love needs, esteem needs and self-actualisation needs. Travelling with family or friends can strengthen personal relationships. Tourists may also forge new relationships on holiday, thus fulfilling social needs. Some holiday types or destinations are prestigious and exclusive – this could gain tourists the respect of others and fulfil their esteem needs. Finally, tourism can be a deep, meaningful experience that makes tourists feel they are achieving their potential – in this case self-actualisation needs are addressed.

Beard and Ragheb (1983) adapted Maslow's model specifically to tourism and leisure needs. They developed a motivational typology of four components to explain people's participation in tourist and leisure activities:

- *Intellectual component*: this motivates people to use tourism to undertake mental activities like learning, exploring, thinking and imagining.
- *Social component*: in this case people undertake tourism and leisure activities for social reasons: to make friends, gain people's esteem or to build inter-personal relationships.
- *Competence-mastery component*: usually this refers to physical activities: people engage in these to master new skills, compete with others or challenge themselves.
- *Stimulus-avoidance component*: these motivators relate to getting away from stressful or problematic environments, for example at work. People engage in tourism to relax and unwind.

McIntosh et al. (1995) developed a similar model with four categories of motivation:

- *Physical motivators*: these relate to the refreshment of body and mind, health purposes, sport and leisure. They are usually engaged in to reduce tension.
- *Cultural motivators*: these concern the desire to learn about new cultures or the music, art, architecture and lifestyles of a destination.
- *Interpersonal motivators*: these are linked to meeting new people, or visits to friends and family. They can also refer to the escape from the home environment, or spiritual reasons.
- *Status and prestige motivators*: these are concerned with the desire for attention and recognition from others in order to boost personal ego. They may include a desire for the continuation of education, or personal development in the pursuit of hobbies.

Physical motivators answered in Montenegro

Source: Lynn Minnaert

Both models link the needs that were highlighted by Maslow to travel and tourism. Beard and Ragheb's (1983) stimulus-avoidance component can be linked to Maslow's physiological needs (rest). McIntosh et al's (1995) status and prestige motivators can be linked to Maslow's esteem needs. The main difference is that where Maslow's needs are presented in a clear hierarchy, the other two models do not make one type of motivator dependent on the fulfilment of other needs. They also leave open the option that tourists are motivated by more than one type of need.

Tourism in Relation to a 'Centre'

Cohen's (1979) model was one of the first to look at the sociological motivations of tourists. Cohen regarded the motivations for travel as the search for certain tourist experiences in relation to a 'centre'. The 'centre' is a theoretical concept that refers to values and meanings that are important and valuable for the individual. The centre is what people value, the principles by which they want to lead their lives, aspects that are 'central' to who they are. The centre can be religious, spiritual or cultural, or entirely personal – whatever gives a deeper meaning to someone's life, can be part of the 'centre'.

Cohen used this concept to critique a common view of tourism at the time he was writing: that tourism was a frivolous, superficial and trivial phenomenon.

He identified five types of tourist experiences and their underlying motivations and relationship to the 'centre'. Together, the five types form a spectrum of motivations for tourism, from the quest for superficial 'mere pleasure', to a search for deep and meaningful, in some cases life-changing, tourist experiences. These five types are:

1 *The recreational mode*: In this form of tourism, the motivation of tourists is to take a break from daily life and come back refreshed and positive. A holiday in this sense is a form of entertainment that is similar in nature to the cinema, the theatre, or television. With regard to tourism, tourists on a sun-sea-sand holiday, who do not engage with the local culture much and just want to relax, could be seen as being in recreational mode. Tourism is in this case far removed from the 'centre': 'Though the tourist may find his experiences on the trip "interesting", they are not personally significant' (Cohen, 1979: 184). Like other forms of mass entertainment, these forms of tourism may be seen as superficial, shallow and trivial: the tourist may be lured by commercialised, contrived, or even inauthentic tourism products in the destination. But rather than seeing this as a sign that the tourist lacks insight, Cohen argues that the tourists in this category get what they want: the pleasure of entertainment. Authenticity may not be all that relevant to them: tourism can be seen as similar to a movie or a play – even though the spectators know what they see is not real, it is still enjoyable. With regard to motivation for travel, tourism is thus mainly seen as a 'pressure valve' (Cohen, 1979: 185): when real life, and everything related to the real 'centre', become too stressful, a holiday takes the pressure off. From this perspective, tourism plays an important role in modern society: by 'getting away' for a period of time, the tourists can, upon their return, fully focus again on their 'centre'.

2 *The diversionary mode*: In this form of travel tourism is seen as a diversion, as an escape from boredom and meaningless routine. This is a rather pessimistic view of travel motivations: it suggests that for some people their professional and personal life is unrewarding, and that tourism is just a way to find temporary oblivion. Whereas in the recreational mode people concentrate fully on their 'centre' after their return, travellers in this mode have lost sight of their 'centre': nothing is important to them any more. The motivation for travel is superficial and non-committed, not thought through: it is entirely a search for meaningless pleasure. This view of tourism often underlies critiques on modern mass tourism: tourism is then seen as 'a symptom of the general *malaise* in modern society' (Cohen, 1979: 186).

3 *The experiential mode*: In this form of tourism, people who have lost their 'centre' start looking for meaning in the life of others via tourist experiences. The motivation to travel is thus a search for meaning outside their own society and culture: it is important that tourist experiences are authentic and meaningful themselves. From this point of view, tourism is almost like a religious quest or pilgrimage, with the difference that tourists may be looking at religions that are not their own, usually without necessarily wanting to be converted to this different way of life. The experiential mode is thus more profound than the previous two, but does not generate 'real' religious experiences (Cohen, 1979: 188).

4 *The experimental mode*: This form of tourism seeks, just like the previous one, new meaning and a new 'centre' through tourism. In this form though, the trip takes on more

of a spiritual significance. The motivation for experimental tourists in this model is to 'find themselves' (Cohen, 1979: 189) via tourism. Often this involves sampling different cultures, different alternatives, in the hope that one will suit their needs perfectly or satisfy their centre. Because of the profound spiritual motivation, the actual tourist activities may take a different form compared to the previous modes: the tourist may spend time in a hippie commune, an Israeli kibbutz, or a small village in a developing country. In some cases, these tourists discover the meaning they are looking for, and for them the experience may become a new way of life. In other cases though, the tourists become drifters, and never find the deep spiritual experience they set out to find.

An Israeli Kibbutz in the 1970s

Source: Rafi Kornfeld

5 *The existential mode*: This mode of tourism refers to tourists who have found a new 'centre' through tourism, and for whom the experience has taken on a deep spiritual meaning. This may mean that the tourists move permanently to a destination where they have found this deeper meaning, or it may mean that they visit the destination periodically on a sort of 'pilgrimage', from a place that is, for them, devoid of meaning to their new 'centre'. The motivation to travel is thus profoundly to 'derive spiritual **sustenance**' (Cohen, 1979: 190).

> **Sustenance:** Something that provides support or nourishment

Cohen (1979) concludes that some tourist motivations are much easier to realise than others. Recreational and diversionary tourists, for example, seek entertainment and pleasure, they require little with regard to authenticity – so as long as the trip was pleasurable, the tourists can be seen to have achieved their goal. For tourists in the other categories, authenticity is crucial – travel has a deeper spiritual meaning. There is a much greater risk in these cases that the trip may not meet the expectations of the tourist, and that tourist experiences do not bring the tourist any closer to a 'centre'.

Snapshot 4.1 Lifestyle Travellers or Tourists? Travel as a 'Centre'

For most people, travel can be seen as a break from everyday life, that takes place either at certain times of the year, or that marks the transition from one life stage to the next (gap years and honeymoons for example). There are a small minority however who see leisure travel as 'a way of life that they may pursue indefinitely' (Cohen, 2010: 64): these people can be seen as 'lifestyle travellers'. For this group, travel is not a way to get closer to a 'centre': travel is the 'centre' itself. As opposed to the 'existential mode' discussed above, they do not tend to relocate to a destination to start a more permanent life – their ideal is to keep moving, to keep exploring. If they take up employment at one of their destinations or in the home environment, they only do this because it allows them to earn enough money to set off again. In each destination, the lifestyle travellers can test a different way of life in their quest for meaning. Lifestyle travellers are usually experienced backpackers who want to distance themselves from the enclaves and routes that are well-trodden by other backpackers in large numbers (Cohen, 2010).

Travel as a 'Career'

The models discussed so far have discussed tourist motivations at one particular point in time – these motivations may affect the tourist when deciding to travel, choosing a destination or engaging in certain activities. Pearce (2005), however, discusses tourist motivations over a longer period: he argues that tourists may change their travel motivations over time, as their experience of tourism grows. His model is based on Maslow's Hierarchy of Needs model to show how tourism experiences can change. Pearce proposes that:

> many people systematically move through a series of stages or have predictable travel motivational patterns. One pattern proposed is that over time some people may be seen as moving towards more self-esteem and self-actualisation needs, while others may stay at a relationship or stimulation level, depending on contingency or limiting factors such as health and financial considerations. (2005: 53–54)

As people accumulate travel experiences, they may thus be able to move to different travel motivations: from this perspective, tourism may be seen as a 'career'. The state of someone's travel career, like a career at work, may be influenced by several factors: previous experience, travel budgets, lifestyle, family commitments, or age. A tourist can be said to reach a higher level in his or her travel career when self-development through tourism becomes more important. Pearce and Lee's (2005) empirical study has shown that it is usually the tourists with more travel experience who see tourism as a form of self-development and self-education, through experiencing different cultures and meeting the local population. This does not mean though that tourists with less travel experience necessarily approach tourism in a frivolous and meaningless way: this group scored more highly in the area of personal development: developing skills and talents, gaining self-confidence, and gaining a sense of accomplishment. A tourist may, for example, learn how to scuba-dive in a holiday resort and gain a sense of personal satisfaction from doing so. It can thus be proposed from this study that as individuals gain more travel experience, it is the motivation to interact with the destination itself which often becomes stronger. The travel career is not hierarchical: tourists with more travel experience may look for self-actualisation on one holiday, but might decide to book a package deal to an all-inclusive resort in order just to relax on their next holiday.

Tourism as a Combination of 'Push' and 'Pull' Factors

The models discussed so far suggest a range of different motivations for tourist activity, but they don't show how these motivations influence the choice of destination. Models with 'push' and 'pull' factors distinguish between the reasons why individuals participate in tourism at all, and the reasons why they travel to a particular destination.

Dann (1977) describes tourist activity as the result of push and pull factors. 'Push' factors are the personal drivers that predispose a tourist to travel, for example a need to escape the daily routine, a need to spend quality time with the family, or the lust for adventure. Dann argues that there were two main push factors for tourism: on the one hand the need 'to get away from it all', to escape the stresses of daily life (he called this an escape from 'anomie'); and on the other hand the search for status and a feeling of superiority (he called this 'ego-enhancement'). 'Pull' factors are the elements that attract a tourist to a specific destination in order to satisfy the push factors. Pull factors could be a sunny climate, a music festival, opportunities for scuba-diving, or a famous art gallery.

Crompton (1979) expanded on this theory by investigating the 'push' factors further. He argued that the tourism industry was too concerned with the attributes of destinations (pull factors), whereas for many tourists, the destination itself can be relatively unimportant. Crompton also argued that in many cases 'respondents did not go to particular locations to seek cultural insights or artefacts; rather they went for socio-psychological reasons unrelated to any specific destination. The destination served merely as a medium through which these motives could be satisfied' (1979: 415). In other words, tourists may decide to travel because they want to relax on the beach with their family or loved ones. Where exactly this activity takes place may be of secondary importance. The beach resort in question may be in Malta, Cyprus, Kenya or Mexico – as long as the needs of the tourist are met, and there are opportunities to relax on the beach, the holiday experience is satisfactory.

The pull of the beach of Ile de la Vache, Haiti

Source: Valérie Svobodová

Crompton (1979) distinguishes between seven types of socio-psychological motives for travel, two of which were also identified by Dann. The seven motives are:

- *Escape from a perceived mundane environment*: this motive refers to the escape from boredom and routine, or from an urbanised environment.

- *Exploration and evaluation of the self*: being in a new environment, and engaging in different activities, can lead to self-discovery – by travelling, tourists can gain a better insight into themselves.

- *Relaxation*: this motive mainly refers to mental relaxation. Some tourists can engage in intense and exhausting sporting activities whilst on holiday, but still feel they have come home 'relaxed'; for others, physical relaxation and 'doing nothing' is equally important.

- *Prestige*: the motivation here is the attainment of status amongst peers by engaging in tourism, or by visiting certain destinations. Crompton argues that in generating regions with a high propensity to travel, the prestige motivation has diminished because participation in tourism is no longer limited to the elite; however the destination, accommodation type or class of travel can be a source of prestige.

- *Regression*: tourists can feel free from obligations on holiday, which encourages some to behave in a more irrational and juvenile manner, such as indulging in heavy drinking or drug use, even though they do not do this at home.

- *Enhancement of kinship relations*: this motive refers to spending 'quality time' with family and loved ones, bonding and reconnecting to others. Family holidays or VFR are examples.

- *Facilitation of social interaction*: for some tourists, holidays are an opportunity to interact with others. These contacts can be rather brief, or develop into friendships or relationships. Group holidays or organised tours can facilitate social contacts.

Apart from these socio-psychological motives, Crompton (1979) also refers to cultural motives for travel, such as exploring new cultures and destinations, or learning about these to become a more rounded individual.

When choosing a destination, the tourist searches for a place where the push factors described above can be matched with appropriate pull factors. Tourists for whom the search of prestige is an important push factor may be attracted by the pull of exclusive and luxurious facilities of exotic destinations such as the Seychelles. On the contrary, tourists for whom evaluation of the self is a push factor may rather be attracted to the pull factors of a meditation facility deep in the Scottish Highlands.

Complex Motivations

From the variety of models that exist (of which a number have been described above) it can be seen that tourist motivations are complex and highly personal constructs. What motivates a person to engage in tourism can change over time and even by trip – many individuals will take several short trips per year and the motivations for each of these trips can be very different. A tourist might, for example, go on a two-week holiday to a Turkish beach resort, to relax and spend time with the family, and later go on a fishing trip to the Scottish Lakes with friends. When travelling in groups, each person's motivations need to be taken into account, which may result in a number of compromises. Models are helpful tools for the analysis of motivations, but may not reflect this highly complex combination of motives. The case study below considers research that has been conducted into the tourist motivations of the gay community.

CASE STUDY 4.1

MOTIVATIONS OF GAY TOURISTS

The models above have shown that tourism motivations can be linked to a range of personal characteristics and personality traits. In recent years, academic tourism literature has shown an increasing interest in the demand and motivations of the gay tourist. This market segment is of particular interest to the tourism industry, as the gay community are generally seen as high spenders – this is often referred to as the 'Pink Pound/Euro/Dollar' (Waitt and Markwell, 2006). Understanding the travel motivations and purchasing decisions of gay tourists is therefore vitally important for destinations that want to attract this market.

The gay tourist market is often seen as desirable because of a number of typical characteristics. Gay tourists are usually characterised by high education and income levels, and they tend to spend more on discretionary items such as holidays. Not only is their travel propensity higher, they also tend to spend more on these trips. This can be linked to the fact that gay people are less likely to have children, and thus have more free time. They are also generally seen as more style-conscious and more individualistic in their purchasing decisions (Hughes, 2002; Pritchard et al., 1998; Waitt and Markwell, 2006).

Several authors have indicated that this view of the gay market may not reflect reality completely. Hughes (2002) highlights that there are differences in class and wealth in this segment of the population, just as in any other: not all gay people are affluent and well educated. He adds that 'defining a market segment by its sexuality conceals a diversity of age, income, occupation, social class, race, family, attitudes and interests, any or all of which may have a more decisive influence on purchasing patterns' (2002: 154). Hughes (2002) and Pritchard et al. (1998) also highlight that many studies focus on homosexual men and that there are differences between the characteristics of this group and those of lesbians, bisexuals and transsexuals. Pritchard et al., for example, emphasise that lesbians are more likely to develop families by having or adopting children.

Clift and Forrest (1999) researched the travel decisions of 590 gay men in the UK, and established the most popular destinations, as shown in Figure 4.2.

(Continued)

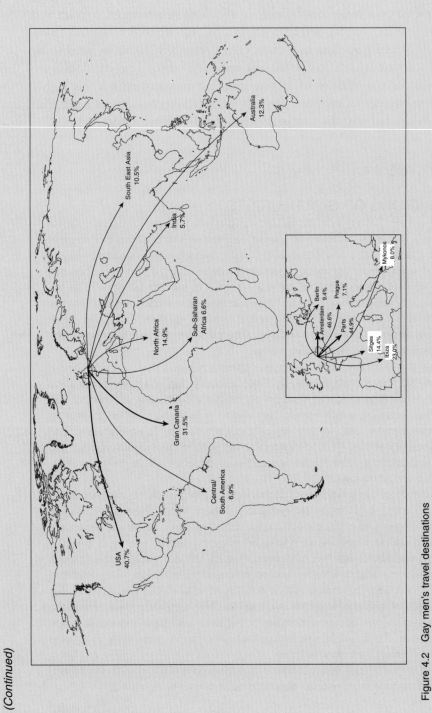

Figure 4.2 Gay men's travel destinations

Source: Clift and Forrest (1999: 619). Reprinted from *Tourism Management* with permission from Elsevier © 1999.

(Continued)

After London, which nearly three-quarters of men had visited in the last five years for a holiday, almost half of the sample had visited Amsterdam, and over 40 per cent had visited Paris. Just over 40 per cent of respondents had travelled to the United States. Next, in terms of popularity, were destinations in the Canary Islands, Gran Canaria (31.5 per cent) and Ibiza (23 per cent), all of which have well known gay resorts. Destinations in Europe and North America were thus the most popular, but smaller groups of gay tourists had visited North Africa, Australia, South East Asia, and Central and South America. This corresponds with travel patterns in the general market (Clift and Forrest, 1999) – even though a number of destinations have a particular appeal to gay tourists (for example Sitges in Spain), many other destinations such as Paris and Amsterdam are equally popular with heterosexual visitors.

Table 4.2 looks in more detail at gay tourists' travel motivations. From the findings, it is clear that a large majority of gay men, no less than heterosexual tourists, place

Table 4.2 Gay men's travel motivations

	Very important (%)	Fairly important (%)	Not important (%)
How important are each of the following to you when you plan a holiday?			
Comfort and good food	70.9	25.1	4.0
Opportunities for rest and relaxation	70.2	22.5	7.3
Guaranteed sunshine	51.4	31.8	16.8
Good night-life	47.9	39.6	12.5
Opportunities to socialise with gay men	36.6	40.2	23.2
Gay culture and venues	39.1	41.1	19.7
Dramatic or beautiful landscapes	38.4	45.0	16.6
Opportunities to see local culture	37.5	46.3	16.2
Opportunities to have sex	29.3	35.3	35.4
Getting away from other people	27.6	36.6	35.8
Getting off the beaten track	27.5	39.1	33.4
Convenient and cheap holiday package	24.9	36.7	38.4
Seeing well known tourist sights	21.1	50.2	28.7
Visiting art galleries and antiquities	17.7	33.5	48.8
Opportunities to see wildlife and nature	13.3	39.1	47.6
Good sporting facilities/ exercise	10.1	23.5	66.5

Source: Clift and Forrest (1999: 620). Reprinted from *Tourism Management* with permission from Elsevier © 1999.

(Continued)

(Continued)

a high value on comfort, good food, relaxation and guaranteed sunshine when planning a holiday. A much smaller proportion appear to be seeking an active holiday which takes them off the beaten track, or which gives them the opportunity to see wildlife and nature, or participate in sports and exercise. The social dimensions of a holiday, and in particular the gay character of a holiday, are important for approximately a third of the sample. It is particularly interesting that the item 'opportunities to have sex' generated a fairly even response across the available answers, with only 29.3 per cent considering this very important, 35.3 per cent fairly important, and 35.4 per cent not important. The more obviously 'touristic' motivations of experiencing different cultures, seeing well known tourist sights, and visiting galleries, gave a wider range of responses, with nearly 40 per cent interested in local culture, but less than 20 per cent being drawn to art galleries and antiquities (Clift and Forrest, 1999: 622).

This study shows that generally, the travel motivations of straight and gay tourists are very similar. This indicates that sexual orientation may not be the primary lens through which people view holiday destinations, and certainly dispels the myth that gay tourists are solely or largely motivated by sexuality when they travel (Waitt and Markwell, 2006). Large proportions of gay men holiday in destinations with an established reputation for being gay, and equally substantial numbers of men also holiday in a wide range of destinations which would not be characterised as gay (Clift and Forrest, 1999). Hughes (2002: 154) supports this view, and states that 'gay men seek holiday destinations that meet the usual requirements of a holiday but which also offer gay space and an absence of homophobia'. It should finally be remembered that many men may undertake two, three or more holidays a year, and the factors influencing choice of destination may vary substantially from one holiday to the next for the same man (Clift and Forrest, 1999).

Reflective Questions

1 On the basis of McIntosh et al's (1995) model, which needs underlie the travel motivations for gay tourists?
2 Some destinations, such as Gran Canaria, are popular with both gay tourists and traditional families. How do the motivations for both groups compare? Can you think of potential conflicts between the two markets?

The research into tourist motivations has led to the development of a number of tourist type models. These will now be discussed.

Tourist Types

Since the 1970s, a range of authors has developed typologies of tourists to model tourism demand. These models aimed to group tourists with similar characteristics and connect them to destinations and activities they would be likely to choose. Some models also focus on the underlying values of tourists, and the meanings they attribute to travel. By grouping tourists with homogeneous needs, different market segments can be distinguished – this process is referred to as segmentation. Even though some models are now fairly old, they are well established concepts in tourism theory.

Cohen's Typology

Cohen (1972) was the first scholar who attempted to divide tourists into different categories. He distinguished between four tourist types, and based his model on the relationship of the tourist with the 'novelty' or 'strangeness' of the visited culture. One of the key attractions of tourism is that the tourist spends time away from the home environment, where certain needs can be better met. How familiar or unfamiliar these places are can vary widely: there will be differences in the level of strangeness or challenge that a tourist seeks.

- *The organised mass tourist*: tourists of this type prefer to stay within a tourist 'bubble', in an environment that has similarities with their routine environment. They tend to travel in groups on pre-arranged trips that are organised by an intermediary (see Chapter 6), often travel on special tourist transport, and are often accompanied by a tour leader or resort representative. They require food that is familiar, and to communicate in their own language or another language the tourist understands. Familiarity is at a maximum, novelty at a minimum (Cohen, 1972: 167).
- *The individual mass tourist*: this type is similar to the organised mass tourist but prefers some flexibility to venture outside of the familiar 'bubble' occasionally during the trip, perhaps by taking local transport to visit a site independently, or sampling a local meal.
- *The explorer*: this type of traveller organises the trip independently, and requires comfortable accommodation and a reliable means of transportation. Explorers try to engage with the local community more and will also try to speak their language – they will attempt to break out of the familiar 'bubble' and experience the 'real' destination. Explorers look for novelty, but still maintain certain routines and levels of comfort from their home life.
- *The drifter*: this type of tourist tries to completely immerse themselves in the host culture: live the way the host community lives, eat the food they eat, and fully share their habits. For this type of tourist, familiarity is at a minimum and novelty at a maximum.

Plog's Typology

Similarly to Cohen, Plog (1974, 1991, 2004) developed a tourist typology on the basis of tourists' willingness to experience unfamiliarity and novelty on holiday. His model additionally connects visitor types to the sorts of destinations they are most likely to visit: it argues that tourism changes destinations, and that very different types of tourists are often attracted to one destination over time.

An allocentric traveller trekking through the desert

Source: Jonathan Collings

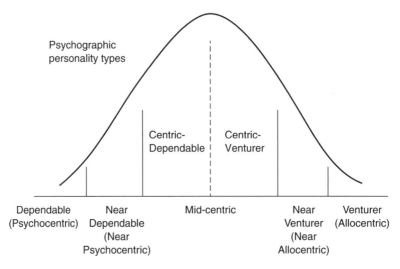

Figure 4.3   Plog's typology of allocentric and psychocentric tourists

Source: Plog (1991). Reprinted with permission of John Wiley & Sons, Inc.

Plog's typology consists of two main types: *allocentrics* and *psychocentrics*. Allocentrics seek out unique and novel travel experiences and are usually the first to discover a destination. When they feel tourism has 'spoilt' a destination, they will seek alternative 'unspoilt' destinations. Psychocentrics prefer a destination with familiar amenities, such as modern hotels, good transport links and well developed attractions. They usually visit destinations with a tourist infrastructure. In the middle of the two extremes are mid-centrics, who are between the two extremes and looking for a destination that is neither wholly familiar, nor wholly unfamiliar.

Table 4.3 summarises the key travel behaviours and characteristics of allocentrics and psychocentrics.

Table 4.3   Allocentric and psychocentric travel motivations

Allocentrics	Psychocentrics
Prefer non-touristy areas	Prefer the familiar in travel destinations
Engage in lots of new activities	Engage in fewer new activities
Want spontaneity and accept unpredictability in trips	Want structured, routinised travel
Want new destinations for each trip	Prefer returning to the same and familiar places
Spend more money on travel	Spend more money on material goods
Seek off-the-beaten-track hotels and restaurants	Want standard hotels and conventional meals

Source: based on Plog (1991: 66–67).

Snapshot 4.2   Tourists, Travellers and Holidaymakers

In his book *Welcome to Everytown*, philosopher Julian Baggini (2008) discusses how, in his opinion, there are not only tourists and travellers but also 'holidaymakers'. His categorisation shows a resemblance to Plog's tourist typology, with travellers standing for allocentrics, tourists for mid-centrics, and holidaymakers for psychocentrics. Baggini pokes fun at these distinctions:

> I have never had much time for the alleged contrast between travellers and tourists, which, according to an old joke, is that tourists go to McDonalds for the food and travellers go there for the toilets. Tourists are the inferior beings in this hierarchy, who follow itineraries set by others and never see the 'real country'. Travellers, in contrast, are free spirits who do what they like and get real with the locals. Of course, this is hogwash. Travellers go where all the other travellers go, following the Lonely Planet Bible. They may stay in more basic accommodation, but that does not make their experience more real, just less comfortable. After all, it's not as though locals live in youth hostels ... Travellers are just deluded tourists with pretentions. I realised that there was another, genuinely different category: the holidaymaker. Whereas tourists and travellers travel in order to see new places and try new things, the holidaymaker goes away simply to have a good time where the weather is better and the problems of home are forgotten. (Baggini, 2008: 145–146)

Krippendorf's Typology

Krippendorf (1984) was one of the first authors to typify tourists by their impact on the destinations they visited. As one of the earliest theorists on the topic of sustainable tourism, Krippendorf argued that because tourism was growing at a rapid pace, tourists were also increasingly likely to impact negatively on host communities and environments. He therefore constructed a typology with the '*much maligned tourist*' on the one hand, and the '*alternative tourist*' on the other.

The 'much maligned tourist' is a combination of all the negative stereotypes that exist about tourists. They are ridiculous with their big cameras and their pale skin. They are naïve and ask dumb questions. They are uncultured, spend whole days at the beach, and show no interest in local culture or food. They are exploiting, polluting, and follow other tourists like sheep. Krippendorf argues that it is easy to poke fun at tourists, because the tourist is always the other person – even if people travel themselves, they do not necessarily identify with this stereotype of a tourist.

At the other end of the spectrum we find the alternative tourist. Even though these tourists show respect for other cultures and people, and do not conform to the negative stereotype, they are not free of negative impacts either: they may have limited negative impacts on destinations, but by discovering new destinations they pave the way for tourism development and the invasion of 'much maligned tourists'.

Krippendorf (1984) concluded that it is too simplistic just to divide tourists into a 'good' and a 'bad' category: he argued for awareness-building and education initiatives that would inform tourists of the consequences of their visit and activities on destinations.

Segmentation in Practice

Tourist typologies can be beneficial for the tourism sector, but these also have a number of limitations. The concept of tourist types as useful generalisations to differentiate between groups of travellers with similar needs and wants is still of use today. It may be helpful for destinations and tourism companies to know more about the type of tourist they attract or want to attract – this way they can adapt the product they offer to the needs and wants of that particular tourist type.

Nevertheless, there are also several limitations attached to the tourist typologies discussed above. First there is their age to consider – all three models were developed in the 1970s and 1980s and travel behaviours have changed significantly since then. They have also been developed on the basis of evidence from one generating region: for all models these were Western, developed countries. It is thus not necessarily possible to apply them generally to tourists today, and it can be argued that they do not span the full scope of tourist types today. As such they may be useful theoretical concepts, but their practical applicability is less clear. When, for example, one would want to research a group of tourists on the basis of Plog's model, it may be very difficult to judge where on the scale between allocentrics and psychocentrics they are situated. And in terms of Krippendorf's model, would any tourist ever identify themselves as a 'much maligned tourist'? Most statistics in tourism therefore will use a more standardised typology of tourists, usually one based on purpose of travel, while many companies and organisations will segment the tourist market using a range of demographic, socio-economic and pyscho-graphic factors. These are discussed in detail in Chapter 13.

Consumer Decision Making

The previous sections explored what motivates individuals to participate in tourist activity and how this influences what they seek from destinations. We have seen that these motivations can be generalised in a number of models, and that tourists have been categorised into typologies based on their motivations and behaviour. Some questions now need to be asked here: how does an individual turn this motivation into a trip? How do the push and pull factors combine to create a purchase decision? How does the tourist make decisions about destination, transport, accommodation, and duration? These are addressed by theories about the tourist decision-making process. This section starts by exploring the different steps in tourism decision making, and then discusses the concept of involvement. A number of models will then be presented which will show the different factors influencing this process.

Steps in Decision Making

Kolb (2006) identifies five steps in all purchasing decisions, including tourism purchasing decisions. These are as follows:

Need recognition: This is when consumers become aware of a need that they would like to see met. These could be simple daily needs, such as to buy food or pay a bill, or they may be more complex: the desire to develop a new career for example, or the organisation of a wedding. In tourism, needs recognition usually refers to the moment when a person realises that the needs we discussed in the first part of this chapter will be met most easily by engaging in tourist activity. Kolb (2006: 130) adds that 'when consumers decide to travel, they are usually fulfilling an internal emotional desire'.

Information search: Consumers search for information about products because they want to make sure their purchasing decision is correct. If the product they are considering buying is very expensive, such as a car or a house, they will try and minimise the risk by gathering as much information as possible about the product they intend to buy. Products they buy routinely and which do not cost much (such as bread or a newspaper) are usually not researched in similar depth. To gather information, consumers may use documentation provided by the producers of the product or intermediaries; they may ask for recommendations from friends or family members, or read product reviews in the specialised press or online.

Evaluation of alternatives: The consumer will then compare a number of potential products or services. Criteria that can be used here are quality, price, design and brand reputation, to name but a few. When choosing a holiday destination, for example, the tourist will usually compare the destination characteristics they seek with those on offer in different places. Of those characteristics, some may be more important than others: a tourist may, for example, be primarily looking for a sunny destination for a family holiday that offers good value for money and does not require more than four hours on a plane. If that destination also happens to offer cultural attractions and a summer festival, this may be an added bonus for the tourist, but it may not have been key to the decision-making process.

Purchase process: The act of purchasing a product or service can be very simple: if you want to buy a newspaper for example, you can just go to the newsagent and do so. Other products however may require a more complicated purchase process: when buying a house, the buyer may need a solicitor or notary to help complete the purchase. In terms of holidays, the purchasing process can be simple when the tourist decides to book a package holiday via a travel agent. In this case, a fixed price is paid, and the accommodation, transport, and in some cases extras like tours or excursions, are all included. When booking independently, however, the process becomes more complicated, as a holiday may include a flight, a hotel and airport transportation. Prices for tourism products can also change very rapidly, so that the tourist may feel under pressure to complete the different elements of the purchase process quickly.

Post-purchase evaluation: This step is where consumers evaluate the products they have bought, and check if these have met their needs and expectations. When buying a holiday, tourists will often only have pictures of destinations and facilities to go on – only on holiday can it be determined if these reflect the reality. The product that was bought can thus not be evaluated after purchase, but only after consumption, and much time may pass between the two activities. The fragmented nature of a holiday, which is supplied by various producers (accommodation, transport, attractions), creates difficulties in evaluating the whole trip. If the expectations of the tourist are met or exceeded, the satisfaction with the purchase will be high, and this may result in repeat business for the destination. If the expectations are not met, this will result in low satisfaction or dissatisfaction.

Involvement

In marketing theory, a distinction is made between *convenience goods* (which are low in price and are bought frequently), and *shopping goods* (which are high in price and are bought less frequently). The purchase of convenience goods is an example of routine problem-solving behaviour, whereas the purchase of shopping goods involves more complex decision making (Swarbrooke and Horner, 2007).

The distinction between convenience and shopping goods can be attributed to differences in consumer *involvement*. Consumer involvement in tourism can be high or low depending on the cost, frequency of travel, and the significance of the trip to the tourist, and consequently there are significant differences in the decision-making process.

Low-involvement tourism purchase decisions happen routinely and are not emotionally significant. Often little research goes into these purchase decisions, and consumers will choose products on the basis of past experience or price. For example, an individual with a second home may purchase transport on an impulse, or if an individual is familiar with a destination and with the usual prices for transport and accommodation the trip may require little research or consultation with others (Kolb, 2006).

Swarbrooke and Horner (2007), and Kolb (2006), suggest that high-involvement tourism products are characterised by:

A higher level of emotional significance: A holiday is often something the buyer will look forward to every year and this is therefore seen as an important decision. If the tourist only takes one longer holiday each year, then the risk involved is rather large: if the wrong destination is chosen, they will need to wait another year before they can go on holiday again. The whole family may also have a say in deciding the destination. A honeymoon is another example of a holiday with a high emotional involvement – the newlyweds will only have one chance to have that perfect trip. Moreover, the money that would be spent on the holiday may be compared to other goods such as a car, a computer, or a TV.

A higher level of information search: Consumers who make high-involvement purchasing decisions will usually be more likely to spend a longer time researching and comparing products. Particularly when the product is unfamiliar, extensive research may be needed. This may also involve consultations with other people such as friends or product specialists.

Long-term decisions: Many high-involvement purchases are decided a longer time in advance than low-involvement purchases. We will often book a holiday a number of months in advance – we do not decide what we are going to have for dinner for months to come. The consumer is thus predicting what he or she will want in the future; this makes the decision more complex. The purchase decision is also more long term because it is made less often: travel products are bought less regularly than convenience goods. The purchase process is thus a more unique experience that is handled less routinely.

More strongly influenced by other people: This aspect has to do with both the nature of travel and with the higher level of information search. Many tourists travel in smaller or bigger groups: couples, families, groups of friends. The motivations and expectations of different individuals will need to be taken into account before purchase decisions are made. Even when tourists travel alone, the choice of travel dates and destination may be dependent on when they can get time off or be free from other obligations. Moreover, in many cases advice will be sought from product specialists (such as travel agents), friends and relatives, or fellow travellers (on travel blogs or review websites).

Decision Making in Tourism

A range of different models of decision making in tourism has been developed that can break down the purchasing process into a number of components or steps. Mathieson and Wall (1982) and Moutinho (1987) are examples of these models. This chapter presents a more recent interpretation of decision making in tourism: the stimulus and response model.

Middleton et al. (2009) compare the human brain to a computer when it makes decisions: when performing a task (making a decision), a computer depends on a certain input of data, from which it presents the user with an output (solution). Simple operations can be carried out quickly, whereas more complex operations, with more input, may take more time to process. The input is referred to as a 'stimulus', and the output as a 'response' (see Figure 4.4).

A detailed exploration of the stimulus and response model can be found in Middleton and Clarke (2001). This can be divided into six steps or 'processes':

Process 1: *Product inputs*: This process refers to the range of products that is available to tourists when they make their decision. These can be travel agents, tour operators, booking websites and businesses.

Process 2: *Communication channels*: This step refers to the different ways a customer can find out about the products on offer. The communication channels can either be 'formal', via brochures and advertisements, or they can be 'informal': buyers may ask the advice of friends and family members, or look for advice from other travellers in online forums.

Process 3: *Communication filters*: In this step, consumers 'make sense' of the wealth of information available to them so that they can make a decision. The brain acts as a mental 'sieve' that filters out information that will be acted upon.

Process 4: *Motivation*: The communication filters in process 3 have strong connections to the personal motivations of travellers in process 4. This step refers to the tourists' needs, wants and goals – these are affected by their socio-economic characteristics (the money they have to spend and their level of education), personality, attitudes, cultural and background. All these factors influence the type of tourism product the tourist is looking for and they drive the selection processes that have been made in processes 1–3.

Process 5: *Purchase decision*: This step concerns the actual act of buying a product at a certain price, within a certain brand, and via a certain distribution channel. This step is likely to be monitored closely by service providers, even though it is only the very last phase of the complex processes described above.

Process 6: *Post-purchase and post-consumption feelings*: In this step, the tourist evaluates their purchasing decisions after consumption of the product, service or experience. If the decision is evaluated positively, this may encourage repeat business and positive word of mouth. If the evaluation is negative, the tourist is unlikely to buy the product again and may discourage other travellers (see process 2) from buying it also.

Measuring and Forecasting the Demand for Tourism

Measuring and forecasting tourism demand is very important for the tourism industry. This is mainly because many tourism products are 'perishable': if an

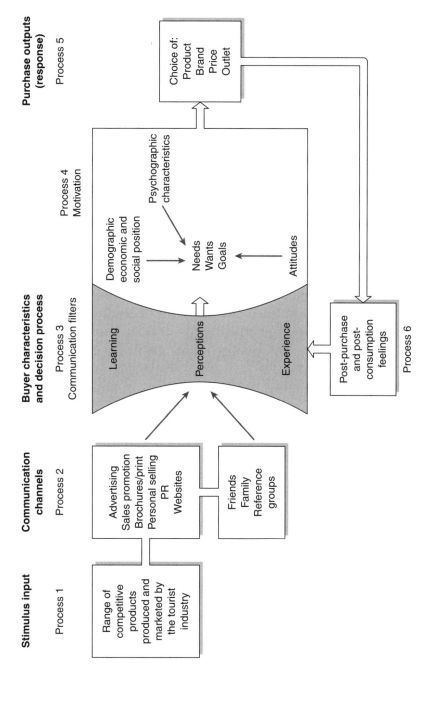

Figure 4.4 Stimulus and response model

Source: Middleton and Clark (2001). Reprinted with permission from Elsevier.

airline does not sell a seat on one flight, it cannot put two passengers in one seat on the next: the loss of revenue cannot be made up. The same goes for a hotel bed or a seat on a sightseeing bus. Adequate measurements and forecasts of tourism demands can help tourism managers with the planning, marketing and selling of their products.

Measuring Demand

International tourism demand is generally measured in terms of the number of tourists from an origin country who visit a foreign destination; or in terms of tourist expenditures by visitors from the origin country in the destination country (Witt and Witt, 1992: 4). Another way of measuring demand is to count tourist nights in the destination country. These data are collected in a variety of ways. Tourist visits are usually recorded via counts at the border (inbound) or by surveying a sample of travellers (inbound and outbound). Records of accommodation establishments (such as hotels) can be used to count the number of visitors and number of nights at the destination. International tourist expenditure data are usually collected using the bank reporting method, or by conducting specialised surveys with travellers. The bank reporting method is based on a registration by authorised banks and agencies of the buying and selling of foreign currency by travellers (Witt and Witt, 1995).

It is very difficult to compile accurate overviews of tourism demand, because there are certain problems associated with each of the methods described above. Counts at the border, for example, cannot always differentiate between transit visitors and visitors to the destination itself. Large airports, for instance, may experience a lot of transit traffic, and tourists may drive through certain countries on the way to their holiday destination, without actually staying or spending any money there. The records of accommodation establishments exclude people who stay at friends' or family members' houses and day trippers. Specialised surveys are often expensive to carry out and may be based on a small sample. The bank reporting methods may not be accurate either, because it can be difficult to distinguish a tourism transaction from another transaction, or relevant transactions may not be recorded at all (Witt and Witt, 1995).

An added problem in the measuring of tourism demand is the fact that data are collected differently in various countries. Tourism arrivals may be registered by their country of residence or nationality, for example. In France and Germany, data are collected through personal interviews, whereas in the UK and the USA, this is done via surveys at airports (Witt and Witt, 1992). Tourism satellite accounts are often proposed as a method to achieve comparable data for different countries (see Chapter 8).

Snapshot 4.3   The UK Passenger Survey

The International Passenger Survey (IPS) is a survey of a random sample of passengers entering and leaving the UK by air, sea or the Channel Tunnel. Over a quarter of million face-to-face interviews are carried out each year with passengers entering and leaving the UK through the main airports, seaports and the Channel Tunnel. Interviewing is carried out throughout the year with a sample that represents about one in every 500 passengers. The interview usually takes three to five minutes and contains questions about passengers' country of residence (for overseas residents) or country of visit (for UK residents), the reason for their visit, and details of their expenditure and fares. There are additional questions for passengers migrating to or from the UK. While much of the content of the interview remains the same from one year to the next, new questions are sometimes added or will appear periodically on the survey. The data collected by the UK Passenger Survey are used not only to compile international tourism statistics, but also to calculate the balance of payments (see Chapter 8) and to estimate the numbers and characteristics of migrants into and out of the UK. The survey results can be accessed via the website of the National Statistics Office (http://www.statistics.gov.uk/ssd/surveys/international_passenger_survey.asp).

Forecasting Demand

Forecasting fundamentally refers to the process of organising information about a phenomenon's past in order to predict its future (Frechtling, 2001: 8). Forecasts can have different time scales: short-term forecasts, for example, are needed for scheduling and staffing, whereas long-term forecasts can influence the level of investment in aeroplanes and hotels (Witt and Witt, 1995).

Two types of methods can be used in forecasting tourism demand: *causal* and *non-causal* methods. Non-causal methods start from the principle that 'a variable may be forecasted without reference to the factors which determine the variable' (Witt and Witt, 1992: 7). In other words, non-causal methods look at the past development of a phenomenon, and predict the future of the phenomenon by extrapolating the trend. If tourism has been growing at a certain rate in the past, it predicts tourism demand based on continuous levels of such growth. The benefit of this method is that it is fairly easy to apply at a low cost. The problem is that it presumes that the causes of growth and decline will just stay the same in the future, which may not be the case. Moreover, historical data for tourism demand are often lacking, which means that there is no trend that can just be extrapolated to the future. Tourism demand is also highly volatile and can be severely affected by events such as wars or crises: demand is thus not stable enough to assume that it will just continue to grow or fall (Frechtling, 2001).

Causal methods link forecasting to a set of determining factors. Forecasts are made up of each of these determining factors and factored into the forecast depending on their impact on tourism demand. This is called an econometric forecasting method (Frechtling, 2001; Witt and Witt, 1992). Econometric forecasts take into account the arrival and expenditure of visitors, but also other factors, such as, for example, the size of the origin population, the income of the origin country per capita, the price of products and services at the destination, and the price of products and services in comparable destinations (Witt and Witt, 1995). This type of forecasting is more complex, but because it incorporates more factors it should be more representative of the complexity of tourism demand. However it is also more expensive and it can be difficult to find forecasts for all the determining factors.

 Snapshot 4.4   New Zealand Tourism Demand Forecast 2009–2015

New Zealand's tourism forecasts for 2009 until 2015 are compiled on the basis of a variety of data sources. From Table 4.4, we can see that New Zealand uses a methodology that combines different types of variables: arrivals, expenditure, visitor nights, GDP in the main originating markets, and exchange rates. The results of this data collection process were then checked via telephone interviews and focus groups with key stakeholders in the industry: this is called a Delphi process.

Table 4.4   Demand forecast data sources

| Data | Coverage | | Source |
	Countries	Years	
Annual expenditure	All	1997–2008	International Visitor Survey. Ministry of Tourism
Annual outbound travel	All	1979–2008	Statistics NZ
Annual visitor arrivals	All	1979–2008	Statistics NZ
Monthly visitor arrivals	Major Markets	1979–2008	Statistics NZ
Annual visitor nights	All	1979–2008	Statistics NZ
Domestic travel	All	1999–2008	Domestic Travel Survey, Ministry of Tourism
Real GDP and exchange rates	Major Markets	1979–2009	Various sources

Source: Tourism Strategy Group New Zealand (2010). Copyright protected by Crown copyright.

Figure 4.5 shows an example of how these techniques are used to forecast international arrivals to New Zealand.

(Continued)

(Continued)

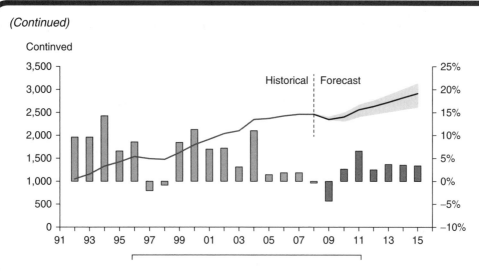

Figure 4.5   International arrivals to New Zealand

Source: Tourism Strategy Group New Zealand (2010). Copyright protected by Crown copyright.

The line beyond the dotted vertical line shows the forecasted growth for international tourism to New Zealand. The grey zone shows the opinions and amendments projected by the specialists in the Delphi process: it can be seen that some specialists are expecting higher levels of growth, others lower levels. The grey zone clearly illustrates the level of uncertainty in the tourism markets after the economic downturn that started in 2008. The historical data also show that even though tourism demand has generally grown steadily since the start of the measurements, there have been years when the growth rate was low, or when there was even a decline. A decline in arrivals between 1997 and 1999 coincided with the Iraq war and an economic downturn.

Summary

This chapter has discussed tourism demand from different perspectives. Firstly it has looked at why individuals engage in tourism activity; at the psychological or social factors that drive them to spend an often considerable part of their income on a product of which they have often little knowledge in advance and thus often includes a certain level of risk. On the basis of motivations, tourists then make a purchasing decision. We have looked at different models that unravel this process, which has been shown to be often complex and time-consuming. Finally, the chapter has explored the measuring and forecasting of tourism demand: it is important for the industry to gain a deeper insight into demand and how it will evolve, so that it can plan its resources effectively.

■ **Self-test Questions** ■

1 Julian Baggini (2008) says that 'travellers are just deluded tourists with pretentions'. What do you think he means by this?

2 Compare a range of adverts for different destinations. What sort of image are they trying to convey for each destination? Is this image realistic and believable?

3 Forecasting the number of tourist arrivals is notably difficult, and often the forecasts will turn out to be inaccurate. What can be the causes for unexpected surges or dips in tourist arrivals?

Further Reading

Kolb, B. (2006) *Tourism Marketing for Cities and Towns: Using Branding and Events to Attract Tourists.* Burlington: Butterworth-Heinemann: (Chapter 6).

Krippendorf, J. (1984) *The Holiday Makers: Understanding the Impact of Leisure and Travel.* Oxford: Butterworth-Heinemann.

Swarbrooke, J. and Horner, S. (2007) *Consumer Behaviour in Tourism.* Burlington: Butterworth-Heinemann.

Useful Websites

http://www.statistics.gov.uk/ssd/surveys/international_passenger_survey.asp
http://www.tourismresearch.govt.nz/

5 Tourism
Suppliers

... tourism involves many different suppliers working across different locations and countries in different industries. (Litteljohn and Baxter, 2006: 23)

Tourist signage in Tamariu, Costa Brava, Spain

Source: Nick Ryan

Learning Outcomes

After reading this chapter you will understand:

■ **the types of suppliers that provide tourism products**
■ **the main characteristics of each tourism supply sector**
■ **common characteristics that affect all tourism suppliers.**

Introduction

Tourism suppliers are providers of the travel products that are consumed by tourists during their trip. Tourism suppliers can be broadly defined by the sector within which they operate – transport, accommodation, non-residential venues, attractions and cruises – however, each of these sectors is highly fragmented and consists of a broad range of distinct suppliers and products.

In this chapter we consider these tourism sectors and the types of suppliers of which each is composed; we have also highlighted significant sectoral issues. We begin by considering the accommodation sector and focus on hotels and the variety of ownership, management and affiliation models that are commonly found. We then discuss non-residential venues, which are often overlooked in discussions of tourism suppliers, and their role in stimulating demand for other tourism suppliers in destinations. We consider the transport sector and the role of government regulation in the airline industry. The visitor attractions sector is then explained, and finally the cruise sector is considered. We end the chapter by considering some of the major common characteristics that affect all tourism suppliers.

Accommodation Suppliers

The tourist accommodation sector consists of many different types of accommodation. A common approach to differentiating between them is to classify them as serviced and non-serviced accommodation:

- *Serviced accommodation*: provides rooms in which to sleep plus other services that are provided by staff on site, such as housekeeping and food and beverage services. Serviced accommodation is most commonly seen in the hotel and guest house sector.

- *Non-serviced accommodation*: often called self-catering accommodation, does not provide these services, although it may be possible to arrange them separately (Middleton et al., 2009).

Serviced and non-serviced accommodation can be broken down further into specific forms of accommodation. Often these forms are used predominantly by either business or leisure tourists. Middleton et al. (2009) identify accommodation types and their main users, and the locations where each type is most commonly located: see Figure 5.1.

The variety of accommodation types creates difficulties in discussing the sector as a single entity. For instance, cottages, villas and apartments are often privately owned by individuals; some may only be used by the owner, and some may be available for rent by tourists. Some providers such as universities

Sector⟍ Market segment	Serviced sector		Non-serviced sector (self-catering)	
	At Destinations	On Routes	At Destination	On Routes
Business and other non-leisure tourists	City/Town hotels (Monday-Friday) Budget hotels Resort hotels for conferences and exhibitions Educational establishments	Budget hotels Motels Inns Airport hotels	Apartment	Not applicable
Leisure and holiday tourists	Resort hotels Guesthouse/ Pensions Farmhouses City/town hotels (Friday-Sunday) Budget hotels Some educational establishments	Budget hotels Motels Bed and breakfast Inns	Apart hotels/Condominia/ Timeshare Holiday Centres/camps Caravan/Chalet parks Gites Cottages Villas Apartments/flats Some motels	Touring pitches for caravans, tents, recreation vehicles YHA Some motels

Figure 5.1　Serviced and non-serviced accommodation by type and market segment

Source: Middleton et al. (2009: 365).

and farm owners use tourism as a source of income to supplement their main activities but are not full-time tourist accommodation operators.

Accommodation providers that operate commercially, that is, with the objective of making a profit, must manage their capacity and availability very carefully. Two methods of measuring the sales performance of a hotel are occupancy rates and revenue per available room (REVPAR).

Occupancy is the percentage of available rooms that were sold during a specific period of time. Occupancy is measured by dividing the number of rooms sold by the number of rooms available (Smith Travel Research, 2011):

Occupancy = Rooms Sold/Rooms Available

For example, a hotel with 100 rooms would have an occupancy rate of 50 per cent if half the rooms were sold on one date. Occupancy rates are a useful tool for describing the demand for accommodation, but they do not measure financial performance; for instance, a hotel that sells its rooms very cheaply could achieve 100 per cent occupancy regularly but may not be profitable.

REVPAR measures the average income achieved at the property by calculating the total room revenue for a specific date and dividing it by the number of rooms available. For example, a 100-room hotel with revenue of

£10,000 on one night achieves a REVPAR of £100; this could have been achieved through a 100 per cent occupancy rate at £100 per room per night, or a 50 per cent occupancy at £200 per room per night.

For the remainder of this section we will focus on the hotel sector.

The Hotel Sector

Hotels are serviced accommodation properties that provide guest rooms and other products such as meeting rooms, bars and restaurants, as well as banqueting facilities. The global hotel sector is estimated to provide more than 18.4 million rooms worldwide (Mintel, 2005) and consists of a variety of types of property. We list the main types in Table 5.1.

Table 5.1   Common types of hotel

Full-service hotels	Provide a range of services such as a restaurant, bar, lounge facilities, meeting space, banqueting facilities, porterage, and room service.
Limited-service hotels	Provide rooms-only operations with few additional services.
All-suite hotels	Provide guest units with one or more bedrooms and a separate living area.
Boutique hotels	Distinct and unique small properties, often style-led and usually full service.
Resort hotels	Properties in holiday destinations with extensive leisure amenities such as pools, spa facilities, sports facilities, restaurants.
All-inclusive hotel	A resort hotel for which all services including food and beverages, entertainment and sport are paid for in advance and are not charged for separately.

Source: adapted from Smith Travel Research (2011).

In addition to describing hotels by type, these can also be categorised according to:

- *Standard and grading*: many countries use a rating system such as stars or crowns to indicate hotel standard and quality, ranging from one to five stars. No formal body awards ratings above five stars, yet in the early twenty-first century self-designated seven star properties have opened such as the Burj-al Arab in Dubai and the Pangu in Beijing. There is no international system for categorising and classifying hotels. Hotel chains with properties in several countries will usually describe their properties as budget, mid-range or up-scale.

- *Ownership*: hotel independents are operators that own and operate fewer than 10 properties, and are not affiliated to any other business. Usually hotel independents are family businesses or partnerships, and they constitute 85 per cent of global hotel supply and range from luxury hotels to guest houses. Hotel chains on the other hand are operators than run a number of properties, commonly defined as 10 or more (Euromonitor International, 2010).

- *Brand*: hotels can be described as either branded or unbranded. Unbranded hotels operate under their own unique name and individual identity whereas branded hotels operate using the identity and format of a nationally or internationally recognised hotel chain, for example a Holiday Inn, Travelodge, Novotel.

Branded hotel chains have grown significantly since the 1980s and many now have a global presence with thousands of hotel properties in the main business and leisure tourism destinations worldwide. Branded hotel chains create a common format, identity and image for their hotels that will be reproduced in all properties that operate under the same name. Knowles (1996) suggests that branding is particularly advantageous for chain hotels for the following reasons:

- Hotel groups expanded in the 1970s and 1980s through the acquisition of existing properties of diverse standards and quality; it was therefore logical to categorise them into distinct types.

- Hotel classification and star ratings vary between countries and can confuse consumers; branding enables a clear indication of the standard and level of service provided.

- Brands communicate specific messages to customers about the standard and quality of the accommodation product; hotel brands tailor their product to the expectations of certain types of customers.

Euromonitor (2010) identifies the leading hotel companies by their value share, that is their share of total worldwide sales (see Table 5.2).

Table 5.2   Leading hotel companies by value share, 2009

Company	Value share 2009 (%)
Hilton Worldwide	4.0
Marriott International	4.0
Intercontinental Hotels Group	3.8
Accor Group	2.9
Starwood Hotels and Resorts Worldwide	2.4
Wyndham Worldwide	1.9
Choice Hotels International	1.6
Best Western International	1.4
Hyatt Hotels	0.9
Carlson Cos	0.8

Source: Euromonitor International (2010) © Euromonitor International 2011.

These hotel companies operate a portfolio of hotel brands which appeal to distinct market segments, for example Accor Hotels has 15 brands across its 4,200 properties in 90 countries: 57 per cent of their hotels are budget (Formule 1, Ibis), 34 per cent are midscale (Novotel, Mercure), and 9 per cent are luxury (Sofitel, Pullman) (Accor, 2010).

Figure 5.2 illustrates the top three hotel companies in each world region.

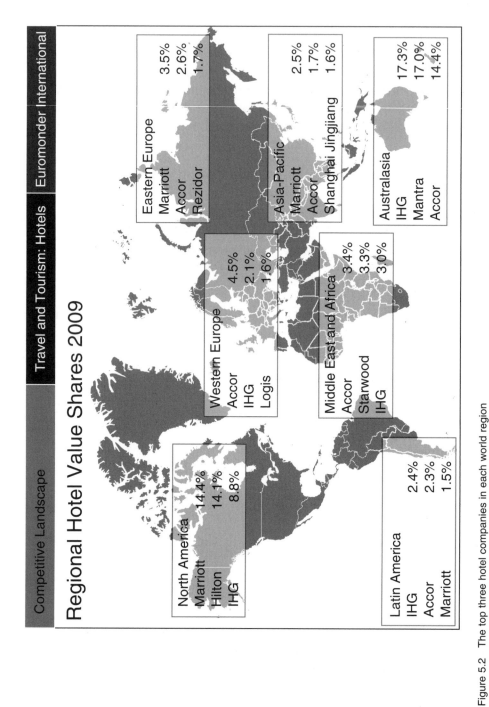

Regional Hotel Value Shares 2009

North America
Marriott 14.4%
Hilton 14.1%
IHG 8.8%

Latin America
IHG 2.4%
Accor 2.3%
Marriott 1.5%

Western Europe
Accor 4.5%
IHG 2.1%
Logis 1.6%

Eastern Europe
Marriott 3.5%
Accor 2.6%
Rezidor 1.7%

Middle East and Africa
Accor 3.4%
Starwood 3.3%
IHG 3.0%

Asia-Pacific
Marriott 2.5%
Accor 1.7%
Shanghai Jingjiang 1.6%

Australasia
IHG 17.3%
Mantra 17.0%
Accor 14.4%

Figure 5.2   The top three hotel companies in each world region

Source: Euromonitor International (2010) © Euromonitor International 2011.

Hotel ownership is complex because frequently hotels that are part of a branded chain may retain their independent ownership. For instance, Accor only directly owns 17 per cent of the properties that operate as one of its brands (Accor, 2010). Most hotels that operate under a brand name actually retain their independent ownership, but are affiliated to a brand for marketing purposes. This is usually achieved in one of four ways: by contracting the brand to manage the hotel; by leasing the hotel to the brand; by becoming a franchisee; or by membership of a consortium.

Management Contracts

Management contracts describe a long-term arrangement where an independent hotel owner contracts a brand to manage and operate the property using their operating expertise. The property owner pays a percentage of their total revenue (usually up to 5 per cent of revenue) and a percentage of their profit (usually 5–10 per cent) to the brand (Cunill, 2006). The brand usually provides the general manager and other senior managers but the hotel owner provides all other staff.

Lease Contracts

Lease contracts describe an arrangement where the brand owner leases the hotel building from the owner, usually for a minimum of three years, and pays rent, calculated as a proportion of revenue, as well as an annual fee (Cunill, 2006).

Franchises

Franchising is a business model that allows hotel owners (franchisees) to run their own businesses with the marketing support of a brand (the franchisor). The franchisor grants the right to the franchisee to operate using their name, design and image. In return, franchisees pay a fee to join the franchise, plus a proportion of their annual revenue and a percentage of their profit. (Cunill, 2006).

Franchising allows independent hotel operators to adopt a brand with a proven track record, established reputation and business strategy. Each franchised property must adopt the brand image, physical appearance and operational procedures of the franchisor, and usually subscribe to the franchise for a period of 20 to 30 years (Cunill, 2006). They are regularly inspected to ensure compliance with the brand's standards.

The snapshot below describes the services provided to franchisees and management contracts by the Intercontinental Hotels Group.

Snapshot 5.1   Intercontinental Hotels Group

In 2011, IHG's total hotel properties numbered 4,422 in 100 countries with a total of 652,456 rooms. A further 1,236 hotels are planned. Only 15 properties are owned by IHG, while 639 are operated as management contracts and 3,768 are franchises.

   IHG operates seven distinct hotel brands that together appeal to all budgets – from economy to luxury:

Courtesy of Intercontinental Hotels Group

IHG's franchisees benefit from a range of services:

- Advice and guidance about which brand to choose.
- Site selection, design and construction for new-build properties.
- Connection to the IHG reservations system which can be accessed by travel agencies worldwide via GDS (a travel agent booking system).
- Sales via IHG's 10 call centres located in major generating regions.
- Promotion via IHG's websites that are presented in 13 languages, and through the large sales team.
- Participation in IHG's loyalty programme – Priority Club Rewards – with 58 million members.
- Advice and training in quality management.
- Participation in IHG's email marketing campaigns and social media.

Franchising provides independent hotel businesses with a number of advantages that they would be unable to achieve alone.

Source: IHG (2011a).

Independent hotels that become franchisees are required to adopt the operating practices of the franchisor, commit to a long-term contract, and comply with very specific product requirements – for instance, the layout, design, decoration and fitting out of rooms and public areas, food and beverage provision, staff uniforms and operating procedures.

   Independent hotels who prefer to retain their individual style, or whose property cannot be easily adapted to match the product specification of franchisors, can obtain similar marketing benefits by joining a hotel consortium.

Hotel Consortia

A consortium can be defined as the collaboration of a number of organisations for a common purpose – 'a kind of mutual self-help organisation' (Knowles, 1996: 304). Hotel consortia are voluntary collaborations between independently-owned hotels who contribute financially to establish and maintain a joint brand and marketing organisation, and achieve marketing benefits that they would be unable to achieve alone. Commonly this involves the establishment of central reservations offices in major generating regions; a brand website featuring all member properties and links to the reservations system of each; the production of a directory listing all member hotels; a sales team who will build relationships with travel agencies, tour and MICE operators, and corporate customers; attendance at travel trade exhibitions promoting the brand; and opportunities to sell via travel agencies worldwide through a GDS presence (Knowles, 1996).

Member hotels benefit from joint purchasing opportunities and access to resources that would be outside their remit individually. Hotel consortia often provide management services too, such as purchasing, HR and training, and marketing. Consortia provide similar benefits to franchises, but do not require product standardisation, therefore allowing each member to retain their individuality: 'Consortia usually make an asset out of the individuality of their member hotels' (Knowles, 1996: 305). Major hotel consortia are Relais and Chateaux, Best Western International, and Leading Hotels of the World.

Full service hotels provide venues for meetings and events and these are a very significant part of the tourism supply in destinations, particularly for business tourism. Venues provide facilities for conferences, conventions, meetings, exhibitions and events and some destinations seek to attract these forms of tourism by building stand-alone, non-residential venues.

Non-residential Venues

Non-residential venues are dedicated convention and exhibition centres, exhibition halls, theatres, arenas and stadiums that are designed to hold large numbers of people. They provide space for conferences, conventions, exhibitions, meetings and events, concerts, stage shows, product launches, sports and team-building events. Venues are very important suppliers for business tourism, in particular through hosting conventions and exhibitions. They also host events for the public which may attract leisure tourists to a destination (Davidson and Rogers, 2006).

The construction and operation of a large venue is capital intensive, and the public sector is often involved in their financing. In many destinations, large venues are owned by the local, regional or national government, and the location of the venue is often selected to regenerate the immediate vicinity and act as a catalyst to attract further investment and development for the benefit of the local economy and community.

There have been three stages to the evolution of venue ownership and management:

1 The first stage was the development of stand-alone dedicated centres that were built and operated under public ownership and management.

2 The second stage required a reduction of state involvement in the management and operation of venues through the development of a model of public ownership and private management; in this situation, state-owned venues are managed and operated by experienced and successful private venue management companies under a management contract.

3 The most recent evolution has seen a move away from standalone venues to developments that integrate venues with hotel, retail or casino developments; the state sells the land surrounding the venue to the private sector in order to finance the construction of the venue, and often leases the venue to a private operator in long-term public–private partnerships (Donaghy, 2007). For example, the Staples Centre at LA Live, London's O2 Arena, the Shanghai Mercedes Benz Arena, the Acer Arena at Sydney's Olympic Park, the Brisbane, Cairns Darwin and Kuala Lumpur Convention Centres, are managed on a long-term lease and operated by one multinational venue operator – AEG Ogden (AEG Ogden, 2011).

The visual appeal of a venue is becoming increasingly important and recently-built venues will often use an iconic design or innovative materials. In addition, venues need to offer a flexible, multi-purpose space that can be used in a variety of ways for different types of event, provide the latest audio-visual (AV) equipment and lighting, and be sound-proof. Venues will usually have a number of rooms for smaller break-out sessions, banqueting, business centres, offices and administration space (McCabe et al., 2000).

The snapshot below presents one of the major convention centres.

 Snapshot 5.2   Vancouver Convention Centre

The Vancouver Convention Centre provides 466,500 square feet of meeting, exhibition, ballroom and plenary theatre space for international conventions, consumer and trade shows, and other meetings and events of all shapes and sizes. The Centre also has 90,000 square feet of retail space, plus over 130,000 square feet of waterfront walkways and cycle paths, as well as over 120,000 square feet of public plaza space. In the fiscal year 2010, over 350

(Continued)

(Continued)

events were held, attracting 225,000 delegates from Canada and worldwide, and $21 million (CAD) in revenue.

The Vancouver Convention Centre is operated by the BC Pavilion Corporation (PavCo), a Provincial Crown Corporation of the Ministry of Jobs, Tourism and Innovation. PavCo's mandate is to create significant economic and community benefits for the people of British Columbia. Research suggests that more than 40 per cent of non-resident delegates intend to return as leisure tourists within a year. The Vancouver Convention Centre provides key services such as food and beverage, electrical and rigging, and audio visual through sub-contracted official suppliers. The Centre employs 70 staff and a further 291 full-time equivalent (FTE) jobs are created for the official suppliers' workforce.

The Centre's environmental impact is significantly lower than industry standards – it has an on-site water treatment plant and its living roof provides a fully-functional eco-system, with six acres of habitat for 400,000 species of native plants and four beehive colonies each with up to 60,000 bees. It has won numerous awards for design and sustainability.

Vancouver Convention Centre

Source: Courtesy of Vancouver Convention Centre (2011)

Accommodation and non-residential venue suppliers are of key importance to the tourism product of a destination. To attract tourists, however, destinations must be accessible. Transport suppliers provide the necessary links between tourist-generating regions and destinations.

Transport Suppliers

In Chapter 3 we identified the main modes of tourist transport as land, sea and air, and explained that within each mode were a variety of types of transport, some of which would be privately-owned like the private car, and some of which would be used by tourists as attractions, for example hot-air balloon flights. In this section we focus on the transport suppliers that enable tourists to travel to destinations, or within destinations, and that are operated along commercial principles, namely high-speed rail services, scheduled and chartered coach services, ferries, and scheduled and chartered airlines. We consider the main differences between types of service and the impact of regulatory systems on the operations of tourist transport suppliers. Table 5.3 identifies the main suppliers of tourist transport.

Table 5.3   Main suppliers of tourist transport

High-speed rail services – High-speed train networks connect major urban centres. The first was introduced in Japan in 1964 on the Tokyo–Osaka route, known as the Shinkansen or Bullet Train (Arduin and Ni, 2005), and more countries have subsequently revitalised their railways by investing heavily in rail infrastructure and high-speed trains; for instance, Trains a Grand Vitesse (TGV) in France, Intercity Express (ICE) in Germany, Eurostar between London, Paris and Brussels, Pendolino trains in Italy, and Alto Velocidad Espana (AVE) in Spain, all of these travelling at speeds of between 280 and 350kph.

Coach services – Technological developments have led to the development of larger and more comfortable coaches with a capacity for up to 79 passengers, a sleeping berth for the second driver, air-conditioning, on-board washroom facilities and refreshments, and wi-fi, making travel by road faster and more comfortable, and through a higher capacity, cheaper per passenger. Coach services can be either scheduled or chartered:

- Scheduled coach services provide a network of domestic or international services that are operated to a published timetable, on which seats are available for purchase by the public. For example, Eurolines provides international services across Europe, from Morocco to Finland, and Greyhound operates domestic routes in the UK, Australia and Canada, as well as the USA.
- Chartered coach services are contracted by a third party, such as a tour operator or the organiser of a group trip, to provide specific journeys. The third party is responsible for filling the seats and the service is not available for sale to the public. Chartered coaches are used extensively for group tours by road lasting several weeks and led by a professional tour manager, as well as for short sightseeing tours within destinations and for transfer services between arrival gateways like airports, ports and railways, to city centres, resorts or specific hotels.

Ferries – Ferries provide services by sea connecting two port destinations on domestic or international routes. Ferries may be passenger only or passenger and vehicle services that can accommodate cars and coaches as well as trucks. The largest passenger ferries are known as superferries, for instance Irish Ferries' Ulysses can carry up to 2,000 passengers and crew plus 1,342 cars. The fastest ferries have smaller capacities (for instance the Stena Voyager with 1,500 passengers and 360 cars) but can travel at twice the speed of conventional ferries, at up to 40 knots.

Airlines – Airlines provide flights between airports on domestic or international routes. Airline services are either chartered or scheduled:

- **Charter air services**: Aircraft are contracted by third parties to operate specific routes for specific groups of tourists. For example, tour operators charter aircraft to transport their inclusive tour customers and small, private aircraft can be chartered for luxury business or leisure travel. Charter flight schedules are not published and tickets are not usually available to the general public for sale.

(Continued)

Table 5.3   (Continued)

- **Scheduled air services**: Operate to a published timetable and seats are available for purchase by the public, either directly or through travel agencies. There are three types of scheduled airlines – full service, low cost and all business class.

  o **Scheduled full service airlines (FSA)**: Operate a comprehensive route network, usually with international and intercontinental services, which follow a published timetable and on which seats are available for purchase by the public. Aircraft are usually configured with two or three classes of cabin – economy, business and first – and seats are usually sold through travel agencies as well as directly. The top 10 airlines by passenger-kilometres flown on international and domestic routes in 2010 are American Airlines, Delta, United Airlines, Air France, Continental, Lufthansa, Emirates, British Airways, North West and Qantas (IATA, 2011).
  o **Scheduled low cost airlines (LCAs)**: Offer a basic no-frills product on domestic or short-haul international routes. Often use less popular (secondary) airports and prices do not include in-flight catering or entertainment. Cabins are configured as economy class only. Usually sell direct using the internet. Southwest Airlines, Ryanair and Easyjet are the largest LCAs (IATA, 2011).
  o **Scheduled all business class airlines**: Offer direct services on a limited number of routes from Europe to the USA. The cabin is configured as all business class, and offers high standards of comfort and service. Notable examples are the British Airways Open Skies service from Paris, the Lufthansa Business Jet from Munich and Dusseldorf, and British Airways Club World from London City Airport.

There are two key concepts that influence both scheduled and charter transport operators – load factor and yield.

Load Factor and Yield

The term passenger or seat load factor is used in the transport sector to measure sales performance. It refers to the proportion of seats sold as a percentage of the seats available on a departure. For example, if 25 seats of a total capacity of 50 are occupied on a ferry, coach or plane departure, the load factor is 50 per cent. Operators seek to achieve as high a load factor as possible but most are unable to achieve 100 per cent load factors on a regular basis. In the airline industry, for example, Continental Airlines' average annual load factor ranged between 74.1 per cent and 81.7 per cent in the period 2002–2008 (Continental Airlines, 2009) while Easyjet's average for 2006–2010 was between 83.7 per cent and 87 per cent (Easyjet, 2010). Some transport operators calculate seat prices based on the minimum load factor required in order to cover their costs, known as the break-even load factor. This is often the approach used by charterers of transport.

Yield describes the average revenue received per seat and is calculated by dividing the revenue achieved on a departure by the number of seats available. Operators seek to achieve as high a yield as possible, but are not always free to determine the prices they sell their seats at because of regulations that govern their activities.

Regulation of Tourist Transport Suppliers

The term regulation refers to the framework of laws and rules that affect how transport suppliers operate. Governments regulate the transport sector in order to:

- Enforce minimum standards of safety for passengers and the communities on the routes served – for instance, laws determine maximum working hours, qualifications, training and licensing requirements, security procedures at terminals and on board, and the performance and maintenance procedures of vehicles and vessels.

- Influence the level of competition between operators providing specific transport services by regulating the economic conditions that they operate under. Economic regulation may prevent transport operators from setting up new routes, adding departures onto existing routes, or adjusting their prices in response to demand. The rail, sea, bus and aviation sectors have a history of government regulation of routes, ownership of operators, control over the number of operators on routes, and controls over frequency of departures and even the prices that can be charged.

The right to operate international services is granted by the government of each state on the route, and therefore the number of transport suppliers operating an international route is often a reflection of government attitudes to the free market. The international passenger aviation industry is a good example of complex economic regulation.

In civil aviation, individual governments traditionally negotiated international air routes over, to and from their territory in a system of bi-lateral agreements that specified the freedoms of the air granted to one or more airlines from each country. The Freedoms of the Air, listed in Table 5.4, were drawn up at the Chicago Convention in 1944.

Protectionist governments restrict the levels of competition faced by their state-owned national carrier, and usually only grant a maximum of the first four freedoms to treaty partners, specifying which airports can be served, and may even specify the frequency and capacity of flights, which airlines can operate on the routes, and even that governments must approve of the fares to be charged.

More liberal bilateral agreements that grant more freedoms to each partner and allow each partner's airlines to respond to market forces are pursued by some countries, particularly the USA. The nature of the bilateral agreement between two countries affects the development of route networks, the number of airlines offering services on the route, the frequency of departures and therefore the number of seats available, and the degree of price competition between carriers.

Levels of economic regulation vary between individual countries and between transport sectors within each country. Many Western economies since the late 1970s/early 1980s have sought to reduce levels of economic regulation,

Table 5.4   Freedoms of the Air

First freedom	The right to fly over another country without landing.
Second freedom	The right to make a landing in another country for technical reasons, for example refuelling or maintenance.
Third freedom	The right to carry commercial traffic from an airline's home country A to the treaty partner's country B.
Fourth freedom	The right to carry commercial traffic from country B back to the airline's home country A.
Fifth freedom	The right of an airline from country A to carry commercial traffic between country B and another country C on a flight originating or terminating in the airline's home country (countries B and C must also agree), e.g. Air New Zealand selling tickets for flights from London to Los Angeles on a flight terminating in Auckland.

Three supplementary rights:

Sixth freedom	The right of an airline of country A to carry commercial traffic between two other countries B and C via country A, by combining third and fourth freedom rights, e.g. Gulf Air selling tickets to British passengers for flights from London to Delhi, via Bahrain.
Seventh freedom	The right to carry commercial traffic between two other countries without the flight originating or terminating in the airline's home country.
Eighth freedom or cabotage rights	The right of airline of country A to carry commercial traffic on domestic routes in country B.

Source: Doganis (2009: 325). Reproduced with permission from Routledge.

state ownership and subsidy, and allow market forces to determine routes, the number of operators, frequencies, capacities and prices. At a domestic level this is known as deregulation and can be achieved through government legislation. At an international level the process is known as liberalisation and is a slow and fragmented process that requires a re-negotiation of existing agreements with all other governments on international routes.

The removal or reduction of economic regulation within the transport sector is often linked to specific benefits for passengers and for tourism. The ability of new entrants to operate routes, of new routes to be set up, for demand to determine the frequency of departures, and for operators to compete on price often results in greater choice, more convenience and lower prices for passengers. For tourism, these improvements are very significant as they stimulate the demand for existing and new destinations.

Arguably the deregulation and liberalisation of civil aviation has had the most significant impact on tourism. Until 1978, all civil aviation was subject to strict economic regulation on a national and international basis. However, a slow process of liberalisation started in 1978 with the US Airline Deregulation Act, the impacts of which have promoted deregulation in other parts of the world, and created new opportunities for airlines (Hanlon, 1996).

The case study below describes the process and impacts of liberalisation of passenger aviation.

CASE STUDY 5.1

LIBERALISATION IN INTERNATIONAL CIVIL AVIATION

The US's Airline Deregulation Act of 1978 removed capacity, frequency and price controls on inter-state routes, and the impact was spectacular: airlines operating inter-state routes increased from 36 to over 120 by 1985; market domination by the top five carriers reduced; fares fell; and with increased efficiencies, costs also fell, increasing the profitability of airlines and giving travellers more choice and lower fares (Hanlon, 1996).

The US sought similar impacts on international routes by renegotiating bilateral agreements with other governments. Country by country, they renegotiated bilaterals with minimum fare controls and no capacity controls and allowed more than one airline from each country to operate the route (multiple designation): with the UK (1977), the Netherlands (1978), Germany and Belgium (1978), and between 1978–1980 with Singapore, Thailand, Korea and the Philippines, and then with Malaysia (1985) and Australia (1989) (Doganis, 1991).

This process liberalised north Atlantic and Pacific routes and some governments began to liberalise their own bilaterals with other countries: Canada/West Germany (1982), UK/the Netherlands (1984), Singapore/the UK (1989).

The impacts of the renegotiated treaties were dramatic. On North Atlantic routes, demand grew by 23.4 per cent in 1978, and by 15.5 per cent in 1979, and by the mid-1980s the number of airlines operating services had increased from three to 12; load factors increased from an average of below 60 per cent between 1960 and 1975, to 67.4 per cent by 1979 (Doganis, 1991). However, price wars on routes with new entrants reduced yields which threatened airline profitability. Between 1979 and 1982, most US airlines made losses on the North Atlantic routes and many new operators collapsed (Doganis, 1991).

Within Europe, liberalisation began with deregulation in the UK and Netherlands in the 1980s and 1990s, and the 1997 EU-wide Three Packages legislation which established the European Common Aviation Area (ECAA). These packages removed government subsidies from airlines and in 1997 granted all eight freedoms of the air to all ECAA registered airlines, stimulating an expansion of the LCA sector, especially Easyjet and Ryanair (Graham, 2009). However, some formerly stable, state-owned airlines suffered from financial instability (Alitalia, Air France), and a number collapsed (Swissair). Since 2006, bilaterals between ECAA and non-EU countries have been negotiated with the EU, and the 2007 Open Skies agreement between the USA and EU has allowed market forces to determine routes, frequencies, capacities and prices, thereby allowing US and EU airlines to operate to any airport in either territory.

EU-type plurilateral agreements are being introduced by regional economic organisations within Asia, South America, the Caribbean and Africa, where liberalisation is progressing.

By the early twenty-first century, domestic airline regulation had reduced in most countries (Forsyth, 2008) although some states do still restrict the number of airlines and retain state ownership. Liberalisation of international routes varies: the USA,

(Continued)

(Continued)

Singapore, New Zealand, United Arab Emirates and Chile have liberal attitudes to aviation, but Japan, China, the Philippines, Africa and South American nations are more restrictive. The remaining countries (Australia, Canada, European and Southeast Asian states) are more pragmatic and will liberalise routes on a case-by-case basis if there are sufficient advantages for doing so, for example, stimulating inbound tourism.

Reflective Questions

1 Liberalisation of an international route often increases demand. Why is this the case?
2 How has liberalisation benefitted low cost airlines?

Accommodation, non-residential venues and transport suppliers provide important supporting roles for tourism to develop in a destination: they allow a visitor to come to the destination and spend time there. The fact that tourists will visit one destination and not another however is closely linked to its perceived attractiveness, and this aspect is usually primarily influenced by a fourth type of supplier, visitor attractions.

Visitor Attractions

The term visitor attraction describes a site that is the focus of recreational activity by tourists and excursionists, and may also be used by the host population of a destination (Wanhill, 2008). There is a diverse range of types of visitor attraction and a huge variety of suppliers, making the study of visitor attractions quite complex. Middleton et al. (2009) refer to 'managed visitor attractions' – which are resources that have been formally designated as permanent sites 'for the enjoyment, entertainment and education of the visiting public' (2009: 409). They identify 10 different types of managed attraction:

- *Ancient monuments*: protected and preserved sites such as fortifications, burial mounds, and buildings; for example, the Pyramids in Egypt, Stonehenge in England, Machu Pichu in Peru, the Great Wall of China.

- *Historic buildings*: also known as heritage sites – castles, houses, palaces, cathedrals, churches, town centres, villages.

- *Designated natural areas, parks and gardens*: national parks, country parks, long-distance paths, gardens, managed beaches. Often these are owned by the state but managed by a designated agency, for example the National Park Authority or local government.

- *Theme parks*: amusement and leisure sites that are based on a particular brand, character, historic period or site. Major theme park suppliers are The Walt Disney Company, Seaworld Parks and Entertainment, Universal Parks and Resorts.

- *Wildlife attractions*: zoos, aquaria, aviaries, wildfowl parks, game parks and safaris, farms.

- *Museums*: sites housing significant collections. Museum content may be subject-specific (science, natural history, transport), site specific (The Forbidden City in Beijing, or the Ironbridge Gorge in England); or area-based, e.g. national, regional or local collections.

- *Art galleries*: galleries with collections built up over many decades. Includes the new wave of modern art galleries in striking new buildings, for example the Guggenheim in Bilbao, Spain. Often state-owned and funded.

- *Industrial archaeology sites*: sites and structures identified with specific industrial and manufacturing processes, such as mining, textiles, railways, from the period post-1750.

- *Themed retail sites*: speciality retail centres, often located in historic buildings or in purpose-built sites. The largest in the UK attract over 30 million visitors a year.

- *Amusement and leisure parks*: parks constructed primarily for 'white knuckle' rides, e.g. rollercoasters, and associated stalls and amusements. Major suppliers are the Merlin Group, Six Flags and Cedar Fair.

  (Adapted from Middleton et al., 2009: 410.)

Visitor attractions are possibly the most important element of the tourism system because they draw tourists to a destination, and stimulate demand for transport, accommodation and other suppliers. Boniface and Cooper (2009: 40) describe attractions as '… the *raison d'être* for tourism; they generate the visit, give rise to excursion circuits and create an industry of their own'.

The visitor attractions sector is polarised between a small number of attractions that draw in over one million visitors a year, and thousands of small attractions that bring in fewer than 30,000 visitors a year and with less than £100,000 in visitor revenue (Middleton et al., 2009). The management and operational challenges faced by different types of attraction, and different sizes of attraction, can vary significantly, and it is therefore useful to categorise attractions that share similar characteristics.

A common approach to categorising attractions is to distinguish between those that are natural and those that are built:

- Natural attractions include beaches, forests, woodland, mountains and lakes, and although they may not provide any built services or charge admission, these still need to be managed and to employ staff to maintain the site, particularly in those that attract large numbers of visitors. Management of natural attractions is often concerned with conserving or protecting the site and with managing visitors effectively to reduce environmental pressure (Fyall et al., 2008).

- Built attractions include historic properties, museums and galleries, farms, gardens, parks, workplaces, leisure parks and wildlife attractions. Built attractions usually focus on increasing visitor spend by attempting to attract demand to match their capacity, and by developing other revenue sources on site to encourage visitors to spend more, for example through food and beverage facilities and souvenir shops. Built attractions can be further sub-divided into those that have been purpose-built as a visitor attraction and those that were originally built for an entirely different purpose.

  o Purpose-built attractions include theme parks, water parks, zoos, aquaria, some museums and art galleries. Purpose-built attractions are designed carefully with a consideration of the most desirable and profitable location and capacity, the most effective location of on-site services such as ticket offices and restrooms, and the provision of revenue opportunities such as food and beverage facilities and shops.

  o Built attractions whose original purpose was not related to tourism include temples, cathedrals, palaces, churches, gardens, farms and workplaces. Some of these may have intentionally developed into visitor attractions as a way of attracting new sources of revenue, while others may be reluctant tourism suppliers. In many cases, these non-purpose built attractions still fulfil their original purpose but have had to adapt in order to provide visitor services as well. Provision must be made for visitors in terms of charging policy, the admissions process, managing visitor behaviour to avoid damage or inappropriate behaviour, control over access to the site, and providing information within the attraction unobtrusively. Some such attractions also exploit revenue opportunities by selling guidebooks or souvenirs on site too.

While it can be useful to classify attractions as natural or built, there are several other characteristics that can also be used to differentiate between them. Leask (2008) illustrates the multiple dimensions by which attractions can be classified, as Figure 5.3 illustrates.

The second main approach to classifying attractions is by charging policy; that is, whether admission is free or paid for by the visitor. Admission charging policies are usually a reflection of the management's objectives. Leslie (2001) identifies the main objectives of visitor attractions as:

- Education and stewardship.
- Conservation and preservation.
- Profit.

Attractions whose objective is to safeguard their contents for the benefit and education of the general public will usually charge low entrance fees in order to encourage attendance. For example, since 2001 all UK museums and art galleries that house national collections have charged no admission fee, in order to implement their objective of providing access to the widest possible public.

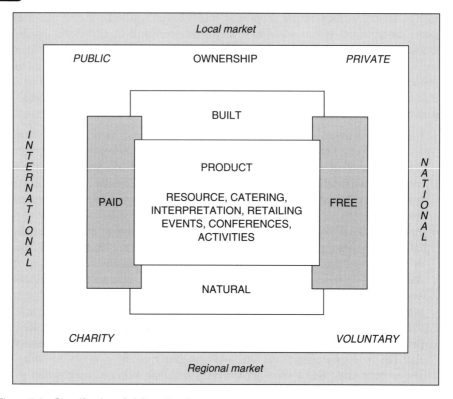

Figure 5.3 Classification of visitor attractions

Source: Reprinted from Fyall et al. (2008) with permission from Elsevier.

Attractions whose objective is to conserve and preserve their contents may use admission fees to raise funds to finance preservation, and may also charge high fees to reduce the number of visitors in order to prevent damage to the resource. For example, in 1994 Kings College Chapel in Cambridge introduced a visitor entry fee to reduce the volume of visitors and to raise funds to maintain the building; in 1995 visitor numbers had reduced by 50 per cent, and a substantial surplus (£300,000) contributed to the conservation of the site.

Profit-seeking attractions charge entrance fees to cover their costs and to generate a return on investment. Many purpose-built attractions, particularly those whose purpose is to entertain, are often, though not always, commercially owned and operated and are therefore required to generate profits. For example, Disney's theme parks earned $468 million in profit in the last quarter of 2010 (Barnes, 2011).

Charging policies are often a reflection of the type of ownership and funding. The model identifies four types of ownership within the visitor attractions sector – public, private, voluntary and charity – and proposes that each operates differently in terms of staffing, priorities, pricing, visitor access and financial resources. We consider ownership in more detail later in this chapter, in relation to all tourism suppliers.

The operating environment of a visitor attraction is influenced by the market that it attracts, for instance whether visitors are mainly local, regional, national or international, or a combination of all of these. The nature of the product, the need to change and update the product regularly, prices that can be charged, the feasibility of additional revenue sources on site, and the way in which information is provided to visitors will vary depending on the source markets attracted (Leask, 2008).

The types of attraction that we have discussed thus far are permanent attractions; that is, they are intended to exist in the long-term. In tourism, there are also a variety of temporary attractions that will have been created specifically for a short period of time – hours, days, weeks or months – that are known as events. Events are a recognised form of tourist attraction.

Events

An event is a non-permanent form of tourist attraction. Events are described as 'an organised occasion such as meeting, convention, exhibition, special event, gala dinner' (Convention Industry Council (CIC), 2003, in Bowdin et al., 2006: 14). Getz (2007) stresses the key principle of events is their temporary and unique nature, and describes events as planned or unplanned activities. Planned events are scheduled, designed and controlled by accountable producers and managers in order to achieve specific outcomes which may be personal, political, cultural, social, or economic; unplanned events are spontaneous and unpredictable, for instance a political demonstration, and are not managed or controlled by a central accountable body. In this section we focus on planned events that are intended to attract tourists to, or encourage them to stay longer in, a destination, or to change the image of a destination.

Events management has become an important field of study in its own right but it overlaps with tourism when an event is staged that draws in leisure, VFR or business tourists. In this section we consider different types of planned events and their suppliers.

The range of types of events is very broad. Getz (2007) developed a typology of planned events as shown in Figure 5.4.

Further approaches to describing events consider their size or function. Bowdin et al. (2006) differentiate between local/community events and major events:

Cultural celebrations (festivals, carnivals, commemorations, parades, rites & rituals) Political & state (political conferences, government summits, VIP visits, royal events) Arts & entertainment (concerts, award ceremonies, theatre, art exhibitions, dance shows, literature)	Business & trade (farmers' markets, trade & consumer shows, meetings & conventions) Educational & scientific (academic & professional symposia, conferences)
Sport competitions (games, meets, matches or festivals at any level, professional or amateur) Recreational (card games, dance & exercise)	Private events/functions (weddings, funerals, barmitzvahs, parties, reunions)

Figure 5.4   Typology of planned events

Source: Getz (2007: 22).

- *Community events*: local or community events are organised, usually by volunteers, for local audiences and are staged in public venues such as schools, streets, sports centres, and parks. Bowdin et al. (2006) stress the community benefits of local events – for example community pride, participation in sports or arts activities, exposure to new ideas or experiences, and appreciation of diversity and tolerance. Local governments often support local events as part of their community and cultural development strategies, and don't attract tourists in significant numbers unless these become so popular that they evolve into a major event, as the Notting Hill Carnival in West London has done.

- *Major events*: these attract large audiences, media attention and economic benefits through visitor spending and a greater awareness of the destination.

Getz (2007) provides definitions for different event types. The main ones are:

- *Hallmark events*: which are staged once or recur at regular intervals and are intrinsically linked to the destination in which they are staged, for example the Munich Oktoberfest, the Rio Carnival, and the Glastonbury Festival. Hallmark events form part of the destination's image, brand and identity.

- *Iconic events*: which describe events that have a strong appeal on their own because of their meaning, and can include hallmark events such as the London Marathon, as well as events that could be held successfully anywhere like the FIFA World Cup or the Superbowl.

- *Premier/prestige events*: which are the top event in the activity that they represent and may be staged in the same place or in different locations. Examples include the FA Cup Final, the Champions League or FIFA World Cup Finals, the World Athletics Championship, or the World Expo.

- *Mega events*: which are events that attract 'extraordinarily high levels of tourism, media coverage, prestige or economic impact for the host community, venue or organisation' (Getz, 2007: 25) Mega events might be staged once or repeated in different destinations, and attract large audiences and media attention, prestige and economic impact. Global events such as the Olympics, the FIFA World Cup Finals and World Expos are usually described as mega events, but Getz (2007) stresses that these can also include smaller events that have a significant impact on the image of the host destination, such as a political conference or a religious or community festival.

- *Corporate events*: which are events produced for a corporation, for example product launches, meetings, conferences, trade exhibitions and grand openings.

 ## Snapshot 5.3   The Glastonbury Festival

Festival crowds at Glastonbury

Source: Simon Inkson

A farm in south west England hosts the iconic music, dance, poetry and theatre event, the Glastonbury Festival. The festival developed from a small community event to a professionally organised and televised event attracting 185,000 people. The festival has a polical message – at first donating funds to the Campaign for Nuclear Disarmament (CND), and subsequently to Greenpeace, Oxfam, Wateraid and local charities.

(Continued)

(Continued)

The first festival in 1970 charged £1 for a two-day event and attracted 1,500 people. In 1971 attendance was free in protest against the commercialisation of music festivals; 12,000 attended. No further festivals were held until 1978 when 500 people arrived for an impromptu festival.

Glastonbury Festivals have been held on an annual or bi-annual basis since 1979 and are now, by necessity, professionally organised. Since 1983 a Public Entertainment licence has been required, specifying the maximum attendance and access road, water supply and hygiene requirements.

Crowd control and safety is a major issue: in 1984 designated car parking and stewards to direct traffic were introduced; in 1985 the site expanded into the neighbouring farm; and 1989 saw police involvement in planning. In 2002 a steel fence was erected around the site to control entry and the introduction in 2007 of a ticket pre-registration scheme prevented touting. In 1992 the festival attracted 70,000 people, rising to 150,000 by 2003.

Source: Glastonbury Festival (2011).

Events can provide a tourism legacy, which will live on for years after the event has been staged (Robinson et al., 2010). Many of today's major permanent tourist attractions were originally built for events that took place many decades ago. The Eiffel Tower, for example, is one of the most iconic tourist attractions in Europe: the structure was built for the World Expo in Paris in 1937. The Olympic Park is Munich is also a key tourist attraction for the city, and was built for the Summer Olympic Games in 1972.

One type of tourism supplier that combines the characteristics of transport, accommodation and visitor attraction criteria is the cruise sector, which we explore in the following section.

The Cruise Sector

The cruise sector has experienced rapid growth in demand since the 1980s as a result of technological and operating developments that have increased the capacity of ships, resulting in lower unit costs per passenger.

Until the 1980s cruising mainly attracted wealthy retired customers because of long cruise durations and high prices. Technological and operating advances have created larger, faster ships, increasing capacity so that the unit cost of each passenger became lower, making cruises affordable to more markets. In 1998 the largest cruise ship ever was launched, Princess Cruise's *Grand Princess*, with capacity for 2,600 passengers. However, by 2008 the capacity on new ships had doubled to over 5,000 passengers; Royal Caribbean

International's latest ships, *Allure of the Seas* and *Oasis of the Seas*, both carry 5,400 passengers.

These megaships are floating cities, with shopping malls, theatres, ice-rinks, water parks and cinemas, and are almost destinations in their own right – they provide transport, accommodation and attractions together in one product. Their size dictates their itineraries as they cannot sail with passengers in unpredictable waters, so remain within the Caribbean and Mediterranean. They also require specific port facilities to accommodate such large vessels and volumes of passengers, and to process the volume of waste generated on board.

In the late twentieth century, cruise tourism experienced rapid growth in demand, stimulated by lower prices, and the development of cruise products to appeal to a range of market segments, for instance families, singles and young couples, and, in northern Europe, the sale of cruises by tour operators. The USA dominates the cruise passenger market, but between 2003 and 2008 the European market grew by 66 per cent from 2.6 million to 4.4 million passengers, with major markets in the UK, Germany and Italy.

The cruise industry is dominated by three large shipping companies that own several brands:

- *The Carnival Corporation*: Carnival Cruise Lines, Holland America Line, Princess Cruises, Seabourn Cruise Line, P&O, Cunard, AIDA, Costa Cruises, Iberocruceros, P&O.
- *Royal Caribbean Cruises Ltd*: Royal Caribbean International (RCI), Celebrity Cruises, CDF Crosieres de France, Azamara Cruises.
- *Star Cruises*: Star Cruises, Norwegian Cruise Lines, NCL America, Orient Lines, Cruise Ferries.

The previous sections have provided an outline of the main forms of tourism suppliers. We will now consider the main characteristics that are common to all tourism suppliers.

Characteristics of Tourism Suppliers

We have seen that the supply of the tourism product is fragmented across several sectors and that within each sector there is also a range of different types of industry. Despite this variety tourism suppliers, regardless of the sector or industry within which they operate, are characterised by the same features. Tourism suppliers are part of the service sector and some of the characteristics that we discuss below are common to all service providers, whether they operate in tourism or not, while other characteristics are unique to tourism suppliers. We start by considering the characteristics of services – intangibility, inseparability, perishability and heterogeneity – and how these affect tourism suppliers.

Intangibility

Intangibility means without physical substance and is used to describe assets that cannot be touched, tested or experienced before or after consumption, and for which no physical evidence exists after consumption. Tourism suppliers' products are often described as intangible because:

- Tourists often make reservations and pay for tourism products before their departure from the generating regions; they are therefore unable to check or test destination-based suppliers products before making the purchase decision. At the end of the trip they will have no evidence of it apart from souvenirs, photographs and memories.

- The benefits that the tourism product provides are experiential and not physical. For example, leisure tourists will seek relaxing, indulgent or challenging experiences, while business tourists may seek professional, efficient or prestigious experiences. These experiences require the use of a tangible physical infrastructure such as transport, accommodation and attractions in destinations, but these are used as a means to achieve more experiential benefits.

Intangibility creates challenges for tourism suppliers. They need to understand the benefits sought from their products by tourists but are impeded from researching consumer needs by the distance between generating and destination regions. In addition, any language or cultural differences creates difficulties in communicating with potential tourists while language, distance and currency differences create practical difficulties in processing reservations and payments. This was particularly challenging before the emergence of the internet and created a role for businesses based in the generating region who sold suppliers' capacity on their behalf. These businesses are known as intermediaries and we discuss them in detail Chapter 6.

The snapshot on p. 106 identified a number of business models that could reduce the problems caused by intangibility. Franchises and consortia are not exclusive to the hotel sector: franchising is common in the airline industry, for example, British Airways franchises its brand to Comair in Southern Africa and Sunair in Scandinavia, while consortia have been created by visitor attractions as a way of improving marketing effectiveness. For instance London Shh is a marketing alliance of small historic houses in central London, and SouthBankLondon is a consortium of venues on the south bank of the River Thames.

Inseparability

Inseparability describes products that are, to some extent, produced and consumed simultaneously. This requires the consumer's direct involvement with the suppliers' employees in interactions known as service encounters.

The quality of the service encounter is affected by the input of both the consumer and the service provider and therefore the interpersonal skills of the suppliers' employees are particularly important.

In tourism, service encounters often occur at different stages of the purchase and consumption experience and often involve interactions with several employees in different roles. For example, a tourist may reserve and pay for a hotel online, receive the confirmation by email, phone the reservations team with a particular enquiry, and on arrival be welcomed and checked-in by the front office, encounter housekeeping staff in corridors or in the room, and be served breakfast by food and beverage staff. Tourism suppliers must monitor and manage the quality of each service encounter to ensure consistency in the customer's experience (Grönroos, 2007).

Perishability

Perishability means that the life of an individual product is limited to a specific deadline and that once that deadline is reached the product ceases to be available for sale. All tourism suppliers' products are perishable; individual units of capacity, for example a hotel room, admission to an attraction or a seat on a transport departure, cannot be stored indefinitely until a consumer makes a decision to purchase it; if it is not sold by a certain time, then the opportunity to sell it disappears. Capacity that is approaching the end of its life without being sold is known as 'distressed inventory' or 'distressed stock'.

Middleton et al. suggest that perishability is a logical result of inseparability and that 'service production is fixed in time and space' (2009: 48). They interpret service production as a 'capacity to produce' rather than a volume of products. If demand is lower than the capacity to produce, spare capacity remains unsold or unused. Conversely, if demand is higher than the capacity to produce, extra capacity cannot usually be added. Perishability creates challenges for suppliers in matching capacity and demand; demand can be forecast based on previous experience and knowledge of the market and the external environment, but these forecasts are unlikely to be exact. It is therefore crucial that effective ways to sell as much available capacity as possible are found, and that prices are set to ensure that optimum yield is earned. We explain a common approach to this on p. 128.

Heterogeneity

Heterogeneity means that each consumer's experience of a supplier or a product is unique to that consumer. As a result of inseparability, tourism suppliers are unable to guarantee that each tourist's experience of their product will be the same. Heterogeneity therefore creates quality control and service quality management challenges for tourism suppliers – maintaining a consistent quality in all service encounters and ensuring that all consumers' experience of the same company is considered to be at least satisfactory or better. Employees providing services to consumers therefore have a crucial role in delivering customer satisfaction. We explore this issue further in Chapter 13.

In addition to service characteristics, tourism suppliers are also affected by demand variations, complementarity, and high fixed to variable costs (Middleton et al., 2009).

Demand Variations

Demand variations mean that the level of sold capacity will vary significantly on dates throughout the year or times throughout the day; that is, the demand for a product is not consistently the same. Most tourism suppliers experience significant demand variations on a seasonal, daily or hourly basis. Middleton et al. (2009) point out that for some tourism suppliers seasonality creates 90–100 per cent filled capacity for some weeks or months of the year, but less than 30 per cent filled capacity for the remainder of the year. Indeed many tourism suppliers choose to close down during their low season.

These demand variations, together with perishability, create pressure on suppliers to earn enough revenue during periods of peak demand to compensate for the lower revenue when demand falls. Many tourism suppliers respond to this challenge through the use of creative pricing to smooth demand (Hoffman et al., 2009), which we discuss later in this chapter.

Complementarity of Suppliers

Complementarity means that there is an inter-relationship or an inter-connectedness between suppliers; decisions made by suppliers in one sector may affect the demand for suppliers in other sectors (Middleton et al., 2009). For example, the decision by a transport operator to terminate a route into a destination will affect the accommodation and attractions sector there, while the range and quality of attractions in a destination will affect the demand for accommodation and transport suppliers too. Therefore tourism suppliers in one destination must depend on each other, even though they may operate completely independent of each other.

This complementarity creates a need for cross-sectoral cooperation and collaboration to ensure that decisions are made that will benefit tourism within the destination as a whole; in particular decisions about product design and quality and the messages about the destination that are communicated to consumers. This collaboration is often led by a department of the local government, a local, regional or national tourism organisation, or by a partnership of representatives from each tourism sector within a destination (Middleton et al., 2009). This issue is explored in detail in Chapter 7.

High Ratio of Fixed to Variable Costs

Tourism suppliers are characterised by the nature of their fixed and variable costs. Fixed costs are costs that must be paid regardless of the volume of units sold, for example an accommodation property must pay the costs of loans, wages, equipment, advertising and energy regardless of its occupancy rates. The price charged for each occupied room contributes to these fixed costs. Variable costs are only incurred when a unit of capacity is sold, for example in our fictional hotel below, the additional energy, water and cleaning costs incurred whilst a room is occupied, and the cost of breakfast.

Most tourism suppliers are characterised by high fixed costs and low variable costs. This is important because it creates opportunities to use flexible approaches to pricing, and potentially to sell each unit of capacity at different prices. The potential to do this, combined with variations in demand and the problem of perishability discussed earlier, allows tourism suppliers to stimulate sales for distressed inventory by selling a proportion of their capacity at lower prices. Figure 5.5 illustrates the concept of fixed and variable costs and their relationship to price and profit in a fictional accommodation property.

Pricing scenarios for a two room property – the published price is £200 and total fixed costs are £120 per night								
50% occupancy			*100% occupancy*			*100% occupancy*		
	Room 1	Room 2		Room 1	Room 2		Room 1	Room 2
Room revenue	200	0	Room revenue	200	54	Room revenue	200	100
Variable cost	20	0	Variable cost	20	20	Variable cost	20	20
Contribution	180	0	Contribution	180	34	Contribution	180	80
Fixed	60	60	Fixed cost	60	60	Fixed cost	60	60
Profit	120	–60	Profit	120	–26	Profit	120	20
Total profit: £60			Total profit: £94			Total profit: £140		

Figure 5.5   Variable pricing in a hotel

Figure 5.5 illustrates the flexibility that tourism suppliers have in pricing their products. Very large companies use sophisticated software to calculate the impact of price on profit and to determine the most profitable prices to charge, in a process known as revenue management.

Revenue management is the name of the process used widely in the hotel, transport, venue and cruising sectors to manage demand profitably. Revenue management forecasts sales, calculates the required yield or REVPAR, and determines the price to charge for each unit of capacity. The aim of the method is to manage demand through pricing in order to maximise revenue (Kimes, 2000).

Revenue management manages demand for and supply of a supplier's capacity by monitoring availability and sales and adapting prices continually, based on the forecasted load factor or occupancy rate and the required level of contribution to fixed costs required by each unit. When demand is high, some consumers will be prepared to pay a much higher price for the limited number of seats/rooms that are available, and the tourism supplier will sell to these customers at the highest possible price. Effective marketing ensures that customers who would pay the higher prices are unable to purchase the product at the lower prices. We discuss this in more detail in Chapter 13.

The characteristics described above create challenges for tourism suppliers in effectively communicating with consumers in order to sell optimal levels of their capacity at the highest prices, before it perishes. Fyall and Garrod (2005) suggest that as a result of IT advances and globalisation, business organisations have the opportunity to overcome these challenges by collaborating with businesses who were formerly regarded as adversaries: 'This trend is particularly apparent in the tourism industry, where the fragmented, multi-sectoral and independent nature of tourism provides a powerful catalytic focus for inter-organisational co-ordination and collective decision-making' (2005: 3).

We have already discussed examples of collaboration between hotels in the form of franchising and consortia. The snapshot below describes another common form of collaboration, the alliance:

 ### Snapshot 5.4   Airline Alliances

Collaboration between airlines is a common feature of the airline industry. Collaboration can take a variety of forms, but among the most common are code-share agreements and membership of a global alliance:

- Code-shares are commercial agreements between two airlines: one airline operates a flight and the other airline sells seats on that flight using its own flight designator code. The airline operating the flight benefits from higher load factors and the code-share partner extends its route network without incurring the costs of operating the flight (Hanlon, 2007). For example,

(Continued)

(Continued)

Virgin Atlantic sells seats under its code 'VS' on flights that are operated by Air China, bmi, Continental, Singapore Airlines, South African Airways, US Airways and Virgin Blue (Virgin Atlantic, 2011).

- Global alliances are consortia of selected airlines operating different routes. There are three global airline alliances – Star, oneworld and SkyTeam – of which Star is the largest with 27 member airlines, including Egyptair, LOT Polish Airlines, Continental, Lufthansa and Singapore Airlines (Star Alliance, 2011). Global alliance members benefit from code-share opportunities, shared facilities at airports, integrated Frequent Flyer Programmes and access to global markets (Fyall and Garrod, 2005).

Lufthansa Boeing 747 with Star Alliance branding

Source: Courtesy of Udo Kröner/Lufthansa

In addition to the characteristics discussed above, ownership is an important factor in the supply of tourism.

Ownership of Tourism Suppliers

The supply of tourism is provided by a range of types and sizes of organisation. In this section we consider ownership in the context of the private, public and voluntary sectors, and explain how the main characteristics of each affect tourism suppliers.

The term 'private sector' or 'commercial sector' describes firms which are owned by individuals or groups of individuals and provide products and services that are purchased by consumers. Profits from their operation are retained by their owners. The survival of private sector firms depends on their profitability and often their growth. The private sector plays a major role in tourism but there is great diversity in the size of firms (Buckley, 1994). Firms are described as large, medium, small or micro and are usually defined by employee numbers, annual turnover and the annual balance sheet. The EU definition of SMEs, established in 2005, is outlined in Table 5.5.

Table 5.5   EU definitions of SMEs

Enterprise category	Headcount	Annual turnover	Annual balance sheet total
Medium sized	< 250	≤ €50 million	≤ €43 million
Small	< 50	≤ €10 million	≤ €10 million
Micro	< 10	≤ €2 million	≤ €2 million

Source: European Commission (2005) © European Communities, 2005.

Large companies are defined as firms that employ more than 250 employees, with an annual turnover of over €50 million. Large companies usually benefit from access to finance and expertise and therefore are better equipped to overcome the challenges created by intangibility, perishability, heterogeneity and inseparability, and to grow and compete effectively.

Throughout this chapter we have identified the major suppliers in each tourism sector and have shown that there are many high-profile multinational tourism suppliers with a portfolio of globally-recognised brands, particularly in the hotel, airline, cruise and theme park industries. However, tourism supply is actually dominated by small and medium-sized businesses, and micro-businesses, known collectively as SMEs.

The domination of tourism by SMEs is very important because these face different challenges to those experienced by large companies. For instance SMEs often:

- Have limited access to financial resources; Haven-Tang and Jones (2005) suggest that tourism entrepreneurs often use personal and family savings as their main source of capital.

- Lack marketing and management expertise; Middleton et al. (2009) suggest that managers of visitor attractions with fewer than 100,000 visitors a year lack formal management and marketing training, and are likely to be knowledgeable enthusiasts who focus on daily operations rather than on strategic growth.

- Lack long-term business ownership experience; Haven-Tang and Jones (2005) found that many SME business owners entered the tourism industry as a lifestyle choice, to escape from what they perceived as the rat race, to semi-retire or to supplement a lifestyle in a more desirable location: their business goals may not prioritise growth.

These characteristics will often restrict an SME's ability to overcome the challenges created by the nature of services and of tourism that we discussed earlier. In addition, SMEs may face difficulties in competing with multinational suppliers which have expanded into destinations worldwide and enjoy a range of operating advantages such as professional management, access to international investment and lower costs through economies of scale and integration.

The potential skills gap in SMEs suggests a need for additional support for SMEs through training provision, marketing research to identify and understand potential markets, and promotional activities to reach consumers effectively. This support is usually provided by the public sector.

The term public sector describes state intervention in the supply of products and services. Public sector provision exists through ownership of shares in a commercially operated enterprise, through local government and other statutory agencies financed by public funding, and through state enterprises. In tourism the public sector has a major role, for example, 54.95 per cent of Singapore Airlines is owned by Temsek Holdings, a state enterprise; the French railway SNCF is wholly owned by the state; national museums in the UK are state owned and funded but operated as non-departmental public bodies; while in China, CITS (China International Travel Service) is a large state-owned tourism group that promotes China as a destination to inbound markets, develops and manages tourism resorts in China, and operates tours within China.

The public sector assumes responsibility for the provision of public goods and services in a variety of circumstances because:

■ The benefits are shared by the whole population – for example, in tourism with well-maintained road networks, access to international transport routes, or in museums and art galleries with collections of national importance.

■ The private sector is unable to provide such goods or services profitably or in sufficient quantity – for example, in tourism because use is free of charge or because demand is low but the economic benefits to the whole community are great: for instance, the state-owned Paradores de Turismo hotel chain in Spain operates 93 hotels in historic properties in rural regions where tourism and other economic activities are low.

■ The private sector is reluctant to invest because of the risk of failure, the amount of capital required and the slow return on investment – for example, airport, resort, venue and attraction construction in new destinations where demand has not yet been established.

The level of public sector provision of tourism products and services is a reflection of government ideology. Many European states have experienced a process of privatisation since the 1980s whereby state-owned activities and assets were sold to the private sector and became commercial entities. For instance, in the UK British Airways and the British Airports Authority were privatised in 1987.

The term voluntary sector or third sector refers to organisations that are independent and self-governing and are comprised of people who have joined together voluntarily to take action for the benefit of the community. A voluntary organisation may employ paid staff or volunteers, but must be established other than for financial gain. In tourism many attractions are provided by the voluntary sector, particularly museums and heritage attractions. The National Trust in the UK purchases and manages historic buildings by using charitable donations and membership fees and charging admission fees to the public.

Summary

Tourism supply is complex and fragmented. It consists of a variety of sectors which can be sub-divided into individual industries and within which a diverse range of ownership types, objectives and resources exist. The private, public and voluntary sectors operate alongside each other and the state has a clear role in providing elements of tourism supply, particularly where the private sector cannot see profitability.

It is clear however that individual tourism suppliers are but one element of a whole tourist experience of a destination and that their inter-reliance creates a need for them to be coordinated and to collaborate. Suppliers that lack the skills or resources to operate, manage or market themselves effectively require additional support from an external source in order to ensure that tourism in the destination is not compromised. In addition, there is a growing trend for alliances and collaborations between operators within the same sector to avoid a duplication of effort, achieve marketing power and economies, and reduce costs in order to compete more effectively with operators outside their alliance.

 ■ **Self-test Questions** ▬▬▬▬▬▬▬▬▬▬▬▬▬▬▬▬▬▬▬▬

1 Consider the place in which you live. Which elements of tourism supply exist there?

2 Describe the characteristics of this supply with reference to ownership, demand variations, and complementarity.

3 Consider the extent to which the public sector plays a role in supplying the tourism product in your home town.

Further Reading

Fyall, A., Garrod, B., Leask, A. and Wanhill, S. (2008) *Managing Visitor Attractions: New Directions*. Oxford: Butterworth-Heinemann.

Getz, D. (2007) *Event Studies: Theory, Research and Policy for Planned Events*. Oxford: Butterworth-Heinemann.

Jones, E. and Haven-Tang, C. (2005) *Tourism SMEs: Service Quality and Destination Competitiveness*. Wallingford: CABI.

Useful Websites

Association of Leading Visitor Attractions: www.alva.org.uk
British Hospitality Association: www.bha.org.uk
Civil Aviation Authority: www.caa.co.uk
Passenger Shipping Association: www.thepsa.co.uk

Intermediaries in the Tourism System

Inexperienced travellers, fearful of adventure ... encouraged the emergence of tour operators who mass-produced, standardised and rigidly packaged tours, removing any element of consumer risk. The tour operator would pre-test and pre-visit the destination and would normally have a hired representative in the destination – someone with a familiar face who spoke the same language and who could relate to the fears and anxiety of the inexperienced – providing an additional sense of security and an added incentive for mass tourism. (Poon, 1993: 40)

Organised tour in the high Atlas Mountains, Morocco

Source: Clare Inkson

Learning Outcomes

After reading this chapter you will understand:

- **the types and roles of travel intermediaries**
- **the constraints under which travel intermediaries operate**
- **how intermediaries are affected by changes in the external operating environment.**

Introduction

In Chapter 2 we discussed the distance between generating and receiving regions that is inherent in tourism. Since tourists often reserve and pay for travel products some time in advance of consuming them, this geographical distance creates practical problems for travel suppliers in selling their products. Where there are language or currency differences between suppliers and the potential consumers of their product, these difficulties may be exacerbated.

Travel intermediary:
A company acting between two separate parties in the distribution of travel products- e.g. between the consumer and supplier

This challenge creates opportunities for companies acting as intermediaries between suppliers and consumers: facilitating the process for tourists of buying travel products, and for suppliers of selling them. **Travel intermediaries** are mainly comprised of travel agencies, tour operators and wholesalers, and are usually, although not always, based in the generating region. Travel intermediaries may serve the leisure market, the corporate market, or both, and are known collectively as the travel trade.

The travel trade has experienced great upheaval since the end of the twentieth century as a result of regulatory changes, new internet and mobile media technologies that created new ways for tourists to research and purchase travel products, and the emergence of more experienced, independent and confident tourists in some generating regions who seek more flexible travel experiences that are tailored closely to their individual needs. Travel intermediary businesses have had to adapt quickly to these changes and as a result the sector is very dynamic and in a state of constant development.

In this chapter we identify each type of intermediary, its role in the tourism system and its main operating features. We consider how the travel trade is regulated, and common structural features of intermediary businesses.

Types of Intermediary in the Tourism System

There are three main types of intermediary in the tourism system: travel agencies, operators and wholesalers (Buhalis, in Buhalis and Laws, 2001). Each of these is defined in detail in Table 6.1.

Intermediaries do not directly produce any individual elements of the travel experience, but they play an extremely important role in the distribution of travel products produced by other companies and organisations. That is, they sell travel products – transport, accommodation, amenities and attractions – on behalf of suppliers, creating a link between suppliers in destinations and the potential consumers of their products in generating regions.

In practice the distinction between wholesalers, operators and agencies is not always clear because there has been some blurring of their activities in

Table 6.1 Intermediaries in the tourism system

Wholesalers	Operators	Travel agencies
Wholesalers buy capacity from one type of supplier, e.g. hotels, airlines, or attractions, and sell the capacity on in its original form to other intermediaries or direct to the consumer.	Operators buy capacity from accommodation, transport and attractions suppliers and combine them together to create an inclusive tour, or package, which is sold at one price. The customer does not know the price of each component of the package.	Travel agencies represent suppliers and process sales on their behalf, usually through computerised reservations systems.
Wholesalers of air seats are known as brokers or consolidators.	Operators may create holidays, short-breaks or day-trips for the leisure market, or organise meetings, incentive trips, conferences and exhibitions for the MICE market.	In some generating regions, travel agencies will often specialise in either the leisure or the business travel market.
Wholesalers of hotels are sometimes known as bed banks.		

Source: Buhalis (2001).

recent years. For example, some intermediaries may act as both a travel agency and an operator and require flexibility in the way they buy capacity and sell it on to the consumer. Legally though, the distinction between types of intermediary is important because the financial risk, contractual responsibilities to tourists, liabilities and regulatory controls will differ depending on the nature of the contract between intermediary and supplier.

Intermediaries negotiate contracts with individual suppliers specifying dates, capacity and rates. Rates given to intermediaries may be:

- *Commissionable rates*: the supplier determines the price at which capacity will be sold and pays an agreed percentage of the sale price to the intermediary. In this case the tourist's contract is with the supplier, known legally as the principal, who is responsible for the fulfilment of the contract (Renshaw, 1992). This was the standard approach used by travel agencies, but is now changing because many suppliers have considerably reduced the commission rates they pay.

- *Net rates*: suppliers give rates that are heavily discounted compared to their published rates and the intermediary adds their own mark up. Legally, the supplier's contract is with the intermediary who then creates another contract with tourists when they purchase the product from them. In this case responsibility for the fulfilment of contractual obligations, and provision of the supplier's product, lies with the intermediary. This is the standard approach used by wholesalers and operators, although it is becoming more common for travel agencies in some generating regions to negotiate net rates too (Beaver, 2002).

- *Inclusive tour rates (ITX)*: net rates given to intermediaries who must use the product to create a package (Beaver, 2002). Usually contracts will specify that the selling price of the package cannot be lower than the supplier's published rate. ITX rates are usually negotiated by operators when they contract capacity from a transport supplier. Again, the legal obligation is with the intermediary for the fulfilment of the contract and supply of the product.

The actual net or ITX rates negotiated reflect the financial value of the intermediary to the supplier. This may be measured in the volume of bookings that the intermediary makes or the type of consumer that the operator brings to the supplier. Some intermediaries have significant power and are able to negotiate very low rates because of the value they can offer to the supplier.

The Role of Intermediaries in the Tourism System

Intermediaries offer a number of benefits to suppliers and to tourists, and consequently in major generating regions, a complex network of travel intermediaries has developed. These networks may serve the leisure or the business travel market, or both.

Figure 6.1 illustrates the network of intermediaries traditionally used to distribute tourist products from supplier to consumer. The figure shows that suppliers of travel products have four options for distributing their products to customers. These are a combination of direct or indirect (sometimes called mediated) distribution. Each option is known as a channel of distribution. Suppliers may use one or more of these channels and intermediaries themselves may also use another channel of distribution to reach their customers.

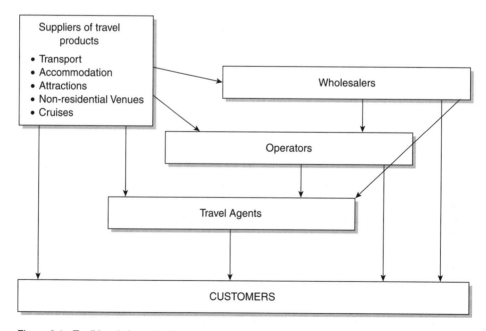

Figure 6.1 Traditional channels of distribution in the tourism system

Benefits of Intermediaries for Suppliers

Yale (1995) and Buhalis (2001) identify a number of benefits that intermediaries offer to suppliers based in destination regions:

- *Sales volume*: by selling large quantities of their capacity either on the same date, or on different dates over a season.

- *Market access*: by reaching certain types of consumers that the supplier would be unlikely to reach alone.

- *Market knowledge*: by understanding the detailed requirements of consumers in a generating region, the prices they are likely to pay, and the most effective ways of communicating with them.

- *Reduced marketing costs*: by incurring the cost of researching markets in generating regions and promoting to consumers.

- *Simplified sales process*: by processing reservations, payments and ticketing on behalf of suppliers.

- *Disposal of distressed stock*: by selling some capacity that would otherwise remain unsold.

- *Complaint handling*: by mediating between supplier and consumer and attempting to resolve disputes.

Intermediaries contract capacity with suppliers in different forms:

- *Allocation*: the reservation of a specific number of rooms, seats or tickets, for specific dates. If the intermediary is unable to sell all of the allocation by a specified deadline, known as the release date, the unsold element is released back to the supplier to sell through other channels (Gale, 2006). Operators and Wholesalers contract capacity on this basis.

- *On request*: intermediaries negotiate prices with a supplier for irregular bookings that cannot be predicted at the time of contracting – also known as ad hoc bookings. No reservations are made until the intermediary receives an enquiry from a customer (Yale, 1995), but if there is no availability then capacity must be sought from an alternative supplier. This form of contract is used by wholesalers, operators and travel agencies.

- *Guarantee*: the reservation of a confirmed number of rooms, seats or tickets which must be paid for whether or not the intermediary has sold the capacity to a customer (Yale, 1995). Guaranteed contracts are effective in negotiating very low rates and were used by large European tour operators during the 1980s to secure cost advantages over their competitors to resort destinations in the Mediterranean with a history of reliable demand (Gale, 2006), but are less popular now because of the financial risk.

In addition to the advantages that intermediaries offer to suppliers, they also provide benefit to tourists who purchase travel products through them.

Benefits of Intermediaries for Tourists

Pender (2001) and Buhalis (2001) identify the benefits to tourists of buying travel products through intermediaries:

- Easier access to information about destinations and the suppliers within them.
- Advice and guidance about the most appropriate travel products to buy.
- The ability to make reservations in their own language and currency in the generating region.
- Possibly obtaining lower prices than if they booked with the supplier directly.
- In some generating regions, financial assurance that payments made to travel agencies or to operators are protected in the event of the intermediary's insolvency.
- Advice and assistance during the trip for operators' customers, from a representative based in the destination.

Internet technology has significantly reduced the perceived distance between supplier and potential customer and has facilitated a process of disintermediation in the travel industry. Disintermediation is a relatively new concept in the travel sector and refers to the growing trend among consumers in some generating regions, and suppliers in destination regions or on transit routes, to remove intermediaries from the travel supply chain by buying or selling direct (Pender, 2001). The relative ease with which consumers and suppliers can reach each other through the internet, plus the increasing demand for travel experiences that are tailor-made to the needs of the consumer, are viewed as a very clear threat to the long-term future of intermediaries (Law, 2009). We return to this point later in the chapter.

We now consider each type of intermediary in more detail.

Wholesalers

Wholesalers have played an important role in tourism for many decades. Until recently however, they were a hidden intermediary in the tourism system because they provided a business to business service (B2B): they sold products to travel agencies and/or operators rather than to the consumer.

The impact of internet technology, together with increased consumer demand for greater flexibility and independence in their travel experience, has created new opportunities for the travel wholesale sector: they can now target the consumer direct via the internet, and now offer enhanced services to agencies allowing them to tailor-make travel packages to the needs of individual customers.

Wholesalers usually specialise in a particular type of product, for example airline seats, hotel rooms or attraction tickets, and are able to negotiate lower rates from suppliers than many travel agencies or operators as a result of the volume of capacity they contract. They then sell the capacity on in the same form to operators, agencies or direct to the customer (Pender, 2001). The original B2B function of wholesalers exempted them from the consumer protection regulation that affected operators and agencies; this has considerable implications for consumers now that wholesalers often sell direct. We discuss this issue in more detail later in the chapter.

Operators

Operators combine tourist products into packages and sell them as pre-arranged inclusive tours (ITs) at one price (Pender, 2001). Usually the package consists of transport and accommodation but could be accommodation and an attraction, or transport and an attraction, or all three. The key point is that the package is sold at one price and the consumer is unaware of the cost of each element.

The operator sector can be subdivided into:

- *Tour operators*: based in the generating region these create holiday, touring or recreational ITs for leisure tourists. These ITs may be mass produced or tailor-made. Mass produced ITs are programmes of hundreds or thousands of identical trips that are sold 'off the shelf' and appeal to a very broad market. Tailor-made ITs are arranged specifically to meet the individual requirements of each customer and are usually more expensive. Poon (1993) describes mass produced ITs as 'old tourism' that stimulated the expansion of mass tourism demand during the 1960s and 1970s in northern Europe.

- *MICE operators*: also known as event organisers, are usually based in the generating region these arrange meetings, conferences, incentive trips or exhibitions for companies and organisations. Usually these are tailor-made to the customer's individual requirements.

- *Incoming or inbound operators*: also known as destination management companies or ground handlers, these are based in the receiving region and provide local expertise and organise local transport and accommodation for tour or MICE operators or travel agencies from different generating regions (Pender, 2001). Buhalis (2001) suggests that the incoming operator sector is the least-known in tourism and one that is often forgotten by researchers, but they actually play a vital role in some destinations as the link between local suppliers and operators in generating regions.

Although tour, MICE operators and inbound operators create products for very distinct markets, they share the same function: they create a link between suppliers and some or all of their potential customers, as well as facilitate the organisation, purchase and operation of the travel experience for their customers.

The practical organisation and operation of an IT requires similar processes regardless of whether the operator is a tour, MICE or incoming operator. The organisation of ITs can be extremely complex, requiring careful planning, often well in advance of the departure date.

The Planning Process

The process of research, negotiating with and contracting the suppliers, pricing the trip, and marketing and selling it, often starts at least one year before departure, particularly for large tour operators whose customer base is made up of hundreds of thousands, or millions, of customers a year (Pender, 2001). MICE operators organising a major conference or incentive trip for hundreds or thousands of delegates, and tour operators planning a programme of continuous departures to a range of destinations throughout a season, may start their planning several years in advance. Operators with small programmes with limited departures are often able to organise ITs and launch them for sale more quickly (Pender, 2001). The snapshot below describes a hypothetical large tour operator's planning process for a programme of holidays to a number of destinations in the May–October 2012 season.

Snapshot 6.1   An Example Planning Process for a Tour Operator's Holiday Programme to a Range of Worldwide Destinations in May–October 2012

TUI Travel representative

Source: Courtesy of TUI Travel Plc

(Continued)

(Continued)

- Late 2010: Forecasting of passenger numbers and decisions on destinations and suppliers to include, based on customer feedback and sales data, consumer trends and political, economic, social and technological influences. Foreign currency requirements and purchases are planned.
- Jan/Feb 2011: Contractors negotiate allocations with destination and transit route suppliers. Auditing of properties for health and safety compliance.
- May/April 2011: Preparation of promotional material – brochures and website for consumers and reservations and sales material for travel agencies. Commission rates negotiated with travel agencies. Calculation of final selling prices. Development of sales promotions to encourage early bookings.
- May–September 2011: Programme launch to travel agencies and/or the public using advertising in selected print media, television, radio and online. Promotional materials and product information supplied to travel agencies.
- May 2011–October 2012: Bookings and deposits received from agencies and direct customers. Sales forecasts are reviewed and adjustments made, e.g. increasing or reducing allocations and reducing prices if necessary.
- Autumn 2011 and Spring 2012: Recruitment and training of staff for each destination – team leaders, resort representatives, childcare providers, entertainers, and office staff.
- March–August 2012: Issuing of final invoices to travel agencies or direct customers, receiving payments and issuing travel documents.
- May–October 2012: Operations department finalises arrangements for each customer; destination staff arrange transfers and excursions. Customers are welcomed on arrival by overseas staff and given information about the destination and excursions.
- May–October 2012: Collection and analysis of customers' quality control questionnaires.
- May–October 2012: Finance department pays suppliers.

This snapshot shows the time lag between the negotiation of rates with suppliers and payments being made by customers. The long time period between setting up and pricing the programme and its operation leaves operators vulnerable to many factors beyond their control which may have a serious effect on their projected profit margins: in particular, exchange rate fluctuations, increases in fuel prices or a sudden collapse in demand for a destination because of political unrest, disease outbreak, natural disaster, or crime or terrorist attacks targeting tourists.

An operator's ability to add **surcharges** to a sale in the event of cost increases is usually governed by consumer protection legislation of the state or country where the sale is made. EU legislation requires operators to absorb the first 2 per cent of the package price and prevents them from adding surcharges within 30 days of departure (ABTA,

Surcharges: The addition of extra costs to the customer, after the original selling price has been agreed

Forward contract:
Future purchases of a currency can be ordered at current rates by payment of a deposit

Stop loss contract:
Specifies the maximum rate at which a currency should be bought

2010). Many operators guarantee no surcharges as a way of competing more effectively. Operators are therefore vulnerable to exchange rate fluctuations or rises in fuel prices (Pender, 2001). To reduce risk, operators may purchase currency strategically using **forward contracts** or **stop loss contracts** (Laws, 1997), however the cost of these financial tools may prohibit small operators, who require relatively small amounts of foreign currency, from using them. Small operators are therefore less able to alleviate the risks of contracting in one currency and selling in another.

Chartering Transport

Operators often reduce the cost of the transport element of an IT by chartering transport. Any mode of transport can potentially be chartered, such as a train and a cruise boat or ship, but this is most commonly used in the coach and air sectors.

If an operator requires a large number of seats on a single departure, series of departures, or a tour, it is often cheaper to hire the required mode of transport for their own use, as a whole charter, rather than buy a number of seats on a scheduled service. In the coach and air sectors, many transport suppliers will specialise in charters and only sell their services through intermediaries, mostly operators. For this reason, many chartered transport suppliers are relatively unknown to the public. For example, many coach companies will hire their coaches and drivers to operators for transfers or for tours and charter airlines will operate on routes and timetables established by an operator. The operator negotiates a rate for the charter and is responsible for filling all of the seats.

Laws (1997: 177) identifies a range of charter agreements:

- *Ad hoc charter*: a one-off contract to operate one leg of a journey, a round trip, or a tour. Used by tour and MICE operators.
- *Series charter*: regular departures operating specific routes within a certain time period, but the coach, ship or aircraft is also chartered to other operators during that time period. Mainly used by tour operators.
- *Time charter*: exclusive use of the coach, ship or aircraft for the whole of a specified period, often a whole season. Mainly used by tour operators.
- *Part charter*: the departure is shared between two or more organisers – this is most common with charter flights. Mainly used by tour operators.
- *Whole charter*: all the seats on one departure are contracted to one operator. Used by tour and MICE operators.

- *Block charter*: operators contract a number of seats on a scheduled departure at ITX rates that must be combined with other travel products to create an inclusive tour. Common in the airline industry but also used on trains and ferries. Used by tour and MICE operators.

Operators select the most appropriate type of charter based on sales forecasts and costs.

Profitability of Operators

Operators work in a very competitive environment and often the basis for such competition will be price. MICE and niche tour operators are less susceptible to price competition because reputation and quality are a priority for their customers whose budgets are usually higher. Operators that organise mass-produced ITs and compete for the same customer markets will often feature the same destinations, and sometimes even the same accommodation and transport suppliers; the only distinction between their ITs is often the selling price. This leads to pressure to reduce costs in order to reduce prices and often results in a precarious profitability (Pender, 2001).Tour operators who compete on price suffer from very slim profit margins (Yale, 1995); northern European mass-market tour operators achieve profit margins that represent 2–3 per cent of their turnover (FTO, 2009). For example, the profit margin on a holiday sold for €500 is €10–15. Consider this slim profit per passenger with the risk of currency fluctuations and fuel price increases discussed above, plus the restriction on surcharging imposed by the EU, and this narrow margin could be quickly depleted, leaving the operator just breaking even, or possibly suffering a loss. If the operator fails to sell all of its capacity and has contracted on a guaranteed basis, this slim margin may be threatened further.

In addition, seasonal revenue patterns create further financial challenges (Yale, 1995). If an operator's product has an identifiable peak season, for example summer sun, or only operates during certain months of the year, for example a winter sports operator, there will be specific times of year when revenue is highest – when customers pay the balance for their trip, usually eight weeks before departure – and other times when little or no revenue is earned, thereby putting pressure on cash-flow.

Such a precarious financial environment creates financial instability in the tour operator sector and there are not infrequent financial collapses of tour operators as a result. In 2008, record oil prices and the impacts of the 2007 credit crunch created volatile operating conditions that led to the closure of a number of tour operators. One high profile tour operator collapse is outlined in the snapshot below.

Snapshot 6.2　The Collapse of XL UK

XL Leisure Group was the UK's third largest travel organiser, carrying 2.3 million passengers in 2007 and employing 1,700 staff with subsidiaries in France and Germany.

The UK company consisted of:

- Supplier: XL Airways – flying to 50 destinations from three UK Airports and with a fleet of 21 planes.
- Wholesalers: Freedom Flights and Medlife Hotels – seat-only to trade; bed bank to trade and public.
- Tour operators: Aspire Holidays, Travel City Direct, Kosmar Holidays, Really Great Holiday Company, XL Holidays, Travel City International.
- Retail: XL.com.

The company was affected badly in 2007 by oil price inflation, the credit crunch and an unsuccessful attempt to refinance, and in September 2008 it ceased trading. Flights were cancelled and planes grounded, leaving 90,000 customers overseas and 240,000 unfulfilled advance bookings.

The majority of customers were repatriated or refunded by the CAA, but customers who had booked seats on XL Airways direct through the website or hotels through Medlife were not protected and could only claim refunds if they had paid using a credit card.

The high-profile collapse has prompted the EC to review travel consumer protection.

XL France and XL Germany were sold and are still operating.

Sources: *Travel Trade Gazette* (2008); *Travel Weekly* (2008); CAA (2009).

XL UK was an integrated travel company that owned different types of intermediary. The snapshot demonstrates the difference in consumer protection offered by wholesalers and operators and the implications of this for their customers. We discuss integration and consumer protection later in this chapter.

Travel Agencies

The travel agency sector has experienced huge upheavals since the last decade of the twentieth century. Traditionally travel agencies provided points of sale in the generating region for suppliers of tourist products, known as principals, and they earned a commission on each sale (Laws, 2001; Pender, 2001). Travel agencies accessed suppliers' inventory to check availability and prices, make reservations, and issue documents using global distribution systems (GDS) such as Amadeus, Sabre, Galileo, and Worldspan. The internet now enables customers to research availability and prices, make reservations and issue travel documents themselves, and consequently the travel agency sector has had to adapt to a new business environment.

Travel agency businesses bear relatively little financial risk as they do not purchase stock and have no contractual responsibility for the products they sell at commissionable rates. In practice, travel agencies have a duty of care to their customers and have responsibilities to their principals (Beaver, 2002), but the contract resulting from the sale is between the principal and the consumer.

Until the 1980s the travel agency sector was relatively stable: most travel agencies represented the same principals and were usually paid the same rates of commission by all principals operating in the same sector. For example, airline commission rates were commonly 9 per cent and tour operators and hotels paid 10 per cent. Travel agencies were unable to reduce the prices quoted by principals and consumers could buy the same product at the same price from most travel agencies.

Changes to legislation in some generating regions, and revised agency agreements with some suppliers, relaxed the business environment in the 1980s and 1990s, allowing travel agencies greater flexibility to compete with each other. Airline deregulation in the USA in the late 1970s and 1980s forced changes to the traditionally inflexible relationship between airlines and travel agencies and greater freedom was given to airlines in the sale of their seats; airlines could in theory sell tickets in the USA through banks, hotels and retail chains (Dilts and Prough, 1991; Hodgson, 1987) and airlines there began reducing commission rates or paying a flat fee to travel agencies (Beaver, 2002). In 2002 in the USA, commission payments by airlines to travel agencies were eliminated (Amadeus, 2007). A similar pattern followed in Europe where several airlines reduced commission from 9 per cent to 7 per cent between 1997 and 1999, with further decreases since 2001; several European airlines now pay a zero rate or 1 per cent commission to travel agencies (Amadeus, 2007). Suppliers in other sectors such as accommodation, attractions and car hire also began to negotiate more flexibility into their relationship with travel agencies, selecting travel agencies strategically rather than selling through them all, and incentivising them through **over-ride commissions** (Renshaw, 1992).

> **Over-ride commissions:** An increase in commission rate when a sales target is reached e.g. from 10 per cent to 12.5 per cent

Agencies responded to this by becoming more selective about the principals they represented (Renshaw, 1992; Yale, 1995). The volume of a travel agency's sales with one principal had a direct effect on the commission rates earned and therefore the profitability of the travel agency and its ability to compete. Travel agencies with more than one outlet and thus larger volumes of customers could benefit from higher commission levels if they directed sales towards specific principals.

Some travel agencies began to charge fees to their customers, to compensate for reduced commission rates. This has been particularly common in travel agencies specialising in business travel.

In theory, one travel agency can serve the leisure and business travel markets because frequently the suppliers used, with the exception of operators, are the same. In some regions, particularly emerging markets such as Brazil and China, this is common (Euromonitor International, 2008) and in mature markets, such as northern Europe and north America, also used to be the case (Laws, 2001).

However, in mature markets a distinction between leisure and business travel agencies has developed since the 1980s, as a result of more selective distribution by principals and the divergence of the needs of business and leisure travellers (Pender, 2001).

Demand for seats on scheduled flights is generally higher from business tourists and the IATA requirement that travel agencies selling seats on scheduled flights must have an IATA licence was regarded as an ineffective investment by travel agencies who mainly sold package holidays. Travel agencies began to specialise in serving either leisure or business travellers (Mayhew, 1987) and although some do still serve both markets specialisation is a growing trend. Leisure travel agencies focus on selling suppliers' products to leisure tourists, while business travel agencies focus on the business tourist market. We now consider each of these in detail.

Business Travel Agencies

Business travel agencies specialise in selling tourism suppliers' capacity to businesses and organisations, for their employees who travel as part of their work. Business travel agencies are also known as corporate travel agencies and more recently, because of changes in the way they work, the term travel management company (TMC) is being increasingly used (Beaver, 2002).

Business travel agencies are not usually visible to the public as they do not require a high street shopfront location, but need to be accessible to companies and organisations they target. Consequently, they are located in business districts, often in office premises, and may even establish an office within the premises of a corporate customer that generates a large volume of business for them; this situation is known as an implant (Pender, 2001).

The reduction in commission rates paid by suppliers to travel agencies that we discussed on p. 145 has forced business travel agencies to adopt a new business model. To replace the reduction in commission revenue, business travel agencies began to charge a service fee to their customers. To justify this fee, they needed to offer greater value to their customers than simply reserving travel products and issuing documents. Consequently business travel agencies have adapted their business model to provide comprehensive travel management services; they still process the purchase of travel products but also offer additional value by advising on and managing their customers' business travel policies and reducing their expenditure on business travel through strategic purchasing. The corporate client pays a management fee to the TMC on a monthly basis, and the commission earned on any sales is shared between the client and the agency (Davidson, 2001).

There are a number of very powerful global TMC providers, for example Carlson Wagonlit, American Express and Uniglobe, who have strong purchasing and marketing power. Independent TMCs can choose to operate under the brand name of a TMC chain by becoming a franchisee. Franchising is discussed in detail in Chapter 5. The snapshot below describes Uniglobe, a global TMC franchisor.

 ## Snapshot 6.3   Travel Agency Franchise

Uniglobe headquarters, Vancouver

Source: Courtesy of Uniglobe Travel International

Uniglobe Travel International is a global travel management company (TMC) franchisor specialising in travel services for small to mid-sized businesses and vacation travellers. Its first location opened in 1981 in Canada and by 2011 it had locations in more than 50 countries across North and South America, Europe, Asia, Australia, the Middle East and Africa, with an annual sales volume of $4 billion.

(Continued)

(Continued)

Uniglobe operates on a franchise model whereby each agency is individually owned and operated. The locations have an agreement with Uniglobe head office that permits them to operate under the Uniglobe brand name and take advantage of the various programmes that the franchisor offers. Such programmes include support in corporate sales, marketing, and technology, along with access to negotiated supplier rates.

Through local ownership, Uniglobe locations provide their clients with better service and accountability, while having access to the tools, programmes and volume benefits of a larger organisation. The franchisees are encouraged to network with other Uniglobe locations to provide global coverage for their accounts and to learn best practices from their colleagues elsewhere in the world.

Source: Uniglobe (2011).

TMCs are able to clearly demonstrate the value they offer to their customers. In the leisure travel agency sector, this value is harder to demonstrate.

Leisure Travel Agencies

The growth in internet use by consumers has made the role of the conventional leisure travel agency unclear (Law, 2009). Consumers are now able to research, reserve, and pay for travel products direct from suppliers via the internet, as well as print their own travel documents. In the UK this is widely known as DIY (do-it-yourself) travel. The value offered by leisure travel agencies has diminished since consumers have been able to fulfil their function themselves.

Changes to leisure travel agencies' operating environment – a reduction in commission rates, competition from suppliers targeting consumers direct through the internet – have forced the leisure travel agency sector to innovate in order to survive. At times the future of the sector has been considered to be very bleak and there is evidence that the number of travel agencies in mature generating regions is declining. However, in emerging markets the sector is still expanding.

Trend data from Euromonitor International (2008) show that in Germany, the UK and the USA the number of travel agency outlets is reducing while in Brazil, China, India and Russia the sector is growing. This may be because relatively inexperienced travellers are more reluctant to buy travel products direct from suppliers and because internet use is less widespread in these emerging markets.

Some leisure travel agencies charge transaction fees to their customers, although this varies between countries; in the UK specialist leisure travel agencies that serve niche markets may charge a service fee, but in general the practice is not yet being used widely.

The process of disintermediation, discussed at the beginning of this chapter, has created a more flexible method of organising leisure travel called dynamic packaging.

Dynamic Packaging

Dynamic packaging is the process whereby an inclusive tour is constructed without the use of an operator, specifically to the individual requirements of the consumer. For leisure travel agencies, the ability to dynamically package has created important new opportunities.

Dynamic packaging allows a travel agency to tailor-make an inclusive tour for a customer by buying individual components of the travel experience at net rates, either direct from the supplier or from wholesalers, thus adding on their own mark-up and selling the package at one price. This responds to the falling demand for a 'one size fits all' approach to inclusive tours by offering flexibility to the customer. It also responds to the reduction in commission payments that some suppliers are pursuing and provides agencies with the opportunity to increase their revenue. Dynamic packaging may alter the consumers' legal relationship with travel agencies, creating the contractual and regulatory liabilities that operators are subject to.

While the growth of internet use is considered to be a threat to the leisure travel agency sector, it has actually created opportunities for travel agencies as well, and in generating regions where internet penetration is high travel agencies must also develop e-distribution to remain competitive (Buhalis and Kaldis, 2008). Travel agencies with websites are able to increase their market penetration by reaching customers in geographic regions that are far beyond the catchment of the traditional agency outlet (Law et al., 2004). In generating regions with a high penetration of internet access travel agencies often have their own websites and some no longer have a physical sales location.

The late twentieth century saw the emergence of a new type of travel agency – the online travel agency (OTA). These agencies have no physical sales outlets and often have a global customer base that targets markets in all of the main generating regions in the world. For example, Expedia was established in 1996 and is now one of the largest travel companies in the world, targeting the leisure market in over 14 generating regions, as well as the corporate market in 12 generating regions with its own corporate travel agency, Egencia.

Some forms of travel intermediary are subject to complex regulations that govern their operations.

Regulation of Intermediaries

In some generating regions, particularly within the EU, intermediaries are closely regulated: their business practices, the accuracy of the information they provide to consumers, and their liability to consumers are stipulated either through self-regulation or government legislation.

Self-regulation

Self-regulation is the voluntary adoption of regulation and is usually implemented through membership of a trade association that stipulates minimum standards of operation for all of its members.

Self-regulation through trade associations is common in the travel agency sector – for example, ABTA in the UK, ASTA in the USA, AFTA in Australia, and TAANZ in New Zealand – and in the tour operator sector – for example, AITO in the UK, and the United States Tour Operators Association in the USA. Regulations establish a code of conduct for members, set standards of training and qualifications for staff, and monitor the financial performance of trade association members. Membership of an association often acts as a mark of quality for its members, providing reassurance to customers about the security of their payments or the reliability of the company.

Some suppliers require travel agencies to be licensed by their own trade association, for example travel agencies that sell scheduled airline seats require an International Air Transport Association (IATA) licence which is granted after inspection of the financial performance of an agency and stipulates the minimum levels of qualification and staff required in order to hold a licence. IATA's Passenger Sales Agency Agreement (PSA) defines the minimum requirements that agencies and airlines must adhere to in their transactions (IATA, 2009).

Legislation

Travel intermediaries are subject to the same laws as non-travel businesses, for example the consumer protection legislation that enforces consumer rights and the responsibilities of manufacturers, retailers and consumers. In some generating regions laws specifically regulating travel intermediaries have been introduced. For instance, in Australia and Malaysia travel agencies require a government licence in order to trade (Humphreys, 2006) and in 1993 operators selling ITs within the EU became subject to very strict legislation governing their business practices, as Case Study 6.1 explains.

The main consumer protection elements of regulation of intermediaries relate to:

- The security of customers' payments.
- The accuracy and clarity of information provided to customers.
- The safety of the tourist during the trip, for operators selling to customers in the EU.

Each of these will now be discussed.

Security of Customers' Payments

Customers booking through intermediaries pay in advance of departure – the reservation is secured by payment of a deposit when the reservation is made and the balance is usually paid six to eight weeks before departure. Intermediaries may not be required to pay suppliers until after the customer has used the product. If the intermediary goes out of business whilst holding these payments, customers who have not yet travelled will lose their reservations and customers who are travelling at the time of the company's collapse will be stranded in the destination with no transport home and probably no accommodation. Suppliers in destinations will also not be paid. When this happens, consumer confidence in travel intermediaries is adversely affected and suppliers in destinations may be less willing to work with intermediaries from the same generating region.

In order to prevent this, some trade associations require operators and agencies to guarantee the security of their customers' payments; in the event of financial failure, all monies paid by customers will be refunded and customers who are in the destination will complete their trip and be transported back as originally planned if possible.

Often financial assurance is provided through a **bond** which is administered by a trade association, for example the United States Tour Operators Association's (USTOA) $1 million Traveler's Assistance Programme which requires all members to post a bond or letter of credit of $1 million as security to refund customers in the event of insolvency (USTOA, 2010). Travel agencies that are members of ABTA in the UK must have a bond (ABTA, 2010) and in Australia licensed travel agencies contribute to the Travel Compensation Fund which refunds customers in the event of the financial collapse of a member (Travel Compensation Fund, 2010).

> **Bond:** A promise from an organisation, a bank or an insurance company to refund payments if an operator collapses

Operators within all EU member states are required by law to provide financial protection to their customers. In the UK, all packaged tours that include flights must be bonded with the Civil Aviation Authority (CAA) through the Air Tour Operator's Licence scheme (ATOL), to which all ATOL holders contribute a fee per passenger. In the event of a company failure, the CAA arranges repatriation and refunds (CAA, 2009). Purchasers of packaged tours that do not include flights can be protected through a bond operated by a trade association, such as the Association of Independent Tour Operators (AITO), through an insurance policy, or through the holding of all monies paid to the operator in a trust account such as the Travel Trust Association (TTA).

Wholesalers are not generally required to be licensed by a government agency, nor to provide financial guarantees for their customers' payments in the event of insolvency, because traditionally they have provided a B2B service. However, the development of online sales of wholesalers' products direct to the consumer, or to travel agents who package them together with transport on behalf of the consumer, is beginning to reveal the vulnerability of wholesalers' consumers. The high-profile collapse of the UK bed bank, Medlife Hotels, in 2008, detailed in Snapshot 6.2, raised important questions about the financial protection offered to wholesalers' consumers, and it is expected that, in the EU at least, legislation to include wholesalers in travel industry financial regulation will be developed (Gray, 2009).

Accuracy and Clarity of Information

Until the emergence of the internet, intermediaries' customers made their decision to purchase a travel product from the information provided by the intermediary themselves. The customer could not verify this information until their arrival at the destination.

Tour operators' customers were particularly vulnerable because their purchase decision was usually based on brochures provided by the tour operators themselves. These brochures depicted destinations and suppliers with photographs and elaborated on these using descriptions. The brochure was a sales tool and some less scrupulous operators exaggerated, misrepresented or withheld some facts in order to sell their holidays (Horner and Swarbrooke, 2004). For example, the fact that a hotel was located on a very busy road may have been omitted, or the photograph may have inaccurately implied that all rooms had balconies or sea views. In extreme cases in the 1960s and 1970s, customers arrived at destinations to find that the building of their hotel was incomplete, and they had to be accommodated elsewhere (Delaney-Smith, 1987)!

Scrupulous operators could be the victims of poor business practices by suppliers: over-bookings were not unusual and last minute changes to the product – for example flight times or the closure of facilities at a hotel – would undermine operators' ability to provide the experience that customers expected. As a result, the tour operator sector gained a reputation for being unreliable and untrustworthy.

Some trade associations, for example ABTA in the UK and the Council of Australian Tour Operators (CATO), fought against this by implementing and enforcing codes of conduct for their members and setting higher standards of clarity, accuracy and reliability. As a result, a tour operator's membership of such an association became a mark of quality that provided customers with assurance about the packaged trip they were purchasing.

Legislation to ensure accuracy was included in the 1992 Package Travel Regulations (detailed in Case Study 6.1) and set comprehensive laws about descriptions, notifications of any changes and contractual terms relating to surcharges, cancellation and compensation for changes (Pender, 2001).

The Safety of Tourists During their Trip

Regulation for the safety of intermediaries' customers is also applied in some generating regions and applies mainly to the operator sector.

Safety is an important issue because operators select suppliers in destination areas on behalf of their customers. These suppliers are governed by the legislation of their own national governments in terms of health and safety, for example of hygiene standards in kitchens, fire protection in hotels, or the licensing of coach drivers. However, these local standards may be lower than the level that tourists are accustomed to in their home regions. In addition, local inspection processes to ensure compliance may not be as rigorous as would be necessary in some regions. Therefore, consumers may be at risk if a supplier selected for them by their operator does not comply with health and safety legislation, or if the local standard is inadequate. This has important implications for the operator because they have a legal responsibility for the fulfilment of the contract.

Many operators ensure that the suppliers they contract comply with acceptable standards by conducting their own health and safety audits when contracting. In the EU this is particularly important for operators because European regulations since 1992 hold the operator legally responsible for the safety of their customers; if a customer is injured or killed as a result of the negligence of a supplier, the operator acting as intermediary is liable to prosecution (Yale, 1995).

The case study below explains the impact of the EC legislation.

CASE STUDY 6.1

EUROPEAN UNION DIRECTIVE ON PACKAGE TRAVEL, PACKAGE HOLIDAYS AND PACKAGE TOURS 1992

In 1993 new EU legislation came into force that had serious implications for the operator sector.

The purpose of the legislation was to create consistency of regulation regarding operators across all EU member states. At the time leisure package travel was

(Continued)

(Continued)

notorious for its high levels of complaints from consumers about the quality of the components of holidays; often the accommodation did not meet the standards that customers had expected. In addition, a number of high profile tour operator insolvencies left customers stranded in destinations or having lost the money they had paid in advance. The sector had been subject to national laws concerning accuracy of descriptions and consumer protection and in many countries the sector was self-regulated through a trade association that prescribed codes of conduct and financial protection for its members. However, this was inconsistent across the EU.

The new EU legislation ensured that all EU consumers of package travel would benefit from the same standard of legislation.

The legislation required improved levels of regulation concerning a number of operator practices and financial protection for consumers and, crucially, held the directors of operator companies criminally liable for any breaches.

The Directive specified operators as 'tour organisers' and this definition was to include leisure operators selling domestic or international travel that lasted for more than 24 hours, and those who sold any two of transport, accommodation and other services, at an inclusive price.

Some regulations became subject to criminal law:

- The accuracy of information provided to the consumer about the product and requirements for travel such as passports, visas, health protection and travel insurance.
- Financial protection for consumers' payments in case of insolvency.

In addition, the Directive formalised the liability of the tour organiser who became liable for all formal aspects of the trip, regardless of whether these were carried out by the operator's employees or a third party. A breach of the regulations could incur a financial penalty and serious breaches, that led to the death or injury of consumers during the trip, could result in the imprisonment of directors of the operator.

The formalisation of liability has been very important in refining operator practices in terms of compliance procedures and information control:

- Operators check suppliers' documents during contracting to confirm the validity of licenses, fire and hygiene certificates and public liability insurance.
- Operators contractually require suppliers to provide accommodation, food and services that comply with the operator's description of them to the consumer.
- Information control systems to ensure information about suppliers gathered in one department are shared with other relevant departments and staff must clearly understand the operators' obligations.
- Complaints are monitored to identify information that may have implications for safety standards.
- Large operators conduct rigorous health and safety audits of suppliers to ensure compliance with local laws and their own minimum standards.

Sources: Gale (2006); Yale (1995).

(Continued)

(Continued)

> **Reflective Questions**
>
> 1 What are the cost implications for operators of the EU legislation?
> 2 How are small operators likely to be disadvantaged by the legislation?

While EU regulation was instrumental in improving standards for tour operator practices, the regulations still exclude some of the new forms of organised travel purchases that consumers now use via the internet, in particular wholesalers and dynamically packaged trips arranged by travel agencies. It is anticipated that the EC package travel regulations will be updated before 2012 to include all intermediaries.

Increasing Concentration in the Travel Intermediaries Sector

The discussion of each type of travel intermediary highlights the significance of buying power in negotiations with suppliers. Buying power allows more efficient production which can be translated into lower, and therefore more competitive, prices or greater profit margins. In addition, the low profit margins and precarious profitability of some intermediaries mean that their survival depends on massive volume of sales. Therefore market power is a key motive in the growth strategies of travel intermediaries.

Table 6.2 presents a summary of the world's major travel intermediaries, showing sales volume, number of employees, the number of generating regions they serve and passenger volume, where these figures were available.

Table 6.2 Global travel intermediaries

Company	Sales	Employees	Passengers/transactions
Carlson Wagonlit 2010	US$24.34 billion	18,500+	57 m+ transactions 151 source markets (Carlson Wagonlit, 2011)
TUI 2010	£13.5 billion	49,000	30 m customers 27 source markets (TUI Travel plc, 2011)
American Express	US$25.7 billion		140 source markets (American Express Travel, 2011)
Japan Travel Bureau	YEN 20 billion	27,323	(Japan Travel Bureau, 2011)
Thomas Cook	£8.9 billion	31,000	22.1 m 21 source markets (Thomas Cook, 2011)
Kuoni	CHF 3.8 billion	9,070	(Kuoni, 2011)

This concentration has been achieved through internal growth and through mergers and takeovers. The result has been a sector dominated by a small number of very powerful companies that are vertically and horizontally integrated and are forging expansion into emerging generating regions in Asia and South America.

We will now consider integration in the context of all intermediaries.

Travel Intermediary Integration

Integration is a form of strategic growth that is prevalent in the tourism system and in particular among the intermediaries sector (Pender, 2001). Integration is the creation of formal links between companies and provides three broad advantages to companies – security, efficiency and monopoly. Integration can be achieved in two ways: horizontally and vertically.

Horizontal Integration

Horizontal integration occurs when a company expands through an acquisition or merger with another company at the same stage of the same industry. Horizontal integration occurs within all types of travel intermediary, on a domestic or international basis, for example, two travel agency companies, two wholesalers or two operators uniting under the same ownership.

Horizontal integration provides a number of advantages that can allow companies to compete more effectively:

- *Economies of scale* – the combined companies reduce costs per sale through rationalising business functions such as reservations, human resources or marketing, or closing down duplicate sites (Yale, 1995). Their increased size may enhance their bargaining power with suppliers (Renshaw, 1992).

- *The opportunity to move into complementary products for which growth in demand is intensifying.* The acquisition of an existing successful company achieves benefits more quickly than setting up a new one (Pender, 2001).

- *A rapid increase in market share by buying into an existing market.* Large intermediaries in mature markets are expanding their geographical spread by acquiring small intermediaries in emerging markets.

Horizontal integration was prevalent in the travel agency sector during the 1980s and 1990s in the UK, often referred to as the 'March of the Multiples' (Humphreys, 2006; Pender, 2001; Renshaw, 1992). For instance, Lunn Poly (now Thomson) expanded rapidly from 180 branches in 1989 to 507 in 1992 (Renshaw, 1992) through the acquisition of independent travel agencies. Northern European tour operators pursued horizontal integration throughout the 1980s and 1990s to create a concentrated business environment that now provides a number of tour operator brands that are owned by just two parent companies, TUI Travel plc and the Thomas Cook Group.

Vertical Integration

Vertical integration refers to the merging of companies that operate at different levels of the stages of production in the same sector, for example a retailer and a manufacturer. Figure 6.1 at the beginning of this chapter, showing the traditional channels of distribution in the tourism system, would demonstrate vertical integration if one company owned subsidiaries that operated within separate channels. For example if an airline, a wholesaler, a tour operator and a travel agency, or any two of these, were owned by the same parent company, the company would be described as vertically integrated, and known as a travel organiser or travel group.

Vertical integration can be described as forward or backward (Pender, 2001). Forward, or downstream, integration occurs when the original company integrates with a company that operates at a later stage of production, for example an airline integrating with a tour operator, or a tour operator integrating with a travel agency.

Backward, or upstream, integration occurs when the original company integrates with another company that operates at an earlier stage of production, for example a travel agency with a tour operator, or a tour operator with an airline.

Frequently, tour operators will integrate forward with travel agencies, followed by a backward integration with charter airlines, and sometimes hotel companies and cruise lines. In the leisure travel market, vertically integrated travel intermediaries are very powerful because of their size. Many destinations, particularly in coastal regions such as the Mediterranean, rely heavily on the two main leisure travel intermediaries in Europe – Thomas Cook and TUI Travel – as a source for their tourists.

Vertical integration is very common in the travel industry due to the competitive advantages that it creates, identified by Pender (2001) as:

- Forward integration that provides a secure source of buyers for all or part of the company's capacity, and may reduce the cost of those sales through the reduced marketing effort required, which may in turn impact on pricing.

- Backward integration that secures the supply of a product, perhaps at a more attractive price than competitors would be able to purchase it for, and controls competitors' access to the product.

- Both of these forms of integration provide control over supply and pricing, and provide the opportunity of maintaining a consistent quality of product and standard of service throughout most of the customer's travel experience.

- Vertical integration provides a competitive advantage over rivals who are not vertically integrated, possibly pushing them out of the market and creating barriers to entry for new entrants.

Consider the snapshot of Thomas Cook UK and Ireland below.

 Snapshot 6.4   Thomas Cook UK's Integrated Structure

Thomas Cook travel agency, north London

Source: Clare Inkson

Thomas Cook is a good example of a horizontally and vertically integrated intermediary. As a tour operator it originally forward integrated by establishing a travel agency brand and backward integrated by establishing an airline. Within each individual sector, Thomas Cook is horizontally integrated and owns several companies that offer the same type of product to distinct market segments (see Figure 6.2).

Figure 6.2 shows that rival companies may also work with companies within the Thomas Cook Group to secure airline seats, accommodation or sales outlets. Competitors targeting the same markets as Thomas Cook are considerably disadvantaged if they are not also vertically integrated as they lack its buying and marketing power.

Since the 1980s the UK travel organiser sector has been increasingly dominated by fewer and fewer companies. Throughout the 1990s and until 2007, Thomas Cook was one of four travel organisers dominating the UK market. In 2007 this reduced to two as Thomas Cook merged with one of its competitors, MyTravel, and TUI Travel merged with First Choice.

Thomas Cook's main competitor is now TUI Travel which is also similarly vertically and horizontally integrated. Together they dominate the European outbound leisure travel market with expansion ambitions into emerging generating regions.

(Continued)

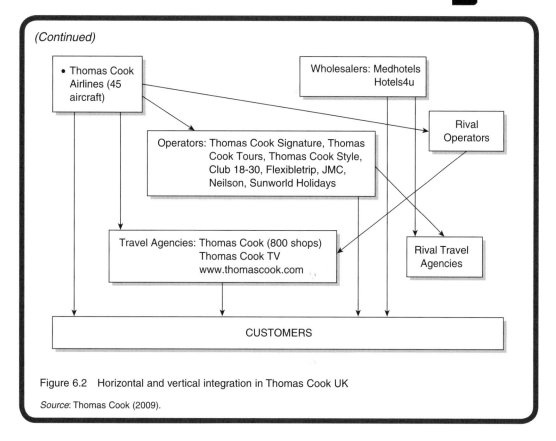

(Continued)

Figure 6.2   Horizontal and vertical integration in Thomas Cook UK

Source: Thomas Cook (2009).

The main threat to these companies is not other travel groups, but increasing demand for independent travel in some markets, facilitated by low-cost airlines, direct sales by suppliers, and the growth in online distributors to serve these markets. In the UK, for instance, the package holiday has been in decline since 2002, and by 2006, the independent leisure travel market was 35 per cent larger than the inclusive leisure tour market (European Commission, 2007). Online distributors, in the form of search engines, target the independent market and offer reduced distribution costs than traditional channels of distribution.

New E-intermediaries – Search Engines

In the early twenty-first century a new type of travel intermediary emerged in response to technological opportunities offered by the internet. These intermediaries are internet search engines that provide a website for customers to request availability and price information about specific products. Transportation, accommodation, attractions, wholesalers and online travel agencies may allow these search engines access to their computerised inventory. When a customer clicks through to a supplier's website to make a booking, the search engine receives a fee from the supplier.

For example, Kayak.com was founded in 2005 as a travel meta search site. It does not sell anything, instead it searches the websites of suppliers and some intermediaries, displays the relevant information, and allows the consumer to click through to the provider to make a booking. It has links to hundreds of airlines, almost 160,000 hotels, and 17 cruise lines, as well as all the major car hire brands, online travel agencies and wholesalers. The consumer does not pay to use Kayak.com; its revenue comes from the site that the consumer clicks through to.

E-intermediaries are not travel agencies, wholesalers or operators and for this reason do not fit easily into the traditional channels of distribution. They create another channel which potentially can be used by other intermediaries and suppliers that provide internet access to their inventory. For suppliers and some intermediaries, the e-intermediary provides an additional channel of distribution that targets a large and increasing market of consumers that they may find harder to reach directly.

Summary

The travel intermediaries sector is a volatile and at times unstable part of the tourism system that has recently experienced frequent change. The ability to compete effectively in mature markets often depends on the expansion of individual companies and the eventual domination of a market by a small number of very powerful companies.

The development of internet technology has had a major impact on the intermediaries sector, not least because it has enabled suppliers to reach some consumers directly and cut out intermediaries. However, through dynamic packaging, the travel agency and wholesale sectors have been able to defend their positions. At the time of writing, e-intermediaries or travel search engines, are in their infancy; as consumers become more sophisticated purchasers of travel products, e-intermediaries will provide an important tool for them to engage in DIY travel purchasing.

The traditional regulatory system governing travel intermediaries has been disturbed by e-commerce and it is anticipated that, particularly in Europe, travel consumer protection legislation will be revised to encompass all forms of travel intermediary.

Although the role of intermediaries has changed, there will always be a role in the tourism system for them. Some markets will never purchase travel products direct from suppliers, some types of product are too complex for individuals to arrange independently, and large intermediaries will continue to offer suppliers' products at prices below those which individuals can purchase directly. While the travel intermediaries sector will continue to evolve in response to external influences, and there will be shifts in the structure of the sector as a whole, intermediaries will continue to fulfil a vital function in the tourism system.

 ■ **Self-test Questions**

1 Select a high street travel agency and consider the value it offers to consumers. Why would you buy travel products from there, rather than direct from the supplier?

2 Identify the ownership of the travel agency and see if you can find evidence of integration.

3 Explain why Western and northern European travel intermediaries are expanding into emerging generating regions.

Further Reading

Campo, S. (2008) 'Tourist loyalty to tour operator: effects of price promotions and tourist effort', *Journal of Travel Research*, 46(3): 318–326.

Pearce, D.G. and Schott, C. (2005) 'Tourism distribution channels: the visitors' perspective', *Journal of Travel Research*, 44(1): 50–63.

Smith, K.A. (2007) 'Distribution channels for events: supply and demand-side perspectives', *Journal of Vacation Marketing*, 13: 321–338.

Useful Websites

Association of Independent Tour Operators: www.aito.co.uk
Association of British Travel Agents: www.abta.com
Thomas Cook Group PLC: www.thomascookgroup.com
TUI Travel PLC: www.tuitravelplc.com

7 Destination Development and Management

Destination areas carry with them the potential seeds of their own destruction, as they allow themselves to become more commercialised and lose their qualities which originally attracted tourists. (Plog, 1972: 8)

Construction of a new tourist resort, Taghazout, Morocco

Source: Clare Inkson

Learning Outcomes

After reading this chapter you will understand:

- **the main tourism destination development theories**
- **the links between destination development and the impacts of tourism**
- **the role of destination management**
- **the importance of collaboration between the public and private sectors in managing destinations.**

Introduction

In Chapter 2 we discussed Leiper's (1979) tourism system and the relationship between generating and destination regions. Destinations are of particular interest in tourism studies because they provide most of the individual components of tourists' travel experiences, and because the majority of the impacts of tourism are concentrated there. Most importantly, tourist destinations are usually also places with a resident community, other industries, and natural or built resources that may be vulnerable to overuse.

Tourism is a dynamic activity that creates economic, social and environmental changes in destinations. Since the emergence of mass tourism in the twentieth century, many places have experienced rapid, dramatic and frequently undesirable change as a result of tourism development. Plog's quote at the beginning of this chapter suggests that the damage caused by tourism may even destroy a destination's tourism potential.

In this chapter we consider how places become destinations, how they change over time, and how intervention is necessary to ensure the long-term success of tourism for the benefit the host community, economy and environment. The chapter is divided into two main parts. In the first part we examine a range of theories and models of destination development, and in the second part consider how destinations are managed.

Destination Development

Tourism destinations are frequently described as dynamic and evolving because of the way they change in response to changes in tourism demand. Plog's quote at the beginning of this chapter, written in 1972, suggests a typical pattern of development in destinations that creates irreversible and often undesirable change, as a result of tourism.

There is evidence of concern about how destinations change and evolve in response to tourism from 1860 in the UK and 1883 in the USA, with concerns about undesirable physical tourism growth in summer resorts and coastal towns (Butler, 2006c). However, research into the process of tourism-led change in destinations was limited until the 1970s, despite some analysis by geographers of how destinations develop, how their tourist markets change, and the dynamics of change, published between 1930s and 1950s, which laid the foundations for future research into destination development (Barrett 1958; Gilbert, 1939, 1954; House 1954; Ogilvie, 1933; Pimlott, 1947; Wolfe, 1952).

In the 1960s and 1970s, research into the dynamics of destination development progressed with studies of flows of tourists (Williams and Zelinsky, 1970; Yokeno, 1968), identification of a pattern of tourism development in destinations (Christaller, 1963), the link between changes in tourist markets and changes in destinations (Plog, 1972), how hosts' attitudes to tourism change as destinations develop (Doxey, 1975), identification of a destination development cycle (Noronha, 1977), and evidence of a destination's rebirth through the addition of new attractions (Stansfield, 1978) Thurot's (1973) study identified tourist class succession in Caribbean destinations, and, in 1977, Miossec developed a framework of destination growth describing phases to changes in tourist behaviour and attitudes of decision makers and host populations as destinations develop.

Drawing on evidence from these earlier studies, in 1980 Butler published a conceptual model that has become the best known and most widely cited theory about the dynamics of destination development – the Tourist Area Life Cycle, known as the TALC, which we discuss in detail later.

It is difficult to generalise about how destinations develop because the transformative effect of tourism is influenced by many factors that are internal and external to the destination. Pearce (1989) refers to these factors as the contextual characteristics of tourism development.

The Context of Destination Development

Pearce (1989) identifies four main contextual characteristics that affect how destinations develop:

- *Physical*: physical context includes location, climate and landscape. Location affects physical accessibility and determines the potential generating regions for a destination. Landscape and climate may be attractions for tourism, and determine the type of tourism that develops. For example, a mountainous region with reliable snow conditions suggests potential for winter sports tourism. The potential physical development and growth of a destination is determined by its topography and the vulnerability of its landscape and ecosystem, particularly in fragile environments such as coastlines and alpine regions. In some destinations, the potential environmental impacts of new development have often determined its acceptability to decision makers and host communities.

- *Social/cultural*: social context refers to local culture and heritage that may be a tourist attraction, and also to the host society's characteristics such as education, demographics, class, attitudes and political influence. The extent of participation of the local community in the planning process will influence the type, scale and timing of destination development, facilitate or limit the involvement of multinational corporations, and subsequently influence the impacts of tourism on the destination.

- *Political*: the political context refers to the ideology of the ruling government, the decision-making process, and the level of public sector involvement in destination development. Political ideology will influence the government's attitude to regulation, commercial ownership and free-market principles, and the right of host communities to influence the development process. For example, governments that deregulate their airline industry, directly influence tourism demand because of the resulting fall in ticket prices to some airports, and subsequent increase in arrivals. (See Chapter 5 for a more detailed discussion of deregulation.) Legislation limiting foreign investment or ownership influences the involvement by multinational corporations in the provision of attractions and amenities such as hotel companies and theme parks, affecting the scale and type of tourism that develops, and the image of the destination. The extent to which host communities are active in the decision-making process will affect the scale, design and timing of new tourism development, and perhaps prevent it or fundamentally change proposals where there is significant opposition to plans.

- *Economic*: economic context refers to the economic system (e.g. free-market, planned or mixed economy), the availability locally of capital and the willingness to invest it in tourism, land prices, land ownership patterns, and the potential of other sectors of the economy. The level of economic development domestically, and therefore the wealth of the domestic market, will determine the potential of domestic markets or the dependence on inbound tourists.

Pearce (1989) suggests that tourism often dominates in regions where there are few or no alternative industries, for instance in tropical and sub-tropical islands and coastal regions, and that the type of tourism development that occurs will be influenced by land ownership structures. For example, the urbanisation of parts of the Majorcan coastline resulted from the break-up and sale of large estates to financial and property speculators (Bisson, 1986, in Pearce, 1989), making small parcels of land available to hotel entrepreneurs. Ownership patterns that are dominated by small and medium-sized enterprises, or micro-businesses, may slow the speed of development because of limited access to capital, or may create a dependency on foreign tour operators for the sale of their product in generating regions (see Chapter 5 for a more detailed discussion of the significance of ownership of tourism suppliers). Where land costs are high, the likelihood of external investment (from other regions or other countries) increases. It is often assumed that tourism development will benefit other sectors of the local economy such as agriculture or fishing because tourism businesses will source produce from local suppliers. However, such economic linkages frequently do not occur because of the quantity, quality or price of the local produce, or the logistics or mechanism for purchasing it (Butler, 1980 , in Pearce and Butler (eds) 1999).

As these contextual characteristics vary from one destination to another, even amongst destinations within the same geographic region, a number of different processes of tourism development have taken place.

Processes of Destination Development

There are several models of destination development providing an analytical framework against which a destination's experience can be evaluated. Models may be useful to destination managers by suggesting the likely effects of policy changes, or to guide decisions on the best value opportunities (Howie, 2003). Many destination development models were based on research into particular types of destination, for example, coastal, ski or urban tourist destinations, but often they share common elements (Pearce, 1989):

- The nature of developers and the resources being used.
- The sequence of development.
- Spatial changes to the destination.

We have selected the best known models to consider.

Barbaza's Spontaneous and Planned Typologies

Barbaza (1970, in Pearce, 1989) identified three types of coastal destination development: spontaneous; planned and localised; and planned and extensive.

Spontaneous Tourism Development

Spontaneous tourism development occurs when demand precedes supply, and the construction of facilities for tourists occurs before planning measures can be introduced, resulting in spatial reorganisation that may be undesirable, and often, degradation of the environment. In some destinations, for example in Cannes and Nice, tourism development of villas for the wealthy occurred in the eighteenth and nineteenth centuries, before the introduction of planning laws, and subsequent new demand after 1945 led to a massive unplanned **ribbon development** of tourism on land between urban centres, resulting in hundreds of kilometres of urbanisation of the Mediterranean coastline. Similar spontaneous development occurred along the Spanish Mediterranean coastline.

> **Ribbon development:** Continuous construction along a road or a coastline

Planned and Localised Development

Planned and localised destination development occurs when tourism development is led by a carefully planned and researched decision-making process that investigates markets and impacts, and the resulting destinations are concentrated in specific locations, with a limited effect on existing urban centres. Barbaza (1970, in Pearce, 1989) identified this development process in resorts along the Black Sea coastline in Romania and Bulgaria during the socialist era, where tourist complexes with 15,000–25,000 beds were rapidly built. The process was facilitated by economic and political contextual characteristics that included collective ownership of the land and the state financing of development.

Extensive Development

Extensive development occurs when planned tourism development involves a spatial reorganisation of the whole area, with the development of new resort complexes and the expansion of existing urban centres and the infrastructural links between them. Barbaza (1970, in Pearce, 1989) identified this form of development on France's southwest Mediterranean coast, Languedoc-Roussillon, where rapid and massive development occurred in the 1960s, led by the state but financed by private sector investment.

Pearce's Integrated and Catalytic Development

Pearce (1978) identified two broad types of tourism development based on studies into the development of ski destinations in the European Alps.

Integrated Development

Integrated tourism development occurs when the impetus for development, and its subsequent management, comes from a single developer, excluding involvement by any other participants. For example, a ski resort, golf course development, marina development, time-share resort, or all-inclusive resort hotel, where the recreational, accommodation, catering, entertainment and retail amenities are owned and managed (although perhaps not operated) by one developer. This requires extensive financial and technical resources which are usually derived from companies based outside the destination or from foreign investors. Opportunities for the local community are limited to employment at the construction and operational stages, and government agencies may finance infrastructure projects such as road and utility provision. The snapshot below describes integrated destination development of a ski resort, La Plagne, in the French Alps.

 ## Snapshot 7.1 Integrated Development in the French Alps

Aerial view of Plagne Centre

Source: Courtesy of www.laplagnet.com

La Plagne is a collection of nine resorts in France's mountainous Savoie region. It provides 225 km of pistes, 130 ski slopes, a snowpark, and 50,000 bedspaces (Powder Blue Ltd, 2010).

(Continued)

(Continued)

Resort development in La Plagne began in the 1960s in response to economic decline and depopulation. Five villages formed an association to regenerate the area and sought a developer. In 1961 the Société d'Amènagement de La Plagne (SAP) was granted exclusive rights to purchase land above the villages and construct lift networks on the surrounding land in return for a percentage of lift pass revenue (Pearce, 1989).

The first resort, La Plagne (now called Plagne Centre) was designed as an integrated resort with ski in/out accommodation complexes linked by covered walkways and with enclosed shopping arcades. The whole resort was built in the same 1960s style and was pedestrianised so that skiers and pedestrians could share the same environment (Powder Blue Ltd, 2010). Accommodation capacity was planned to reflect ski field capacity, and designed to reduce land and energy use and servicing costs.

By 1968 La Plagne had 5,000 beds mainly in self-catering apartments, and lift capacity for 9,000 skiers per hour (Pearce, 1989). Subsequently eight more integrated resorts were developed, the most recent one in 1990, connected to each other by ski lifts and cable cars (Powder Blue Ltd, 2010).

Pearce (1989) suggests that integrated development and management offer several advantages for the single developer:

- Balanced development through capacity consistencies (recreational and bed capacities are matched).

- Quality consistencies through control of all elements of the destination experience.

- Financial synergies – the return on investment can be achieved more rapidly through the provision of more profitable amenities such as accommodation, as well as the basic amenities like ski lifts.

Integrated developments create a functional, concentrated and localised destination where all amenities and attractions are close together, but this usually occurs in isolated areas away from existing residential and economic communities. This isolation may incur higher development costs but these can be offset by the provision of high standard facilities targeted at higher spending tourists. Pearce (1989) suggests that the relative isolation of an integrated destination development may enhance its image and allow premium prices to be charged.

Catalytic Development

Catalytic tourism development describes development that is initiated or dominated by one developer, but allows complementary development by other participants. Pearce (1989) identified three stages in catalytic development:

1 Conditions for 'take off' are provided by a single developer through the provision of specific amenities in a destination. For instance ski lifts, a golf course, marina moorings, a theme park, or large-scale accommodation units such as a large hotel or villa and apartment complexes, in accordance with the local government's development policy.

2 Demand for these stimulates opportunities for other participants providing complementary amenities such as catering (restaurants, cafes and bars), entertainment (nightclubs, casinos, theatres), retail (shopping), recreational (golf, water parks, excursions and tours, guides and instructors, equipment hire), and other accommodation facilities.

3 Further expansion and success depends on the initial and secondary developers meeting and satisfying demand, and possibly an increase in the number of participants. To avoid excessive expansion, planning regulations should be in place to control growth.

Catalytic tourism developments usually occur in areas with an existing residential and economic community. The involvement of several participants in the provision of tourism amenities and attractions creates a more diverse destination, but also creates challenges in coordinating quality, prices and promotion.

The distinction between integrated and catalytic destination development is an important one because of their influence on the impacts of tourism in a destination. Catalytic development creates potential for the local community to participate in the tourism economy through ownership of amenities (in theory at least: limited availability of capital or the poverty of the host population may constrain this). Integrated development offers many advantages for a single investor but limits local community participation in the tourism economy to employment, and often requires external funding, with the subsequent leakage of profits to the investor's source region.

Miossec's Tourism Development Model

Miossec describes the development of tourism regions over time and space, identifying specific phases with distinct changes in the number of destinations within the region, transport links to and within the region, tourist behaviour or knowledge of the region, and the attitudes of decision makers and the host community in the region (Miossec, 1977). His research was based on specific regions at a time when understanding of the impacts of international mass tourism was emerging.

Miossec's model (Figure 7.1) identifies five phases:

- *Phase 0* – the region has few or no transport links, is not known by tourists, and therefore has no tourism development. The host community regards potential tourism development either very positively or very negatively.

- *Phase 1* – development of a pioneer destination, either by accidental discovery by explorer type tourists (see Chapter 4 for a detailed discussion of types of tourists), or as planned development policy. Transport links to and within the region begin to develop, along with awareness of the region by tourists. At this stage the host community will observe to assess the impact of the pioneer resort.

- *Phase 2* – the multiplication of **identikit destinations** with more infrastructural developments creating transport links between resorts. Visitor numbers increase as tourists become aware of the range of the tourism destinations in the region, and the introduction of policy and infrastructure to service the resorts.

Resorts	Transport	Tourist behaviour	Attitudes of decision makers and population of receiving region
Phases	**Phases**	**Phases**	**Phases**
0 A B territory traversed distant	0 transit isolation	0 ? lack of interest and knowledge	0 A B mirage refusal
1 pioneer resort	1 opening up	1 global perception	1 observation
2 multiplication of resorts	2 increase of transport links between resorts	2 progress in perception of places and itineraries	2 infrastructure policy servicing of resorts
3 organisation of the holiday space of each resort, beginning of herarchy and specialisation	3 excursion circuits	3 spatial competition and segregation	3 segregation demonstration effects dualism
4 hierarchy specialisation saturation	4 connectivity ↓ maximum	4 disintegration of perceived space, complete humanisation, departure of certain types of tourists, forms of substitution, saturation and crisis.	4 total tourism development plan

Figure 7.1   Miossec's regional tourism development model

- *Phase 3* – host community attitudes to tourism change. They accept, reject or call for planning controls to limit or direct further development. Where tourism is accepted, tourism development and growth continues across the region; where control is demanded, further tourism growth is confined to specific destinations. Destinations in the region compete for tourists and some restructuring results in each destination targeting specific tourist markets. The region as a whole has a well known tourism image, and this image becomes the main attraction. The original tourist types no longer visit.

- *Phase 4* – specialisation continues with distinct tourist types in each resort, each resort is served by a network of transport links across the region, and the region has a well-known tourism image.

> **Identikit destinations:** A term used to describe destinations that are so similar that they are almost indistinguishable from each other

Pearce (1989) identifies several regions that have developed in line with Miossec's model. In the late 1980s, Provence, in France's Mediterranean south, showed evidence of an advanced stage of Phase 4, with a coastline saturated with tourism development, an integrated network of road, rail and air transport links, and the strong influence or even domination of the economy by tourism. Individual destinations appealed to specific types of tourists, attracted by the type of accommodation and related amenities in each. Pearce (1989) suggests that by the late 1980s, Languedoc-Roussillon in southwest France, and the Costa Brava, Costa Blanca and Costa del Sol in Spain, were at an earlier stage of development but were showing growth patterns in terms of transport and destinations that mirrored Miossec's model. The snapshot below illustrates the development and distribution of tourism destinations in Phuket, an island in the Andaman Sea in southwest Thailand.

Snapshot 7.2 Regional Tourism Development in Phuket, Thailand

Phuket's sandy bays

Source: Courtesy of www.tourismthailand.co.uk

(Continued)

(Continued)

Tourist accommodation capacity has increased rapidly in Phuket. In 1975, there were 555 rooms, increasing to 18,959 by 1994 (Uthoff 1997 in Gormsen, 1997), and by 2010, approximately 30,000 (Phuket Tourism, 2010). Phuket attracts over 4 million tourists a year and offers 'every conceivable style of resort and activities to appeal to all types of clients' (Tourism Thailand, 2010).

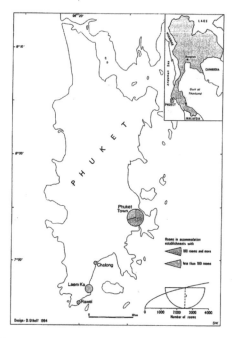 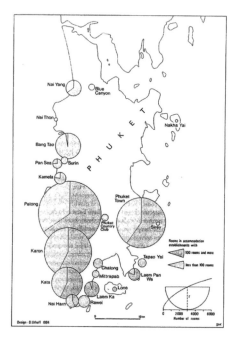

Figure 7.2   Hotel capacity on Phuket in 1975 (left) and in 1993/94 (right)

Source: Reproduced with permission from Professor Dieter Uthoff (1997, in Gormsen, 1997: 44).

Uthoff mapped the scale and speed of regional tourism development in Phuket between 1975 and 1994 and showed the location of tourist development – (see Figure 7.2).

Development was facilitated by improved access: in 1967 by a road bridge connecting the mainland, and in 1979 by construction of its airport. The first large hotel, in Phuket Town, was followed by more hotel construction there and along Patong Beach on the west coast. Accommodation capacity has expanded in existing destinations, and new resorts along the southern and western coastlines have developed.

Individual destinations vary in capacity and accommodation type, and attract different tourist markets. Small destinations on the northwestern beaches are currently constructing luxury hotels with over 100 and 200 rooms (Phuket Tourism, 2010).

Purpose built attractions include the Blue Canyon Championship golf course plus four other golf courses, the Fantasea theme park, a zoo and aquarium.

Phuket International Airport receives direct charter flights from Europe and low-cost scheduled flights from southeast Asian cities and Sydney, and plans to expand its current capacity of 24 flights per hour by 2016 (www.phuketairportonline.com).

Miossec's model is useful because it describes a number of factors that influence destination development, and shows how these may change over time and in response to further physical development. In particular, he identifies the role of transport in stimulating demand, and the link between transportation and the growth of destinations (Prideaux, 2000).

Many academics (Brenner and Aguilar, 2002; Davidson and Maitland, 1997; Pearce, 1989) suggest that Miossec fails to identify the context of tourism development – that is, who invests in building resorts, who owns the amenities within them, and the purpose of the investment.

Butler's Tourist Area Life Cycle (TALC)

> ... the TALC is one of the most cited and contentious areas of tourism knowledge
> ... (it) has gone on to become one of the best known theories of destination growth
> and change within the field of tourism studies. (Hall, 2006: xv)

The TALC demonstrates the process of change in destinations as the volume of tourist arrivals increases. The TALC suggests that destinations evolve through a number of stages, depicted in the model as a life cycle that starts with the 'birth' of tourism in a destination and ends with its decline, leading to 'death', or, if action is taken to prevent this, the resurrection of tourism, usually in another form. The TALC is presented in Figure 7.3.

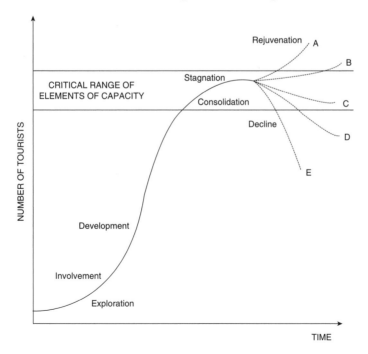

Figure 7.3   Butler's hypothetical evolution of a tourist area

Source: Reprinted from Butler (2006a: 5). Reproduced with permission from Channel View Publications.

The TALC is a hypothetical model, derived from Butler's research and experience of British and northern European coastal and mountain tourist destinations, during the period that Mediterranean resorts were developing as competitor destinations. Butler was interested in flows of tourist demand – that is, volumes and patterns of visitation – and the implications for destinations when flows expand or decrease or when their characteristics change. The model doesn't specify a time period or numbers of tourists, as these vary for each destination.

There are six stages to the lifecycle. Each stage is characterised by:

- Different volumes of tourist arrivals.
- Different capacity levels and types of accommodation and other amenities.
- Different levels of involvement in tourism by the host population.
- Different types of tourists.

As tourist arrivals increase and the destination moves through the life-cycle stages, greater stress is put on the environmental, infrastructural and social carrying capacities, reducing the quality of the tourists' experience and increasing the resentment of the host community. These issues are discussed in detail in Chapters 8, 9 and 10.

Tourists who were attracted to the destination during one stage, find the changes taking place undesirable and no longer visit, seeking alternative destinations that they consider to be unspoilt by tourism. The characteristics of each stage are as follows.

- **Exploration:** small numbers of independent tourists (Plog's allocentrics or Cohen's explorer types: see Chapter 4) who use local facilities and have close contact with the host population. Irregular visitor patterns are seen throughout the year. The physical appearance of the destination is unchanged by tourism. The economic and social life of the host community remains relatively unaffected by tourism. At the time of Butler's research, parts of the Canadian Arctic and Latin America showed evidence of the exploration stage.

- **Involvement:** the host community begins providing facilities primarily or exclusively for tourists, with close contact between the host community and tourists, especially those directly involved in tourism. An identifiable tourist season begins to emerge, to which suppliers and their employees adjust. Advertising is undertaken to stimulate demand in specific generating regions. Organisation by tour operators or travel agencies of some elements of the tourists' visits increases. Pressures increase on government and other agencies to provide or improve particular services, e.g. transport infrastructure, water or electricity supply, or refuse collection and beach maintenance. Butler identified this stage in some small, less developed Caribbean and Pacific islands, and more remote areas in North America and western Europe.

- **Development:** attracts tourists from specific generating regions. Local involvement and control decreases as external organisations invest in larger and more modern facilities, particularly accommodation. Natural and cultural attractions are supplemented by man-made attractions, e.g. water parks, nightlife entertainment or shopping centres. The destination's physical appearance changes noticeably, which may not be welcomed by the host community. Planning decisions and the provision of facilities may become more remote from the destination, passing to regional or national governments, and tourist volumes during peak season may equal or exceed the host population. As this stage progresses, more labour is imported, and the type of tourist attracted reflects Plog's mid-centrics and Cohen's institutionalised or Smith's Incipient Mass type. Butler identified this stage in parts of Mexico, the developed Pacific islands, and the north and west coasts of Africa.

- **Consolidation:** the growth in tourist arrivals slows, but total visitor numbers now exceed the destination's resident population. Much of the local economy is dependent on tourism and marketing and advertising is used to lengthen the season and attract tourists from other generating regions. The supply of many amenities is provided by national or international chains, but expansion of the destination stops and a distinct tourist district can be identified. Older facilities may be perceived as outdated and undesirable and therefore attract the lowest spending tourists. Tourist domination is opposed by parts of the host community, particularly those not involved directly in the industry and whose own activities may be restricted by tourism. Butler identified this stage in areas of the Caribbean and on the northern Mediterranean coast.

- **Stagnation:** visitor numbers stop growing and capacity levels are reached or exceeded, creating social, environmental and economic costs. The destination is well known but no longer fashionable as new destinations develop and the destination now attracts Cohen's organised mass tourist and Plog's psychocentrics (see Chapter 4). Suppliers struggle to maintain high occupancy rates, using pricing and advertising to maintain demand. The destination's original attractions are probably less important than the man-made attractions that complement them. New tourist developments are on the peripheries of the original tourist district and ownership of the original facilities changes frequently. This stage was identified in 1980 in the resorts of Spain's Costa Brava and the cottage resorts of Ontario. At this stage action can be taken to rejuvenate the destination, or it can be left to enter the decline stage.

- **Decline:** visitor numbers decrease and the length of stay decreases as day-trips and short-breaks replace holidaymakers. The supply of tourist facilities shrinks as properties are converted for other uses, such as residential homes for the elderly or children, or for housing, jeopardising the viability of the remaining tourism plant. Local involvement in tourism increases as facilities can be purchased at lower prices but if facilities are not updated or more attractive destinations are available, ultimately the destination 'may lose its tourist function completely' (Pearce, 1980). In 1980, Butler identified this stage in the older resort areas in northern Europe, and in Miami Beach (Curve D). Curve E represents a catastrophic event such as war, long-term political instability or disease, from which a recovery in demand is very difficult to achieve (Butler, 1980).

There are several examples of destinations that have declined in line with the TALC, but the economic and social consequences of this in destinations are now regarded as morally unacceptable. Sustainable destinations need to be proactive in anticipating changes in demand, in understanding the needs and expectations of the host community and tourist markets, and in monitoring the environmental, socio-cultural and economic 'health' of destinations, and intervening where necessary to avoid the decline stage being reached (Howie, 2003).

The TALC also identifies a potential rejuvenation stage that restores tourism demand to a destination. If action is taken, usually through the collaboration of the local public and commercial sectors working in partnership, tourism demand may be restored. This often requires 'a complete change in the attractions on which tourism is based' (Butler, 2006a: 8).

Successful rejuvenation can be achieved in three ways:

- Continued growth and expansion beyond capacity limits (Curve A), through adding a new attraction and drawing greater volumes of tourists; in 1980, Butler identified this stage in Atlantic City in the USA, where casinos were developed to restore tourism demand by attracting a new visitor market.

- Continued growth at a slower rate (Curve B) through the modification of resources and capacity levels – for example, in Aviemore in Scotland and some spa towns in Europe, where the reduction in demand from traditional summer tourists was compensated for by the promotion of the destinations for winter sports and the addition of the necessary amenities.

- A reduction in capacity levels and decrease in tourist numbers (Curve C), attracting new tourist types (Butler, 2006a: 7).

In destinations where rejuvenation has been successful in restoring tourism demand the cycle begins again and Butler acknowledges that, over time, the destination will again lose its competitiveness, potentially leading to a decline or further rejuvenation.

Butler (1980)) acknowledged that the shape of the TALC curve would differ for each destination depending on the context of development – the speed of development, the rate of increase in transport accessibility, types of amenities, government policies, and the number of competitor destinations. The exploration stage may be particularly long if there is local opposition, capacity constraints in access or accommodation, or a lack of external investment. Some destinations demonstrate the stages of the TALC more explicitly than others; Butler described Cancun in Mexico as an 'instant resort' that started the cycle at the development stage, virtually omitting the exploration and involvement stages, and suggested that in developing countries this was often the pattern of destination development (Noronha, 1976: 27). Resort destinations in developed countries, for example in western Europe, the northern Mediterranean, northeast USA and parts of Florida, show evidence of having moved through all stages of the TALC.

Publication of Butler's TALC in 1980 attracted much attention from tourism academics and since then it has been scrutinised, evaluated, criticised, and adapted by numerous researchers. By 1990, 15 research studies had been published that assessed the TALC's applicability, with a further 33 during the 1990s (Lagiewski, 2006). Modifications to the model have been suggested, for example using length of stay rather than tourist numbers, amending the characteristics of each stage, adding on more stages, or applying it to distinct products in a destination (Legiewski, 2006).

The TALC is widely regarded as a useful descriptive tool to understand how destinations have changed and how decline is likely to occur in the absence of appropriate intervention (Howie, 2003). Importantly, the TALC reflects common destination development scenarios that occurred in destinations before the 1980s, where destination development was frequently led by entrepreneurs in destinations without an appropriate planning and policy framework. Its relevance to more complex destinations with several economic sectors that compete for resources, such as cities and towns, is less clear (Howie, 2003).

Since the 1980s, understanding of the role of the public sector, and of multi-sector partnership organisations, in planning and managing destination development has increased considerably and the evolution of destinations through the TALC to the decline phase is no longer inevitable.

Managing the Demand for Destinations

Until relatively recently, it was accepted practice in many destinations that the responsibility for attracting and serving tourists lay with the commercial sector – individual suppliers of attractions and amenities in the destination, transport operators to the destination, or intermediaries in generating regions (Ritchie and Crouch, 2003). Many of the models of destination development referred to earlier in this chapter were based on observation of destinations with limited or no active management which became victims of commercial responses to changes in demand from their tourist markets.

Reliance on the commercial sector creates several challenges for destinations:

- Some tourism SMEs and microbusinesses may have difficulties in researching and meeting the expectations of tourists, which affects the ability of a destination to consistently provide satisfying experiences through all its components.

- Tension between the financial objectives of individual suppliers and the interests of the host community, economy, or environment may create local opposition to tourism, resistance to new development, or perhaps detrimentally affect the relationship between the host population and tourists.

- Individual operators may withdraw from a destination if demand begins to decline, for example hotels may close down or be converted to apartments or residential care, transport operators may close down routes or tour operators may stop operating to a destination, thereby compromising the destination's tourism sector's ability to survive.

The fragmented nature of destinations, their vulnerability to long-term changes in demand, the need of host populations for a tourism sector that meets their economic, social and environmental needs, and the tourists' need of destination experiences that provide consistent product and service quality have each created a need for effective management of destinations.

While the type and volume of tourists to a destination will change over the long term as a destination grows and changes, many destinations will also experience regular fluctuations as a result of seasonality.

Seasonality

Seasonality refers to the cyclical changes in demand for a destination over the course of a year, or 'the temporal concentration of tourism' (Pearce, 1989: 123). In destinations this is reflected by the creation of peak periods, when demand is at its highest, and off-peak periods when it is at its lowest. The intervening period is known as the shoulder season. Some destinations effectively shut down in their off-peak season, with accommodation and other amenities closing for a number of months.

Destinations whose attractions depend on climate and weather conditions, for example heat, sunlight hours, low rainfall, snow, wind or wave conditions, develop identifiable patterns of demand, where tourist arrivals are high at certain times of year but significantly lower at other times, creating surplus capacity and an under-utilisation of attractions, amenities and transport. The length of the high season influences the economic impact of tourism on a destination and the investment potential it offers; longer seasons enable a greater utilisation of tourism infrastructure and higher returns on the capital invested (Pearce, 1989).

In addition to climatic influences, seasonality is also caused by patterns of leisure time in the generating regions, for instance institutional holiday periods such as school or religious holidays or business shut-downs, creating a surge in demand for tourism from particular tourist markets. The snapshot below illustrates seasonality in the US Virgin Islands.

 Snapshot 7.3   Seasonality in the US Virgin Islands

The US Virgin Islands (USVI) are located in the Lesser Antilles, between the Atlantic Ocean and the Caribbean Sea. Tourism centres on the three principal islands – St Croix, St John and St Thomas – whose attractions include pristine beaches and bays, coral reefs and tropical forests. Hotel accommodation predominates, although villa rentals are also significant, and

(Continued)

(Continued)

there are port facilities for cruise ships. Climate in the USVI is warm and stable with little temperature variation; average temperatures range between 25°C and 28°C, with higher rainfall from August to October, and a hurricane risk between June and November.

The islands attract sunseekers, adventure tourists, MICE groups and cruise day-trippers. Annual arrivals from 2003 to 2009 fluctuated between 1.5 and 2 million cruise visitors, and 600,000–700,000 visitors by air (US Virgin Islands Bureau of Economic Research (USVIBER), 2010). The USA constitutes more than 80 per cent of the total market. Variations in demand throughout the year are reflected in the hotel occupancy rates shown in Figure 7.4.

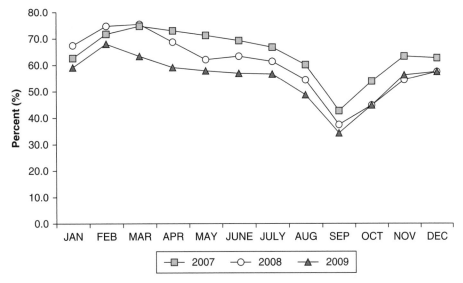

Figure 7.4   USVI occupancy rates, 2007, 2008 and 2009

Source: US Virgin Islands Bureau of Economic Research.

Although the summer is the main holiday period in the USA, demand for the USVI drops significantly. This may be explained partly by the less favourable weather in the destination, but also by improved weather elsewhere.

While seasonality is more pronounced in destinations with outdoor attractions, other types of destination also experience seasonal fluctuations in demand. Urban destinations that attract business tourism in the form of meetings, conferences and exhibitions usually experience reduced demand during traditional holiday periods and at the weekend.

Seasonality is considered to be a problem because:

- Peak tourist volumes can create environmental and social pressure through congestion, overcrowding and higher prices. Acute seasonality can exacerbate the negative social and environmental impacts of tourism. This is discussed in detail in Chapter 9.

- Tourism employment is unstable with high levels of temporary and part-time positions, creating unemployment during the off-peak season, labour shortages during the peak season, and difficulties in attracting and retaining trained and professional staff.

- Reduced income during the shoulder and off-peak seasons creates cash flow problems and therefore less stable profitability and a higher investment risk for businesses and investors. Destinations with severe seasonality may struggle to attract investors.

- A short season means that revenue opportunities are concentrated into a short operating period when income for the whole year must be earned, requiring tourism business managers to be adept at financial and marketing management. Destinations with many SMEs and microbusinesses may be less able to manage seasonality.

- Appeal in the off-peak season may be reduced as many amenities may be unavailable, creating difficulties in reducing seasonality.

Butler (2001) suggests that seasonality is perceived as negative mainly for economic reasons, but that in some destinations the host community regards seasonality positively because it gives time for rest, recuperation, social bonding and environmental recovery after a period of intense tourist arrivals.

One of the greatest challenges for destinations is to reduce fluctuations in demand by balancing demand and supply. This can be achieved in a number of ways:

- Using pricing to encourage some tourists to visit at a different time, thereby redistributing some demand from the peak period to the shoulder periods.

- Extending the high or shoulder seasons through the development of additional attractions, for example some destinations host annual events in order to attract visitors in the shoulder or low season, or develop all-weather attractions that are not affected by climate.

- Attracting new markets through the provision or promotion of particular activities, for example ski destinations that promote their summer lakes and mountains attractions to the coach tour market, or to outdoor pursuit markets, for example those for mountain biking, hiking and bird watching.

Pricing decisions are made by individual operators, while the development of new attractions or promotion to new tourist markets usually requires the involvement of public sector agencies. Public sector management is discussed in detail in Chapter 12. In order to ensure that decisions that affect the whole destination are coordinated and consistent, there is a need for leadership and direction of the destination through destination management.

Destination Management

We have seen from the previous discussion that the conditions in which tourism destinations exist are often unstable and unpredictable. These conditions create particular challenges in ensuring the long-term success of destinations.

Gilbert (1984) conducted research into destination success and found that in order to compete effectively destinations needed to differentiate themselves from other destinations. His 'Differentiation Strategy' placed destinations on a continuum between two points – commodity and status – and suggested that the more unique a destination's products were, the greater the willingness of tourists to pay a higher price for them (see Figure 7.5).

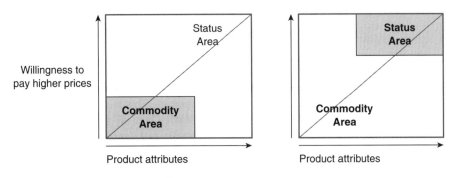

Figure 7.5   Gilbert's Differentiation Strategy

Source: reprinted from Gilbert (1984) with permission from Emerald Group Publishing.

According to Gilbert's model, commodity destinations offer standardised attractions that are available in many other destinations. They attract price-sensitive markets that will visit if the destination's products are among the cheapest, but are easily substitutable if the other destinations offer the same benefits at a cheaper price. Demand for commodity destinations is therefore highly price elastic (see Chapter 3). Suppliers in commodity destinations often seek to reduce costs wherever possible in order achieve competitive prices and consequently risk reducing the quality of the tourists' experience of the destination, damaging the destination's image and creating obstacles to its success. Commodity destinations would be considered 'old tourism' using Poon's (1993) approach that we discussed in Chapter 2.

Gilbert suggests that the long-term success of a destination depends on it developing unique, high quality product attributes, for which some tourists are prepared to pay more, and because of their positive experiences, will return to the destination in later visits or recommend it to others. This uniqueness may be a particular attraction that is not available elsewhere, although few destinations are endowed with such advantages. Alternatively, the differentiation may be achieved through higher quality resources, for example well-maintained beaches, the hospitality of the local community, the service skills of tourism employees, or the range of shopping facilities. Destinations should strive to be a status area in order to attract higher spending, loyal tourists and increase the economic benefits of tourism.

Ritchie and Crouch (2003) investigated the features of a destination, and the pressures on it, that will affect its ability to sustain success and compete with other destinations:

> what makes a tourism destination truly competitive is its ability to increase tourism expenditure, to increasingly attract visitors while providing them with satisfying, memorable experiences, and to do so in a profitable way, while enhancing the well-being of destination residents and preserving the natural capital of the destination for future generations. (Ritchie and Crouch, 2003: 2)

The quote identifies some important points:

- Destinations compete with other destinations for the same tourist markets; indeed Kotler et al. (1993) refer to 'place wars', suggesting that places must adopt a marketing approach in order to compete more effectively. This requires the production of a range of high-quality attractions and amenities that will meet the needs of desired markets and the promotion of a distinct image that draws together various disparate elements of the destination.

- The quality of the tourists' experience of all elements of a destination is a crucial part of a destination's success, requiring coordination and collaboration between the components to ensure consistent standards and quality.

- Tourism must make a positive contribution to the host community and environment, as well as to the host economy. Fundamentally, tourism in a destination must be guided by the principles of sustainability – that is, its resources must be carefully managed to avoid their degradation. In this approach, evaluation of the likely impacts of new developments and activities is required along with careful management of the tourism resources. Sustainability replaces the traditional focus on the volume of tourist arrivals with an emphasis on the value that particular tourists bring to a destination. Therefore the type of tourists, the benefits they seek, their activities and the impacts of these on the environment, host community and economy, and the volume and pattern of their spending locally, become more important determinants of planning and management decisions.

Ritchie and Crouch's quote illustrates the multiple indicators of a destination's success – preservation of resources, high levels of tourist satisfaction, resident well-being, the profitability of local tourism suppliers, and increased tourist expenditure in the destination. In reality however individual stakeholders do not always view these equally and may prioritise some over others. In destinations where stakeholders are not all working towards the same goals, it is less likely that the destination will be able to compete effectively and sustain success.

Destinations therefore face a number of challenges: to create cohesion amongst all stakeholders, to balance their diverse priorities, to develop a single image from fragmented resources, and to ensure consistent high quality experiences for tourists throughout their visit. How destinations achieve this in practice is a relatively new area of research in tourism. Traditionally, the public sector has taken a leadership and coordinating role in destinations, although recent research suggests that partnerships between the public and private sector may be more effective. The public sector's role in tourism development and management is discussed further in Chapter 12.

What is Destination Management?

Destination management refers to the activities, programmes and processes that are implemented across all of the tourism industries in a destination to create supportive and enabling conditions that will achieve policy goals and the destination's long-term success (Keyser, 2002).

Ritchie and Crouch (2003: 183) describe destination management as 'the key to maintaining a sustainable competitive advantage', and its role has become more significant as the number of destinations has increased and the competitive environment in which they operate has intensified.

Research into destination management is relatively recent as its contribution to a destination's long-term success is being increasingly recognised (Howie, 2003). Until the late 1990s, destination management was widely interpreted to mean either promotion or planning, and while these roles are still important, destination management is actually much broader.

The role of destination management includes:

- Co-ordinating the fragmented supply that together provides the tourists' experience in a destination, for example local transport, hospitality and attractions providers, the local government whose decisions affect the destination's tourism resources, and the local community, to create a single cohesive vision and voice for tourism.

- Providing information about the destination to prospective and actual tourists and to provide information about markets and trends to destination stakeholders.

- Developing and maintaining high quality resources for tourism and an effective image to promote the destination.

- Liaising with agencies inside the destination, for example trade associations, chambers of commerce and local government departments, or with agencies outside the destination such as regional or national tourist organisations or funding sources.

- Leading the tourism sector and be its advocate to the local community and local government (Gartrell, 1994).

While individual activities to fulfil these roles are often implemented by a number of organisations or by separate departments within the local government, many destinations have recognised the value of a separate single body to lead and coordinate these activities to ensure that tourism policy goals are being achieved. Ritchie and Crouch (2003) suggest that leadership and coordination of a destination is achieved most successfully by a destination management organisation (DMO) made up of commercial and public sector partners that represent local tourism.

Destination Management Organisations

There is no widely accepted definition of the structure or activities of a DMO. Until relatively recently, a DMO was understood to mean a destination 'marketing' organisation and was usually understood as either the tourism unit of a local government, or a local tourism trade membership organisation that collectively represented the interests of the local tourism industry, often known as a convention and visitor bureau (CVB). Often CVBs also received some public funding. The primary role of these organisations was the provision of information to promote the destination.

DMOs are now increasingly interpreted as autonomous partnership organisations whose membership represents public and private sector tourism interests in the destination. Public/private partnership organisations are considered to provide a number of advantages:

- The sharing of stakeholders' knowledge, expertise, capital and other resources to collectively strengthen the destination's ability to compete effectively (Kotler et al., 1993).

- Efficient use of resources through collective activities that stakeholders would be unable to achieve independently, or at a lower cost than could be attained individually, for example promotional, training and networking activities.

- Participation by all sectors in strategic decision making about the destination's future.

- A sense of ownership of tourism policies and strategies across all of the tourism industries in a destination, leading to 'empowerment, equity, operational advantages and an enhanced tourism product' (Bramwell and Lane, 2000: 2).

While destination partnerships may in theory seem straightforward, they can be very difficult to implement in practice. Dredge (2006) studied the struggles to form an effective DMO in a seaside destination in Australia. The case study below is based on her findings.

CASE STUDY 7.1

THE DEVELOPMENT OF A DESTINATION MANAGEMENT ORGANISATION IN LAKE MACQUARIE, NEW SOUTH WALES

Lake Macquarie is a vast lake in New South Wales, 200km north of Sydney and 40km from the Hunter Valley. Tourism resources include sandy beaches with good conditions for outdoor activities like cycling, hiking, diving, fishing, surfing and sailing. Tourism supply is dispersed around the lake in over 90 towns and villages which are governed by Lake Macquarie City Council. Several have their own chambers of commerce. Accommodation is provided by small boutique and resort hotels, guest houses, self-catering apartments, campsites, houseboats and cottages (Lake Macquarie Tourism, 2010).

Since the 1970s several attempts to establish a cooperative local organisation integrating diverse interests and representing tourism holistically have failed:

- 1972 – the first industry organisation set up but closed within a year because it lacked council support. Soon after, the council set up a temporary tourism committee to improve signage.
- 1977 – council's second tourism committee set up to encourage tourism growth but limited involvement in decision making discouraged industry support.
- 1981 – the council established a formal tourism committee with industry membership and a board representing industry and the council. The council controlled the board structure and membership and decisions often reflected the council's priorities. Industry support was limited and it was dissolved in 1982.
- 1984 – Lake Macquarie Tourist Association set-up by suppliers with regional government funding, as a membership organisation supported by the council with whom tourism advice would be exchanged. However, disagreement over priorities, leadership and representation created tension, and industry support faltered. In 1989, it restructured without council input and in 1990 it disbanded.
- 1990 – the council established another tourism committee, but support for it was weak and its activities were limited.
- 1994 – public sector restructuring focused on economic development. The tourism committee was replaced by an Economic Development and Tourism Task Force. Its committee lacked tourism expertise, and its relationship with suppliers deteriorated.
- 1999 – Lake Macquarie was one of few councils in the region with no local tourism organisation, and political pressure increased. In 2000 the Lake Macquarie Tourism Association (LMTA) was established (Dredge, 2006).

Progress has been made. By 2010 LTMA's cross-sectoral membership exceeded 130. Its mission is to develop a cohesive tourism sector working together for long-term profitability and sustainability. Supplier membership provides training through seminars, networking

(Continued)

(Continued)

and information events, and cooperative marketing programmes. Four of the 13 LMTA board members are council representatives (Lake Macquarie Tourism, 2010).

The council's tourism unit works with the LMTA under the brand name Lake Macquarie Tourism. Together they create and implement the tourism strategy, promote the destination, encourage improvements to tourism supply, advocate tourism to the community and other council departments, and improve industry cohesion. They also operate the visitor information centre (VIC) and website with an online booking facility, www.visitlakemac.com.au. LMTA members are represented in printed promotional materials distributed through the VIC and with a presence and online reservation facility on the website (Lake Macquarie Tourism, 2010).

Lake Macquarie Tourism is a member of the Hunter Regional Tourism Association which promotes the whole region.

Source: Adapted from Dredge, D. (2006) Policy networks and the local organisation of tourism, *Tourism Management*, 27: 2, pp. 269–280. © Reprinted with permission from Elsevier.

Reflective Questions

1 Why is industry support for a DMO important?
2 How should a DMO be structured to facilitate the fair representation of all tourism interests in the destination?

Lake Macquarie's experience clearly illustrates the complexity of establishing a DMO. The difficulty of finding consensus amongst diverse stakeholders, power struggles between members, and the challenge of recruitment and retention of members is not easily resolved. However, it is crucial that destinations do resolve these difficulties because recent research identifies clear links between the quality of destination management and a destination's success (Bornhorst et al., 2010). Regular and clear communication with stakeholders, strong and dynamic leadership, political astuteness and a balanced representation of stakeholders are highlighted as key determinants in a DMO's success (Dredge, 2006). The importance of networks and balanced partnerships in DMOs is now becoming apparent.

Dredge (2006) suggests that the DMO is the leading tourism body in a destination, supported by other formal and informal networks that span the public and private sector, for example Lake Macquarie Tourism as a partnership between the public and commercial sector is supported by the council and LMTA whose membership represents all commercial tourism sectors in the destination. Each member may also be part of another formal or informal network, for example a chamber of commerce or a trade association. Dredge suggests that the linkages between a DMO and local government 'represent one of the most important and influential networks shaping the development of the industry at a local level' (2006: 270). This is supported by Augustyn and Knowles (2000) who identify five criteria for the success of a destination partnership organisation:

- *Expert preparation*: the partnership must be carefully developed with a simple and legal agreement that establishes an official body involving the public and commercial sectors equally.

- *The right underlying objectives*: the objectives of the partnership are long term and derived from detailed research and forecasting. The objectives balance the interests of all partners and therefore directly address economic, social and environmental well-being for local residents, as well as the profitability of local suppliers.

- *Developmental structure*: control and decision making are shared, the responsibilities and roles of each partner are clear and coordinated to avoid a duplication of tasks, and effective information and consultation processes are in place to inform decision making.

- *Effective and efficient actions*: appropriate activities must be undertaken to achieve partnership objectives at the lowest cost, while also developing a social network of external contacts to inform decision making.

- *Sustainable nature*: long-term and successful partnerships need to be dynamic and able to respond to internal and external changes. Constant monitoring and feedback is needed in order to adapt objectives, structures and activities.

We will now consider how the DMO's roles are implemented.

Destination Management Activities

Ritchie and Crouch (2003) suggest that destination management involves nine key activities: organisation; marketing; the enhancement of quality of experience and service; information and research; human resource development; finance; visitor management; resource stewardship; and crisis management. Each of these are interdependent and some are more important than others. These activities may be implemented by the DMO itself, or be the responsibility of its member organisations overseen and led by the DMO.

Organisation

Destination management involves strategic and operational activities, and requires an organisational structure that facilitates this. For example, strategic activities include the development of a strategic vision for the destination, a long-term strategy to achieve the vision, and short-term plans of activities to progress through the strategy, while operational activities may include training provision, quality enhancement and promotional activities.

There is no prescribed structure for destination management as it should be customised to the needs and nature of each destination in accordance with the destination's tourism policy. Tourism policy is discussed in detail in Chapter 12. However decisions about structure, funding and membership are very significant, as Case Study 7.1 has shown.

The proportion of commercial/public sector financing often influences the focus of the DMO. For example, where public funding dominates, the DMO's focus is more likely to centre on public service and community well-being, while domination by commercial sector funding will centre on the return on investment, cost controls and accountability (Ritchie and Crouch, 2003).

The relationship between the DMO and its members, and the stakeholders that its members represent, will affect its credibility with industry and therefore its viability. Howie (2003) suggests that a DMO's authority largely depends on its ability to influence and persuade stakeholders, therefore clear and regular communication of the DMO's activities and performance is very important.

Marketing

Marketing and promotion is traditionally considered to be the most important DMO activity (Bornhorst et al., 2010) and this is often implemented through the operation of information services to tourists through information centres or a website, the development of printed promotional material, representation of the destination at trade and consumer travel exhibitions, and PR through press releases and 'fam trips' for the media and intermediaries. The DMO is usually a member of a regional tourism organisation that provides particular marketing functions, for example promotion to international markets. Marketing activities are directed by the objectives of the tourism strategy, for example to increase the value of each tourist's visit, or reduce seasonality.

However, DMOs are unable to control all aspects of marketing in the destination because individual suppliers are likely to engage in their own independent marketing activities (Fyall and Garrod, 2005). This is particularly the case with large commercial suppliers, for example national or international hotel or attraction brands, who may market themselves unilaterally and perhaps not support local trade associations or the DMO.

The marketing role of DMOs has become more powerful since the development of e-tourism platforms in the form of destination management systems (DMS). DMS facilitate flexible marketing opportunities and a customer-centred approach by tailoring information to the needs of the enquirer through dynamic mapping, itinerary planners, and product descriptions that are designed for particular segments. DMS allow the destination to be presented with a single consistent image to reinforce the brand image, and this is particularly beneficial to small independent suppliers who would be unable to achieve the same promotional opportunities on their own.

DMS allow information to be distributed through different channels depending on the stage of booking – for example, on the website at the enquiry stage or on touch screen information kiosks or on hotel TV in the destination during the consumption stage. DMS also provide availability searches and booking and secure payment functions.

DMS aid marketing research through tracking website visitors, monitoring enquiries and reservations and analysing data on bookings, customer profiles, availability, and response to promotional campaigns, to allow the DMO to monitor the effectiveness of their activities.

Industry members of the DMO have a presence on the DMO website and can update their inventory or change content and prices as required. The DMS can be used to manage communications with industry and customise electronic services for members.

Enhancing the Quality of Service or Experience

Much of the tourists' experience of a destination is beyond the direct control of the DMO. However the importance of consistent quality of service and of standards across the whole of a tourist's experience of a destination is becoming increasingly recognised (Ritchie and Crouch, 2003).

DMOs can influence the quality of tourists' experience of a destination in a variety of ways:

- By including quality enhancement as a strategic objective in the destination's tourism strategy with targets for improved tourist satisfaction levels and monitoring the effectiveness of activities designed to improve quality.
- By overseeing the provision of training for service providers to tackle particular issues, for example language skills or service skills.
- By requiring promotional opportunities to include only those suppliers that have been inspected and registered by an approved body.
- By influencing tourists' expectations of a destination through the descriptions used in promotional materials.

Information and Research

DMOs manage vast amounts of information that inform their activities and support the marketing activities of their members; for example, they collect information that monitors demand to the destination – on tourist satisfaction, tourism impacts, destination image and the activities of competitor destinations. This information is disseminated for their members, to stakeholders, and for potential investors, and is used to inform tourism policy and planning. DMOs also conduct research to investigate specific issues and concerns (Ritchie and Crouch, 2003).

The Lake Macquarie case study identified the need for DMOs to demonstrate the value they provide to stakeholders to encourage membership and improve retention. The provision of useful information that enhances members' planning and performance is a key tool to achieve this. Additionally, evidence that demonstrates tourism's contribution to the local economy can be used to justify public funding of the DMO and to enhance local residents' understanding of the role of tourism in community well-being. Recent research suggests that a DMO's management of its relationship with suppliers, the local community and government bodies helps to achieve the committed support without which the DMO will fail; information and research is a valuable tool in building this relationship (Bornhorst et al., 2010). DMS facilitate the information, analysis and dissemination of information.

Human Resource Development

DMOs organise training support to suppliers to improve the service skills of tourism employees and training programmes to enhance the management skills of owners and managers.

The role of DMOs in human resource development is closely linked to their quality enhancement role. Some DMOs implement training programmes and promotional campaigns aimed at the wider community to influence the quality of their interactions with tourists. For example, in Jamaica a series of print, radio and TV adverts emphasised the economic value of tourism to the whole community, and a 'Team Jamaica' training programme has been made compulsory for all tourism workers including taxi drivers and craft sellers to teach them appropriate behaviour and attitudes, customer service skills, product knowledge, and the history and geography of the country in order to enhance their interactions with tourists (Government of Jamaica, 2009).

Finance

DMOs rarely provide financial support directly to tourism businesses but are able to provide advice on potential sources of funding and investment through links with financial organisations and public sector agencies that fund particular projects (Ritchie and Crouch, 2003).

Visitor Services and Management

Visitor services are a cornerstone of a DMO's role. The provision of information before and during the tourist's visit via a tourist information centre or website and provisions of reservations services for accommodation and activities, and the organisation of guided tours, are common examples of visitor services.

DMOs are also in a position to influence visitor behaviour in the destination through the information they provide, for example by dispersing tourists more widely throughout the destination via the promotion of particular attractions or activities, or to influence their length of stay. Visitor management is discussed in detail in Chapter 11.

Resource Stewardship

Resource stewardship refers to the management of the impacts of tourism to ensure that the physical and human resources for tourism in a destination do not deteriorate. Often DMOs do not have direct responsibility for this as the owner of the resource is ultimately responsible. Where the public sector owns or manages a tourism resource, for example a beach, it will be responsible for its operational management.

Stewardship may include visitor management techniques implemented by a department of the local government or by individual site operators, for example zoning a beach for different activities or signposting to direct tourists along a particular route to an attraction. Some destinations use environmental certification and awards to encourage suppliers to reduce the impacts of their operations, which may be co-ordinated by the DMO.

Crisis Management

Destination management occasionally involves steering the destination through the aftermath of a crisis. As the link between the public and private sector, the DMO is well placed to disseminate information to the trade and media, present a single voice to the media, and anticipate marketing activities to manage changes in demand as a result of the crisis. Young and Montgomery (1998, in Ritchie and Crouch, 2003: 223) developed a crisis plan for a Convention and Visitor Bureau that identified four key elements: physical emergency procedures (chain of command, formation of a safety team, communication procedure); internal communications with employees and public officials; external communications with the media, travel trade, members and consumers; and local assistance (helping with recovery, communications with local suppliers, information provision to tourists). The role of the public sector in crisis management is explored in detail in Chapter 12.

Destination management activities are diverse and may be carried out by different organisations overseen by the DMO. The snapshot below describes the structure of destination management in Bournemouth.

The DMO is the centre of the network of diverse tourism suppliers in the destination, creating a framework for communication between suppliers and the DMO through their industry representative. Bournemouth was the first destination in the UK to introduce this form of partnership and it has since been adopted by other destinations.

Summary

Destinations are complex entities whose long-term success is determined by a number of contextual internal and external influences. Plog's quote at the beginning of this chapter suggested a cycle of commercialisation and decline that is common to many destinations, and many of the theories and models of destination development identify how destinations expand and change over time.

 ### Snapshot 7.4   Destination Management in Bournemouth

Bournemouth beach

Source: Courtesy of Bournemouth Tourism 2010

(Continued)

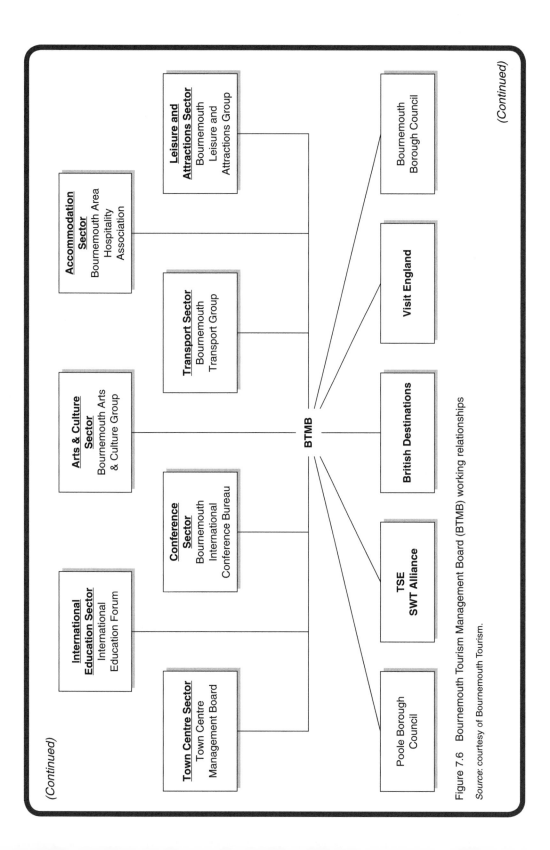

Figure 7.6 Bournemouth Tourism Management Board (BTMB) working relationships

Source: courtesy of Bournemouth Tourism.

(Continued)

(Continued)

Bournemouth is a coastal resort on the south coast of England. It attracts the MICE market for conferences and exhibitions, educational tourists to English Language Schools, and leisure tourists to its beach. The local council owns the conference centre and manages the beach, and is responsible for marketing Bournemouth through its tourism unit, Bournemouth Tourism. The private sector provides built attractions and accommodation.

In 2006, Bournemouth introduced an innovative new destination management structure, Bournemouth Tourism Management Board (BTMB). The board consists of public and private sector representatives with a collective responsibility for managing the resort. The board's structure is illustrated in Figure 7.6.

Each tourism supplier sector is represented by its local trade association, while the public sector is represented by officers from the local council's environment and economic services, tourism services departments, and elected councillors. Experts from the national government tourism organisations and the neighbouring destination are also on the board.

BMTB is a steering group that develops the tourism strategy and creates a single voice for tourism in the destination. It oversees the tourism strategy's implementation and monitors the effectiveness and value of the marketing activities of Bournemouth Tourism.

What is clear from the models is that unless preventative action is taken, some destinations change so much, or don't respond sufficiently to changes in demand, that their tourism sector is damaged irreversibly.

While there are several examples of destinations whose pattern of growth have mirrored the cycle of development and decline, it is now clear that sustainable tourism involves proactive management of the destination as a single entity.

Destination management involves a range of activities that may be implemented by a number of organisations but are guided by a single vision and a tourism strategy with clear objectives that synergises the complex tourism supply and balances the needs of all interests. Successful destination management requires a close collaboration between the various sectors that comprise tourism in a destination, their combined involvement in its strategic development, and the maintenance of a close working relationship. In practice this is not easy to achieve. Research into effective destination management is increasing and many destinations are introducing innovative management partnerships with cross-sectoral representation and shared goals.

 ■ **Self-test Questions** ▬▬▬▬▬▬▬▬▬▬▬▬▬▬▬▬▬

1 Consider a destination or a region that you have visited as a tourist – is there any evidence of its development through different stages?

2   As a tourist there, which destination management activities were you aware of?

3   How could you identify whether your visit was in the high, low or shoulder season?

Further Reading

Bornhorst, T., Ritchie, J.R.B and Sheehan, L. (2010) 'Determinants of tourism success for DMOs and destinations: an empirical examination of stakeholders' perspectives', *Tourism Management*, 31(5): 572–589.

Bramwell, B. and Lane, B. (eds) (2000) *Tourism Collaboration and Partnerships: Politics, Practice and Sustainability*. Bristol: Channel View Publications.

Ritchie, J.R.B. and Crouch, G. (2003) *The Competitive Destination: A Sustainable Tourism Perspective*. Wallingford: CABI.

Useful Websites

Bournemouth Tourism: www.bournemouth.co.uk
La Plagne: www.laplagnenet.com
Tourism Thailand: www.tourismthailand.org
Visit Lake Mac: www.visitlakemac.com.au
VisitBritain: www.visitbritain.com

8 The Economic Impacts of Tourism

It has become a cliché to state that tourism is the world's largest industry. Does the claim really matter? Perhaps it was made simply to attract the attention of the politicians and those who fund the research. (Ryan, 2003: 148)

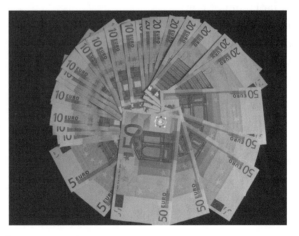

Source: Lynn Minnaert

Learning Outcomes

After reading this chapter you will understand:

- the economic benefits tourism development can bring to a destination, but also the disadvantages that tourism development may bring
- two ways used to measure the economic impacts of tourism: the multiplier effect and Tourism Satellite Accounts
- the value of tourism as an economic regeneration tool for urban and rural areas
- the basic principles that can help a destination optimise the economic benefits of tourism.

Introduction

In Chapter 2 we saw that tourism arises as a consequence of the physical movement of individuals from the generating region to the destination region to engage in tourist activities. This physical flow of tourists into a destination is usually accompanied by flows of their money too; money that is earned in the generating region, but spent in the destination on products that would be unlikely to exist without tourism, such as commercial accommodation, attractions and conference facilities, and also on products that primarily serve the local community, for instance shops, restaurants, and local transport.

The injection of tourists' spending into the local economy has great economic potential and for this reason tourism is viewed by national, regional and local governments as a sector with the potential to stimulate or revive economic growth. The potential economic impacts of tourism are often the main motive for the planned development of destinations by the state, but many destinations have developed in response to entrepreneurial opportunities created by visits by allocentric or explorer type tourists who require accommodation and catering services during their stay.

In this chapter we consider how tourism may benefit the destination economy and the reasons why these benefits may not be fully realised. We discuss how the economic impacts of tourism are measured and end the chapter by considering how economic impacts can be managed to ensure that the benefits for the host community are optimised.

Types of Economic Impact

Before we consider how tourism affects a destination economy, it is useful to understand how these impacts are described by economists. The economic effects of any sector on an economy can be direct, indirect or induced:

- *Direct economic impacts*: this refers to the impacts that are generated directly via tourism expenditure. Tourist income directly generates income and jobs in hotels, attractions, tour companies and travel agencies. Much of the passenger transport in airlines is tourism-related – be it for leisure or business purposes. Tourists' expenditure may also generate direct economic impacts in places that are not strictly part of the tourism industries, such as health spas, clothing stores, cinemas and internet cafes.

- *Indirect economic impacts*: this refers to instances where tourist expenditure indirectly augments the local economy, via purchases made by the businesses that cater for tourists. If a hotel, for example, buys in foodstuffs from a local producer or wholesaler, it will increase its order if business is going well: either because there are more tourists or because the tourists are spending more. Similarly, if a museum has more visitors it may need to hire extra staff. In both cases businesses that are not within the tourism sector are benefitting from tourism indirectly.

- *Induced economic impacts*: this refers to the economic impacts that are the result of expenditure by residents of the region, who have been directly or indirectly affected by tourist expenditure. This type of economic impact is the least visible of the three: it refers to the general economic situation of the region. If through tourism many residents of a region are better off (because of income that is generated directly or indirectly), they are likely to spend more and make many local businesses flourish. They may in turn hire more staff or pay more taxes. The idea is thus that because the region is generally better off because of tourism this affects almost everybody, even people who do not benefit directly or indirectly from tourism income.

Vanhove (2005) classifies the economic impacts of tourism into six types (see Table 8.1). We will now consider each of these and how their impact may be positive or negative.

Table 8.1   Economic impacts of tourism

Income generation	The income that is generated via tourism activities, where it is generated, and how it is distributed.
Employment generation	The number of jobs that are generated via tourism activities, the type and quality of the jobs, and the type of employees that work in them.
Tax revenue generation	The revenue that the government makes via taxation of tourist activities, and the products and services that are taxed.
Balance of payments	A record of the financial transactions between one country and the rest of the world.
Improvement of the economic structure of a destination region	The development of different linkages between tourism and other sectors in the economy of the destination.
Encouragement of entrepreneurial activity	The extent to which tourism encourages entrepreneurs in the host community to start or expand their business.

Income Generation

The economic significance of the tourism industry can be clearly demonstrated by the level of income or revenue it generates. In 2007 international tourism generated US$856 billion, which equalled 30 per cent of the world's exports of services (www.unwto.org). This statistic only includes the revenue generated from international tourism: domestic tourism revenues are often less frequently or accurately recorded, but are in many countries very significant.

Eurostat, the European Union's statistical office, recorded that in 2006 the then 27 European Union countries recorded a total tourism revenue of EUR 243.2 billion. Of this revenue, 90 per cent was generated within the EU-15 area: this is a term that is used to describe the first 15 countries that joined the EU. These are Austria, Belgium, Denmark, Finland, France, Germany, Greece, Ireland, Italy, Luxembourg, the Netherlands, Portugal, Spain, Sweden and the United Kingdom. Even though the biggest revenues may be recorded in these countries, the highest growth rates were noted in the new member states

(Eurostat, 2008). This means that the new EU member states are quickly gaining a share of international tourism income. These countries are Cyprus, the Czech Republic, Estonia, Hungary, Latvia, Lithuania, Malta, Poland, Slovakia, Slovenia, Bulgaria and Romania.

Tourism Australia calculated that international tourists spent AU$23 billion in the country in 2007. Domestic tourists spent an even larger amount: figures range between AU$58 billion and AU$62 billion. This consumption has caused tourism to contribute 3.7 per cent to the Australian **GDP** in 2007 (www.tourism.australia.com).

> **Gross Domestic Product (GDP):** A term used to indicate the overall economic performance of a country. Takes into account consumption, investments, government spending, exports and imports

Employment Generation

As tourism plays an increasingly important role in the economy of many countries, its role as a creator of jobs is becoming widely apparent. Tourism is often seen as particularly suitable to tackle unemployment and underemployment by policy makers, because:

- It is a growing sector in many destination regions.
- It is varied and resilient.
- It is labour-intensive.
- It provides many jobs with low entry possibilities – many tourism jobs are relatively low-skilled, and employees do not need extensive training or experience. These jobs are especially suitable for individuals at the bottom of the labour market, such as unemployed young people, the long-term unemployed, the less-skilled, ethnic minority groups and, to some degree, women (re-entering the labour market) (OECD, 2008b: 127).

Worldwide, the tourism sector was estimated to directly and indirectly generate 8.1 per cent of all jobs in 2010. This is expected to rise to 9.2 per cent in 2020. China, India and the United States are the countries where tourism generates the highest numbers of jobs. However the proportion of total employment supplied by tourism is often very high in island economies: in Aruba in 2010, 92.2 per cent of the population was directly or indirectly employed in the tourism sector (www.wttc.org).

Even though tourism can be used to increase overall employment and reduce the number of people on unemployment benefits, not all tourism labour achieves this. Critical labour shortages in the peak season are often filled by immigrant seasonal workers. Such workers may be hired to fill poorly paid, insecure and unpleasant jobs. Sometimes they are employed illegally. Immigrant seasonal workers, and also casual or student workers, can be used by employers to keep their costs down (OECD, 2008b: 131). This sort of employment has little impact on the overall employment levels in a destination.

The impact of tourism on employment can be measured by counting the number of individuals employed, or the number of jobs generated. The two figures can be different, as several people can be employed in a part-time capacity to fill one job. The structure of tourism in a destination creates problems in measuring employment because it is a heterogeneous sector, with a wide variety of types and sizes of businesses. Some jobs are *directly* generated by tourism (by businesses selling products and services directly to tourists, for example hotels, travel agents and cruise operators), whereas other jobs are *indirectly* created (with the suppliers of tourism businesses, for example food producers, wine merchants or printers of promotional material). Therefore it can be very difficult to get an overview of all the jobs directly and indirectly linked to tourism. An added difficulty here is that tourism incorporates many sub-sectors: accommodation, food and beverage, transport, retail and insurance, to name but a few.

To overcome the fact that direct and indirect tourism jobs cannot be easily counted, tourism employment is often measured by translating expenditure or consumption into a number of jobs using a labour coefficient or ratio. This means that the total expenditure of tourists is divided by a figure that is calculated to represent how many direct jobs this expenditure would normally generate. The result of this calculation is an approximate number of *full-time equivalent* jobs. The ratio can then be used to predict how many extra jobs an increase in tourism expenditure would create. It can also be used as the basis of an estimate of indirect employment (OECD, 2008b: 137). It is important to note here that by using a ratio of tourist expenditure one can only estimate the number of jobs in the sector: although this process will lead to a rigorous estimate, it is important to remember it is an estimate nonetheless.

VisitBritain reports that in 2007, the tourism industry generated over 2.6 million jobs approximately: 1.4 million of those were direct tourism jobs, while 1.3 million were indirect tourism jobs. The direct tourism jobs represented 4.3 per cent of overall employment within the UK. The combined direct and indirect employment of tourism represented about 8.4 per cent of the UK's overall employment (www.tourismtrade.org.uk).

Tax Revenue Generation

Tourism can be a source of income for the government via taxes. A tax, as opposed to a user charge, is an involuntary payment to the government that does not entitle the payer to receive a direct benefit or equivalent value in return (Mak, 2004: 149). Taxes related to tourism can be levied on tourism businesses, or directly on tourists. The World Tourism Organisation has identified 40 different types of these taxes. Examples of tourism businesses and products that can be taxed are airports and airlines, hotels, accommodation, food and beverages, and gambling facilities. Although most taxes are payable by residents of a country and tourists alike, some are specifically targeted at tourists. A common example is entry/exit charges and visa fees. Accommodation taxes, such as a 'bed tax', or taxes on car rentals, are also mainly aimed at tourists (Gooroochurn and Sinclair, 2005). The practice of getting non-residents to pay tax is called tax exporting (Mak, 2004: 149).

Taxation aims to create revenue, which may correct market failure. The term market failure refers to a situation where markets provide either too little or too many of the specific goods and services we desire (Mak, 2004: 153). Tourists, for example, use a range of public goods that they do not pay for: they use roads, pavements, parks and beaches; their rubbish and waste needs to be collected; they expect certain security measures to be in place at free events, and require the provision of signage, parking facilities and information about the destination. While tourists generate costs for the destination economy, the local population pays for them via taxation: it is clear that here the market system is 'failing' to divide these costs fairly. This is why taxes targeting tourists can be seen as a justified way to recuperate these costs. Moreover, tourists tend to have no voting power in the local area. Local politicians can thus easily target them for taxation, without losing local support. Local tourism businesses however may be against taxing tourists, as this may affect the destination's ability to compete with other destinations.

In 2008, Statistics Canada published a detailed report on the portion of government revenue that is directly attributable to tourism. Taxes play an important role in the generation of this tourism revenue. The biggest source of revenue was found to be taxes on products (or final sales) – in most countries this is referred to as Value Added Tax or VAT. These taxes accounted for CAN$4.7 billion for the federal government, which represented 50 per cent of all its revenue from tourism. For provincial governments, taxes on products brought in another CAN$1.9 billion, or 60 per cent of their tourism revenue (Statistics Canada, 2008).

Balance of Payments

A country's balance of payments is 'a systematic record of all transactions between residents of one country and the rest of the world' (Begg et al., 1994: 513). In this record money coming into the country is entered as credits, whereas money leaving the country is entered as debits. A balance of payments record can be compiled specifically for tourism: in this case, the money foreign tourists spend in a country will be compared to the money residents of that country spend on holidays abroad. In some countries, the tourism balance of payments will be positive, because inbound tourists' expenditure is greater than that of outbound tourists. Often developing countries whose residents have low propensities to travel internationally and where inbound tourism for leisure or business is well established will have a surplus on their tourism balance of payments – burgeoning tourism industries such as Kenya and the Gambia are examples here. This is called a surplus. Other countries can have a negative tourism balance of payments: their residents spend more abroad than inbound tourism earns. Developed economies whose residents have a high propensity to travel internationally, for example Japan, are likely to be in this position. This is called a deficit. The following case study identifies the countries with the highest surplus or deficit on their tourism balance of payments.

CASE STUDY 8.1

INTERNATIONAL TOURISM BALANCE OF PAYMENTS

UNWTO figures show the tourism balance of payments for a number of important tourism-generating and tourism-receiving countries. Figure 8.1, with figures from 2006, shows the countries that have a significant surplus: in other words, they receive more revenue from tourism than the money their residents spend on holidays abroad. These are usually popular 'sun and sea' tourism destinations (for example Spain and Turkey). Italy and Turkey also have beaches and mountain regions, as well as popular city break destinations. Countries that have strong domestic tourism industries (France, Italy, Spain) also benefit in terms of the tourism balance of payments: if a resident of a country takes a domestic holiday, the money spent does not leave the economy, and thus does not cause a deficit.

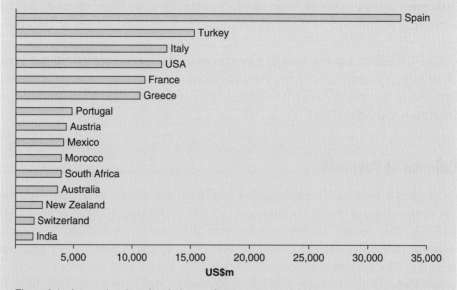

Figure 8.1   International tourism balance of payments: surpluses

Source: UNTWO.

(Continued)

(Continued)

Germany, the UK and Japan recorded the largest deficits in 2006 (see Figure 8.2). The table mainly includes Northern and Western European countries, as well as developed Asian economies.

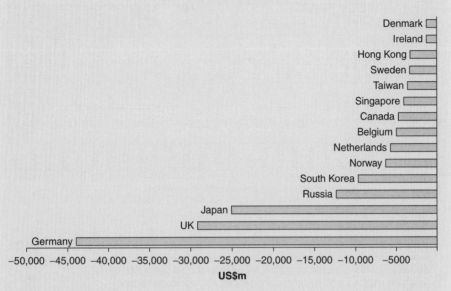

Figure 8.2   International tourism balance of payments: deficits

Source: UNWTO.

VisitBritain researched the Tourism Balance of Payment for the UK and recorded a significant increase in the deficit between 1998 and 2005. The main reasons for this were growth in demand for outbound tourism fuelled by a booming economy and a more affluent population, on the demand side, and cheaper flights provided by low-cost airlines, on the supply side, so more people had the opportunity to travel internationally, with a whole range of new destinations to explore. In the 1970s the UK had a temporary surplus in its balance of payments, as shown in Figure 8.3. This was due to worsened economic conditions in the UK, rising unemployment, restricted access to credit and a restriction in the amount of sterling that could be taken outside the UK, resulting in fewer people travelling and a weaker pound (VisitBritain, 2006b).

Even though overall the UK tourism balance of payments had a deficit of almost £18 billion in 2004, this deficit does not exist with every trading partner. Figure 8.4 shows the countries where the UK has the biggest deficits.

For some countries, the amount of money their residents spent in the UK was slightly higher though than the money British residents spend with them. The scale of Figure 8.5 is much smaller though than the scale of Figure 8.4: this highlights that

(Continued)

(Continued)

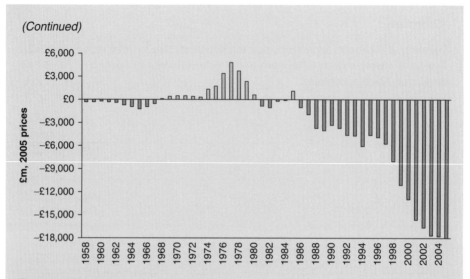

Figure 8.3   The UK's international tourism balance of payments

Source: VisitBritain (2006b).

By far the largest deficit is with Spain and its islands. Indeed, the difference between what UK residents spend in Spain and Spanish residents spend in the UK amounted to over £5 bn in 2005, that represents 28% of the total UK deficit. Among the top 15 countries with which the UK has an international tourism balance of payments deficit are a number of European' 'sun' destinations, but long-haul countries such as India, South Africa, Australia and Thailand feature in the list too.

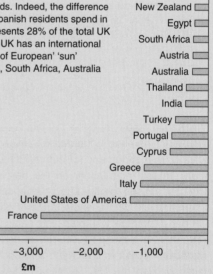

Figure 8.4   UK tourism balance: deficits

Source: VisitBritain (2006b).

the surplus with these countries is much smaller than the deficit with these countries. As such the overall tourism balance of payments for the UK is clearly negative, even though for a few countries surpluses are noted.

(Continued)

(Continued)

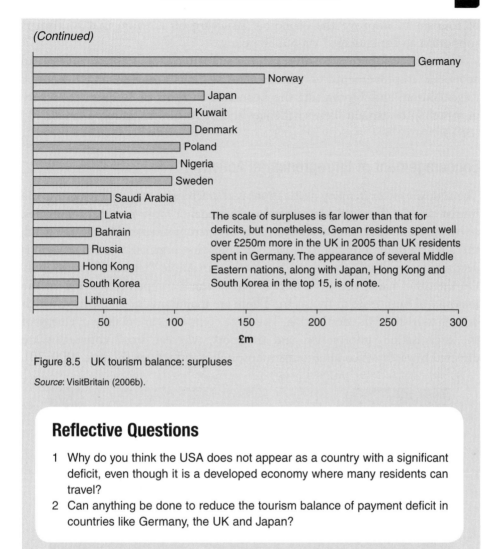

The scale of surpluses is far lower than that for deficits, but nonetheless, Geman residents spent well over £250m more in the UK in 2005 than UK residents spent in Germany. The appearance of several Middle Eastern nations, along with Japan, Hong Kong and South Korea in the top 15, is of note.

Figure 8.5   UK tourism balance: surpluses

Source: VisitBritain (2006b).

Reflective Questions

1   Why do you think the USA does not appear as a country with a significant deficit, even though it is a developed economy where many residents can travel?
2   Can anything be done to reduce the tourism balance of payment deficit in countries like Germany, the UK and Japan?

Improvement of the Economic Structure of a Region

This economic impact refers to the contribution one industry or sector can make to other sectors in the economy of the host community. Tourism can be seen as a sector with a lot of 'backward linkages' to other sectors in the destination's economy (Wall and Mathieson, 2006: 84). A local hotel, for example, may establish close working relations with local food and drink suppliers, entertainers, tradespersons and employment agencies. Developing tourism in a destination can thus bring economic benefits not only to those who are directly involved in the tourism industry, but can also have wider indirect impacts on the economy of a region. It is often because of this perceived ability of tourism to improve the economic structure of a region that tourism is supported and encouraged via public policy.

Tourism development however is not a guaranteed way to bring widespread economic improvements to regions. The sections 'Tourism and Economic Regeneration' and 'Optimising the Economic Benefits of Tourism' elsewhere in this chapter explain these challenges and opportunities in more detail.

Encouragement of Entrepreneurial Activity

The tourism sector in many destinations is characterised by a dual structure: the tourist product is supplied by either large national or multi-national companies, or by small and medium-sized enterprises or microbusinesses. On the one hand, there are a limited number of large companies that organise tourism to various destinations or supply the tourist product, for example TUI and Thomas Cook. On the other hand, there is a large group of small companies, making up the majority of businesses in the sector. These are mainly micro-enterprises, which deliver tourism at the destination. The large companies are mainly in charge of the organisation, information and transport, whereas small companies are directed towards welcoming tourists, hospitality and leisure (Ecorys, 2009: 20).

A shop along a tourist road in Mali

Source: Lynn Minnaert

The smaller companies in the tourism sector are mostly characterised by self-employment and small family firms (Boer et al., 1997; OECD, 2008a). This is often due to the fact that many tourism businesses do not require large amounts of investment to set up: a food and beverage outlet, bed and breakfast or souvenir shop has a relatively low entry level, which makes it an attractive business to start up as an independent entrepreneur. In developing countries, tourists may be a particularly attractive market for producers of foodstuffs, handicrafts and souvenirs – or for tourism services such as those of tour guides, taxi drivers and entertainers. Pro-poor tourism is a form of tourism that is particularly aimed at bringing the economic and social benefits of tourism to poor communities in the destination via enterprise and entrepreneurship (for a fuller exploration of pro-poor tourism, see Chapter 9).

The presence of multinational businesses can make working as an independent entrepreneur rather difficult: this is particularly true for all-inclusive resorts, which often encourage their guests to stay on the property and only consume the products and services offered there. Cabezas (2008) has researched the experiences of independent guides in the Dominican Republic and found that local entrepreneurs were at times displaced by foreign-owned businesses.

> The agents of these corporations are talking bad about us, about assassinations, assassinations, and such things. We are walking guides; we provide a service. My friends and I speak different languages. Why is it that all the hotels and the travel agencies and the stores in the resorts have to use foreigners to work there? Why, if I speak German, I can defend myself in Italian, I am excellent in English? I can sell anything in German. It is something that I do not understand. I used to sell horseback riding tours; now all those are owned by Germans. They are displacing us in our own country. (Cabezas, 2008: 30)

Disadvantages

Although the development of tourism can bring a range of economic benefits to a region, not all the economic impacts are always positive. Tourism development is also associated with a number of economic disadvantages – the most prominent disadvantages will be reviewed here.

Costs

While tourism may be able to bring money into the economy, there are also certain costs to the local community associated with it. These are usually paid by public money, which in turn is often reliant on taxes paid by the local community. These costs can be divided into three categories: direct, indirect and opportunity costs.

Direct costs are costs that are directly linked to the provision of tourism products or services. A museum, for example, that is run by the local government needs to be staffed, cleaned, marketed and maintained. Most destinations have a tourist office or tourism information centre: again, this is mostly funded by public money, although in many destinations tourism suppliers may contribute voluntarily through membership. The reasoning is that the provision of these goods and services stimulates the local economy, resulting in higher consumption by tourists and increases in employment. As stated in the previous section, some of these costs can be recouped via taxation on tourist activities.

Indirect costs are costs that are not directly linked to the provision of tourism goods and services, but that rise when the volume of tourists in the destination rises. Waste collection is an example: this service is not there purely for the tourists, but will be more intensively used when there are large numbers of tourists around. Another example is policing costs: staging events may require the police to be at hand to guarantee the safe running of the event, which may result in the need to pay overtime or extra staff.

Opportunity costs are costs of the opportunities that are lost because of the development of tourism. Instead of investing in a tourist information centre, for example, the destination could invest in a job centre that helps unemployed people find employment. If this option or opportunity had been chosen, the costs to the local community could have been reduced, as fewer unemployment benefits may have needed to be paid. If the savings made by the job centre would have been higher than the income from tourism, then those surplus savings can be seen as an opportunity cost. The concept of opportunity costs is particularly useful when thinking about encouraging tourism in developing countries, as a vehicle for economic advancement. Policy makers need to weigh up the projected costs and benefits of developing tourism up against the projected costs and benefits of other industries (e.g. agriculture, manufacturing, etc.).

Inflation

Inflation can be described as a rise in the general level of prices or a fall in the purchasing power of money (Tribe, 2005: 272). Tourism can cause inflation, because it can make the demand for a certain product or service go up sharply, where it may be in limited supply. A typical example would be tourists buying holiday homes in a foreign destination. Because the demand for homes goes up the prices will generally rise, unless the supply of homes keeps up. As the prices for homes go up, it may be difficult for local people to buy a home, as they may be priced out of the market by foreign tourists who may be more affluent or come from countries with a stronger currency. This type of inflation, caused by an economy that is growing so rapidly that supply cannot follow demand, is called demand-pull inflation (Tribe, 2005).

Over-dependence

Although tourism has been shown to potentially bring a range of economic benefits to a region, over-dependence on tourism can make the area more economically vulnerable. A decrease in demand for the product, a new competitor or an economic downturn in the source markets can all cause impacts on revenues and employment – and if tourism is the only major industry in the destination, then there are few other options to make up for the losses.

 ## Snapshot 8.1   Tourism in Marrakesh

Marrakesh, known as the 'Red City', is one of Morocco's prime tourism destinations, mainly famous for its old fortified city (the medina). It is an example of a destination that has grown rapidly and strongly, and that has now become very dependent on tourism. Tourism is currently the biggest industry, with 72 per cent of all investments between 2003 and 2007 being used to develop tourism products and services. Originally positioned as an affordable destination, prices in Marrakesh have increased drastically because of tourism: tourists, as opposed to many locals, can afford to pay higher prices. This has caused prices to keep rising steadily and Marrakesh is now perceived as the most expensive city in Morocco. This more expensive image may deter tourists, causing a range of economic problems. Indeed, in 2008, because of the financial downturn, overnight stays decreased – making Marrakesh vulnerable due to its high inflation rate and rocketing real estate prices. Because of the lack of other major industries, employment opportunities in other sectors are severely limited (http://www.morocconewsline.com/index.php?option=com_content&task=view&id=209&Itemid=26). To increase economic stability in the destination, Marrakesh should aim to diversify its industries more and become less dependent on tourism alone.

Source: Senija Causevic

Seasonality

Many destinations do not have the same influx of tourists all through the year: they are busy during the peak season and may then be rather deserted during the low season. Seasonality can have various negative economic impacts on destinations, listed by Baum and Lundtorp (2001: 2) as:

- A short business operating season with major periods of closure or a reduced level of operation.
- The consequent need to generate a full year's revenue within a short operating season while servicing fixed costs over a 12-month period.
- Under-utilisation of capital assets which are inflexible, and, generally, do not have obvious alternative uses.
- The consequent problem of attracting inward investment in tourism.
- Problems in maintaining **the supply chain** on the basis of a short operating season.
- Problems in ensuring sustained support from transport providers such as airlines and shipping companies, who are reluctant to maintain their commitment to and invest in highly seasonal operations.
- Short-term employment rather than sustainable long-term jobs, creating high levels of either off-season unemployment or temporary outward migration.
- Problems of maintaining service and product quality standards in the absence of permanent, long-term employees.

The supply chain: Is made up of the business processes that get a product from the producer to the consumer

Increased Propensity to Imports

The economic benefits of tourism can be diminished strongly if the destination becomes more dependent on imports because of tourism development. If a luxury hotel, for example, builds a resort hotel in a developing country, many of the luxury goods the tourists desire and expect may not be available locally. In this case they will need to be imported from other regions, which causes the economic benefits of tourism to 'leak' out of the destination. This may cause a situation whereby the destination bears the disadvantages of tourism development (in terms of resource use, congestion and pollution) whereas the local population enjoys few of the economic benefits that are caused by tourism.

Measuring Economic Impacts

This section will discuss two methods that can be used for measuring the economic impacts of tourism: the multiplier effect and Tourism Satellite

Accounts (TSA). These are not the only two methods that can be used for this purpose: for a more in-depth review of measuring tools see Vanhove (2005: 193–199).

Multiplier Effect

Vanhove (2005) states that the multiplier concept is based on the idea that different sectors in the economy are interdependent. This would mean that tourism does not stand on its own in the economy: a hotel, for example, needs to source foodstuffs from the agricultural industry, a tourist attraction may need a website and therefore make use of the telecommunications industry, or a travel agency may take out loans and other products in the financial industry. The income that is created through tourism is thus dissipated (or multiplied) throughout the local economy via many of its sectors. The same idea can be applied to employment: a strong tourism industry creates jobs in the area, and as the employees of the tourism industry become financially better off, they may start using more services in the local area, thus creating jobs in other sectors and industries. In this section we will take the income multiplier as an example. At its most basic level, this multiplier can be seen as the sum of *direct, indirect and induced income generation* (Vanhove, 2005).

The concept of the multiplier is based on the work of the economist John Maynard Keynes, who saw the economic wealth of a region (also called GRP or Gross Regional Product) as determined by injections (money coming in), and leakages (money flowing out) (Ioannides, 2003). The equation for calculating GRP is:

$$GRP = C + I + G + E - M$$

The following sections describe the meaning of the different components of the formula.

C = Consumption

Consumption stands for the money that is spent by consumers on goods and services (direct consumption) and by the producers of these goods and services (indirect consumption). For example: when consumers (in this case, tourists) spend money on tourism goods and services, this leads to direct income generation; when money is spent within the region to produce tourism goods and services, this leads to indirect income generation (see above).

Levels of consumption vary between different purposes of tourism and different types of tourist; for instance, leisure tourists usually use their own financial resources, whereas business tourists are funded by their employer.

Business tourists tend to spend more than leisure tourists: 'As a rule of thumb, the ratio of daily expenditure by business travellers to that of leisure visitors is generally situated somewhere between 2:1 and 3:1. It has been estimated for example that business visitors to the UK spend on average three times more per day than leisure visitors' (Davidson and Cope, 2003: 14).

The sum of all consumption related to a trip is called *gross* consumption. Gross consumption also includes expenditure in the home environment before travelling (for example, buying a sun tan lotion or new clothes before the holiday, or booking travel via an agent at home who earns commission on the trip) or after returning (for example, getting your photos developed). The money that is spent at the destination is called *net* consumption: to calculate net consumption, the consumption at home is thus deducted from the gross consumption (Mihalič, 2002). To calculate GRP, it is the *net* consumption that is of importance, as expenditure at home does not impact on the economy of the destination.

I = Investment

Tourism development can attract investment from individuals or businesses who consider tourism as a way to make a profitable return. Investors can be local, or can come from outside the region. Small destinations that attract large numbers of tourists are particularly prone to attracting outside investment. The risk with outside investors is that the profits may leak out of the region, thus reducing the multiplier effect (see M = Imports/leakages).

Destinations in early stages of development, for example in developing countries, usually need substantial financial investments to develop accommodation, infrastructure and attractions. Staff training may also be needed (Wall and Mathieson, 2006). This type of investment is often long term and risky: not only is there no guarantee that the destination will be successful, the tourism industry is also heavily reliant on the general state of the economy and can be very seasonal. Private investors are usually not keen to tie up large sums of capital in investments that will only yield profits in the longer term. This is why the public sector may provide certain **incentives** (such as subsidies, tax concessions or low-cost loans) to encourage private investment. (See also: G = Government Spending.)

Investment incentives: Government schemes that are aimed to encourage the interest of private investors in certain sectors or projects

G = Government Spending

National, regional and local governments can decide to spend money on developing tourism in a region. This is often seen as an investment, in the hope that tourism will generate substantial income or employment opportunities or economic restructuring. Public investments in tourism usually take one of the following forms:

- *Incentives to attract new suppliers*: as discussed in the section above, tourism investments can be risky and public bodies may provide incentives to stimulate investment from private suppliers. Tax concessions, for example, are schemes whereby the government (temporarily or permanently) reduces taxes on certain business activities so that they become financially worthwhile. The government may also make available loans with low interest rates, or put in place a grants scheme whereby businesses can apply for money for tourism projects.

- *Promotion*: governments may stimulate demand by investing in destination promotion and branding. Tourism promotion campaigns are often largely (or even completely) publicly funded. The services of tourist information centres, tourist offices and convention bureaus can all be seen as ways to stimulate demand for and promote the destination.

- *Planning and regulation*: the public sector plays an important role in the planning and regulation of tourism (see Chapter 11 for a fuller discussion of this subject). The public sector covers the costs of providing this role.

- *Infrastructure*: finally, the government may invest in tourism-related infrastructure such as airports, roads, attractions, the maintenance of historic buildings and green spaces, museums, attractions, convention centres, festival halls.

Source: Lynn Minnaert

E = Exports

Inbound tourism is an export because it involves the flow of money into the national economy from outside. This may seem like a paradox: after all, tourists are coming to visit the destination, and goods and services are thus not physically shipped (or exported) to them in their home country. International tourism however causes foreign consumers to buy a local product with foreign money – as such, this can be seen as an export, even though the tourist travels to consume the goods and services in the destination.

For many developing countries, generating foreign currency is particularly vital to pay for those goods and services that they import. Tourism can be an important generator of foreign currency. In Japan in the 1980s, tourism was used to redress the international balance between imports and exports in the opposite direction: the country incurred an extreme trade surplus, which meant that it exported many more goods than it imported (mainly due to the popularity of the cars and technological products that were produced in the country). To offset this surplus, it sponsored the 'Ten Million Programme' – it encouraged 10 million Japanese citizens to travel abroad by 1990 (Milner et al., 2000).

M = Imports/leakages

In tourism economics, 'leakage' is the part of national income that is not spent on domestically produced goods or services (Aramberri, 2005: 145). The term refers to tourists and tourism businesses buying imported goods and services, and the repatriation of profits by foreign owners (Mowforth and Munt, 2008). If tourists or tourism businesses buy imported goods, the indirect income generation of tourism is not achieved locally. If a hotel in Trinidad, for example, serves its guests asparagus imported from Peru, rather than vegetables that are grown locally such as ochroes or patchoi, then it is the farmer in Peru who indirectly benefits and not the local producer. Money that could have been multiplied within the region is thus instead 'leaked' out of it. Similarly, if the hotel in Trinidad is owned by a foreign corporation, then the profits of the hotel may leak out of the destination.

Leakage can already start before a tourist reaches the destination (Holden, 2008). If the holiday is booked by foreign intermediaries, such as tour operators and travel agents, then a share of the revenue leaks out of the destination here. If a tourist uses a foreign airline, that share is increased even further. This may mean that the main portion of the tourist's expenditure never reaches the destination.

The level of leakage in a destination is not always static and may change over time. When the destination is in the early stages of development, for example, it may be reliant on short-term imports of goods and services that are not available locally. As the destination develops, there may be more entrepreneurial activity and those goods and services may become available at the local level. Certain tourism products (for example high-end, luxury tourism) may require more foreign imports, but in some cases this may result in higher profits – in some cases, a higher level of leakage may thus cause a higher level of income, because the profit margins are higher (Benavides, 2002).

Tourism Satellite Accounts

Tourism Satellite Accounts (TSAs) are a set of tables, which, taken together, enable the user to understand the true economic significance of tourism within a nation, a region or a specific destination (VisitBritain, 2006a). In other words, TSAs describe the structure of a nation's tourism activity and measure its economic size and contributions (Mak, 2004).

The method originated in the 1990s because many organisations and tourism scientists felt that the sector was underestimated (Vanhove, 2005). This underestimation was mainly due to the fact that different countries estimated the economic impacts of tourism using various definitions and methodologies – this made valid comparisons between nations impossible (Frechtling, 1999). Using TSAs, the direct contribution of tourism to the economy can be measured on a more consistent basis with more traditional industries such as manufacturing, agriculture and the retail trade (Tribe, 2005: 260).

TSAs are constructed on the basis of a number of tourism surveys and statistics. When fully built a TSA can have up to 10 separate but often inter-related tables as shown below (VisitBritain, 2006a):

- Table 1: Inbound tourism expenditure (equivalent to an export).
- Table 2: Domestic tourism expenditure (one element of overall domestic consumption).
- Table 3: Outbound tourism expenditure (equivalent to an import).
- Table 4: Domestic 'tourism final consumption' (based on Tables 1 and 2).
- Table 5: Production of tourism commodities (services and products of tourist and non-tourist industries).
- Table 6: Domestic supply and consumption by product (a key TSA table, based on Tables 4 and 5).
- Table 7: Employment and labour use.
- Table 8: Tourism fixed capital formation (equivalent to 'investment').
- Table 9: Tourism collective consumption.
- Table 10: Non-monetary tourism indicators (for example, the total number of inbound or domestic visits).

Collecting these different tables can be expensive and time-consuming, and can usually only be achieved via multi-agency cooperation. No single organisation can develop a functioning TSA in isolation, nor can a TSA be constructed without the input of considerable resources in terms of finance, time and expense (VisitBritain, 2006a). This is why, although the UNWTO has been calling for a uniform and comprehensive measurement methodology for the economic impacts of tourism since 1983, the first comprehensive TSA was only developed in Canada in 1994 (Frechtling, 1999).

The main benefits of TSAs is the measurement of the economic impacts of tourism that is comparable across countries, consistent over time, and compatible with the standard measures of a national economy (Frechtling, 1999). TSAs allow a country to ascertain:

Final consumption: Goods and services used by households

Capital investment: Money invested to buy a capital asset, such as real estate or machinery – Usually longer-term investment

Output: Amount of work, goods or services produced

- Tourism's contribution to its gross domestic product.
- Tourism's role in **final consumption**.
- Tourism's part in **capital investment**.
- The productivity of the tourism supply sector.
- The tourism's impact on its transactions with the rest of the world.
- The tourism sector's net **output** relative to the output of other industries.
- Tourism-related employment.
- Tourism-generated tax and other government revenue.
- How the above are changing over time (Frechtling, 1999: 167).

In 2000, the United Nations Statistics Division (UNSD), the statistical office of the European Communities (Eurostat), the Organisation for Economic Cooperation and Development (OECD) and the World Tourism Organization (UNWTO) developed a common conceptual framework for the design of TSAs. In 2008, this framework was updated. The framework includes international recommendations which should increase consistency and comparability across nations.

Snapshot 8.2   Australia's TSA 2007–2008

Figure 8.6 shows the different elements that make up the Tourism Satellite Account for Australia. Starting at the top, we see that tourism consumption is divided between the consumption of international tourists and the consumption of domestic tourists. Domestic tourism consumption is almost three times larger than inbound tourism.

(Continued)

(Continued)

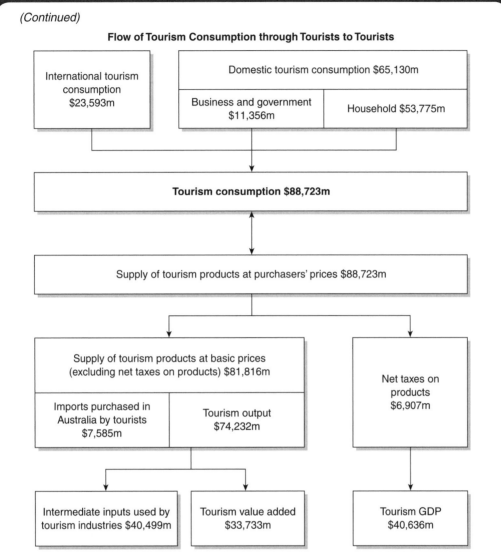

Figure 8.6   Australia's Tourism Satellite Account

Source: Tourism Australia (www.tourism.australia.com).

The total tourism consumption is then equalled by the total supply of products at purchaser's prices. This just means that the money tourists, businesses and government clients have spent on tourism products is equal to the money tourism suppliers have received when they sold their tourism products – the money spent and the money received is the same money, after all. The model then divides these receipts into tourism products and the taxes levied on these tourism products. In the discussion of the multiplier effect, it was shown that imports can be seen as leakage: this is why the model differentiates between the imported goods tourists have bought, and the contribution of Australian products and services to the economy: the tourism output.

(Continued)

(Continued)

To produce tourism goods and services, Australian businesses have used goods and services supplied by other businesses or other industries – this is indirect revenue. To calculate the direct revenue generation of the tourism sector (and only the tourism sector), the intermediate (indirect) outputs are then deducted from the total output: this then results in the value tourism adds to the total economy, in terms of outputs at basic prices. Combining this number with the tax revenue that is generated through tourism results in a figure that reflects the total contribution of tourism to GDP.

Tourism and Economic Regeneration in Urban and Rural Areas

This section will discuss tourism as a tool for economic regeneration in two types of destinations: urban and rural areas. For each type of destination, the macro-economic circumstances that have encouraged tourism development will be reviewed. The advantages and disadvantages of tourism development will also be considered for both cases.

Urban Areas – Deindustrialisation

Law (1996, 2003) states that cities may be attractive to tourists because they can be seen as 'multi-purpose centres' with a wide range of attractions and amenities. Cities tend to have museums, hotels, entertainment facilities such as cinemas and nightlife, and cultural attractions such as theatres and museums, and sometimes they also have a political importance for the nation or the region (parliament buildings and royal palaces). Cities are often well-connected via transport links as well. There is thus a clear case for developing tourism in cities.

For some cities, however, tourism has become more than just an economic product worth exploring and selling – it has in some cases become a central part of economic regeneration. This has particularly been the case for many former industrial cities that have lost much of their industrial income and employment during the deindustrialisation period. Deindustrialisation can be defined as 'the decline in the importance of manufacturing' (Worthington and Britton, 2006: 278) in some regions. This decline was particularly notable in cities in the Western world in the 1970s and 1980s, because of a range of factors such as increased international competition (with countries where wages were lower, so that production units were moved to these countries), a lack of skilled workers, and a lack of investment in research and development.

The snapshot below describes how tourism was used as a tool to regenerate the economy of a city in northern England during the 1980s.

 ## Snapshot 8.3   Bradford

Bradford is a city in Northern England with a strong industrial heritage. In the nineteenth century it became famous as the 'Wool Capital of the World', because wool was imported to its textile mills to be turned into worsted cloth. In the twentieth century however the textile industry in Bradford fell into decline. Recently though, Bradford has turned its industrial heritage into a cultural attraction: the Salts Mill is a historic mill that has received UNESCO World Heritage Status and is now an important tourist attraction for the town. This historic building has been transformed into a thriving shopping, dining and arts complex. Bradford has also developed a range of cultural events and has profiled itself as a cultural destination. Although, like many other post-industrial towns, Bradford lacks the attractive image of many tourist-historic cities, tourism has become of major importance to the local economy and an important employment generator. The industry generates about £409 million for the local economy per year and employs over 10,000 people. The National Media Museum is one of the most visited British museums outside of London and it attracts over 600,000 visitors per year (Bradford Council, 2002). The museum also improves the image of Bradford and makes it more attractive for inward investment.

Source: Graham Miller

Tourism development in cities can have several advantages. It can contribute to economic diversification, which is particularly important for cities that used to rely on manufacturing and warehousing in the past. Cities also have a product that is interesting to tourists because they are multi-purpose centres. In large cities tourists may blend in well with the local population, as the facilities there will be better equipped to deal with large numbers of people than, for example, those in small coastal resorts.

This is not to say tourism development has no disadvantages. Tourism for example is a fickle industry: in many destinations it is highly seasonal and often dependent on the general economic situation. Leakages and the reliance on low-paid, low-skilled labour are also aspects that make tourism less attractive. Finally, a disadvantage can be the increased competition between cities, so that an investment in tourism is less likely to pay off. Page and Hall (2003) refer to the phenomenon of 'serial reproduction' in cities whereby all cities are starting to look the same, with, for example, a shopping mall, a redeveloped waterfront, and a flagship cultural attraction.

Rural Areas – the Decline of Agriculture

Rural areas have many attractions for tourists: visitors may look for a peaceful and quiet way of life, enjoy the fresh air and the scenery or engage in outdoor activities. Rural tourism has seen strong growth over the past 20 years. One of the reasons for this is that tourists have started to look for an alternative to the typical, overcrowded sun-sea-sand holiday (Lane, 2005). This increased demand has gone hand in hand with a decline in the agricultural industries in many Western nations, and a subsequent need for economic diversification. Page and Getz (1997: 18) state that:

> With changes in the economic structures of rural areas, as agricultural employment declined in the post-war period, rural planning has adopted a more positive strategy towards rural tourism as a form of employment generation to off-set out-migration and a declining population base, and to sustain thresholds for service provision.

Tourism can thus be used to diversify the economy. Intensely farmed or prosperous areas with a diverse rural economy may be less in need of (and less suitable for) tourism development. However, tourism can be a suitable economic regeneration strategy for economically marginal areas which depend on traditional, small-scale agrarian industries (Sharpley and Sharpley, 1997) and suffer from out-migration, an ageing population, and poverty.

Apart from economic diversification, tourism development in rural areas can have a number of added benefits. Rural tourism is characterised by a large number of private **SMEs** and microbusinesses that are locally owned and therefore

SMEs: Small to medium sized enterprises

reduce leakages (for example, accommodation providers, restaurants, attractions and facilities). Through the creation of jobs, tourism may encourage employment and stop outward migration in the area. Tourism can also valorise conservation (Lane, 2005: 13): revenue from certain tourism products, for example taxes or entry fees to national parks, can be used to maintain the natural environment.

Page and Getz (1997) however highlight that tourism in rural areas is not necessarily a magic solution for economic regeneration. As discussed above in relation to urban tourism, tourism is a fickle and seasonal industry and one typified by low-waged, low-skilled labour and leakages. Moreover, rural tourism takes place in a fragile natural environment. This not only has environmental but also commercial implications: the tourist is looking for an unspoilt environment and tourism can be an urbanising influence (Lane, 2005). Limited transport networks mean that tourists must often rely on private cars, and alternatively there is a need to supply public transport for tourists. Due to the large number of SMEs in the sector, it may be hard to coordinate an effective strategy to ensure environmental sustainability (Hall et al., 2005). Finally, the costs for development and operations are often higher in rural areas, hence obtaining finance may be difficult. A range of public grants and assistance programmes is often put in place to help rural communities diversify their economy through tourism (Page and Getz, 1997).

Snapshot 8.4 Lavaux Vineyard Terraces

An example of a rural area that has diversified its economy through tourism is the Lavaux area in Switzerland, stretching for about 30km along the northern shore of Lake Geneva. Vineyards cover the terraced mountain slopes that run down to the lakeshore, providing a peaceful and picturesque region for hiking and cycling. There are a few small villages and in the tourist season there is now a tourist train that provides tours with wine tasting sessions. The area is careful to avoid the negative impacts of tourism like congestion and environmental damage: strict land use laws on a local and regional level are in place to protect the environmental assets of the area. Moreover, the local tourism authority adopts a 'low volume – high value' approach to tourism development. Francois Margot, president of Montreux-Vevey Tourism, explains: 'We can't welcome hundreds of thousands of additional tourists. The structures do not allow it. Our communication is targeting quality tourism – individuals or small groups' (http://www.swissinfo.ch/eng/Specials/UNESCO-World_Heritage/Sites_in_Switzerland/ Lavaux_celebrates_its_Unesco_status_in_style.html?cid=7664614). Planning laws prohibit the construction of further hotel accommodation in the area, which means that a rapid growth rate is impossible. The aim is to attract high spending visitors by offering a quality experience. Margot adds: 'The most important thing is that we respect the people who live in

(Continued)

(Continued)

the region. It's not going to be a kind of prostitution of the region, it cannot be a zoo, and people just coming through like Disneyland' (http://www.swissinfo.ch/eng/Specials/UNESCO-World_Heritage/Sites_in_Switzerland/Lavaux_celebrates_its_Unesco_status_in_style.html?cid=7664614).

Sources: http://www.swissinfo.ch/; http://whc.unesco.org/

Source: Lynn Minnaert

Optimising the Economic Benefits of Tourism

The previous section highlighted some of the challenges for destinations that want to use tourism as a way to regenerate or diversify economically. The seasonal nature of tourism, the fact that it is often income-elastic, the reliance on low-skilled and low-paid labour, and the possibility of leakages are just a few of these challenges. This section will review three strategies that aim to optimise the economic benefits of tourism for the destination.

Reducing Leakages – Increasing Local Linkages

One of the reasons why tourism may not fulfil its potential as a tool for economic regeneration is the fact that foreign imports of goods and/or labour may result in income leaking from the area. To counter these leakages, the tourism industry has been encouraged by the UNWTO to develop greater linkages: in other words, to build relationships for sourcing goods and labour locally.

Linkages are central to the tourism industry in general: tourism intersects with a number of other industries to provide the goods and services tourists need on holiday. Industries such as transport, retail, catering, agriculture and arts and crafts, for example, can benefit from linkages with tourism. The key to avoiding leakages is to make sure that these linkages are formed at the destination level. One example could be to encourage hotels to serve local, seasonal ingredients in their menus, bought from local suppliers, rather than importing foreign foodstuffs, and to employ local residents.

There are two types of linkages: backward and forward (Kweka et al, 2003). Backward linkages are the linkages between tourism businesses and their suppliers. A local attraction, for example a museum, can have backward linkages with printing companies for the production of the museum maps, with catering companies that provide products for the café, and with the merchandising company that supplies the items in the gift shop. Forward linkages are linkages between the tourism business and business in other sectors that will benefit if tourism volumes increase. A local shopping centre with clothing and gift retailers, for example, may generally benefit if there are more tourists in the area.

To increase the benefits of tourism, it is important to foster backward linkages can are local and can reduce leakage. Local Chambers of Commerce may be well-placed to encourage these links. Not only may the use of local suppliers come with economic benefits for the area, it can also be an environmental policy as transport emissions may be reduced.

Equitable Distribution of Income

As already indicated with regard to the social impacts of tourism, it is elementary that the local community can participate in and influence tourism planning and development, so that the costs and benefits of tourism are evenly distributed. In too many destinations the economic benefits of tourism are allocated to a happy few, whereas a great number of local people have to bear the costs in terms of congestion, environmental and cultural degradation, or inflation.

Encouraging local businesses to trade with tourists or tourism businesses in the area is one way of achieving a wider distribution of the economic benefits of tourism. Tourism is an industry that is largely characterised by a high number of small businesses with low start-up capital – locals may, for example, start selling arts and crafts in a small shop, or start up a surf or dance school. Godfrey and Clarke (2000) suggest that if local suppliers are available, they should be given the chance to renegotiate their prices so that they can become more competitive. This can apply to suppliers on all levels, from financial services providers to construction contractors. Government policies can encourage equitable distribution and several tourism charities could also encourage local entrepreneurship and provide training sessions for local populations.

Better Employment Opportunities

One of the important economic benefits tourism can bring is access to employment opportunities. In many cases, though, employment in tourism is low-paid and low-skilled, part-time or seasonal, and with unsociable hours. The more high-skilled jobs in tourism may go to foreign employees, particularly in developing countries. By training local people and giving them opportunities to progress in their jobs, tourism employment can bring much greater value to local populations.

Tourism can also be used as a way of accessing employment. Tourism was used as a specific employment strategy in Edinburgh in 2004. At that time, the city was faced with a lack of skilled tourism workers, and many employers hired employees from overseas. 'Deal Me into Tourism' was a campaign that aimed to give unemployed people in Edinburgh a chance to develop skills and gain experience. The programme lasted for 36 weeks and included 10 weeks' training and 26 weeks' paid work experience. The public and the private sector worked together to provide the places for participants (http://edinburghnews.scotsman.com/latestnews/Move-to-pull-in-locals.2582587.jp).

Summary

This chapter has highlighted the many economic benefits tourism can bring to destinations and also the disadvantages that go hand in hand with tourism development. Evaluating tourism's economic impacts is dependent on how well we can calculate these impacts and two different methods have been reviewed here: the multiplier effect and Tourism Satellite Accounts. Tourism was then assessed as a tool for economic regeneration – an idea that was applied to both urban and rural environments. Again, this emphasised that tourism was not a magic solution to all the economic difficulties that destinations faced: it had to be planned and coordinated carefully if the benefits from tourism development were to outweigh the costs. Three basic strategies for optimising the economic benefits of tourism concluded the chapter.

■ Self-test Questions

1 Tourism can bring a range of economic benefits to destinations. Why is it that in some destinations, though, these benefits do not seem to reach the local population? Do you know of initiatives that work towards a more equitable distribution of the economic benefits of tourism?

2 What can rural/urban destinations with few famous or popular attractions do to attract tourists? Are there other ways in which they can regenerate?

3 What are the strengths and weaknesses of multipliers and Tourism Satellite Accounts to calculate the economic impacts of tourism?

Further Reading

Gooroochurn, N. and Sinclair, T. (2005) 'Economics of tourism taxation: evidence from Mauritius', *Annals of Tourism Research*, 32(2): 478–498.

Vanhove, N. (2005) *The Economics of Tourism Destinations*. Oxford: Elsevier.

Wall, G. and Mathieson, A. (2006) *Tourism: Change, Impacts and Opportunities*. Harlow: Pearson Education.

Useful Websites

swissinfo.ch: www.swissinfo.ch
Tourism Australia: www.tourism.australia.com
UN World Tourism Organization: www.unwto.org

9 The Social and Cultural Impacts of Tourism

Should we have stayed at home and thought of here? Where should we be today? Is it right to be watching strangers in a play in this strangest of theatres? (Bishop, 1968: 32)

Jacmel carnival, Haiti

Source: Valérie Svobodová

Learning Outcomes

After reading this chapter you will understand:

- the different socio-cultural impacts tourism can have, both positive and negative, on the destination and the tourists themselves
- the factors that influence how destinations, and the individual members of the host community, are affected by the socio-cultural impacts of tourism
- the underlying views and theories that influence how one sees the role and responsibilities of the tourism industry and the tourist with regard to socio-cultural impacts
- a range of strategies that can be used to manage the socio-cultural impacts of tourism on destinations.

Introduction

Of the three main types of impact, the socio-cultural consequences of tourism are the least obvious and hardest to measure. While the economic impacts of tourism are often the main objective of tourism development in destinations, and its environmental impacts are often visible, the impacts of tourism on the host community and culture emerge more slowly, affect each destination and individuals within it in different ways, and are difficult to isolate from other causes.

Although the social and cultural impacts of tourism are often discussed together, there are certain differences between the two. Social impacts usually refer to interpersonal relations, social conduct, crime, safety, religion, language and health. Cultural impacts usually refer to material and non-material forms of culture (for example, heritage and religious buildings, artefacts, rituals) and processes of cultural change (Wall and Mathieson, 2006). A body of literature regarding the socio-cultural impacts of tourism has developed since the 1970s, with key scholars such as Cohen, Mathieson and Wall, Piznam, Pearce and Moscardo.

Like all impacts, tourism's social and cultural impacts may be positive or negative. Major claims have been made for tourism as a force for peace and greater understanding between communities but the experience of tourism in host communities in many destinations shows that, in reality, tourism can be a force for rapid and undesirable social change.

In this chapter we identify the potential positive and negative social and cultural impacts that are linked to tourism development and consider the factors that determine the extent of these impacts. We conclude the chapter by discussing how the social and cultural impacts can be managed effectively to ensure that tourism development adheres to the principles of sustainability.

The Socio-cultural Impacts of Tourism on Host Communities

Tourism can be seen as a form of meeting: between people from different places, between cultures, and between lifestyles. In tourism the nature and quality of personal contact between tourists and the host community form an important part of the tourists' experience of a destination and many destinations promote the friendliness of the community as an attraction. For example:

'Indonesia: Just a smile away'
'South Carolina: Smiling faces, beautiful places'
'The Gambia: The smiling coast of Africa'
'Taiwan wears a smile'

These slogans imply that the host community is welcoming to tourists and happy that tourism has developed, and that every encounter between tourists and members of the host community will be positive. Tourism can bring people together, foster friendships, and enable contacts between people from all around the world. However, in many cases, the contacts between hosts and tourists are superficial and formalised. For example, tourists who do not venture outside of the 'tourist bubble' may only encounter the local community in their role of employees or in commercial transactions. The duration of a tourist's visit may limit the opportunity to have close contact with members of the host community, and the opportunity to communicate may be restricted by language or cultural barriers. These factors can limit deep, meaningful contacts between hosts and tourists. The contact that the two groups have can leads to social and cultural impacts on both sides, which can be positive as well as negative.

Positive Impacts

Potential positive socio-cultural impacts of tourism for host communities include:

- A better understanding between cultures.
- Revival of culture.
- Improved standard of living.

Better Understanding Between Cultures

The UNWTO names the 'contribution of tourism to the mutual understanding and respect between peoples and societies' as the first article in its Global Code of Ethics. Tourism can be seen as a chance to understand unfamiliar people, places, and cultures. From this can grow a deeper understanding, tolerance and respect for different religious, and moral and philosophical beliefs. This, however, is only possible if the different stakeholders in tourism are accepting and appreciative of these differences and needs to be supported by tourists' sensitivity to the cultural and social norms of the destination.

A better understanding between cultures can potentially lead to the breaking down of negative stereotypes. Mark Twain, the nineteenth-century American author, said: 'Travel is fatal to prejudice, bigotry, and narrow-mindedness, and many of our people need it sorely on these accounts. Broad, wholesome, charitable views of men and things cannot be acquired by vegetating in one little corner of the earth all one's lifetime' (Twain, 1869: 129). By increasing the cultural awareness between hosts and visitors, tourism can contribute to reducing stereotypes and prejudices about nationalities, religions and, cultures. Prejudices are often inaccurate and tend to emphasise the negative attributes, whereas the positive attributes are ignored. They may lead to discrimination or rude and hostile behaviour (Reisinger, 2009).

Tourism has not only been claimed to encourage a better understanding between cultures, it has also been described as a force for peace. The link between tourism and peace dates back to the 1980s. The year 1986 was the UN Year of Peace, an initiative that followed several severe instances of terrorism around the world, many of which were aimed at tourism. The first global Peace Through Tourism conference took place in this year and the International Institute for Peace through Tourism was founded (www.iipt.org). Although the evidence claiming that peace can be achieved through tourism is contested, many scholars argue that tourism can achieve an attitudinal change in tourists and promote cross-cultural understanding (Higgins-Desbiolles, 2006a). It has been argued, however, that when the host and destination country are in conflict with each other, greater cultural understanding is not always achieved: Causevic (2010) highlights examples of studies that have shown that Israeli tourists visiting Egypt, and Greek tourists visiting Turkey, do not necessarily alter their opinion of the visited culture. It is thus clear that in some cases tourism leads to greater cultural understanding, whereas in others it does not.

Revival of Culture

The admiration of tourists for local culture, arts, traditions or customs can increase the cultural pride of the local community and revive aspects of this culture that might have been declining. Certain art forms or traditions, for example, can be mainly kept alive by an older generation: the positive attention of tourists can encourage young people in the host community to become actively involved as well. The snapshot below describes tourism's role in the preservation of an Indian art form.

 ## Snapshot 9.1   Bundi Miniature Painting

An example of an art form that has been encouraged and supported by tourism is miniature painting in Bundi, Rajasthan (India). The Bundi style of painting, characterised by rich colours and intrinsic detail, became an established art form between the seventeenth and nineteenth centuries. Most miniatures depict hunting or palace scenes. The Bundi school of painting used traditional hand brushes and hand-made colour, and even today no modern instruments are used.

(Continued)

(Continued)

This means that one picture can take one month to one year to make. Tourist guides for the area usually recommend the miniatures as souvenirs and gifts. The *Frommer's India* guide for example advises: 'If you want to take home a few miniature paintings (and you do – the style is exquisite and the prices are laughably cheap), Bundi is one of the best places to do so' (De Bruyn et al., 2008: 431). Because of increased interest from tourists, making miniatures in Bundi has once again become a profitable profession. This is important as government support for the artists is low, although the Rajasthani government explicitly considers the commercialisation of tourism as a way to promote culture (www.rajasthantourism.gov.in/).

Improved Standard of Living

Tourism development often requires infrastructural improvements that improve the host community's standard of living if the resources that tourists use are shared with them. These improvements include: better accessibility through the provision of new roads, new services or new transit routes; the provision of new amenities and attractions that may also be used or enjoyed by the host community, for example cultural, sport or entertainment events, or the construction of facilities for cultural, sport or leisure activities; the redevelopment or improvement of neglected buildings and areas; and the improved provision of water and electricity supplies.

Tourism development may also bring new employment opportunities to the destination for the local population – these are discussed in more depth in Chapter 8. Finally, tourism development can support the conservation and enhancement of the local environment, thus improving the quality of life of the local residents (see Chapter 10).

 Snapshot 9.2   Tourism in Albania

Albania is an example of a country that may benefit from tourism development. At present the country is one of the least developed in Europe; but with its mountains, lakes and Mediterranean coast line, it has great potential for tourism. Albania also has a relatively mild climate and a strong cultural heritage, influenced by the Greeks, the Romans, the Italians and the Turks. At present the infrastructural limitations of the country (for example electricity shortages) hinder its development, but investment has now increased with tourism in mind. For example, Tirana International airport is being modernised and international arrivals are increasing. The development of the airport has led not only to improvements for tourist arrivals, but also for facilities

(Continued)

(Continued)

for cargo flights – from this perspective, it can be seen as a boost to the Albanian economy as a whole, as it allows an increase in the export of goods. This modernisation has gone hand in hand with the construction of new road infrastructure (including a new access road that substantially shortens the travel time between Tirana and the airport), a new bridge, and a new water supply and sewage plant – thus simultaneously improving the infrastructure for the local community (Euromonitor, 2006).

Although tourism can thus be linked to a range of socio-cultural benefits, it is not always a positive socio-cultural force. We will now review the potential negative socio-cultural impacts of tourism for host communities.

Negatives Impact

Potential negative socio-cultural impacts of tourism for host communities include:

- Conflict of interests.
- Pressure on limited resources.
- Resentment.
- Loss of cultural pride.
- Staged authenticity.
- Demonstration effect.
- Commodification – trinketisaton – cocacolonisation.
- Displacement.
- Crime and prostitution.
- Begging by children and child labour.

Conflicts of Interest

Relations between tourists and the host community are not always problem-free. Tourists may see the destination as a place of rest, relaxation and enjoyable activities, but for many locals it is a place of work and this can cause tensions between the two groups. Tourists enjoying a beach holiday may complain about noise created by fishermen when they bring in their catch in the early morning, or may be deterred by a new farm building erected in a rural landscape. The conflict here is that many of the things tourists enjoy in a destination, such as the beach, the sea, the landscape or the view, are not actually owned by tourism suppliers. (Private beaches and gardens are notable exceptions here.) This implies that the tourist sector has little control over these resources and has to compete for them with other industries. Often the economic importance of the industry to the local community is thus a key factor. Especially when these resources are limited, this can cause conflict and negative social impacts. It is usually the task of governmental bodies in charge of tourism planning to address these conflicts of interest (Gunn and Var, 2002).

In 2008, locals protested in Cuzco, Peru, burning tyres and blocking roads. In Machu Picchu, a destination world-famous for its Inca heritage, access to the tourist sites was blocked by protesters and tourists had to be escorted out by police vehicles. The reason behind these protests was a new tourism law that would ease restrictions on tourism-related construction. Tourism in Peru has gone through a strong period of growth, with visitor numbers to Machu Picchu doubling over the past decade. The Peruvian government wanted to encourage further tourism development because of the employment opportunities and economic benefits it can offer; in many of the highland tourism destinations, poverty is still widespread. The local population, however, is largely dependent on agriculture and considered that the money should be spent on better heathcare and education. Tourism jobs were generally seen as an insufficient benefit, because they tended to be low-paid and low-skilled (http://news. nationalgeographic.com/news/2008/02/080211-AP-peru-machu.html).

Pressure on Limited Resources

Tourists put extra pressure on local resources such as public transport, parking facilities, waste collection and hospitals, particularly during periods of peak demand. In large cities these extra pressures are often more easily dealt with than in small coastal or rural destinations or historic towns where local residents may experience delays and inconvenience when going about their daily activities.

In developing countries, where resources may be scarce, the pressure from tourism can be very significant. A common example is the development of golf tourism in climates with limited rainfall. Golf courses in these places require constant irrigation to keep the fairways and greens up to standard. It is estimated that an 18-hole golf course can consume more than 2.3 million litres of water per day (UNEP, 2008). In Kerala in India, Kerala Tourism Watch, a coalition of civil society activists and local community members in this tourism destination, is lobbying against the increased construction of golf courses in the area. Maintaining a golf course puts heavy pressures on the water supply, and Kerala is an area where many residents experience acute water shortages (www.keralatourismwatch.org).

Resentment

The negative social impacts of tourism can cause a feeling of resentment against the tourist within the host community. The Irridex model, discussed later in this chapter (p. 245), illustrates how resentment can build up, especially when the economic impacts do not benefit the host community directly. Where it is felt that the benefits brought by tourism do not outweigh the social costs, the local community may become frustrated and dissatisfied with tourism and express this in their relations with the tourists. In areas that are dependent on tourism and where the economy relies on the income derived from it, negative attitudes of the host community towards tourists can undermine the quality of the tourists' experience and the success of the destination. This resentment can also be increased by possible racial tensions, if the tourists and the host population are from different racial backgrounds.

Resentment within the local community can also be caused by the behaviour of the tourist, which can be seen as inappropriate or in breach of local customs and traditions. In Zanzibar, for example, an island in the Indian Ocean off the Tanzanian coast, the cultural values of predominantly Western tourists do not always match the predominantly Islamic and Swahili culture of the island. The consumption of alcohol in public, for example, and the tourists who stroll around the town in shorts and bikini tops, can cause offence to the people of the local community and put a strain on relations between hosts and tourists. Even though many tour operators advise tourists to cover up and respect local customs not all tourists follow these guidelines, which can then lead to discontent within the host community. This is the case, for example, in Muscat, Oman: a destination that has recently started promoting itself for tourism. Compared to nearby Dubai, Muscat is more traditional, with most men wearing white dishdashas and women black veils. In the hotels, bikinis, shorts and T-shirts are accepted, but when going into the town, tourists are advised to wear respectful clothing and cover their legs and shoulders (http://www.rte.ie/travel/nofrontiers/ 20080309_muscat.html /).

Loss of Cultural Pride

It has already been highlighted that tourism can increase local cultural pride, but tourism can also have the reverse effect and cause a feeling of inferiority in the host population. This is often the case when there is a big difference between the financial power of the tourist and the host community. Local residents may feel that they are objectified in front of the camera and that their culture is overly commercialised (Cole, 2008). A contributing factor to this loss of cultural pride may be that the local population does not feel a part of tourism development and does not share in the benefits it brings: tourism development may be in the hands of foreign investors or large corporations, or the policy makers may not have consulted the locals in their decision making. To encourage a feeling of ownership and pride trough tourism development, community participation should be a key element of socially sustainable development.

Staged Authenticity

Authenticity: In tourism, aspects of culture and the tourist experience (such as cuisine, festivals, housing, artifacts) are said to be **authentic** when they are considered to be traditional, original, unique, and intrinsically linked to the culture that is visited

Many tourists are attracted by what is called the **authenticity** of other cultures: they want to see and experience events, customs, traditions and other aspects of culture that they perceive as genuine, real, and meaningful. Often these events, customs and traditions will be different from what the tourist is used to at home. Cultures in less developed countries may be seen as more 'primitive' and 'pure' and representing certain values that the tourist might feel are lost in the home society.

When tourism is developed, however, culture becomes a selling point for many destinations. This means aspects of culture might be commercialised and lose their true meaning: events for example that used to take place annually may be *performed* weekly, for the benefit of the tourist; or local delicacies that are only cooked at certain times of the year may be made available all year around. In many cases the tourist still experiences the core of an authentic aspect of culture, but it may have been adapted to some extent so that it becomes more easily 'consumable'.

The staged authenticity of many Polynesian cultural experiences is also referred to as 'The Bali Syndrome'. In these mature tourist destinations, resorts have developed that protect the tourist from unpleasant encounters with beggars and street sellers, and instead offer an enclave that is seen as pure and unspoilt. In those enclaves, tourists typically experience artificial cultural experiences and stylised representations of local people, which do not necessarily match reality. Rosenbaum and Wong (2008) argue that, in reality, contemporary locals in Polynesia are quite similar to people in Western urbanised areas. The cultural experience that is sold in the tourist enclaves does not always respond to actual culture, but rather to tourists' romanticised expectations of that culture. The tourism sector responds to this by providing a cultural product, that itself is a form of staged authenticity.

Another example is the Paduang tribe in Northern Thailand: this tribe is famous for its tradition of beautifying women by elongating their necks. This is achieved through adding brass rings to a girl's neck from the age of 5, pressing down the collarbone and ribs, and pushing up the chin. This traditional custom is now mainly practised for commercial reasons: each girl who decides to wear the rings is paid by the tourist boat operators (www.tourismconcern.org.uk).

Authenticity is an issue not only for intangible aspects of culture such as cultural customs and norms, but also for tangible aspects of culture. The development of cultural sites, such as heritage sites, for tourism needs to balance commercial interests with the conservation of the authenticity of the site, and those two objectives may be in conflict with each other. Over-commercialisation may reduce the authenticity of the visitor experience. In 2009, a plan was proposed to develop the Taj Mahal site in India with a Ferris wheel, a suspension bridge, and cable cars. This plan met with a lot of opposition, as many were concerned that the original significance and meaning of the site would be lost. The Taj Mahal was built by the grieving Mughal emperor Shah Jahan in memory of his wife, Mumtaz, who had died in childbirth. Its white marble minarets, dome, jewel-inlaid mosaics and classical Persian garden took thousands of craftsmen from 1632 to 1652 to complete. It is protected from surrounding development by a 500-metre conservation zone. The development of the tourist park was proposed at a distance of 800 metres from the site. In 2008 about 3 million people visited the Taj Mahal but officials hoped to increase the figure by linking it to neighbouring historic buildings and adding the Agra Eye – a Ferris wheel modelled on the London Eye. Cable cars between the Taj Mahal and other attractions were expected to increase tourist spending at each. Conservationists and other activists however strongly opposed the plans, arguing the development would not be in keeping with the ambience of the attraction (http://www.telegraph.co.uk/travel/destinations/asia/india/5976407/Taj-Mahal-doesnt-need-a-theme-park-India.html).

The Taj Mahal, India

Source: Sandra Charrasse

Demonstration Effect

Originally this was a term used in sociology and economics when describing the effects on behaviour from observing other people's actions. In tourism, it is used to refer to the copying of tourists' behaviours, dress codes or preferences by the host community. An example could be that younger generations stop wearing traditional dress and adopt the clothing style of visitors.

In contemporary society, the power of tourism as a medium for the demonstration effect must not be overestimated. Television and the internet are now much more likely to contribute to the changing tastes and behaviours of host populations than tourists alone. Only a few destinations and host communities (for example primitive tribes) mainly have contact with the wider world via tourism – now that technology is more common and widespread, tourism is only likely to be a contributing factor, if that, to the demonstration effect. Even tribes that do not tend to have contact with tourists can still be exposed to different cultures via TV researchers and film crews. The BBC programme *Tribe*, for example, focused on some of the most isolated peoples in the world. The presenter of the programme, Bruce Parry, lived with each tribe and explored their cultural traditions and way of life. Even though great care was taken not to cause any negative socio-cultural effects on the participating tribes, they were still exposed to technological equipment, cultural habits and artefacts they were not accustomed to.

Commodification – Trinketisaton – Cocacolonisation

Commodification means that a value, a cultural aspect, or an artefact is turned into a commodity: in other words, that it is commercialised. This can cause changes or mutations in those values or cultural aspects and may lead to staged authenticity (see p. 234). Another consequence of commodification may be standardisation: this means that everything becomes consumable and thus similar and familiar. A clear example of standardisation can be seen in popular souvenirs: in many tourist destinations the same souvenirs are sold and only the name of the destination differs. Think of T-shirts with 'My girlfriend went to … and all I got was this lousy T-shirt', or black bags with the name of the destination printed on them in colourful letters.

Trinketisation is a term that refers to the commercialisation and trivialisation of culture. Cultural motives and traditions are still recognisable, but they are no longer linked to their history and meaning. Artefacts and crafts that are supposed to be the expression of a destination's rich cultural heritage may for example be mass-produced and sold as mere trinkets. Fake native American dream catchers may have been produced in an Indian factory, and the Murano glass a tourist brings home from a trip to venice might have been made in China.

The commodification and trinketisation of culture can also be linked to a process of Cocacolonisation (also referred to as McDonaldisation or Disneyfication). In the field of tourism, these terms refer to the spreading of Western cultures and values throughout the world: just as these brands are present everywhere, so are Western cultural values increasing their influence worldwide. These values often represent (over-) consumption and the free market, materialistic wants,

Source: Lynn Minnaert

Source: Lynn Minnaert

Source: Lynn Minnaert

homogeneity, and a distancing from nature and the natural environment. Disneyfication additionally refers to the sanitising of environments into clean and safe places, removing all risk, until these places feel like a Disney theme park. Although safety and cleanliness are no doubt positive attributes for a destination, the term is used negatively to refer to the modification of what is authentic and complex into easily understandable and consumable chunks.

Displacement

Displacement means that local residents, because of the development of tourism, are forced to move away from their homes. This may be because they have been evicted, to make way for a hotel complex for example. Another reason could be that because of the influx of tourists, property and land prices have gone up, so that local residents can no longer afford to buy or rent in the area. They might be priced out of the market by developers, or by tourists from wealthier areas looking to buy a second home.

In some cases, this may mean the local residents not only lose their homes, but also their livelihoods. Tourism Concern, a charity that fights exploitation through tourism, raises awareness of the displacement of tribes in Eastern Africa. Several tribes in Kenya and Tanzania for example were evicted from their homes to make way for game reserves for tourists. They received no compensation and in many places had to move with large amounts of cattle and livestock. Because the cattle are no longer allowed to graze in the new wildlife reserves, this impacts on the livelihood of the tribal community. According to Tourism Concern, 'this is a pattern that has been repeated throughout East Africa. National parks and wildlife are being conserved at the expense of the people who have lived there and been guardians of the land and the wildlife for centuries, and who understand the bush in much more detail than western wildlife "experts" and have a low-impact, sustainable lifestyle' (http://www.tourismconcern.org.uk/index.php?page=displacement-of-people).

Crime and Prostitution

Tourism development can lead to an increase in crime in the destination community. Tourist-related crimes include theft, robberies and assaults on tourists: although these affect the tourist rather than the host directly, it can lead to an increased sense of a lack of safety within the host community. Members of the host community may also be victims of crime. Sports events, for example, are sometimes linked to an increase in crime, and football matches are sometimes blighted by hooliganism, violence and vandalism (Barker, 2004).

Although prostitution is not solely linked to tourism, in many destinations the problem gets worse as tourism increases. In some destinations, this may include child prostitution. This is mostly the case when there is a big financial divide between the tourist and the host community, and when the fact of being in another country gives the sex tourist a feeling of being 'untouchable'. ECPAT International is a global charity that aims to protect children from sexual exploitation. Although child prostitution is mainly linked to the tourism industries of Asian (e.g. Thailand) and Latin-American countries (e.g. Costa Rica), this negative impact of tourism is now becoming noticeable in growing tourism destinations in Africa and even Europe (e.g. Estonia and the Czech Republic) (www.ecpat.net).

Begging by Children and Child Labour

Tourism opportunities can divert children from education by encouraging them to sell souvenirs, provide street entertainment, or beg for money rather than going to school. Begging by children is common in tourism destinations in developing countries – in some cases for money, in others for sweets, pens and other small items. In several countries, such as Morocco and Mexico, giving money to begging children is often frowned upon, because it is seen to encourage a culture of dependence on hand-outs.

Tourism can also encourage child labour. Many children are not officially employed by the tourism industry, but are working in the so-called 'open air economy': they derive an income from the recreational spending of the tourists. Children can earn money as street sellers, car attendants or shoe-shine boys and girls. Tourists may be more generous than the locals and pay them much more for their services (Black, 1995). Children may also be involved in prostitution and the sex industry: see above.

A child vendor in Peru

Source: Sonia Rosiers

Snapshot 9.3   Children and Slum Tourism

The 2008 film *Slumdog Millionaire* shocked its viewers with images of children being deliberately blinded by a criminal gang, because they would receive more money begging. Unfortunately, these scenes are not rooted in fantasy: in big Indian cities like Mumbai, criminal gangs are said to be operating, abducting, maiming and blinding children, in some cases even amputating healthy limbs (http://www.dailymail.co.uk/news/worldnews/article-1127056/ The-real-Slumdog-Millionaires-Behind-cinema-fantasy-mafia-gangs-deliberately-crippling-children-profit.html). Tourists often give money, food or small gifts to the children, and so help to sustain this practice. Slum tours are now being offered in an increasing number of destinations: the favela in Rio de Janeiro and the shantytowns in Cape Town are examples. The slum tour organisers usually donate a share of their profits (if they make any) to local charities or initiatives that will help the slum community. The slum community gets the opportunity to show their way of life to the tourists and sell handicrafts. These different income streams can help to improve the quality of life for the residents of the slum. Proponents of slum tourism highlight that a first-hand experience of poverty can be an educational experience. However, opponents say that slum tours can sensationalise the horrors of living in a slum.

Socio-cultural Impacts on Tourists

Tourism can have profound impacts on the host communities and destinations, but travelling can also have impacts on the tourists themselves. After all, if tourism does not do the tourist any good, why do so many people travel and love to travel? Tourists may decide to travel for different reasons (see tourist motivations, Chapter 4), and the types of holidays they take may be very different; still, we can distinguish some general impacts on tourists. Positive impacts mostly have to do with a sense of psychological and physiological well-being, negative impacts with feelings of anxiety and disturbance.

Positive Impacts

Many tourists will decide to go on holiday because of the positive effects of travelling on their well-being. A holiday is something we may look forward to all year, save up for, and plan carefully; it can also be a source of happy memories that are treasured long after our return. Hazel (2004) discusses common positive impacts of holidays on tourists:

Rest and renewal: Holidays provide a break from routine and an escape from the daily surroundings and activities that may seem stressful or just rather boring. On holiday the tourist has a chance to relax, to take a break from it all. This allows tourists to rediscover themselves and what is most important in life (recreation is after all linked to the word re-create). On holiday, the tourist has a chance to recharge their batteries and return to the daily routine refreshed and motivated.

Mental and physical health: Rest and renewal can also be important at a mental level. Holidays have been linked to improvements in health – mainly mental health and mental strength. There is also isolated evidence that holidays can reduce the risk of stress-related illnesses such as heart disease.

Social interaction – strengthening relationships: Holidays can provide opportunities to meet new people, be it fellow tourists or people from the host community. This can increase the tourist's social support network and contribute to higher confidence levels. The tourist can also gain a better understanding of peoples and cultures he or she was not familiar with before, which may increase intercultural understanding and counteract incorrect negative stereotypes (see p. 228). Tourism can also mean spending quality time with loved ones – a partner, friends or family. Being away from the home environment and the stresses and routines it represents often encourages tourists to purposely make time for each other.

Broadening experiences: On holiday, tourists not only get the opportunity to visit a place they might not have been to before, they can also easily engage in activities that are new to them. Trying out windsurfing on holiday, or picking up a few words of Italian, may, for example, lead to the development of a new hobby or a new skill. The tourist may also be more inclined to try a different cuisine or take an interest in a new art form whilst on holiday. Back home, these new interests and skills may lead to increased well-being and confidence.

Developing independence: Travelling, especially for young people, can also increase independence. On holiday, tourists may be faced with new situations or unexpected problems that need to be dealt with: luggage may get lost, or the dishes on menu will be written in a language the tourist does not understand. Dealing with these requires a certain level of independence and confidence. When a young person travels alone, he or she may develop new skills by having to be independent in a new environment.

Negative Impacts

Tourism can also have negative socio-cultural impacts on tourists. Certain holiday situations can lead to tension, stress and anxiety instead of relaxation and well-being.

Terrorism: Tourists, because of their high visibility and their capacity to attract large amounts of worldwide media attention, can be prime targets for terrorism. Examples of destinations that have experienced terrorist attacks specifically targeting tourists are Sharm el-Sheikh, Istanbul, Mumbai and Bali (see also Chapter 12, p. 333). Tourists that have a close experience of these attacks may experience high levels of anxiety and tension in their daily lives after their return from holiday. Bongar et al. (2007: 6) explain just how extensive the psychological effect of terrorism can be, even for persons who were not affected by an incident directly. He states that military psychologists have long known that fear, stress and exhaustion do much

Psychogenic:
Resulting from an
emotional conflict

more damage than guns and bullets. For example, in 1995, a chemical attack in the Tokyo subway killed 12 people, but more than 4,000 non-affected individuals went to hospital afterwards with **psychogenic** symptoms. The long-term effect of this increased stress can be linked to lower activity rates, depression, and suicide.

Crime against tourists: Several elements of the tourist destination may result in increased levels of crime. If there is a large discrepancy between the wealth and lifestyle of the tourist and the local population, for example, tourists may run an increased risk of having their belongings stolen via pick-pocketing or burglary of their holiday home. Some tourist destinations are famous for their nightlife and clubs, which may lead to an increase in alcohol-related violence during the tourist season. Tourists may also not be aware of more dangerous areas in a destination, or perhaps take more risks on holiday, and so put themselves in a more vulnerable position. Experiencing or witnessing a crime on holiday may lead to fear and anxiety, even after a tourist has returned home, and thus counter the positive impacts of the holiday.

Scams: Scams are schemes that are aimed at conning tourists out of their money. They influenced to hand over the cash voluntarily, only to find out later that they have been duped. Because many tourists are unfamiliar with the destination and its customs, they are prime targets for scams. They may, for example, be asked to hand over their passport by a fake police officer, who will subsequently disappear with it. Another famous scam is the fake holiday club, which mainly targets older tourists in the Canary Islands. The tourist are offered a scratch card, and by scratching off three equal symbols they win a luxury holiday. To get this holiday, they are asked to sit through a lengthy sales presentation, where they are offered membership to an exclusive holiday club with exclusive offers at bargain prices. After paying the expensive membership fee, they find they have only bought access to an online booking service, offering no better deals than the average travel agent. The UK Office of Fair Trading has launched a campaign to warn British tourists not to sign the contracts offered in this scam (http://www.safefrom-scams.co.uk/HolidayClubScam.html).

Factors Governing the Extent of Socio-cultural Impacts on Host Communities

It has been established that tourism can have a range of positive and negative socio-cultural impacts on destinations. Not all of these impacts are present in all destinations; and in some the overall balance will be positive, whilst in others the balance will be negative. A range of destination characteristics can be distinguished that determine the extent to which positive and negative socio-economic impacts of tourism will develop. Inskeep (1991) suggests that these mainly depend on the magnitude of the differences between the hosts and the tourists in terms of:

- Basic value and logic systems.
- Religious beliefs.
- Traditions.
- Customs.
- Lifestyles.
- Behavioural patterns.
- Dress codes.
- Sense of time budgeting.
- Attitudes towards strangers.

Faulkner and Tideswell (1997) developed an alternative model and divided the factors that would determine the extent of socio-cultural impacts of tourism on destinations into two groups. On the one hand there are factors that apply to the host community as a whole, as an homogeneous group. But destinations are made up of individuals and within communities different groups might experience tourism in different ways. This means that on the other hand there are factors that apply to some individual members of the host community, but not to others.

Characteristics of Destination

Whereas Inskeep (1991) focuses mainly on the differences between the hosts and the tourists in his model, Faulkner and Tideswell (1997) have extended this to include a range of characteristics of the host destination. These characteristics are the stage of development of the destination, the tourist type it attracts, the pace of development, the dominance of tourism, the relationships between hosts and guests, the ratio of tourists to residents, and the level of seasonality.

Stage of Development

The intensity of certain socio-cultural impacts can be linked to the stage of development of the destination. The Tourist Area Life Cycle (see Chapter 7) is a representation of how resorts may develop: starting with low visitation and limited tourism development, the destination becomes ever more established and reaches a peak in tourist numbers, after which it either declines, or rejuvenates via further investment.

Many of the negative socio-cultural impacts, such as commodification of culture, staged authenticity and displacement, will only appear when tourist numbers and the level of development have become significant. In the earliest stages of development, the number of tourists, their impacts and their visibility may be low. In further stages of development these negative impacts may become ever clearer and it is important that the host community is protected from them via effective policy and destination management.

Tourist Type

The type and level of socio-cultural impacts of tourism on destinations is often linked to the type of visitor to those destinations. Here the Faulkner and Tideswell model is similar to Inskeep's model, as it examines the magnitude of the cultural differences between the host community and tourists, and how far tourists are willing to adapt to the host culture. The type of tourist the destination attracts is thus important from the perspective of these cultural similarities/differences.

A range of tourist typologies exists (see Chapter 4). A typology that is helpful to estimate the level of socio-cultural impacts of tourism on host communities addresses such questions as: are the visitors very different from the host population in terms of wealth, race, religion, or cultural background? Are the visitors adapting to the culture of the destination, or do they want that culture to adapt to them? Smith's (1977) model specifically focused on the socio-cultural impacts of different tourist groups to the destination. For every tourist type, the model links the number and visibility of the tourists to their willingness to adapt to the local culture. The further down the model, the more pressing negative socio-cultural impacts may become, and the higher the need for effective policies and management (see Table 9.1).

Table 9.1 Tourist types

Tourist type	Visibility/pressure	Attitude towards local culture
Explorer	Very limited	Adapts fully
Elite	Rarely seen	Adapts fully
Off-beat	Uncommon but seen	Adapts well
Unusual	Occasional	Adapts somewhat
Incipient mass	Steady flow	Seeks familiar amenities
Mass	Continuous influx	Expects familiar amenities
Charter	Massive arrivals	Demands familiar amenities

Source: adapted from Smith (1977). Reprinted with permission of the University of Pennsylvania Press.

Pace of Development

The pace of development is another factor that influences the level of socio-cultural impacts. If tourism develops slowly and gradually, the local community is given the opportunity to develop policies and management strategies to deal with the socio-cultural impacts, maximising the positive impacts and minimising the negative impacts. If the development of tourism is sudden and fast (for example, if an investor is allowed to build a big hotel complex in a small and little-developed destination), it may be more difficult for the local community to consider effective ways to deal with the influx of visitors.

Dubai is a typical example of a tourist destination that has developed very rapidly. Dubai is one of the seven autonomous sheikhdoms in the United Arab Emirates. Since the 1990s it has started to develop tourism in response to fluctuating oil prices and revenues. Since then, it has become one of the fastest growing tourism destinations worldwide. The main markets are other Gulf States, Europe, and Africa. From 2003, earnings from tourism have surpassed those from oil in most years. Even though rapid tourism development is thus undeniably linked to economic benefits, it has also caused a degeneration of the urban environment and negative social impacts. The influx of tourists has caused congestion, pollution, and noise. The futuristic new developments push emblems of traditional culture, such as the Persian wind towers, into the background (Henderson, 2006). Therefore the negative impacts in this case are inconvenience and Westernisation.

Dominance of Tourism

Destinations can also experience different levels of socio-cultural impacts depending on the dominance of tourism as a source of income. If the area is economically largely dependent on tourism, it may become more difficult to slow down tourist development, even if it is seen to bring negative impacts to the local area.

The example of Dubai can again apply here: due to over-construction of accommodation, prices in many older hotels have recently fallen. The cruise terminal, built to attract stopover tourism, is underutilised over the summer. By becoming more and more dependent on tourism instead of oil, the tourism industry is now of vital importance as a source of revenue and employment: this may mean that the need for economic benefit could override socio-cultural concerns in the future (Henderson, 2006).

Host–tourist Relations (Irridex)

Doxey (1975) proposed a model to describe the different community reactions to tourism. He suggested that as tourism develops and the industry becomes bigger, the attitude of the local population is expected to become more negative (see Figure 9.1).

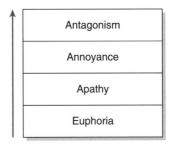

Figure 9.1   Doxey's Irridex Model

Source: adapted from Doxey (1975).

Doxey suggested that when tourism first develops (in the earliest stages of the Tourist Area Life Cycle), the host community is likely to welcome the positive impacts this has on the area and the relationship between hosts and visitors will be positive (Euphoria). As the tourism industry becomes more established and the local population gets used to the visitors, this positive relationship may be transformed into a state of Apathy. If the tourist industry then develops even further and more negative impacts start to become clear, the local attitude towards visitors may turn into Annoyance, or in the most extreme cases Antagonism (for example violence against tourists).

Doxey's model applies most to destinations where the impacts of tourism are not managed. It can be seen as pessimistic, because it seems to indicate that tourism development will necessarily lead to Antagonism within the host community. Still, this does not have to be the case: with careful planning and management in the destination (see Chapters 11 and 12), it is possible to foster positive relationships between hosts and visitors.

The Ratio of Tourists to Residents

This ratio refers to the number of tourists versus the number of local residents in a destination. In a large city like London, Tokyo or New York, this ratio is much lower than in a small seaside or island resort with a small population. If the ratio is high, it becomes more likely that the socio-cultural impacts of tourism on the destination will be more pronounced.

In 2007, Estonia had an overnight tourist ratio of 0.014: this meant that for every Estonian resident, the country received 1.4 overnight tourists (www.stat.ee). This was a relatively low and manageable number compared to Phillip Island, Australia (home of the Australian Grand Prix): here, the tourist ratio at the weekend can be as high as 0.35 (www.dse.vic.gov.au). This means that at peak times, there are 35 tourists for every resident. The pressures of this influx of additional space users may be very high in this example, and unless the tourists are carefully managed, the chance of negative impacts occurring is substantial.

Seasonality

If tourism in the destination has a distinct seasonal pattern, such as, for example, in beach or ski resorts, the impacts on the community will be accentuated during peak periods. The destination may become congested, it may become more difficult for the local community to carry out daily tasks or worship, and feelings of resentment may grow.

Tourism in Spain is highly seasonal and geographically concentrated, which causes a particular set of social problems. The main season is from June to September, when tourism employment levels are high and a lot of the bed space is likely to be occupied (Hudman and Jackson, 2002). In response to this seasonality, the Spanish government supports a social tourism programme called IMSERSO: this programme allows older people to travel off-peak, via special grants, to destinations that would otherwise be under-visited. The programme provides holidaymakers with a grant of 30 per cent of the total cost of the holiday. It thus achieves the social aim of increasing the mobility of older people and supports out-of-season employment. Because this means that the government has to pay less unemployment benefit, and receives income via taxes, the scheme has directly or indirectly generated more than 30,000 jobs in the tourist sector alone (Minnaert et al., 2010).

Characteristics of Individual Host Residents

This section refers to the characteristics of individual members of the host population. These may influence how they perceive the socio-cultural impacts of tourism on the destination. The section highlights that even though some characteristics will apply to the destination as a whole, this does not mean that all members of a host community will have the same views of tourism development and its impacts. Ap (1992) has described this as an adaptation of the *social exchange theory*: he sees the relationships between hosts and tourists as a trade-off between positive and negative impacts; and how far an individual benefits or suffers from tourism development will determine his or her attitude towards tourism and tourists.

Involvement in tourism: If persons in the host community are dependent on tourism for their livelihood – if they are employed in the tourism industry or if they operate a tourism business themselves – they are more likely to be more accepting of the negative socio-cultural impacts of tourism. For them the benefits of tourism often outweigh the costs, meaning the *social exchange* is positive.

Period of residence: Depending on the destination, the period of residence may be a positive or negative factor in determining the socio-cultural impacts of tourism on residents. If individuals move to the destination because they seek peace and tranquillity, the development of tourism there may seem rather threatening. However, if the tourism destination is rather developed already, new residents are often aware of the impacts of tourism before they move, so they may be more prepared to accept these than the residents who have lived there longer.

Residential proximity to tourist centre: This characteristic refers to how far from the tourist centre the resident lives his or her daily life. If the resident lives far away and has limited contact with tourists, he or she may experience fewer impacts of tourism development. Residents who live and/or work in the tourist centre and have frequent interactions with tourists are likely to experience the impacts of tourism more acutely.

Socio-economic characteristics: This characteristic is mainly applicable to tourism in developing countries, where the socio-economic gap between the visitors and the hosts can influence the relationships between the two groups. More educated and affluent groups in the destination may, for example, experience more positive contacts and impacts, whereas more disadvantaged groups in the destination might mainly experience negative impacts.

Underlying Theories

Cultures and societies are complex entities and tourism is just one factor that influences them. This is why tourism and its impacts do not operate independent from the ideas and ideologies that shape the rest of our social worlds. Tourism, as a relatively new industry, can be seen as an expression of ideas and theories that have influenced society for much longer – tourism researchers have thus frequently looked towards other disciplines, such as history, sociology and ethics, to frame the moral and philosophical aspects of the socio-cultural impacts of tourism. Sometimes this leads to opposing views of how tourism affects/should affect host communities and tourists – two examples are discussed here.

Tourism as an 'Industry' Versus Tourism as a 'Social Force'

Higgins-Desbiolles (2006b) argues that since the 1960s, tourism has increasingly been seen as an 'industry', a phenomenon that is created and governed by the private sector and driven by profit. As such, tourism is industrialised, and just like many other industries it is normal that damage to the environment and culture will occur in its development. Tourism is seen as a discretionary activity: in other words an activity we will choose to engage in if we are willing to pay the price for it. Tourism can thus be seen as a commodity and in this sense it is no different from a car or a plasma TV.

According to Higgins-Desbiolles (2006b), tourism can have other impacts than just income generation. Tourism can be seen as a way to gain human enrichment and education, and as a stimulus for a better understanding between cultures and a better society. Tourism can even be seen as a human right: the Universal Declaration of Human Rights mentions the right to leave and return to one's own country (Article 13.2) and the right to leisure and recreation (Article 24). In this paradigm, tourism is not private sector-led, but led by the public sector and community organisations. It emphasises the potential of tourism to bring a multitude of benefits to the tourist and the host community. It does not see tourism as a commodity, but rather as a social force with transformative capacities.

Neo-colonialism Versus Tourism as a 'Sacred Journey'

Tourism for some can be seen as a 'sacred journey', as a means to find oneself and make meaningful connections with places and people in other parts of the world. Researchers like MacCannell and Graburn link the origins of tourism to pilgrimages and argue that current forms of tourism are modern interpretations of these religious quests (Cohen, 1984). If tourism is seen this way, it should be able to bring positive impacts to both the tourist and the host community: the tourist gains a meaningful experience and visits the destination with respect, looking for a better way of life. The focus in this interpretation is on a search for meaning and truth, and the belief that these may be found in the destination culture.

It would seem that in some destinations, mostly in developing countries, this balance is not always retained. It often seems as if the tourists come to a destination and use and enjoy all that is good about it with little regard to the negative impacts of tourism: they then go again, leaving the destination to pick up the pieces. The power balance is often in favour of foreign developers and tourist dollars, forcing the local community into a subservient role. Tourism can also be considered a way to spread Western culture, consumption patterns and behaviours around the world: Western eating habits and products find their way around the globe via tourism. The globalisation of the tourism industry also plays a role here: the increased bargaining power of multinational tour operators means they can pressurise local providers to charge the lowest possible price. They may block-book a large amount of rooms to sell to their customer base, which gives them great power over the local accommodation provider. On the basis of this, tourism and the tourist industry have been compared to a form of neo-colonialism or imperialism: the focus is on the role of tourism in creating dependencies between tourism-generating, 'metropolitan' countries and tourism-receiving, 'peripheral' nations that replicate colonial or 'imperialist' forms of domination and structural underdevelopment. This was first argued by researchers such as Nash and Matthews (in Cohen, 1984) and is still prominent in tourism studies today.

An example of a destination where tourism could be seen as a neo-colonial force is Cyprus. The great majority of tourists travel to Cyprus on inclusive tour (package) arrangements. This is particularly the case for UK and Scandinavian visitors: about 80 per cent of the UK market and 100 per cent of the Scandinavian market in Cyprus are typically on package holidays. This means the island, and its tourism industry, have become increasingly dependent upon a small number of major overseas tour operators. In 2000, although over 60 specialist and mainstream operators (including some 20 Cypriot-owned companies) in the UK alone offered holidays to Cyprus in their programmes, it was observed that, as a result of restructuring within the tour operating industry, some 30 per cent of all arrivals in Cyprus were controlled by just one company, the German group Preussag (O'Connor, 2000). The strong position of this tour operator gives it a lot of bargaining power, thus reducing the freedom of Cypriots to develop new products or their own revenue streams. Although there is no immediate cultural conflict between tourists and local residents, resentment can be the result of this type of development, as the local community is faced with the negative impacts of tourism whereas the bulk of the revenue goes to multinational companies.

Managing Socio-cultural Impacts

Tourism development in a destination should aim to minimise the negative socio-cultural impacts of tourism and maximise the positive socio-cultural impacts – in other words, it should aim to be sustainable. Different stakeholders are involved in this process. The *public sector*, through planning and policy, often plays an important role. The public sector is not out to make a profit, and their responsibility is to represent the views of different groups in the destination. The *private sector*, for example accommodation providers, service providers and tour operators, can also have an influence over how impacts are managed. Although these businesses are profit-driven, there are ways for them to reduce their negative impacts. In areas where drinking water is scarce for example, hotels may decide to fill pools with sea water, so as not to put an excessive strain on resources. The *host community* is another stakeholder. Already it has been discussed that a host community is not an homogeneous group (see p. 247) – some residents will experience more positive or negative impacts than others. The final stakeholder is the *tourist*, who influences the destination socio-culturally via his or her behaviour and consumption pattern.

Visitor Management

Visitor management aims to minimise the negative impacts of tourism in three ways: controlling the number of visitors at a given place or time; modifying the way tourists behave; and adapting tourist resources to cope with visitor numbers (Mason, 2008).

Diversifying the product offer of a destination can be a first strategy to spread the numbers of tourists more evenly throughout the year, day or week. This could be achieved for example by promoting the destination in the off-peak season, by offering price promotions during these periods, or by staging events. Business events such as conventions, conferences, trade exhibitions and consumer fairs, for example, often run outside the leisure tourist season. By focusing on the niche of the business traveller, destinations may also avoid certain negative socio-cultural impacts of tourism. Seeing that business travellers often stay indoors for most of the day, they are less visible and less likely to cause congestion than leisure travellers for example. Visitor numbers can also be regulated via pricing strategies and advance-booking systems. These ensure that the number of tourists does not exceed the attraction's or destination's carrying capacity (see Chapters 10 and 11 for a full exploration of this concept).

A second visitor management strategy can be to modify the way tourists behave. This aim can be achieved in different ways. Education and information provision to the tourist is a first strategy: making visitors aware of their negative impacts makes it more likely that they change the behaviours that cause them. Positioning the destination to a different visitor type is another strategy: by replacing clubs and bars with more family-friendly facilities, for example, a destination can reduce the number of tourists who come to party and may cause a disturbance.

A third visitor management strategy could be to adapt tourism resources to minimise damage: certain areas of historic sites may be cordoned off, for example, or replicas may be provided to protect the original attraction. Wardens and guides may also be put in place to stop unruly behaviour.

For a full exploration of visitor management concepts and techniques, see Chapter 11.

Protecting Culture

It has been discussed here how tourism can have profound impacts on the culture of a destination: commodification, staged authenticity and the trinketi-sation of culture and its expressions are some examples. To counter these impacts, a range of strategies has been developed in many host communities to protect cultures from the negative impacts of tourism. Boissevain (1996) describes these strategies as covert resistance, hiding, fencing, organised protest and aggression.

Boissevain (1996) presents *covert resistance* as a first, uncoordinated defence against the negative impacts of tourism on culture. Covert resistance is not direct defiance or an organised form of protest, but rather a subtle but clear message to the tourist in the host community's behaviour. The local taxi driver might not challenge tourists directly, but may be sullen or rude towards them. The locals may gossip about or ridicule the tourists to express their feelings of discomfort or hostility.

Hiding is another strategy to protect culture and happens when certain aspects of culture become 'insider only'. Religious or cultural events may, for example, be purposely held before the tourists arrive or after they leave. Tourists are not informed about these events and they may function as alternatives to other events that have been expropriated by tourists.

Fencing is a more explicit strategy to protect culture. It can literally refer to fencing off certain areas of the host community to stop tourists from accessing them: restricting access to (certain parts of) a religious building, for example, or not allowing them to disturb fisherman at work. Fencing can also be used in a figurative sense, referring to preventing certain behaviours by tourists. Tourists may for example be discouraged from taking pictures of residents.

Organised protest mostly occurs when the negative impacts of tourism have overshadowed the positive impacts. This strategy may take the form of campaigns, demonstrations or boycotts. In extreme cases, the feelings of frustration and anger within the host community may even lead to *aggression* and violence.

Snapshot 9.4   Organised Protest in Malia, Greece

Malia is a resort on the northeastern coast of the Greek island of Crete. Because of its many nightlife facilities and its young visitor profile, it is often referred to as 'the Ibiza of Greece'. In July 2007, hundreds of local residents took to the streets to protest against the lewd and violent behaviour of young British tourists. They closed off the main highway and handed out leaflets. These explained that many young tourists, often under the influence of alcohol, would engage in public sexual acts, vandalism and violence. This had made the local residents feel unsafe, because the local police force was overstretched and was struggling to maintain order. The behaviours of the tourists had direct impacts on the everyday family life of the locals, many of whom would not venture out in the evening to go to a café or for a walk with their children. The protest aimed to put pressure on the government to stop travel agencies promoting Malia as a destination for sex and fun (http://uk.reuters.com/article/2007/07/25/uk-greece-britain-tourists-idUKL2588436920070725).

Community Participation

A further principle in the management of socio-cultural impacts is community participation in tourism. The basic idea is that if the local community are more involved in the decision-making process, tourism development will be more adapted to their needs and circumstances. The participation of the local community can take different forms, depending on how many local residents participate, whether these participants are representative of the community as a whole, and how much weight their views carry when making decisions. The community may, for example, be asked for their views in a public consultation that informs decision making, or they may be involved in the complete tourism development process.

Although extensive community participation is a theoretical ideal for equitable tourism development, there are often practical problems in destinations to achieve this. Destinations are not homogeneous groups (see p. 247) and it is not always possible to reconcile the different interests of all the community members. In destinations in developing countries, it is also possible that not all community members will have the educational skills or the confidence to participate in tourism decision making. They may be unclear about the procedures and ways to have their say, or there may be a profound distrust between the community and the decision makers. The views of

stakeholders with more financial power (such as the business community and local investors) might also carry more weight than the views of members in the community who live in poverty. In certain cases, it would thus be more useful to include community members in the tourism development process in a practical way, rather than via consultations and negotiations, to build on the involvement of the local community and make further participation possible. The example of pro-poor tourism below is one way to achieve this.

> **Stakeholder:** A person, group or organisation that is affected by (has a direct 'stake' in) an organisations' actions

CASE STUDY 9.1

PRO-POOR TOURISM

The Pro-Poor Tourism Partnership (www.propoortourism.org.uk) defines pro-poor tourism as tourism that results in increased net benefits for poor people. It is not a specific tourism product, but rather an approach to tourism management that improves the socio-economic and socio-cultural quality of life for poor people in the host community. In other words, pro-poor tourism is not a new type of holiday, but rather a way of doing business differently. It is this focus on new business strategies that makes pro-poor tourism different from many other approaches: pro-poor tourism allocates a central role to business and trade, not public sector support and interventions by voluntary organisations, to bring positive impacts to poor communities in a destination.

Pro-poor tourism strategies have economic and socio-cultural aspects. The economic impacts mostly have to do with building linkages with local suppliers (see p. 205) – such as sourcing food and other products locally rather than relying on imports. Another important economic aspect is job creation for the local community: employing local staff, training them, and paying them a fair salary. The increased income for the local community can lead to socio-cultural improvements such as a better infrastructure and quality of life. A socio-cultural aspect of pro-poor tourism can be the development of excursions and cultural attractions in the local area, increasing the local population's opportunities for finding pride in their culture and developing their own business. This can increase positive contacts between hosts and visitors, encourage capacity building within the poor population, and improve the balance between tourism and other forms of resource use.

Ashley et al., in a report for the Overseas Development Institute (2001), have compiled a report with guidelines for the development of pro-poor practices in the Caribbean. Examples of these guidelines include:

- Pay smaller, local suppliers regularly. Hotels often pay for goods 30 to 90 days after these have been delivered, but small producers do not always have the working capital to wait that long for payment.

(Continued)

(Continued)

- Local producers often offer goods that can be used in hotels, but the quantity, quality and reliability of the supply are often inadequate. Consider working with smaller contracts and appointing a facilitator who can inform and work with the local suppliers.
- Develop and implement a policy which encourages openness and a lack of stigma towards HIV. Educate managers as well as staff about HIV/AIDS, safety in the workplace, and working with HIV+ colleagues.
- Integrate local interaction and local shopping into existing excursions. Visiting local craft markets or workshops can enhance tourists' experience and expenditure. Offer retail space to local craftspeople and advertising space to local taxis, excursions and guides.
- Find out about the goals local people have: these may be different to what tourism operators expect. In several pro-poor tourism projects local income has been welcome, but poor people also have non-financial priorities such as training, dignity, access to natural resources, access to infrastructure, and the ability to participate in decisions.

Reflective Questions

1 Think of a place you have visited or tourism in your own country. Can you think of any examples of measures that aim to include poorer groups in society in tourism?
2 Pro-poor tourism is aimed at bringing benefits to poorer groups in the host community. Can you think of any benefits pro-poor tourism brings to the private businesses who engage in it?

Summary

This chapter has highlighted the socio-cultural impacts of tourism on destinations and host communities, some of which are positive (a better understanding between cultures, a greater appreciation of the own culture), and some of which are negative (commodification of culture, prostitution, Disneyfication). It has also explained the positive and negative socio-cultural impacts tourism can have on tourists: positive in terms of confidence, relaxation and relationships with others; negative in terms of anxiety due to violence or scams. The extent to which these impacts affect destinations can be linked to certain destination characteristics, such as how dominant tourism is, which type of tourists visit the destination, and the pace of development. Some members of the host community have also been shown to be more tolerant of these impacts than others, depending on, for example, their involvement in tourism or their proximity to the tourist centre.

The way we look at these impacts, and to what extent we see them as inherently linked to tourism, will depend on our underlying theory of tourism itself: is it an industry with unavoidable externalities? Or is it a social force, a sacred journey that affects both the tourist and the destination? The chapter has concluded by highlighting ways to manage the socio-cultural impacts of tourism, so that the positive impacts outweigh the negative impacts for both the destination and tourists.

 ■ Self-test Questions

1   Think about the countries you have visited, or about the tourism industry in your own country. Which of the above socio-economic impacts of tourism on destinations have you noticed? Can you give examples of these?

2   When you travel, how does that affect you as a person? How long do the effects of a holiday last after you get back home?

3   Think of a destination you have visited. Do the positive socio-cultural impacts of tourism outweigh the negative socio-cultural impacts it brings?

Further Reading

Boissevain, J. (ed.) (1996) *Coping with Tourists: European Reactions to Mass Tourism.* Providence: Berghahn Books.

Faulkner, B. and Tideswell, C. (1997) 'A framework for monitoring community impacts of tourism', *Journal of Sustainable Tourism*, 5(1): 3–28.

Holden, A. (2005) *Tourism Studies and the Social Sciences.* London and New York: Routledge.

Mason, P. (2003) *Tourism Impacts, Planning and Management.* Amsterdam: Elsevier.

Useful Websites

ECPAT International: www.ecpat.net

International Institute for Peace through Tourism: www.iipt.org

Office for Fair Trading – Safe from Scams: www.safefromscams.co.uk

Pro-Poor Tourism Partnership: www.propoortourism.org.uk

UN World Tourism Organization Code of Ethics: http://www.unwto.org/code_ethics/eng/global.htm

10 The Environmental Impacts of Tourism

Many tourists who visit such places become fascinated by, and protective of, reef fish, corals, nesting turtles, migrating cetaceans, whale sharks and so on. They will often actively support conservation initiatives; but they may also be the unwitting necrotic travelling agents of change. (Mair, 2006: 1)

Nature-based tourism near Freiburg, Germany

Source: Lynn Minnaert

Learning Outcomes

After reading this chapter you will understand:

- **the potential environmental impacts of tourism, both positive and negative**
- **the role of environmental sustainability in new tourism forms, and the different characteristics of these tourism forms**
- **a number of key concepts and management tools for the environmental management of tourism.**

Introduction

Tourism experiences are intrinsically linked to the environment they take place in: we often travel to experience places and environments that are different from the one we are familiar with. Many destinations are popular because of their natural assets: beaches, lakes, mountains, rolling countryside and empty plains are all examples of natural environments that can make a destination popular with tourists. At the same time, however, many of these environments are fragile, and by introducing tourists and their activities to them, we run the risk of damaging them. Tourism can also cause changes to the built environment, such as resort towns or parts of cities. This chapter reviews how tourism impacts on the environment it takes place in, and how these impacts can be managed.

This chapter also provides an overview of the different impacts tourism can have on the environment of a destination. Both positive and negative impacts are reviewed. The concept of sustainability is examined, and linked to new tourism forms such as eco-tourism, responsible tourism and agro-tourism. Finally the chapter discusses how environmental impacts can be managed in the destination, by maximising the positive impacts and minimising the negative impacts. Key management concepts and tools to achieve this aim are presented.

Environmental Impacts of Tourism on a Destination

The rapid growth of international tourism in the past 50 years or so has gone hand in hand with its ever more visual impact on the environment. Several once popular and beautiful resorts now seem to be typified by polluted beaches, an over-developed seafront and hordes of tourists who are not always respectful of their surroundings. This has led to an interest within tourism studies in how sustainable tourism is: although the concept of sustainable development has been around much longer, the debate about sustainable tourism is a phenomenon of the 1990s (Swarbrooke, 1999). This section will present the negative environmental impacts of tourism on the natural and the built environment, as well as on animal life. It will also highlight how tourists, via their behaviour, may exacerbate the negative environmental impacts of their holiday, although the extent of these impacts depends strongly on the scale of development in the destination, the environmental controls that are in place, and the visitor management techniques that are employed. Even though these negative impacts of tourism attract a lot of attention and are not to be minimised, tourism can also make positive contributions to the natural and built environment. The section will give examples of these positive environmental impacts of tourism.

Negative Environmental Impacts of Tourism

Tourism can cause a wide variety of negative environmental impacts. These are most visible within destinations but may also occur within the generating region and along transit routes. This section will start by reviewing the negative environmental impacts of tourism on three aspects of the destination:

- *The natural environment and resources*: air, water and soil pollution, waste/litter, over-use of resources.

- *Animal life*: habitats, animal behaviours, eco-systems, and the dangers of the souvenir trade.

- *The built environment*: over-development, pollution via building work, aesthetic pollution.

The Natural Environment

Tourism, and most particularly mass tourism, is being increasingly acknowledged as a human activity that poses huge threats to the natural environment. Not only does tourism often develop in fragile natural environments, such as lakes, beaches and mountains, it is also reliant on transport via air, sea or road. Tourism can cause damage to the natural environment via pollution, an increase in waste, and an over-use of resources.

Air Pollution

Air pollution has been linked to a range of environmental problems: acid rain, smog, the greenhouse effect, and 'holes' in the ozone layer. The increase in emissions via transport has also been linked to global warming, which again has been connected to environmental problems such as the melting of the ice caps and an increased level of natural disasters.

One of the main sources of air pollution is the release of particles in the air when energy is burnt. Because of is its heavy reliance on road and air transport, tourism contributes greatly to the global levels of emissions. The negative environmental impacts of transport are known as externalities; they create costs that are borne by society or the environment that are not paid for by the producer or user. The following sections review the externalities of different forms of transport with regard to air pollution.

Air transport mainly contributes to air pollution through the emission of carbon dioxide (CO_2) and nitrous oxides (NOx) that create global warming and ground-level pollution at airports. The contribution of aviation to carbon dioxide emissions is relatively low compared to other sectors, for example it is considered to be around 3–4 per cent of total emissions in the EU (Hanlon, 2007). However, the projected increase in demand globally suggests that aviation's contribution will increase. The UK government in 2003 estimated that by 2030, the contribution of UK aviation to UK greenhouse gas emissions could be as much as 25 per cent (DfT, 2003). In addition, while greenhouse gas emissions in the EU fell by 3 per cent between 1990 and 2002 overall, emissions from international aviation increased by 70 per cent (these figures include freight traffic). According to the UK's Energy Saving Trust, a return flight between the UK and Thailand produces more than two tonnes of CO_2 per passenger; this is more than the average annual carbon footprint of most non-flyers. Despite technological, regulatory and operating advances that reduce the emissions of individual flights, these have not neutralised the additional emissions caused by the increased volume of flights. In addition, it is widely believed that the climate change effects of aviation may be worse than those of other industries because of the altitude at which they occur, and the resulting cloud formation and condensation trails.

Motorised road transport contributes to greenhouse gases and climate change through exhaust emissions, reduces air quality through the release into the atmosphere of fine particulates that cause respiratory illnesses, and creates congestion and environmental damage. Tourism by road increases these negative environmental impacts which within destinations affect the quality of life of local residents and visitors' experience of the destination. However, tourists who travel by coach, on public transport or private group tours, reduce the number of equivalent tourists' cars on the road, and Page (2005) suggests that the occupancy level of cars used for tourism purposes is often higher than when used for other purposes such as commuting. Greyhound Lines in the USA claim that one departure removes the equivalent of 34 cars from the road and achieves 184 passenger miles per gallon.

Rail transport is becoming increasingly acknowledged as a viable sustainable alternative to road and air transport. The environmental impacts of rail transport are significantly lower than most other modes of transport, for instance high speed rail uses one-third of the energy requirements of flights over 500–1,000km, and trains using coal-fired electricity emit almost half the greenhouse gases of many aircraft, with non-fossil electric trains emitting substantially less (Friends of the Earth, 2000).

Sea transport makes considerable contributions to air pollution, particularly because of the volume of shipping globally. According to the International Maritime Organization (IMO), international shipping emitted 2.7 per cent of global man-made emissions in 2007 (IMO, 2009), and this is expected to increase alongside global trade. It should be noted, though, that most sea transport is for freight rather than passengers, however the growing popularity of cruise travel has led to the increasing importance of sea transport for tourism.

The Japanese bullet train – Shinkansen
Source: Valerié Svobodová

An additional moral issue is that transport does not only pollute the air in the tourism-generating areas, in other words the tourist's own geographic region, but also in the destination countries, some of which produce a lot less CO_2. Tourists who visit developing countries, for example, pollute the air by flying to the destination, thus causing air (and noise) pollution for people who pollute a lot less themselves. The same goes for countries tourists tend to drive through on the way to their destination: many northern Europeans for example drive to southern Europe via the **Benelux** countries. In these countries, emissions due to tourism will thus be high, even though tourists do not bring many environmental, social or economic benefits to the local communities. In both cases, the tourists do not pay for the environmental damage they cause to these destination or transit regions.

> **Benelux:** Belgium, the Netherlands and Luxemburg

Water Pollution

Tourism often takes place in areas close to water, such as seas or lakes. Still, it is usually not the activities of tourists in the water that have the biggest negative impacts. Pollution tends to be caused by inadequate facilities that are unable to cope with the large influx of tourists at peak times. Holden (2008) indicates that inadequate sewage systems may result in human waste being disposed directly into the sea. Rapid development in the past, to keep up with growing numbers of tourists, has sometimes left destinations with infrastructure that cannot cope with the demands tourism places on it. Another form of water pollution results from the use of fertilisers and herbicides for hotel gardens and golf courses. These chemicals seep down to the ground water lying between five and 50 meters under the surface, and from there flow into rivers, lakes and seas.

The Mediterranean Sea is one of the most heavily polluted, semi-enclosed basins in the world. According to Greenpeace, thousands of tonnes of toxic waste are pumped directly into it – mainly by industry. Tourism is a contributing factor to this: the Mediterranean is one of the most popular tourism destinations in the world, and accounts for up to a third of the global tourist arrivals. Overcrowding and inadequate facilities, often built at a distance from population centres and amenities, result in increased pollution in the peak months (www.greenpeace.org). A more recent example is Dubai, a fast-expanding tourist destination which was rocked in 2008 by a sewage dumping scandal. One of its most prestigious sections of beach (including the Jumeirah Beach Hotel and the Offshore Sailing Club) was closed due to the presence of raw sewage, toilet paper, and chemical waste. The dumping of the waste had been done illegally, by truck drivers who instead of queuing for a lengthy wait at the city's only sewage treatment plant, resorted to dumping it in the storm drains. These drains were meant to collect excess water during the short rainy season. The incident led to accusations that due to Dubai's rapid development, the local authorities were unable to enforce environmental regulations adequately.

The Blue Flag programme is an internationally used quality label for beaches that guarantees good water quality, environmental education and information, environmental management, safety, and other criteria. It is awarded by the independent charity Foundation for Environmental Education. In 2008, over 3,200 beaches and marinas were awarded Blue Flag status. Most of these were in Europe, but some were located in other parts of the world, for example, Canada, New Zealand and South Africa (www.blueflag.org).

 ## Snapshot 10.1   Surfers Against Sewage

Surfers Against Sewage is a not-for-profit organisation campaigning for clean, safe recreational waters, free from sewage effluents, toxic chemicals, marine litter and nuclear waste. Surfers and recreational water users who come into contact with sewage or other toxins may contract health problems, ranging from ear, nose and throat infections, eye and wound infections, and gastro-intestinal complaints such as diarrhoea and vomiting, to more serious illnesses such as bacillary dysentery, pneumonia, botulism, hepatitis A, meningitis, and septicaemia. Research by the organisation showed that surfers were three times more likely to

(Continued)

(Continued)

contract hepatitis A than the general public. Surfers Against Sewage highlight that popular British destinations such as Guernsey and Brighton discharge raw sewage in the sea, and campaign for greater awareness and regulation. The organisation also campaigns against marine litter and water pollution via the flushing or dumping of chemicals. The majority of these chemicals can be found in everyday household products such as shampoos, skin care creams, washing detergents, and paints. Some chemicals have been found to change the hormonal balance of wildlife: they are partly responsible for the feminisation of around one-third of the male fish population in Britain (www.sas.org.uk).

Soil Pollution

Soil pollution, or soil contamination, refers to the presence of chemicals or other man-made substances that interfere with the natural soil environment. This type of pollution is often caused by underground storage tanks (for example containing fuel), the application of pesticides, and the dumping of industrial waste. Although the tourism industry is not the biggest cause of soil pollution, certain of its activities can contribute to the problem. The use of pesticides on golf courses and hotel grounds is an example. Boniface and Cooper (2005) have also linked the use of artificial snow in ski resorts to soil pollution. Because ski seasons are becoming shorter and less reliable, ski cannons are increasingly used to top up the snow in these resorts. Not only do these snow cannons use a large amount of water, there are also chemicals in artificial snow that speed up the crystallisation process. These chemicals can then contaminate the soil in an already very fragile natural environment.

Waste/litter

Tourism, and in particular mass tourism, increases the destination's population size temporarily, and therefore the level of waste that is generated too. This can cause environmental problems if not properly managed. Some waste (such as food) can be classified as organic, whereas other forms (such as packaging) are inorganic. Litter can have various effects on a destination: in some cases, it will just make the environment unpleasant for tourists and the local community – for example if the beach is littered with bottles, papers and cigarette butts. Ultimately, there is no completely safe method of waste disposal, and the only way to truly avoid environmental harm from waste is to prevent its generation (Ceballos-Lascuráin, 1996).

One of the most famous effects of litter and waste caused by tourism is the widespread pollution in the Indian Himalayas. Mount Everest, the highest mountain in the world, is also referred to as 'the highest junkyard in the world'. Solid waste management is a problem, particularly along the trekking routes. During the tourist periods, food stalls pop up along these routes, selling their wares in disposable containers (Cole and Sinclair, 2002). Even though a large amount of the waste could technically be recycled, it needs to be transported to the main road and then to recycling centres, making this an intensive and costly enterprise. According to Kuniyal et al. (2003), visitors need to be educated more about the impacts of waste so that they can change their attitudes. Environmental groups have called for access to the mountain to be halted to tourists altogether until the waste is cleaned up.

Over-use of Natural Resources

When large numbers of tourists come to a destination with limited resources, increased competition for these resources may ensue. Energy resources, such as gas and electricity, and water reserves, may come under severe pressure. In destinations with limited water supplies, for example, the construction of large resorts with swimming pools may place disproportionately high demands on this resource.

In Cyprus, the tourism industry is placing a heavy burden on the scarce water reserves of the island. Because of limited rainfall, demand has outstripped supply for many years. The island has a number of desalination plants to supply drinking water, but these plants are energy-heavy and thus cause their own environmental impacts. The situation has at times become so drastic that tanker ships from Greece have been sent to relieve the water shortage in the southern part of the island (BBC news, 16 July 2008). The tourism industry has been forced to adapt to the restrictions of water use, but these are less stringent than those placed on the local population.

Animal Life

Tourism development and tourist activities may affect the behaviour and habitat of animals, particularly if the animals have become an attraction and part of the destination product. It can also be the cause of foreign life forms and micro-organisms (such as viruses and bacteria) that may be introduced in the environment via tourism.

Animal Behaviours

Contact with tourists may alter the behaviour patterns and habits of animals, especially when that contact is frequent and intense. Orams (2002) classifies human contact with animals in the context of tourism in three broad categories: *captive* (in zoos, aquariums, aviaries and oceanariums), *semi-captive* (in wildlife parks or sea pens), or *wild* (in wildlife parks, along migration routes, and at breeding/feeding/drinking sites). Animals in the wild may seem to be least affected by tourists, but because seeing the animals is not as guaranteed in a wildlife park as in a zoo, the animals are sometimes fed by the tourists, in order to allow closer contact. This practice may affect the behaviour of the animal profoundly. The animal needs to spend less time hunting and foraging, which can result in increased breeding, higher population levels or a change in migration patterns – the animal may stay in one place throughout the year, rather than migrating to another place where usually food would have been more abundant. The danger is that the animal becomes dependent on these human hand-outs and does not develop or maintain the necessary skills to feed itself. Another risk is that the animal becomes habituated to human contact and even approaches humans where they would usually keep a safe distance. This may result in animals being hurt or killed. Finally, there are also reported cases whereby animals fed by people have become aggressive towards humans.

CASE STUDY 10.1

FEEDING BY TOURISTS AND ITS IMPACT ON THE BEHAVIOUR OF MONKEYS IN GAMBIA AND GIBRALTAR

Bijilo Forest Park is a small nature reserve in Gambia. It was opened in 1991 to preserve the area from deforestation, and to provide safe habitat for several species of wildlife, amongst which are the green monkeys. These monkeys, also called velvet monkeys, are medium-sized primates, and were threatened by dogs and hunting. Now they are a key attraction for the country, featuring on marketing materials for the marketing campaign 'Gambia, the smiling coast of Africa'. The park receives about 2,000 visitors per year, most of whom stay in nearby hotels. The park, and with it the monkeys, was meant to be a place to enjoy the animals in their natural environment, but now seems to have become a victim of its own success. Although feeding the monkeys is officially forbidden, tourists can buy bags of ground nuts especially for this purpose. The monkeys have understood that rather than foraging for their own food, they can just sit along the path that leads from the hotels and wait for hand-outs. Tourist guides do not enforce the environmental rules and let tourists feed the animals. This practice has profoundly altered the behaviour of the monkeys: their travel range has become much smaller, and they are overfed and overweight, risking illness and diabetes. They have also become more aggressive, both amongst themselves and towards tourists (http://www.telegraph.co.uk/travel/destinations/africaandindianocean/gambia/748406/Gambia-on-the-trail-of-the-green-monkey.html).

The Gibraltar Upper Rock Nature Reserve is home to over 200 Barbary macaques. The macaques have free range throughout the reserve, and occasionally move into areas in the neighbouring urban zones. Interactions with humans have been a substantial factor in the daily lives of the Gibraltar macaques for several generations, and this has impacted on their social behaviour. Fuentes (2006) highlights how the presence of tourists affects breeding patterns, and may lead to physiologically stressful outcomes. The rise of tourists in Gibraltar, and their interest

(Continued)

(Continued)

in the monkeys, has resulted in an explosion in their numbers. Although there are signs indicating that feeding the monkeys is forbidden, and that they may bite, taxi and coach drivers tend to encourage interactions by luring a monkey onto the shoulder or the head of a tourist for a picture. This behaviour culminated in 2008 in the Gibraltar government ordering a group of aggressive monkeys to be killed, after 25 broke into hotel rooms and were found scavenging in bins in the town centre. The motivation behind the cull was that tourists and children were frightened and that the monkeys would damage the tourism sector. The killings resulted in protests from researchers and animal rights groups, who argued that the animals would have returned to the hills if tourists and locals had stopped feeding them.

Both stories show how tourism and tourist activities can profoundly impact on the lives and behaviours of monkeys in certain tourism destinations, and in both cases the interactions with tourists have resulted in negative outcomes for the monkey population.

Reflective Questions

1 Which strategies could be adopted to minimise the negative impacts of tourism on these monkey populations?
2 Can you think of other examples where interactions with tourists have changed the behavioural patterns of animals?

Animal Habitats

Tourism and tourism activities can be a threat to animals when their **habitats** are cleared to make way for tourism infrastructure. Habitats may be destroyed during the construction of hotels, lodges, camping grounds, roads or attractions. Trees, shrubs and other elements that are vital to the lives of the animals may be removed during the construction process.

> **Habitat:** Ecological surroundings that are inhabited by an animal or plant species

Tourism facilities might also fragment the habitat of certain animals, and make it harder for some of them to access sources of food and water. The use of off-road vehicles may damage vegetation in the habitat. All these factors can severely impact on breeding and feeding habits (Higginbottom, 2004).

Certain types of sports tourism can be seen as particularly intrusive from this perspective, because they are intrinsically linked with the natural environment they take place in. Water sports are an example – several of these (e.g. diving and snorkelling) take place in animal habitats, as viewing the animals is one of the attractions of engaging in the activity. Egypt's Red Sea coast, for example, is famous for diving and snorkelling, and attracts thousands of visitors each year. Hunting and fishing are other examples.

Sports activities like these need to be carefully managed so that the activities of tourists do not endanger the animal habitats they have come to visit. Trophy hunting (tourists hunting for specific animals that are seen as trophies, because of their body size, large tusks or skull length) is often presented as a source of income for conservation areas, but causes a set of problems. It is difficult, for example, to set reliable hunting quotas in areas where there are insufficient data about animal populations, and because of corruption the quotas that are set may be exceeded. In the developed world, there is also a growing ethical resistance against the idea of killing animals for sport (Lindsey et al., 2006).

Snapshot 10.2   Diving Tourism and Coral Reefs

Coral reefs are an example of habitats that are under threat from tourism, mainly from water sports and diving tourism. Some destinations, like Australia, Egypt, Mexico and Belize, have developed thriving niches for diving tourism. Particularly in destinations like these, where there is intensive diving, the activity can lead to broken coral and sediment covering the reefs. Most of the damage is accidental and involves unintentionally touching, trampling and hitting corals with loose equipment. This damage not only affects the corals, but also the fish, for which the reef is a vibrant habitat. Harriott et al. (1997) studied the behaviour of recreational divers in Eastern Australia and although most divers did not damage any coral, a minority damaged between

Diving tourism in Egypt

Source: Roger Louis

(Continued)

(Continued)

10 and 15 corals each per 30 minute dive. Contact with the sea bed was more common and was usually caused by fins. This form of contact can cause the sediment on the sea bed to move, which may result in the smothering of plants and coral. Damage caused by divers to coral reefs may also lead to higher fish mortality, or cause them to migrate to other reefs (Hasler and Ott, 2008).

Introduction of Foreign Life Systems

Most countries operate strict rules for tourists who want to export or import foodstuffs, seeds, bulbs, or live animals and plants. One of the reasons for this is that these can carry microbes, bacteria, viruses, pests and diseases that can deeply impact on the environment of the area they are introduced to. When tourists, for example, bring exotic flowers home, this may cause invasive micro-organisms that were once confined to a small area to spread around the world.

The introduction of new life forms is particularly danger-ous in pristine and fragile environments, for example, the Galapagos Islands. These islands were studied by Darwin, who found a wealth of **endemic** species there. Tourism activity in the islands has been steadily growing, and although care is taken not to disturb the environment unnecessarily, it is not without its problems. The Darwin Foundation has highlighted how tourist boats in the Galapagos introduced new insects, mainly moths, to the islands, from countries such as Ecuador. The boats also transport insects from one island to another, because the insects are attracted by the lights on them. In fragile ecosystems, the introduction of a new species with no natural predators can cause its numbers to grow rapidly, in time endangering or even replacing domestic species. A simple solution to the problem would be to equip the boats with lights in colours that are less attractive to the insects (www.darwinfoundation.org).

> **Endemic:** Native to a certain region. Because of the isolated location of the Galapagos Islands, there are a great number of species here that cannot be found anywhere else

Souvenir Trade

The trade in certain souvenirs can pose a direct threat to animals in the destination. Ivory, exotic leathers and fur, animal teeth and claws, and foodstuffs such as shark fins can be offered to tourists, who may buy them because they are unaware of the environmental impacts of this, or because this adds to their value as a novelty item. Tourists may also be invited to eat endangered species in local restaurants, such as turtle eggs, shark's fin soup, or iguana meat. Because the products are sold so openly, many tourists do not realise that they are driving up the demand for these products and so putting the environment in danger.

IFAW, the International Fund for Animal Welfare, runs the campaign 'Think Twice – Don't Buy Wildlife Souvenirs' to educate tourists about the environmental impacts of certain behaviours and activities. The campaign website offers an extensive list of souvenirs and foods to avoid whilst on holiday and gives tips on how to be a more responsible tourist. There is also a link for travel agents and tour operators to support the campaign (www.ifaw.org).

The Built Environment

Tourism impacts not only on the natural environment, but also on the built environment. The development of tourism often requires extensive development of supporting facilities such as accommodation, attractions, roads and airports. In some destinations, the extensive and rapid development of these facilities has caused the built environment to deteriorate. This section will look at the effects of over-development and aesthetic pollution. It will also address the problem of sedimentation caused by construction activities and how this impacts on the destination.

Over-development

Most long-established tourism destinations have developed tourism facilities and infrastructure over time on a large scale, to cater for the large numbers of tourists that visit them. In many cases, faced with the strong economic benefits of mass tourism, this development has taken place in a rather unplanned fashion, resulting in long strips of poorly built hotels, cafes and shops that are not always in keeping with the local environment. Not only does this cause the built environment to look ugly (see 'aesthetic pollution' below), it can also negatively affect the quality of life of the local community, for example through a lack of green space, a loss of local pride, and overcrowding and congestion.

In some destinations, action is being taken to remove inappropriate developments. The Spanish coast is one of the most over-developed tourist destinations in Europe and the coastline is largely built up. Even though there is a law that forbids buildings to be erected within 500 metres of the water, it is estimated that about 300,000 holiday homes have been built within this zone. The Spanish government has threatened several times to demolish these holiday homes, but so far only limited demolition has actually taken place. The effects on the natural and built environment can be far-reaching, as Charles Clover, columnist for the *Telegraph* newspaper, commented:

> I was driving down an obscure part of the coast of Almeria last year, one of the driest and so least developed parts of the Mediterranean coast, when I came across a hill in the middle of nowhere being consumed by bulldozers and cranes as if by maggots. White tourist homes with no connection to existing settlements were sprouting out of bare rock and scrub. [I drove] around the rows and rows of largely empty new tourist homes, the golf courses, shops and restaurants most with British names which are devouring the last hillsides around La Manga del Mar Menor. ('Earthlog: A Spanish Tragedy', the *Telegraph*, 3 May 2007)

Aesthetic Pollution

Tourism development can also lead to what Holden (2008) refers to as 'aesthetic pollution': a decline in the visual, aesthetic appeal of a destination. This can be particularly apparent in destinations that have developed rapidly for tourism, where hotels and infrastructure have been constructed without much planning and regulation, often resulting in over-developed and built-up environments. Many coastal resorts have also started looking very similar, with little sensitivity shown towards local cultures or building styles. Aesthetic pollution not only adversely affects the built environment for the local population, it also influences the overall popularity of the destination and the type of tourists it will attract. Uncontrolled growth and aesthetic pollution are often connected to the 'decline' stage in Butler's Tourist Area Life Cycle model (see Chapter 7). An example of a destination that can be argued to be in this phase is Bugibba in Malta. The *Lonely Planet* guide for Malta and Gozo describes this destination as follows:

> The unattractive sprawl of Bugibba, on the eastern side of the bay, is the biggest tourist development in Malta. Bugibba is the heartland of the island's cheap-and-cheerful package holiday trade, and is absolutely mobbed in the summer. It is not the prettiest or most inspiring of places to end up on a holiday (and there are no sandy beaches) but at least it's cheap, especially in the low season when there are some real accommodation bargains and the swimming areas are not so crowded. (Bain and Wilson, 2004: 99)

A viewing point in Buggiba, Malta

Source: Lynn Minnaert

Sediment and Destabilisation After Building Work

Construction activities such as dredging, digging and land clearing can cause large amounts of sediment to settle over the surrounding areas. This sediment can smother vegetation, or be washed away via runoff water from rainfall and pollute waterways and aquatic life. Hotels, runways, roads, and other tourism facilities are often constructed in naturally fragile areas such as beaches, mountains or around lakes, where sediment can threaten the natural environment. Rogers (1990) examined the effect of unprotected development along tropical shorelines on coral reefs, and noted that excessive sedimentation led to fewer coral species, less live coral, lower growth rates, and lower productivity of coral. Sediment control measures, such as the installation of sediment fences, can reduce this potential damage.

The construction of new tourist facilities may also involve the removal of certain natural barriers against erosion, thus causing a destabilisation of the area. On beaches and in dune areas, for example, palm trees and dune grasses are key stabilising elements that stop beach erosion: in other words, they stop the sand from being washed or blown away. Beaches that suffer from erosion often need to be artificially replenished to maintain their tourism appeal. Daby (2003) discusses how the removal of seagrasses has destabilised the lagoon seabed in Mauritius. These seagrasses are crucial for the natural environment because their roots bind and consolidate the soil, but many hotels remove them because they are seen as unsightly, or dangerous for bathers. To provide an aesthetically pleasing environment for swimmers an increasing number of hotels are removing the seagrass bed, resulting not only in destabilisation but also generally in a less robust ecosystem that is more vulnerable to environmental change and extreme weather.

Positive Impacts

Although tourism, as described in the sections above, is often linked to negative environmental impacts, it can also have a number of positive impacts for the natural environment. Even though it is hard to argue that tourism makes the environment better per se, tourism can replace or prohibit activities that are even more damaging, such as mining, logging or heavy industries. The economic benefit from tourism can also be a stimulus for destinations to appreciate the local environment and enforce stronger environmental controls. Tourism can encourage the protection or enhancement of the environment in two ways: it can conserve and protect the natural environment on the one hand, and regenerate and enhance the built environment on the other hand.

Conservation/protection of the Natural Environment

Although tourism, as explained in the previous paragraphs, can often be seen as a threat to the natural environment, it can also act as a driving force for conservation and protection. This is because, via tourism, leisure and recreation, the natural environment can become a source of income for the local community – this means that there is less need to replace the natural area with housing, industry or commercial uses. For many destinations, natural attractions like beaches, mountains, lakes and countryside are important elements of the tourism product. If these destinations want to experience the economic benefits from tourism, it is important that they take good care of this asset. Tourists who visit the area can also play a role in the awareness-building process, if they are being told about the fauna and flora in the area and the various threats that may affect their habitat.

 Snapshot 10.3 Cyabeno Wildlife Reserve

The Cyabeno Wildlife Reserve in Ecuador's Amazon region is a protected natural area on the border with Peru and Colombia. The reserve is a complex of rivers, lagoon and floating forest and spans over 600,000 hectares. It is characterised by its rich biodiversity: it is, for example, home to over 500 types of birds and 240 species of plants per hectare. This area came under pressure from foreign oil companies and their exploration and drilling activities. Oil exports are an important source of income for Ecuador and provide much more income than tourism ever could. Still, the tourism sector (represented mainly by responsible tourism agencies) has played a big role in the lobbying activities of environmental pressure groups. It has also been shown that tourist activities in the area can increase the awareness of the local community about the value of natural resources and lead to the adoption of zoning and regulation schemes (Wunder, 1999). It can thus be said that although tourism activities can have a negative environmental impact themselves, a trade-off with an increased local and national awareness of environmental issues is sometimes possible.

Regeneration of the Built Environment

Tourism can be a driver for the protection and enhancement of not only the natural environment, but also the built environment. The term 'regeneration' refers to the revitalisation of run-down urban areas, so that they become an attractive place to live, work and visit. Regeneration projects usually include impressive buildings, hotels, shopping malls, and entertainment and cultural facilities. In many former industrial cities, regeneration schemes became popular after the deindustrialisation of the Western economy: with many industries moving production to countries with a cheaper labour force, and the growth of the service economy, much of the industrial infrastructure was no longer needed. Tourism, leisure and recreation spending increased rapidly in

> **Disposable income:**
> This is the income of a person after taxes and bills for necessities (food, rent/mortgage, utilities)

modern society as the **disposable income** of many families grew. This resulted in a range of industrial buildings being transformed into museums and cultural attractions. In London, for example, a former power station along the river Thames has been transformed into a major cultural attraction: the Tate Modern museum of modern art. This is an example of how tourism development may create new uses for existing buildings and make an area more aesthetically pleasing via the removal of graffiti and the prevention of dereliction.

Regeneration can involve the conservation and restoration of heritage buildings, but is often associated with grand projects of modern architecture that become symbols (also called flagships) of the city. The Guggenheim museum in Bilbao, for example, is often used as an illustration of how flagship buildings can enhance the image of a city and increase visitor flows. Even though these developments are usually not purely aimed at tourists, their cost and scale can often transcend the needs of the local population. They often become tourist attractions, thus strengthening their symbolic function as showcases for cities.

Although regeneration projects can bring a range of benefits to the destination, some have also been linked to a number of negative environmental and social impacts. Certain urban regeneration projects have been criticised because of the 'placelessness' they can create: the regenerated area of one city,

> **Gentrification:** The rebuilding of an area leading to an influx of more affluent people, often resulting in an increased living cost which may drive out the original residents

with its modern architecture, waterfront apartments and entertainment complexes, may look exactly like that of another city. There are sometimes few links between the culture of a place and the regenerated area, so that landscapes become increasingly 'global' (Smith, 2007). Regeneration can also lead to **gentrification** and displacement: as the area becomes more and more desirable as a place to live and work, the local residents who used to live there may be forced out of the area due to increased rents or housing costs.

 ## Snapshot 10.4   Valencia's City of Arts and Sciences

Valencia is the third largest city in Spain, situated on the south-eastern coast. From the 1980s, the city aimed to reinvent itself after a period of deindustrialisation and a rapid transition from agriculture to a service economy (Prytherch and Huntoon, 2005). Tourism was seen as a key sector that could support Valencia in its overall regeneration. Valencia has a number of established attractions, such as its sandy beach, historic buildings in the city centre and an

(Continued)

(Continued)

authentic cuisine – Valencia is said to be the birthplace of paella. The city is also building a strong reputation as a host city for sports events. One of the latest additions is the City of Arts and Sciences: a culture and entertainment complex, designed by Santiago Calatrava, consisting of a science museum, an IMAX theatre, a planetarium, an oceanarium, a performing arts centre, and an urban garden. The whole complex is located in the dry river bed of the Turia, a river that was diverted away from the city after a flood in the 1950s, and which now runs as a green lung through the city. The aim of this project was to develop cultural attractions in Valencia of a national and international standard that would put the city firmly on the political and economic map (Lapunzina, 2005).

Source: Lynn Minnaert

On the basis of these examples, it can be stated that tourism can have a variety of negative impacts on the natural environment. Mass tourism moves a large number of people to an often fragile natural environment, which may put pressure on resources, cause pollution, affect animal life, and cause detrimental changes to the built environment. There is a growing awareness of these negative environmental impacts of tourism and a mounting pressure on tourism to protect and enhance the natural and built environment. The remainder of this chapter will discuss the concept of environmental sustainability and examine how the environmental impacts of tourism can be managed so that the positive impacts are maximised and negative ones are minimised.

Environmental Sustainability

In the face of a relentlessly growing tourism industry, and the growing awareness of its negative environmental impacts, the concept of sustainability has become central to the tourism debate. A fuller exploration of sustainability can be found in Chapter 1. This section will briefly introduce environmental sustainability and discuss three recent approaches to tourism that aim to provide alternative and more environmentally sustainable tourism choices.

The Focus on the Environment in Defining Sustainable Tourism

The term sustainability is defined in Chapter 1 as 'the term chosen to bridge the gulf between development and environment' (Rogers et al., 2008). The concept has an economic, social and environmental component, but when it is applied to tourism, the environment has for a long time taken a central role in the debate. The term sustainable tourism has come to represent and encompass a set of principles, policy prescriptions, and management methods which chart a path for tourism development such that a destination area's environmental resource base (including natural, built, and cultural features) is protected for future development (Lane, 1994). Hunter (1997, 2004) has long argued that this overemphasis on the environment in tourism needs to be rebalanced and that the tourism industry should take a more holistic view of sustainability.

Pro-poor tourism:
Tourism in which the poor are key stakeholders, and that particularly aims to achieve net benefits for poor people in the host community, often by building partnerships between them and the private sector

Recently, a new emphasis on social sustainability can be noted within the tourism industry, with forms of tourism such as community-based tourism, **pro-poor tourism** (see page 253) and social tourism receiving increased attention from scholars and practitioners. This evolution, together with a continued focus on environmental issues, should move the tourism industry towards a more general implementation of the sustainability concept. The following forms of tourism may focus mainly on environmental conservation and protection, but each of these also includes economic and social elements.

Responsible Tourism

Responsible tourism is a term that does not tend to refer to a product in particular, but to a new attitude to tourism. This attitude sees tourism not as a mere product, that is consumed and then discarded, but as an activity with far-reaching consequences, for which all stakeholders are in part responsible.

This means that the tourists are responsible for their behaviour at the destination; the tourism providers for their operations, sourcing policies, and developments; the local communities for their involvement in tourism; and finally the governments for planning and regulating tourism in a responsible fashion. Responsible tourism, just as with the concept of sustainability, has an environmental, social, and economic element.

Although responsible tourism is thus an umbrella term for different forms of tourism, the environmental aspect plays an important role. Wheeller (1991) points out that responsible tourism tends to favour small-scale, slow, steady development. This should go hand in hand with tourist education so that they are more aware of the impacts of their activities. Even though these are laudable objectives, Wheeller highlights the great difficulty of turning these into reality: small-scale and paced development may be more responsible, but how will this speed of development keep up with the ever-increasing volume of tourists? And educating tourists so that they behave in a more responsible way is also a mammoth task, which would take a long time to achieve. There is also the question of whether raised awareness will automatically lead to a change in behaviour by tourists. Many will have a certain understanding of the environmental impacts of tourism, but this does not always mean they will be willing to change their habits or behaviour.

Despite the practical challenges for responsible tourism, there are some indications of an increasing acceptance of the need for it. In 2002, a large group of tourism stakeholders (inbound and outbound tour operators, emerging entrepreneurs in the tourism industry, national parks, provincial conservation authorities, all spheres of government, tourism professionals, tourism authorities, NGOs, and hotel groups and other tourism stakeholders) from 20 countries in Africa, North and South America, Europe and Asia signed the Cape Town Declaration on responsible tourism. This comprised a list of guiding principles that all subscribers agreed to adhere to (www.gdrc.org). Since 2004, responsibletravel.com has organised the Responsible Travel Awards. Tourists can nominate tourism businesses and destinations they perceive as being particularly responsible, from niche to mainstream. The categories include hotels, cruises, destinations, technologies, and individuals. In 2008, New Zealand was crowned the overall winner for successfully implementing the Cape Town Declaration on Responsible Tourism in Destinations (www. responsibletourismawards.com).

Eco-tourism

France (1999) highlights that there is no single definition for eco-tourism: a range of definitions and approaches exists. Weaver (2006) also highlights a range of characteristics that typify eco-tourism initiatives: these tend to be centred on nature-based attractions, but, as opposed to other nature-based tourism forms, there is usually an educational element involved in the experience. This educational element can be intensive or rather light, but learning about the environment is usually one of the motivations for tourists to participate in eco-tourism. The eco-tourism project should also make a credible attempt to be environmentally sustainable.

One of the key benefits of eco-tourism is that it presents a revenue stream that can be used to fund conservation activities. Eco-tourism can also encourage the tourist to adopt a more environmentally friendly attitude in general. Finally, if the local community is involved in providing the eco-tourism experience, they may take on the role of environmental advocates and stewards (Weaver, 2006: 202). On the flipside of eco-tourism development is the fact that tourism – even eco-tourism – increases the likelihood of negative environmental impacts on the destination's environment. It may increase pollution, change the behaviour of animals, and put pressure on limited resources. This has resulted in eco-tourism sometimes being criticised as being a mere marketing ploy – indeed Wheeller (1991) goes even further and points to eco-tourists as an inherent part of the problem. He says eco-tourists add to the environmental damage of tourism by constantly looking for the new, the exotic, the unspoilt, and the vulnerable. By their very presence in a vulnerable natural environment, they risk causing the most irreversible damage.

Agro-tourism

Agro-tourism is sometimes confused with rural tourism, but the two are inherently different. Rural tourism is the more general term and refers to tourism activities that take place in rural areas. Agro-tourism refers to a specific set of activities, organised by farmers for tourists: the tourist stays on the farm and engages in everyday working activities. This form of tourism is firmly based in the customs and culture of the area and tends to involve close contact between hosts and visitors. The customers for this type of tourism, who usually travel with their families, tend to be educated and of predominantly urban origin. They avoid mass tourism and tend to be environmentally conscious (Lopez and Garcia, 2006).

Israel was an important destination for agro-tourism in the 1960s and 1970s, when many young people travelled to the country to volunteer in kibbutzim, or communal farms. Each kibbutz was run by a community of families who aimed to be self-sufficient. Tourists who visited the kibbutz helped with the farm work and learnt about the traditions, language, history, and customs of the residents. A traditional kibbutz experience like this still exists, but increasingly kibbutzim are inviting tourists to stay as guests and not volunteers. Although ecology and the working of the farm usually still takes a central place, the guest can also engage in leisure activities, such as relaxing by the pool, going on hiking tours, or playing sports (www.agrotour-israel.co.il).

Managing Environmental Impacts

Source: Lynn Minnaert

Because of the new emphasis on the need for environmental sustainability within the tourism sector, the purely economic view of tourism is increasingly being left behind in favour of a more realistic view, that also takes the environmental costs of the industry into account. The management of negative environmental impacts therefore becomes central. Part of this will be achieved via efficient visitor management (discussed in more detail in Chapter 11). This section will specifically look at managing environmental impacts and will examine three key steps in achieving this: determining carrying capacity, policy and planning, and the role of partnerships.

Key Concepts in Environmental Management _____

Carrying Capacity

Carrying capacity can be defined as the maximum pressures a tourism destination, attraction or resource can be subjected to before irreversible damage is inflicted. Carrying capacity can be interpreted in different ways: socially, economically, and environmentally. On an environmental level, it can refer to the maximum number of people that can visit or make use of a natural area before it is damaged irreversibly, or it can refer to the maximum level of development (in terms of constructing buildings, roads, and other infrastructure) before the same effect ensues (Coccossis and Mexa, 2004).

Although carrying capacity is a widely used concept in tourism studies, scholars are increasingly agreeing that a fixed, quantitative view of it is not useful: in other words, the notion that there is a fixed ceiling, a threshold number of visitors, which tourism should not exceed, has been largely discredited (Holden, 2008: 190). Instead, a more flexible view of the concept is now often adopted: carrying capacity assessments today usually allow for a gradual increase in visitation, whilst management strategies are implemented to make this possible in a sustainable way. However, it needs to be emphasised here that this more flexible approach may not be suitable for highly fragile natural environments or destinations where there are no resources available to allow for environmental management strategies (Weaver, 2006).

Limits of Acceptable Change

An alternative to the concept of carrying capacity is 'limits of acceptable change' (LAC). Where carrying capacity is focused on keeping the destination the same and not causing irreversible change, this model projects which changes would be desirable or acceptable, considering the potential of the area for tourism. LAC does not view the environmental needs of the destination as separate entities, but links them with social and economic factors: some level of environmental change may be accepted if there are significant social and economic benefits. In practice, the system adopts a set of indicators (e.g. pollution levels, tourist satisfaction, employment, etc.) that are regularly monitored to see if the (environmental, social, and economic) aims of the project are being achieved (Holden, 2008).

Within environmental management, determining the carrying capacity or the limits of acceptable change should be the first task. Together with Environmental Impact Assessments, these can form the basis of effective environmental management via policy, planning, and partnerships. The complexity and expense of managing this process has led to it mainly being implemented in destinations in developed countries.

Environmental Impact Assessments

Environmental Impact Assessments (EIAs) systematically examine the potential future environmental impacts of development on the destination. Where carrying capacity assessments are carried out for existing facilities and attractions, an EIA is often (but not always) conducted ahead of new developments – the positive and negative impacts on the local environment are predicted and evaluated. Although there is no set structure for how an EIA should be conducted, this usually includes five stages:

- Identifying the impact.
- Predicting/measuring the impact.
- Interpreting the significance of the impact.
- Displaying the results of the assessment.
- Developing appropriate monitoring schemes (Holden, 2008: 192).

Conducting an EIA is an intensive process that includes the participation of, and consultation with, the different stakeholders in the development – as such it is a time-consuming and expensive exercise. Nevertheless, because of the growing emphasis governments place on reducing the negative environmental impacts of tourism, it has now become a part of the legal requirements for new developments in many countries. EIAs are mostly used in the planning stage, where they play a role in identifying environmentally unsound proposals, or in supporting planners in making amendments to proposals to make them more environmentally friendly. Despite their benefits as a planning tool, EIAs have also been criticised: because of their cost, they are difficult to enforce in developing countries. Butler (1993) also highlights that small-scale enterprises, which make up a large part of the tourism industry, are not subjected to EIAs, thus making their environmental impact incremental and cumulative.

Policy and Planning

The public sector can play an important role in minimising negative environmental impacts via effective policy and planning. (The role of policy is discussed in more detail in Chapter 11.) These strategies can usually be divided into two main groups: land use strategies (how the space is used and which new developments are allowed) and visitor management strategies. Visitor management strategies are explained in more detail in Chapter 12. This section will focus more specifically on land use strategies such as zoning and development standards. Apart from policy and planning, the public sector also has a range of practical management tools at its disposal, such as legislation and taxation. These will be discussed later in this chapter.

The negative environmental impacts of tourism tend to increase as tourism develops in the destination. *Land use planning* refers to the actions and decisions governments take with regard to how the land is used, which types of uses are allowed, and which guidelines for development are set. A good way to control the negative environmental impacts of the tourism industry is to regulate where and how it is developed in the first place. *Zoning* is a tool for land use planners: the term refers to regulating land use by dividing the area into zones with specific uses. The guiding principles of zoning are usually to conserve environmental features and to not mix uses that are incompatible. A nightlife area, for example, would not necessarily be compatible with residential developments built very close by. Similar activities may be clustered, the access to certain areas may be restricted, and undesirable buildings may be relocated to alternative areas (Jafari, 2003). To achieve a sustainable balance of tourism use and natural conservation on beaches, for example, specific zones may be allocated for boating and water sports. Jet skis and recreational boating could lead to foreshore erosion and water and air pollution (Lück, 2008). Planners can reduce the pressure on the natural resources by providing an alternative space for the water sports activities – this is referred to as space zoning. On top of this, the activity may be only allowed at certain times of the day – this is referred to as time zoning (Hall and Page, 2002). It needs to be noted here that environmental concerns may not be the only reason for establishing different zones: a separate zone for water sports might also improve the safety and enjoyment of both the sports users and recreational users of the beach.

Development standards are another tool that governments and local communities can use in land use planning. These are conditions and restrictions that are set for different aspects of new developments. Weaver (2006) gives the following examples:

- *Density controls*: the number of accommodation units that are allowed per hectare or square kilometre. These apply not only to residential developments, but also to hotels.

- *Height restrictions*: although high buildings are not necessarily environmentally unsustainable, they can cause aesthetic pollution in areas where they are inappropriate, such as rural areas.

- *Site coverage*: the amount of space that is covered by buildings, compared to the level of open space.

- *Setbacks*: the amount of space that needs to be maintained around landscape features. An example here is the mandatory distance between a tourism development and the beach.

- *Building standards*: these can relate to energy efficiency, waste management, and building materials.

- *Landscaping*: the conservation of open spaces, trees, and native plants.

- *Noise regulations*: restrictions on the levels of noise that are allowed and the times during which they are allowed. Theme parks, airports, and nightclubs may be affected by these regulations.

Partnerships and Collaborations

The provision of tourism depends on a range of different stakeholders – for example transport providers, accommodation facilities, public sector planners, and attractions. All of these stakeholders potentially have an impact on the environment, and there is a growing consensus that to achieve environmental sustainability all of these stakeholders need to work collectively. Partnerships or collaborations are often cross-sector initiatives, including representatives from the public and private sector, and from the local community: 'This is not to say that sustainable tourism development cannot result from partnerships within one sector. Examples from the tourism field abound, such as recent initiatives by hotel and restaurant associations to promote environmental responsibility through recycling and other eco-efficiency measures. However, the negotiation, mutually determined goals and actions, and monitoring resulting from cross-sector partnerships make it more likely that these initiatives will result in sustainable outcomes' (Selin, 1999: 261).

Bramwell and Lane (2000) highlight a number of benefits of partnerships and collaborations. The involvement of a wide range of stakeholders gives a better overview of the problems under discussion, improves democratic decision making, and may increase the likelihood of a successful implementation. A more creative solution may be found by working together. By pooling their resources, the different stakeholders in the partnership may also put these to more effective use. Nevertheless, there are also a number of potential problems. It is important that a wide range of stakeholders take part in the collaboration or partnership for it to be effective. There is also the risk that the collaboration is mere window-dressing, because the more powerful stakeholders do not take the views of other stakeholders into account. The process can also be costly and time-consuming.

Management Tools

Environmental management strategies can be executed via two approaches: these are also called 'hard' and 'soft' measures (see also Chapter 11). Kuo (2002) summarises the differences between the two approaches as follows. Hard measures aim to regulate tourist activities in a destination: they can take the form of access restrictions, rules and regulations, zoning and patrolling.

These measures are firm and binding, and not voluntary. Soft measures aim to educate and influence the visitor and can take the form of information provision, recommendations and declarations, and marketing. Soft measures are moral rather than legal and cannot be easily enforced. The following sections will discuss examples of both hard and soft measures that are used in environmental management. Legislation, taxation and the idea of carbon credits are introduced as hard measures, whereas labelling schemes and codes of conduct are introduced as soft schemes.

Legislation and Regulations

Tourism businesses, like other businesses, are required to comply with environmental legislation and regulations. In most countries, legislation exists regarding air quality, noise levels, land contamination, planning and land use, vehicle emissions, and waste management. So far the industry has largely relied on self-regulation and soft measures (such as recommendations, codes of ethics, and eco-labels), but due to the size and rapid growth of the industry perhaps more hard legislation is necessary. Unsurprisingly, the tourism industry generally fears the restrictive effect these laws could have. Holden (2003: 105) comments that increased litigation and more extensive environmental legislation, including the requirement for more detailed Environmental Impact Assessments, would be likely to restrict tourism development and increase the likelihood of a denial of access to nature areas for tourism. Subsequently, there would seemingly be little direct benefit or incentive for the majority of tourism stakeholders, including government, industry, and local communities.

Taxation

Environmental taxation puts into practice the 'polluter pays' principle: the person who causes the environmental damage is here also the person who needs to pay to rectify that damage. Taxes can be levied on tourism businesses or directly on tourists. Both methods may be implemented either through the general tax system of the economy or through specific plans. The World Tourism Organization has identified 40 different types of taxes applied to the tourism industry in both developed and developing countries (Gooroochurn and Sinclair, 2005: 479). Of these 41 forms of taxation, three are environmental: eco-tax; levies on CO_2 emissions; and landfill tax. Economists have long argued that taxes and charges can achieve the same goals as regulation and in a shorter time (Mak, 2004).

The levy of environmental tourist taxes is a popular notion, but so far the implementation of these taxes has proved to be problematic. A tourism tax was introduced in the Balearic Islands (Mallorca, Minorca, Ibiza, and Formentera), but was soon dropped. The Balearic Islands, and Mallorca and Ibiza in particular, are well-established mass tourism destinations, but also ones that are characterised by poor planning and overdevelopment. Tourism here is highly seasonal and the high visitor numbers in the peak season lead to pollution and water shortages. The eco-tax was introduced in 2002, after heavy political resistance, and was charged via accommodation providers. The tourist paid an average of €1 per day – the cost ranged from €0.25 to €2 depending on the accommodation classification. The proceeds were used to support green marketing, clean up beaches, encourage energy-saving projects in hotels, and contribute to the acquisition of areas of natural beauty in the countryside and the revitalisation of agriculture (Boniface and Cooper, 2005). Even though the tax raised almost €25 million in its first year, it was dropped in 2003 as soon as a new government was elected.

The most common form of environmental tourist tax is probably levies on transport. Aviation in particular has been targeted due to its high level of carbon emissions compared to other transport modes. In February 2007, the British government doubled Air Passenger Duty to reflect the environmental cost of flying. The intra-EU economy rate was raised from £5 to £10 and the non-economy rate from £10 to £20, while the long-haul economy rate was raised from £20 to £40 and the non-economy rate from £40 to £80 (HM Treasury, 2006: 176). In Montenegro, tourists, like residents, pay an eco-tax on motorised vehicles. The revenue from the tax is invested in environmental improvements (www.ecotax-montenegro.gov.me).

Carbon Credits/Carbon Trading

Carbon credits and carbon trading are concepts that play a role in the creation of an international carbon market: this market-based system is proposed as a potentially effective way to reduce carbon emissions. In theory, the mechanism is simple. Under existing or future international agreements, participating nations agree to reduce their carbon emissions to a certain level. Nations that struggle to meet their emissions targets can buy carbon credits from other nations, which either have no emissions target (as is currently the case for developing nations under the **Kyoto Protocol**), or have reduced their emissions below their agreed target. Like any tradable commodity, the price of carbon credits is largely determined by supply and demand (Laurance, 2007: 20). The Kyoto Protocol encourages these trading schemes on a national and international level, but some commentators have also called for trading schemes between individuals (also called personal carbon trading). This would involve allocating every individual a number of tradable energy units per year (Egger, 2007). An

Kyoto Protocol: An environmental treaty aimed at reducing carbon emissions and tackling climate change

individual who takes a large number of flights per year, for example, would have to pay for extra credits, or try to reduce their carbon credits somewhere else, by using public transport or using less energy. Several schemes are currently in operation, but have as yet had little direct impact on travel habits and carbon emissions via tourism.

Labelling/Auditing Schemes

Eco-labels can be awarded to tourism providers and destinations. A range of eco-labels exists, targeting different aspects of the tourism industry: beaches, hotels, camping sites, marinas and events. Font and Buckley (2001) describe the role of eco-labels as threefold:

- *For the consumer*: to guide consumers in choosing more environmentally-friendly product choices.

- *For the suppliers*: to market and promote the environmental efforts of companies and destinations, to incentivise them to improve their economic performance, and to support and guide their efforts.

- *For the government*: to provide a voluntary instrument that encourages environmental sustainability, that can complement legislation.

Most labels are funded by the public or the voluntary sector. This funding is needed to pay for the development of the label, to manage the verification process, and to hire staff to do the administration. Most labels cannot fund these activities via membership fees alone.

'Greenwashing': Companies are said to 'greenwash' when they make green claims to improve their image, but do not make profound changes to the way they operate

These labels are often presented as a way to standardise and validate the green claims companies make: as consumers are becoming more environmentally aware, it is often said that 'green sells' – still, many companies are accused of **'greenwashing'**, so that consumers do not always know which claims to believe. The labels can help tourists to make an informed choice. This can only happen if a label is credible: because many labels exist, the interest and knowledge of the public about them can be rather low – in the worst case, it may even put customers off. At present, there is no label that is globally recognised and subscribed to, although there are some that have gained popularity on a more local level. NEAP (Nature and Ecotourism Accreditation Programme) in Australia, for example, is a dominant label for tour operators. Europe has the largest number of eco-labels, most of which are small-scale and apply to the accommodation sector. Eco-labels are also appearing in the developing world: Kenya, for example, has its own Eco-rating Scheme, which awards accommodation providers with a bronze, silver, or gold rating. The Smart Voyager scheme also certifies eco-friendly cruise ships in the Galapagos Islands.

Developing one global eco-label for tourism may be beneficial in terms of credibility, but is hard to achieve in practice. It would be difficult to ensure, for example, that the verification process would be carried out to equal specifications in different countries, and misuse may be likely. The tourism sector consists of complex and varied industries: it would be hard to develop one eco-label that could certify a ski chalet, a beach, and a marina at the same time. It may be more realistic to aim towards a range of eco-labels that could be used on a wide geographical scale by their product category.

Codes of Conduct/Codes of Ethics

Weaver (2006) describes codes of conduct (also called codes of ethics) as a set of guidelines that aim to influence the attitudes and behaviour of those claiming adherence to these. Such codes are voluntary: people or businesses can choose to sign up to them, but there are no legal penalties for not adhering to them. They can be useful awareness-building tools and are quick and easy to implement as opposed to hard legislation. From this perspective they offer many advantages for the tourism industry, but there are also disadvantages: because they are not binding, it is easy for a tourism business to sign up to a code of ethics and not significantly change their business behaviour. As with any form of self-regulation, the success of the code is dependent on how serious the business decides to be in implementing it. Mowforth and Munt (2003) highlight that most codes of conduct are not even monitored by independent bodies and can be seen as covert marketing exercises. Codes of ethics can also be rather general and focus on environmental principles, rather than providing real help and support mechanisms that are also economically sustainable.

A wide range of different codes of conduct is in use, some of which focus particularly on tourists or communities involved in tourism, whereas others target tourism businesses. For tourists and the local community, codes of conduct will usually promote a responsible use of resources, showing respect for wildlife and local cultures, reducing waste, and using local products and suppliers. For tourism businesses, they tend to focus on the same issues, in addition to the use of environmental auditing and business practices.

An increasing number of eco-tourism tour operators have developed their own code of conduct that is sent out to clients before their holiday. These may provide a form of 'moral suasion' (Weaver, 2006: 114) for the tourist: even though these codes are not legally binding, on a group holiday there is a form of social control, and not following the code could result in disapproval from fellow travellers and a loss of face. Many of these codes include practical guidelines instead of focusing on more general environmental principles. Asia Adventures, a private tour operator in Cambodia, sends its travellers a code of conduct before departure that includes (amongst other advice) the following environmental guidelines:

> Consider what you pack in your suitcase before leaving home. Waste disposal systems in many developing countries are ill equipped to deal with the increased pressures that tourism brings, and a few simple measures can make an enormous difference to the effect you have on your destination. Where possible remove the wrapping of packaged goods before you leave, e.g. unwrap soaps and take bottles/tubes out of boxes. Please take more harmful waste, such as batteries, back home with you where they may be disposed of or recycled more responsibly;

> Consider bringing a refillable water bottle with you as these can often be refilled hygienically from large water containers in hotels and certain attractions, this limits the amount of plastic bottled water you would use;

> Try to reduce other plastic use, for example when shopping use your own bag to carry purchases, and refrain from having straws with your drinks;

> On our tours we have a 'zero litter' policy – 'carry in, carry out', so please do not drop litter. As well as being unsightly, bottles, cans, plastic, cigarette butts, etc. can be deadly to wild animals;

> Remember that in many places water is a very precious commodity and should not be wasted, use a minimum both in your accommodation and whenever possible throughout your trip, e.g. turn off the tap when brushing your teeth, take a shower rather than a bath;

> In addition where toilet facilities exist, however unsavoury, they should be used. Where they do not, always bury your waste and make sure it is never near (at least 30m) from a water source. (www.asia-adventures.com)

Summary

This chapter has provided an overview of the environmental impacts of tourism. Many of these are negative: tourism may increase pollution, disturb animal life and habitats, and have a detrimental effect on the built environment. The activities and behaviours of tourists may add to the environmental cost of tourism. Nevertheless, tourism can also have positive impacts, by increasing protection and conservation, or encouraging regeneration. The concept of environmental sustainability has been discussed and linked to a number of new tourism forms that have this concept at their core. Finally, a number of guiding principles of environmental management were reviewed and a set of management tools discussed.

In brief, it can be said that the development of mass tourism has tended to take the natural environment, on which it is often very dependent, for granted.

Tourism operators and tourists themselves nowadays often show a greater awareness of these impacts and positive signs of change can be noted. However, with the industry growing at a relentless pace, much still needs to be done before the industry can pride itself on being environmentally sustainable.

 ■ **Self-test Questions**

1   The environmental problems caused by tourism are often highlighted in the media and there are groups who discourage regular foreign travel. How do you think this has impacted on tourist behaviour? Has it affected the travel choices you make?

2   This chapter has discussed hard and soft measures to reduce the negative environmental impacts of tourism. Which do you think are most effective and why?

3   Regeneration schemes have been accused of leading to placelessness and an homogenisation of the built environment. Do you feel this is true in the case of Valencia? Would this be a place you would be inclined to visit?

Further Reading

Font, X. and Buckley, R. (2001) *Tourism Ecolabelling: Certification and Promotion of Sustainable Management.* Wallingford: CABI.

Holden, A. (2008) *Environment and Tourism.* London and New York: Routledge.

Smith, M. (2007) *Tourism, Culture and Regeneration.* Wallingford: CABI.

Weaver, D. (2006) *Sustainable Tourism.* Oxford: Elsevier Butterworth-Heinemann.

Useful Websites

Blue Flag: www.blueflag.org
The Darwin Foundation: www.darwinfoundationorg
Greenpeace: www.greenpeace.org
The International Fund for Animal Welfare: www.ifaw.org
Responsible Tourism Awards: www.responsibletourismawards.com
Secretariat of the Antarctic Treaty: www.ats.aq
Surfers Against Sewage: www.sas.org.uk

11 The Management of Visitors

The voyage of discovery lies not in finding new landscapes, but in having new eyes. (Marcel Proust, 1923: 53)

The Red Fort in Delhi, India

Source: Sandra Charrasse

Learning Outcomes

After reading this chapter you will understand:

- that visitor management is made up of two elements: the needs of the tourism resource (e.g. an attraction, destination, natural area) and the needs of the visitor
- the concepts of carrying capacity and quality management with regard to visitor management
- the different strategies and tools that can be used in visitor management plans, both at the level of the visitor and at the level of the site
- examples of how technology can support visitor management.

Introduction

The previous chapters have discussed the positive and negative economic, social and environmental impacts tourism development can have on destinations. Visitor management is an area of tourism studies that is specifically aimed towards limiting the negative impacts of visitors on destinations, and ensuring that the visitor has an enjoyable experience. Growing global tourism demand has reinforced the importance of visitor management, as it plays a central role in sustainable tourism management, particularly in established and successful tourism destinations, where resources may be stretched or over-used due to the volume of tourists that make use of them. Different types of destinations can be vulnerable to the negative impacts of tourists and tourism: visitor management can be applied to destinations with natural, historic or purpose-built attractions.

In this chapter we discuss the aims of visitor management and how these are implemented in practice, and specify some of the negative impacts that a visitor management plan can aim to limit. One of the aims of visitor management, the safeguarding of quality tourism experiences, will be presented in detail. We also give examples of different visitor management tools and techniques destinations can make use of. Finally, the role of technology in visitor management is examined.

The Need for Visitor Management

'The dilemma of visitor attractions is that, generally speaking, the greater the exposure of the site to visitors, the greater is the potential for negative visitor impacts to arise' (Garrod, 2008: 166). Indeed, the previous chapters have shown that tourism can have many positive as well as negative impacts. In many cases, the negative impacts will be felt more strongly when the pressures of tourism, or the volumes of tourists, increase. Visitor management strategies aim to limit the negative impacts of tourism and tourists by balancing the needs of tourists with those of the destination or attraction. The concept thus consists of two equally important parts: protecting the destination, specific sites and the local population; and ensuring that the tourist is offered a quality experience. This section will mainly concentrate on the first element, the needs of the destination; the following section will discuss the quality of the visitor experience in more detail.

Visitor management plans can address a wide range of pressures that are caused by tourists, and which pressures are included often depends on the type of destination the plan is developed for: natural parks, for example, experience different problems from those of historic cities. Even though it is thus hard to generalise the objectives of visitor management plans, these often include the following: to avoid overcrowding; to influence tourists' behaviour; and to address traffic-related problems. Garrod (2008) also mentions objectives to address social impacts and authenticity issues – these concepts are discussed in Chapter 9.

To Avoid Overcrowding

When tourist numbers increase, it is not always possible to increase the space or facilities for these extra tourists at the same rate. Historic cities, for example Bruges or Venice, are often typified by small winding streets. In smaller seaside resorts there may be enough parking for residents, but not necessarily for all the extra tourists during the peak season. In these conditions overcrowding may become a problem for the destination or attraction: it may cause negative environmental impacts, reduce the visitor experience, and affect the quality of life of the residents. The overcrowding may occur only in certain areas (e.g. at the entrance of an attraction, near a popular facility) or throughout the destination or attraction. Overcrowding can be a problem at certain times of the year, such as during festivals or in the peak season, or may be a constant problem. What constitutes overcrowding is, up to a certain point, subjective: some tourists like the buzz of a crowd, whereas others would find this rather stressful or unpleasant. It will also depend on the type of destination or attraction and how severe the impacts of overcrowding are: in cities, crowds may not have the same detrimental environmental impacts as in fragile natural environments.

Crowds visiting the Sacré Coeur in Paris

Source: Sandra Charrasse

Snapshot 11.1 Visitor Management in Venice

A typical example of a destination that is faced with overcrowding is Venice. In 2006 it attracted 15 million visitors, in a city that covers just three square miles. For many years the government has tried to implement initiatives to reduce the negative impacts of mass-visitation on the built environment of the destination and also on the visitor experience. Mass tourism has also changed the actual fabric of the city: many residents have moved out of Venice because they feel the pressures of tourism are just too overwhelming. Overcrowding thus affects the city on three levels: firstly, it causes damage to the natural and built environment; secondly, it reduces the visitor experience and thus damages the appeal of the destination; and thirdly, it threatens to turn Venice from a functioning city into an open-air museum. In November 2010, a resident organisation protested that the city had become a theme park: they handed out Disney-style maps and 'free tickets' to what they ironically called 'Veniceland'. The group claimed that the 55,000 day trippers double the population each day in the historic centre, while at night it is an empty ghost town (http://www.telegraph.co.uk/news/worldnews/europe/italy/8119924/ Protesters-invite-Venetians-to-the-Veniceland-theme-park-in-bid-to-save-the-city.html).

Visitor management techniques can be used to discourage one type of tourist whilst attracting another. As the snapshot above shows, big groups of day visitors bring many negative impacts to the destination, like overcrowding, but do not always bring many benefits: they tend to spend much less than overnight visitors. To discourage day visitors destinations may put a range of visitor management techniques in place, such as limiting access for coaches or marketing overnight packages.

To Influence Tourists' Behaviour

This refers to general damage that may occur to a destination or attraction due its everyday use by visitors. Visitors do not necessarily aim to do damage to the destination or attraction, but because of the sheer volume of them they can still have a negative impact. Garrod (2008: 168) gives as examples of wear and tear, trampling, handling, humidity, temperature and pilfering.

Trampling refers to when tourists walk on certain areas (usually in more fragile natural areas), damaging vegetation and preventing nature from naturally recuperating.

Handling in this context refers to tourists touching historic artefacts, buildings or plants, and thus causing damage to them.

Humidity and *temperature* can cause damage because visitors, just by being there and breathing, can change the temperature and humidity levels that support the conservation of an attraction or resource. The thousands of tourists who are breathing every day inside the tombs of the Egyptian kings are causing damage to wall carvings and paint. The grave sites of the boy king Tutankhamun and of Queen Nefertiti and Seti I have so much humidity that fungus is growing on the walls. The Egyptian authorities are now expected to announce plans to close at least those three tombs to the public completely, replacing them with replicas – otherwise the tombs could disappear in between 150 and 500 years (http://www.guardian.co.uk/culture/2011/jan/17/tutankhamun-tomb-to-close?INTCMP=SRCH).

Pilfering is used to describe tourists taking home elements of a historic or natural attraction as souvenirs. Usually this is done without malicious intent, but can cause damage to the destination or the attraction. Haspengouw, a rural region in Belgium famous for its apple orchards, noted a big increase in visitors in 2009 after featuring in a popular TV series. Many farmers complained that some tourists were leaving the area with bags full of apples, thus damaging their business. A local government initiative was started to make tourists aware of the impacts of their actions for the farmers, and the police put extra patrols in place during the tourist season (http://www.nieuwsblad.be/article/detail.aspx?articleid=173BD1LS).

Finally, visitor management techniques may be used to keep visitor groups with different behaviours separate in different areas. Zoning (as discussed in Chapter 10) may be a way to achieve this. One example of zoning policy is that of Leicester Square in London. This area, together with neighbouring Soho, is central in London's nightlife, with a wide variety of bars, clubs, restaurants, and cinemas. In the late 1990s, Westminster Council attempted to create a 24-hour economy by creating a nightlife zone and granting licences to many large-scale drinking establishments. This policy created heavy pressures on the area as alcohol-fuelled violence and anti-social behaviour became common. More recently Westminster Council has changed its approach by attempting to turn the area into a more family-friendly entertainment zone. They are encouraging al fresco dining on the square and have insisted at least one family movie is shown every evening. The council has also become more cautious when granting licences to nightclubs and bars (Carmona et al., 2008).

To Reduce Traffic-related Problems

Natural environments or historic sites may not be equipped for the traffic that is generated by tourism. There may be lack of suitable parking spaces, or the roads may not be suited to heavy usage (e.g. by coaches). Exhaust fumes from motor vehicles can also cause damage and pollution. It is not only the destination or attraction that is at risk: traffic-related problems may also lead to an increased risk of accidents for visitors and staff.

Historic cities often struggle to provide sufficient car parking spaces and coach parking spaces for visitors. There is often a lack of suitable drop-off points for coaches as the streets are usually narrow, so these may need to park rather far away from the city centre. In some destinations, park and ride schemes are used to improve visitor flow, or local 'ambassadors' will provide a welcome to coach groups. The visitor management strategy for the Royal Borough of Windsor and Maidenhead ('Our Vision of 2012 and Beyond') mentions this as a particular weakness of the destination:

> Limited parking and congestion are significant concerns as this can have a negative impact on the visitor experience. The cost of parking varies significantly between different operators and transport links between hotels, town-centre and attractions are inadequate. This encourages visitors to use their cars (53% arrive by car and 23% by rail). Coaches can't get close enough to the castle and the coach drop-off point does not provide a good first impression of the destination. (Royal Borough of Windsor and Maidenhead, 2008: 65)

Respecting Carrying Capacity

Visitor management can thus be defined as the combination of measures that aim to reduce negative impacts such as the above. Alternatively, visitor management can be seen as aiming to establish and respect the *carrying capacity* of a destination or attraction. This concept is also discussed in Chapter 10.

Richardson and Fluker (2004) define carrying capacity as the level of tourist activity an area can sustain without lasting economic, social or environmental impacts, or without reducing the quality of the visitor experience. They distinguish between five different types of carrying capacity:

- *Physical*: the maximum number of visitors that can be physically accommodated on site. For some attractions, this is fairly easy to establish: for example in a planetarium the carrying capacity per session is likely to be similar to the number of seats in the theatre, but for other attractions, such as national parks, or for whole destinations, this number is often harder to establish precisely. The physical carrying capacity may often be higher than the four other types of carrying capacity that follow below.

- *Ecological*: the number of visitors an attraction or destination can sustain before unacceptable or irreparable damage is done to its ecological resources.

- *Social*: the number of visitors an attraction or destination can sustain before the tolerance of the host community is surpassed.

- *Psychological/perceptual*: the number of visitors an attraction or destination can sustain before the visitor experience declines for the majority of visitors. This type of carrying capacity is most dependent on the tourist: what for one tourist may be an unacceptable number of people, could be for another a pleasant crowd. Nevertheless, one can state that the psychological carrying capacity of a destination or attraction is surpassed when the majority of visitors consider that the number of tourists is affecting their experience negatively.

- *Economic*: the number of visitors an attraction or destination can sustain before other desirable economic activities are squeezed out. This type largely refers to the dependency of certain destinations on tourism, and the fact that it is usually better to rely on a diverse economy with different active sectors, than to rely overly on one sector alone.

Of these different types of carrying capacity, the *physical* carrying capacity is usually the higher number. It is likely that many destinations can physically accommodate more people than are suitable on an ecological, social and psychological level. It is also interesting that the concept of *psychological* carrying capacity focuses, not on the needs and characteristics of the destination, but on the needs of the visitors, and the quality of their experience. The next section will focus further on the quality of the visitor experience and how it can be managed.

Quality Management

Williams and Buswell (2003: 19) describe quality management as working towards 'continuous improvement, never being satisfied with what the organisation is delivering, and striving to do "better" to meet customers' needs'. Visitor management is aimed at meeting not only the needs of the destination, but also those of the visitor: a good visitor management policy is able to combine and respect both interests. This section will discuss the concepts of product and service quality and introduce approaches to quality management.

Product Quality

Quality management for tourism is often discussed from the viewpoint of service quality: tourism is after all a service sector. This does not mean that product quality is an unimportant concept for tourism. The main tourism product is the destination: the difficulty here is that this product is not delivered by one provider, but by a whole range of stakeholders: hotels, restaurants, taxi-drivers, attractions and natural resources. Many of these destination components offer a tangible product that can be assessed on quality, as well as a service.

Product quality has two aspects: functionality and appearance. On a basic level, products can be seen as lacking in quality when they are not functional: when they do not do what customers expect them to do. A customer, for example, will expect a comfortable night sleep, but if the bed in the hotel is uncomfortable, or the heating does not work, or the air-conditioning is too loud, then this expectation will not be fulfilled. Customers may also expect a product to be free from blemishes and cosmetic defects. In terms of tourism, this could refer to a tourist expecting a meal that looks appetising, or a beach that is not littered. When their expectations are not met, this is called a 'quality defect' (Twigg-Flessner, 2003). These concepts are usually applied to manufactured products such as cars or washing machines, but can, to a certain extent, also be applied to tourism.

Service Quality

If destinations aim to provide tourists with quality and enjoyable experiences, particular attention should be paid to the quality of the service provision. A great meal can easily be spoilt by a rude or unhelpful waiter and the most beautiful hotel will not be enjoyed much if the staff are unpleasant. Understanding that service quality can be key in customer satisfaction, many businesses now aim to monitor and enhance service quality. The basic principle thereby is often that 'customer perceptions should equal or exceed customer expectations for them to be satisfied with the service provided' (Williams and Buswell, 2003: 178). The extent to which expectations and service performance are similar or different will influence the extent to which customers are satisfied or dissatisfied (Wuest, 2001: 53).

The SERVQUAL model was developed in the 1980s and measures gaps in service delivery based on a number of criteria. The model was originally developed for the financial industries, but later adapted for tourism (Williams and Buswell, 2003). By comparing the expectations of the customer with the actual performance of the organisation at the time of the visit, customer satisfaction can be measured numerically, and areas where service is lacking in quality can be easily identified. Methods that can be used to measure service quality include, amongst others, questionnaires and focus groups.

Managing Quality

Different theories of and approaches to quality management have developed over time. The most recent approaches tend to focus on quality management as an integrated concept: quality management is not just the duty of the customer service staff or the quality manager, but can only be achieved by the organisation as a whole. This means that the entire organisation has to work together to meet (or surpass) the expectations of the customer. In most tourism organisations, this process is monitored and managed in-house: the business sets their own targets and trains their own staff. It is not only in the private sector that quality management is an explicit goal: quality is an increasing priority for the public sector too, where it can be enforced through, for example, tendering processes (Williams and Buswell, 2003).

One of the main tools that can be used in the quality management process is education and training. If quality is seen as the duty and responsibility of the whole organisation and every staff member in it, then staff need to be trained and informed about the standards the organisation is striving to achieve. In many organisations this would happen internally. In-house systems are non-accredited: this means they are developed by the organisation itself and not monitored by external organisations.

Accredited systems, involving training and quality control, have third-party certification (Williams and Buswell, 2003). The quality management process needs to be documented in accordance with the chosen system, and if all the requirements are met this can lead to certification. Organisations may choose to participate in accredited systems because an external quality certification is an objective proof of quality, and this may carry more weight with customers than the internal systems do.

Ezeego1 (http://www.ezeego1.co.in), India's biggest online travel website, was the first travel portal to be certified using the international quality management standard ISO 9001:2008. This standard 'gives the requirements for quality management systems, and is now firmly established as the globally implemented standard for providing assurance about the ability to satisfy quality requirements and to enhance customer satisfaction in supplier–customer relationships' (http://www.iso.org/iso/iso_catalogue/management_standards/quality_management/iso_9001_2008/faqs_on_iso_9001.htm). The standard lays down the quality requirements a system should meet, but does not dictate how exactly these should be achieved: ISO standards are thus not 'tick the box' lists. The organisation is invited to audit its own quality management systems and may also seek audits from clients or external organisations. The different aspects of quality management for this certification are: customer focus, leadership, the involvement of people, a process approach, a system approach to management, continual improvement, a factual approach to decision making, and mutually beneficial supplier relationships (www.iso.org).

Businesses engage in quality management not only to safeguard the experience of the visitor, but also to maximise their profitability. High quality products can demand higher prices whilst still maintaining customer satisfaction. Laws (2000: 74) points out that price and quality are closely related in customers' buying decisions, and that the price that is charged for a product affects their quality expectations. At a normal price, a high standard of service and amenities will please the client, but those same standards will only 'satisfy' clients paying premium rates. Customers enjoying normal or superior standards on a holiday for which they paid low prices will be pleased or delighted. In contrast, customers receiving normal levels of service in return for high prices will at best feel exploited, and if standards fall further, they are likely to experience (and express) anger. Low levels of service or amenities are likely to provide negative responses whatever the price paid for them.

Visitor Management Measures and Techniques

The previous sections have highlighted how visitor management strategies aim on the one hand to protect the resources (natural, historic and built environment) of an attraction or destination, and on the other hand to safeguard the quality of the visitor experience. In this section we will now concentrate on the practical tools and techniques that can be used to achieve successful visitor management. These can be categorised in different ways. Many authors make a distinction between hard and soft measures – both terms are explained below. Other authors also distinguish between visitor management techniques that impact on the level of the site (making physical changes to the site) and those that impact on the level of the visitor (changing behaviour).

Hard Versus Soft Measures

Richardson and Fluker (2004: 303) give the following definitions of hard and soft visitor management techniques:

- *Hard measures*: measures that can be enforced, that are firm and binding. Examples are physical restrictions on visiting attractions or destination areas, such as closing at certain times, the declaration of no-go zones, requirements for permits, selective parking, and the prohibition of vehicles in certain areas. There may also be financial restrictions such as entrance fees and pricing policies.

- *Soft measures*: measures that cannot be enforced as easily and are not as binding – they are, by contrast, persuasive. They may offer incentives for taking some action or sometimes act as a deterrent without the need for actual prohibition. Examples are directional signage, codes of ethics, codes of practice, and information sheets.

Soft measures are usually easier to introduce as there is no need for an enforcement mechanism. The idea is that by informing visitors about the impacts of their actions, and suggesting low-impact behaviours, they will behave in ways that will cause fewer negative impacts to the attraction or destination. The advantage of soft measures is that they do not come across as being very draconian; the disadvantage may be that one has to rely on visitors' goodwill.

Hard measures, however, need enforcement mechanisms: for example, if parking is prohibited in certain areas this needs to be enforced by parking wardens. Dedicated staff have to be on hand to enforce no-go zones or charge the entrance fee. This makes hard measures more complicated to introduce, but in return the guidelines may be followed more closely.

Snapshot 11.2   Yellowstone National Park

Attractions and destinations can choose to use just hard or just soft measures, or they can combine both. The Yellowstone National Park for example adopts a combined approach for the management of visitation in areas that are the habitat of grizzly bears. The purpose of bear management areas is to reduce the human impact on bears in high-density grizzly bear habitats. Grizzly bears can become aggressive when they feel that they or their cubs are under threat, so careful management of both the bears and the humans in their habitat is needed to provide a safe environment. Although incidents are rare (there are more visitors hurt by bison than by bears in Yellowstone), a female grizzly bear attacked three tourists on a campsite in the park in 2011, fatally injuring one. Eliminating human entry disturbance in specific areas prevents human/bear conflicts and provides areas where the animals can pursue natural behavioural patterns and other social activities free from human disturbance. Examples of hard measures include area closures and trail closures, and only allowing visitation in daylight hours or on established trails. Examples of soft measures include education and only allowing party sizes of four or more people, which will make more noise and are less likely to surprise bears (http://www.nps.gov/yell/parkmgmt/bearclosures.htm).

Visitor Management Techniques

There is a range of visitor management techniques that destinations and attractions can make use of. Often different techniques are combined to effectively address the problems caused by intense visitation. These techniques include:

- Increasing capacity.
- Making capacity more flexible.
- Site hardening.
- Restricting/forbidding access.
- Demarketing.
- Charging/pricing.
- Quota systems and timed entry.
- Queue management.
- Education and interpretation.

Increasing Capacity

In some cases the negative impacts of intensive visitation can be limited by increasing the capacity of an attraction. It may be possible to add a new building to a site, or to build an extension. If, for example, the quality of the visitor experience is reduced due to long queues at the lavatories or the catering facilities, this can be avoided by providing more facilities or making the existing facilities better. This is, of course, not an option for all destination areas or attractions. It may not be suitable for historic buildings to add a modern day extension, for example; nor is it possible to make a natural park or a lake bigger than it is.

In 2009, the Natural History Museum in London increased its capacity by opening the Darwin Centre in a landmark glass extension. The focal point of the extension is a giant cocoon structure, built to house 20 million specimens, encased in a glass box. In the cocoon, visitors can study live specimens such as tarantulas and metre-high plants. There is also a studio for events and a climate change wall (www.nhm.ac.uk). This extra facility has created more space for a popular museum that welcomed over 3,800,000 visitors in 2008/2009.

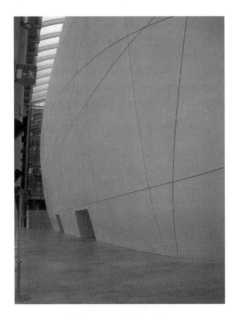

The Darwin Centre at the Natural History Museum in London

Source: Lynn Minnaert

Making Capacity More Flexible

Garrod (2008: 171) provides the following examples of making capacity more flexible, so that the negative impacts of tourism can be reduced without negatively affecting the visitor experience:

- *Extending opening times*: this reduces heavy visitor pressures by allowing visitation during a longer period of the day. For example, The Louvre museum in Paris is open until 10pm on Wednesdays and Fridays (www.louvre.fr).

- *Increasing staff levels*: staff, just like space, can be seen as a resource for an attraction or destination. Having more staff available can allow for increased interpretation or support, act as a deterrent against damaging behaviours by visitors, and enhance the visitor experience.

- *Opening more tills*: if queues at tills need to be managed, these can be reduced most easily by constructing or opening extra tills. This may require increased staffing levels. In some cases, automatic ticketing machines where customers can pay via credit card may reduce queues at tills, without the need for extra staff.

- *Opening additional areas for facilities, such as cafés*: at peak times of the year or day visitor pressures on facilities can be reduced by opening up a second area or space. This allows attractions to manage the space flexibly: if there are many visitors, there is extra space; if not, there is no need to staff this extra area. In many zoos, for example, some of the catering facilities are only open during the summer season.

- *Cross-training staff*: by training staff to perform a range of different tasks, the attraction or destination allows for greater flexibility in dealing with overcrowded areas when this is needed.

- *Managing flows of visitors and offering different routes*: if visitors take different routes through a museum, city, or natural park, this can improve the general visitor flow and avoid everyone being in the same place at the same time. This can be achieved through maps or signage. The location of toilets, souvenir shops, and meeting points at attractions is also an important element in the optimisation of visitor flows.

Site Hardening

Site hardening is often used to protect vulnerable natural environments, such a natural parks, from the negative impacts of tourism. Visitor managers may decide to protect the natural resources of the park by 'constructing a well-designed trail or recreation site, surfacing it with gravel, wood or pavement and adding fencing to keep visitors from trampling sensitive off-trail environments' (Cahill et al., 2008: 233). Trails are likely to have been positioned so as to protect sensitive habitats and vulnerable wildlife; the durable surfacing makes sure that visitors do not destroy vegetation by walking over it. Putting site hardening measures in place 'virtually severs the relationship between the amount of use and its associated resource degradation' (Cahill et al., 2008: 233). Other benefits are that trails provide a safe passage over inhospitable terrain and can accommodate a range of visitors who would otherwise be less likely or unable to visit the site (http://www.chebucto.ns.ca/recreation/orchid-congress/conserv5.pdf).

Even though site hardening has these benefits, there are also a number of disadvantages attached to this technique. If large numbers of visitors use the trails for example, they may start walking outside their edges when there is more use, and this can cause muddiness, widening, and erosion. Site hardening may also affect the visitor experience: paths and trails may be seen as artificial, ugly, or a barrier between the visitor and nature. And because tourists have to stick to set trails, they may feel they are limited in their freedom to explore the landscape (Cahill et al., 2008).

Restricting/Forbidding Access

The most drastic way to stop the negative impacts of tourism is to forbid access to a site, or part of it, altogether. Some commentators feel that tourism is by its nature opposed to conservation and that the needs of the resource are always more important than the needs of the visitor. This point of view reduces visitor management to one of its two functions: although it still protects the building, landscape or destination, the quality of the visitor experience is disregarded as visitation becomes impossible.

Tourism destinations and attractions are often very reluctant to close their doors to tourists altogether, and in practice this rarely happens – other means of achieving better visitor management are opted for. For some attractions, such as natural parks, forbidding access is also very difficult to achieve as these are too large to be cordoned off with fences or other barriers.

In 2006 there were calls to stop tourism on Mount Everest, the highest mountain in the world. The peak has also been described as the 'highest junk yard in the world': conservationists warn that the pollution and damage caused by tourists need to be halted for a few years, at least until the mountain is cleaned up. However, Sherpas in the area often rely on tourism for their livelihood – they oppose any sort of reduction in the number of climbing permits that are assigned each year (http://www.guardian.co.uk/world/2006/oct/27/outlook.development1?INTCMP=SRCH).

  Snapshot 11.3   The Lascaux II Show Caves

The Lascaux caves are a famous tourist attraction near Montignac in the Dordogne region of France. The caves were discovered in 1940 and contain primitive paintings of large animals from the Upper Palaeolithic era. They were opened in 1948, but by 1955 the paintings

(Continued)

(Continued)

had been visibly damaged by the effects of intense visitation – the main cause of the damage was the carbon dioxide in the breath of the visitors. To protect the paintings the caves were closed in 1963 and a replica of two of the cave halls was built about 200 metres away. Lascaux II, as this replica cave was named, opened to the public in 1983. The replica was produced over 10 years, using the same materials and techniques as the original cave painters. Demand for tickets to Lascaux II is high and the number of tickets sold per day is limited to 2,000. Even with these measures in place, the pressures of visitation have started to affect the replica caves: since 2008 the site has been closed several times per year to remove the dust caused by 270,000 visitors per year that covers the walls and damages the paintings (www.lascaux.culture.fr).

Source: Jack Versloot

Demarketing

Demarketing is a term used to describe a form of marketing that reduces the demand of visitors to be more in line with supply by raising prices or reducing advertising. Other strategies that can be used are introducing the need for reservations when tourists want to visit a site, or making the press aware of the negative impacts of tourism on the resources of an attraction or site (Richardson and Fluker, 2004). Demarketing can be used to decrease the overall number of visitors, or can be used to discourage certain types of visitors. It is also an important tool for influencing the expectations and attitudes visitors will bring to a site *before* they visit (Beeton, 2006), thus influencing their behaviour during the visit. Demarketing is also sometimes used to refer to a combination of different visitor management techniques in terms of pricing, entry controls, marketing, and behavioural education (Beeton, 2006).

Although the concept of demarketing is sometimes referred to as a total halt in marketing efforts, this rarely happens in practice. In most cases it is the shift from attracting as many visitors as possible via marketing, to attracting the right type of visitors via marketing, that is the key aim. In recent years, for example, Tunisia has repositioned itself as a destination rich in culture and history rather than just a beach destination. The website of the National Tourist Office of Tunisia includes categories about adventure travel, history, culture, and spa and golf tourism (www.cometotunisia.co.uk). The examples of the promotion campaign for Tunisia below focus on these exact elements, rather than just sun, sea, and sand.

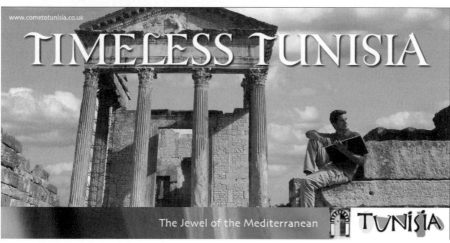

Source: © Courtesy of the Tunisian National Tourist Office.

Charging/Pricing

The demand for a product or service can be directly influenced by pricing. Destinations and attractions that aim to improve visitor flows and reduce the negative impacts of overcrowding can charge fees or increase prices to reduce demand at certain times of the day, week, or year. In this case, charging and pricing are used as mechanisms to steer demand away from peak periods, rather than to attract extra visitors in off-peak periods. Many tourism companies operate *seasonal pricing*, whereby prices go up during the peak season. This is apparent in the sector of inclusive holiday packages, where prices are often presented in tables by departure date. In the peak season few discounts are offered because there are enough customers who are willing to pay a premium fare. In the shoulder season the demand may be smaller, but there is an opportunity to stimulate demand via a variety of discounting practices (Laws, 2000: 69).

Pricing strategies may also be used more generally to influence demand: by lowering the price, demand for the tourism product can sometimes be increased; by increasing the price, the demand for the tourism product can sometimes be lowered. Some attractions will decide to apply high entrance fees to reduce overall visitor numbers and thus reduce the negative impacts of excess visitation. In the case of Bhutan (see the case study below) this principle has even been applied to the destination as a whole.

This approach is not always popular as it is sometimes seen as conflicting with the aim of providing equal access to all layers in society. This means that the higher price will impact much more on visitors with low incomes than on visitors with high incomes who can afford the fee anyway, whereas one group of visitors usually does not cause a more negative impact on the resource than the other. High prices are also sometimes discouraged for economic reasons: the secondary spend (in a shop and café for example) may go down if entrance prices go up (Garrod, 2008).

One example of a pricing strategy that could reduce visitor numbers is the Grand Palace in Bangkok, Thailand. The palace is one of the most famous attractions in the country, and home to the Emerald Buddha. The entrance fee to the attraction in 2008 was 300 Baht – a lot more expensive than many of the other temples and attractions in Bangkok, which can often be visited for 20 to 50 Baht (www.tourismthailand.org). The case study of Bhutan (see below) is another example of a destination using pricing to manage visitor numbers.

CASE STUDY 11.1

VISITOR MANAGEMENT IN BHUTAN

The kingdom of Bhutan is a small, landlocked country in the Himalayas, between India and China. After being cut off from the rest of the world for centuries, it started

(Continued)

(Continued)

to open up to outsiders in the 1970s, but is still fiercely guarding its ancient traditions (http://www.bbc.co.uk/news/world-south-asia-12480707). It has an exceptional visitor management strategy that relies heavily on hard measures and restrictions on visitor levels which go much further than those of most other destinations in the world.

The unusual nature of Bhutan's visitor management policy is linked to the history of tourism in the country. The tourism industry in Bhutan is still relatively young: the first tourists were allowed in 1974. At first, the tourism sector was fully controlled by the government, but is now increasingly run by operators in the private sector. In 2009, there were nearly 200 private tourism businesses (www.tourism.gov.bt).

Bhutan is ranked as one of the poorest countries in the world in terms of Gross National Product and the national poverty rate is estimated at 32 per cent (Bhutan Country Strategy Paper, 2007). Instead of striving towards material richness, the Bhutanese monarchy has famously promoted the philosophy of 'Gross National Happiness' (GNH), which strives to achieve a balance between the spiritual and the material (http://www.bbc.co.uk/news/world-14243512).

The country's main tourist attractions are its stunning natural beauty and its ancient Buddhist culture and architecture. Tourism is the main foreign investment sector and an important generator of foreign exchange revenue. However, instead of developing tourism at a rapid rate to maximise the economic benefits, Bhutan has adopted a restrictive, 'low volume, high value' approach to tourism. This is mainly due to the government's concern for the environment and cultural preservation (Bhutan Country Strategy Paper, 2007). In 2008, just over 27,600 tourists visited the country. Even though visitor numbers are now growing, the rise is limited when it comes to overall visitor numbers.

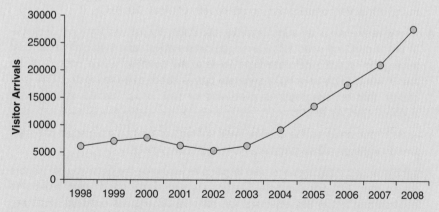

Figure 11.1   Tourist arrivals in Bhutan

Source: Tourism Council of Bhutan (2008: 15).

(Continued)

(Continued)

In terms of tourism revenue, it is clear that the average spend per tourist is high – see Table 11.1

Table 11.1   Tourism revenue in Bhutan

Year	Arrivals	Gross earnings ($US millions)	Growth/decline in annual revenue
2001	6,393	$9.195	−12.4%
2002	5,599	$7.980	−13.2%
2003	6,261	$8.324	+4.31%
2004	9,249	$12.502	+50.19%
2005	13,626	$18.546	+48.34%
2006	17,344	$23.919	+21.11%
2007	21,094	$29.846	+24.78
2008	27,636	$38.829	+30.1%

Source: Tourism Council of Bhutan (2008: 15).

Tourism management is Bhutan is achieved via the following measures.

The country mainly regulates the influx of visitors via its pricing strategy. Bhutan can only be reached by its own national airline, Druk Air. Due to this monopoly, visitors have no choice but to use the rather expensive flights that are on offer. Another form of pricing strategy is the imposing of tourist tariffs on all visitors. Tourists must come to Bhutan on a package tour, organised by a Bhutanese tour operator (foreign companies may not operate in Bhutan itself). The whole itinerary is then organised by this tour operator. The government has set a full inclusive price of $200 per visitor per day – of this price, 10 per cent goes to the foreign travel agent as a commission, 35 per cent goes to the government, and the rest is paid to the local tour operator. The tariff increases if the visitor wants to travel in a very small group or individually (Tobgay, 2008).

A second restriction is an administrative restriction. Tourist visas are not available at the airport and need to be arranged before travel, and visa clearance must have been received before a flight ticket to the country can be booked. If the tourist wants to go trekking, a separate permit needs to be requested. This is to ensure that no one route is over-used or new ones opened without prior approval (Tobgay, 2008).

In terms of demarketing, the country does not market itself on a big scale to attract foreign visitors; rather, targeted marketing is employed.

A number of soft measures are also in place to influence the behaviour of visitors during their trip. For example, visitors are requested not to give sweets to children and not to buy antiques. On national or religious holidays, tours are suspended. The presence of tour guides adds interpretation of these regulations for the tourists and increases understanding of why these guidelines are important. Selling tobacco in Bhutan is forbidden by law.

(Continued)

(Continued)

Visitor numbers in Bhutan and tourism infrastructure have risen in recent years but the rate of growth has been managed carefully because of the regulations above. The majority of visitors to Bhutan are over 60 years old, university educated, with a middle to high income, and very aware of sustainable tourism (Tourism Council of Bhutan, 2008; Tobgay 2008).

Reflective Questions

1 Think about the positive and negative social, environmental, and economic impacts of tourism. Which ones are maximised and which ones are minimised in Bhutan? Consider the advantages and disadvantages of this protectionist visitor management system.
2 What is the typical visitor profile of tourists in Bhutan? Is this a desirable visitor profile? Why?

Quota Systems and Timed Entry

Quota systems refer to the setting of visitor quotas, either daily or over a shorter period of time, that cannot be surpassed. The number of visitors may be limited, or the maximum size of a group may be limited. For attractions, one way of managing a steady flow of visitors throughout the day without surpassing the set quota, is by requiring visitors to pre-book a time for their visit. Immediate access is given if the capacity has not been reached, otherwise the entry may be delayed (Richardson and Fluker, 2004).This avoids the attraction being overcrowded at peak times of the day.

Timed tickets are common for popular attractions and also for exhibitions that may only be accessible for a short period of time. They may also be linked to a compulsory guided tour. An example of an attraction that uses this approach is the harem of the Topkapi palace in Istanbul. The palace dates from the fifteenth century and is one of the top attractions in the city. Although visitors can explore all the other parts of the palace freely, a visit to the harem needs to be booked in advance and is only possible as part of a guided tour. There is also an extra charge for visiting the harem. There are limited spaces available on this tour and visitors are recommended to book their place early (http://www.topkapisarayi.gov.tr).

Queue Management

Queues are often linked to tourism experiences: attractions, theme parks, airports, and toll booths are examples of tourism settings where queuing often

Queues at the Taj Mahal, India
Source: Sandra Charrasse

occurs. When this takes a long time or happens often, it can spoil the tourist's experience considerably. Badly managed queues can also become disorganised or disorderly. All this means that visitor managers should pay particular attention to queues when they plan their service provision.

Pearce (1997) points out that it is mainly a lack of control over the situation, and a lack of information, that will cause people in queues to experience stress and negative feelings. Individuals in long queues will often not know how many people are before them and how long the queue will take, and usually they cannot easily judge how long they have been in the queue already. They can also get bored because they are passive and not active.

Dawes and Rowley (1996) distinguish two goals in queue management: minimisation of the waiting on the one hand and optimisation of the waiting experience on the other hand. They give the example of Disneyworld as an attraction that has excellent queue management practices. Visitors there will regularly queue for long periods, sometimes even one to two hours for the most popular rides. Minimising the queues, for example by increasing the capacity with extra rides, is not something that can be done easily, so Disneyworld uses a range of techniques to make the waiting time at least *feel* shorter: they snake queues around barriers and corners and hide one section of the queue from another. They also install distractions for visitors to pass the time: there may be screens or displays to look at, or glimpses of the ride can be seen. Distractions can also be in the form of music, entertainment, or the screams of people on the rides that can heighten the sense of anticipation. Finally, there are signs that announce how long visitors will have to wait – and usually the time queuing is less than the time advertised. This means that when visitors become aware of the time, it is usually in a positive manner: rather than having to wait one hour for example, they will actually access the ride in 40 minutes.

Some tourism companies have made the reduction of queues a separate product, an option for which the customer can decide to pay a surcharge. Budget airlines like easyJet and Ryanair for example offer 'priority boarding' passes. Because these airlines operate free seating systems, whereby no specific seats are allocated to passengers, boarding the plane first not only avoids queuing, it also leads to passengers having a wider choice of seats. A similar system is operated by several theme parks, where tickets can be bought at an extra cost that will allow visitors to skip the queues for certain rides. The more rides are included in the ticket, the more expensive the surcharge becomes. At Thorpe Park in the UK, a 'Fast Track' ticket that can be used all day long on all applicable rides added £66.00 per person to the entry price in 2011 (www.thorpepark.com).

Education and Interpretation

The term 'interpretation' in the context of visitor management refers to the communication process that helps visitors understand the meaning of attractions, exhibits and heritage. Moscardo and Ballantyne (2008) give the examples of guided walks and tours, lectures and audio-visual presentations, signs, panels, guidebooks, pamphlets, brochures, and information centres. Cooper (1997) also adds interpretive media such as self-guided trails and reconstructions of the past. A more recent example is applications for electronic devices such as mobile phones and MP3 players.

Interpretation and education can also be provided by tour guides. Tours can be optional, or attractions can make them obligatory in certain areas or across the whole site. The Blue Badge guild is a membership organisation for tourist guides across the British Isles. All Blue Badge tourist guides have been trained and hold a specific qualification that informs them of the impacts of tourism and the importance of interpretation in the visitor management process.

The provision of interpretation can make the visitor experience more rewarding and increase sustainability as a soft measure: by informing visitors of the negative impacts of tourism, they can be encouraged to behave in a more sustainable fashion. However, simply providing information does not necessarily guarantee these improvements: 'The presence of on-site guardians does not guarantee the effectiveness of visitor management policies, any more than the presence of a guide guarantees that the visitor will receive adequate and appropriate information' (Shackley, 1998: 8).

The Role of Technology for Visitor Management

Visitor managers can make use of technology in a variety of ways to determine the best strategy for their attraction or destination. As many of the visitor management techniques described above may result in increased staff costs for the organisation (for example, if opening times are extended or extra facilities need to be provided), automation can help to make processes more effective and keep costs down. The following examples will illustrate how technology can help to count visitors, to monitor and restrict where they go, and to facilitate bookings both on and offline.

Counting Systems

Counting systems can support visitor management by providing an exact overview of the number of visitors that make use of a certain site during a certain time period. The data that are gathered with counting systems can be helpful in establishing a realistic and sustainable visitor quota and give an idea of the carrying capacity of the facility. By counting how many visitors there are at certain locations at various times of the day, managers can also determine visitor flows and use the data to see where extra staff may be needed. Counting systems come in a variety of forms, from rather basic to the more sophisticated. Visitors can, for example, be counted by having to pass through turnstiles. More sophisticated systems include sensors on walls or near doors, or under carpets. These sensors usually blend in with the surroundings and tend to go unnoticed by visitors; which means they do not affect the visitor experience.

 ### Snapshot 11.4   Mechanical Versus Video Turnstiles

An example of an attraction that successfully uses a mechanical counting system for visitor management is the Sauvabelin Tower in Lausanne, Switzerland. This tower is made completely out of locally sourced wood and offers a panoramic view of the city (www.tour-de-sauvabelin-lausanne.ch). The viewing platform is reached via 302 steps and measures 12 metres in diameter – this attraction can thus only be used safely by a limited number of visitors, as otherwise congestion would occur on the steps which could make the ascent or descent dangerous. To avoid accidents or spoiling of the experience, a metal turnstile at the entrance lets through 50 visitors at any one time. If more visitors try to enter, the turnstile will lock – only when one visitor leaves the attraction can another gain access. A mechanical turnstile like this one is highly suitable for the Sauvabelin Tower as this is an unstaffed, free attraction. Staffed attractions can use more advanced counting methods such as video turnstiles, whereby CCTV

(Continued)

(Continued)

cameras above entrance doors to attractions, shops and nightclubs are linked to intelligent people counting systems. In this case there are no physical barriers, but the system counts how many people enter and leave and calculates queues and waiting times. These data can then be used by staff to monitor visitors efficiently.

Source: © Courtesy of Lausanne Tourisme

Cameras

CCTV cameras can be used to track where overcrowding usually occurs and where bottlenecks appear. The images need to be monitored and can be used to regulate when extra staff are needed in certain areas or when additional facilities need to be opened. Cameras can also be used as a security measure: they can deter visitors from behaving in an inappropriate manner (e.g. littering, causing damage, or pilfering).

> **CCTV:** Closed Circuit Television. This means that the images are not broadcast publicly

One of Scotland's leading tourist attractions, the Falkirk Wheel, has used CCTV cameras to reduce queuing and improve the customer experience. The Falkirk Wheel is the world's only rotating boat lift that provides a connection between two canals. The wheel can carry up to eight boats at a time and visitors can see the structure in action on board of one of the specially fitted tourist boats (www.thefalkirkwheel.co.uk). The attraction uses CCTV as a security measure in the retail area, and after opening hours, but also uses the images to supervise boat traffic and manage visitor flows. When bottlenecks form, this allows for a rapid response and a redeployment of staff (http://www.securitysa.com/news.aspx?pklnewsid=14819).

Visitor Badges

For some forms of tourism, visitor badges may be a useful visitor management tool. In trade shows and exhibitions, for example, badges are commonly used to determine which groups of visitors will have access to certain areas: only important buyers may, for example, have entry to a VIP room, while other areas may be staff-only. Badges may be read through barcodes or **RFID** tags: these are microchips that can trace the movements of an object or person. This technology is mostly used at events, where the information on the badges is often read via portable scanners.

> **RFID:** Radio Frequency Identification

Online Reservation Systems

Another important technological tool is the implementation of advance booking systems. Technology is used to manage reservations in attractions and increasingly reservations can be made online by the tourists themselves. They may even be able to print off a ticket at home, or collect their tickets at self-service ticket machines. The use of this online technology has a double benefit: on the one hand it avoids overcrowding visitors at peak time and allows a better visitor flow; on the other hand it reduces the queues at entrances or tills because a number of visitors will have printed off their tickets themselves, either on-site or at home.

Madame Tussauds in London is an attraction that encourages visitors to book their tickets online as it avoids long queues and reduces the pressures on staff. When visitors book tickets online in advance, they receive a 10 per cent discount. They are then allocated a half-an-hour time slot and can enter the attraction via a dedicated entrance, so that they do not have to queue needlessly. For the attraction this means that visitors are staggered more evenly during the day (www.madametussauds.com).

Summary

This chapter has discussed visitor management as finding a balance between the needs of the tourism resource and the needs of the visitor. For a tourism resource to achieve sustainable success, it is imperative that the quality of the visitor experience is maintained without putting excessive pressures on the resource, or surpassing its carrying capacity. Visitor managers have a range of tools, techniques and technologies at their disposal, both at the level of the site and at the level of the visitor, which can be used to make sure both needs are met successfully. Success in visitor management refers to minimising the negative environmental, social and economic impacts of tourism, whilst maximising the positive impacts.

 ■ Self-test Questions

1 In destinations like Venice, the large number of day trippers results in high pressures on the natural and built environment, whilst the economic benefits they bring to the destination are often rather small. What can Venice do to manage tourism better, whilst safeguarding the visitor experience?

2 The Abu Dhabi Tourism Authority achieved the ISO 9001 standard of quality management in 2010. What could be the benefits of having this certification? Are certifications a worthwhile investment for tourism companies?

3 Think of a destination or attraction you have visited, where you feel that you as a visitor or the destination or attraction itself was negatively affected by tourism pressures. What could this destination/attraction do to improve visitor management? What would be the challenges of implementing these ideas?

Further Reading

Garrod, B. (2008) 'Managing visitor impacts', in A. Fyall, B. Garrod, A. Leask and S. Wanhill (eds), *Managing Visitor Attractions: New Directions*. Oxford: Butterworth-Heinemann.

Richardson, J. and Fluker, M. (2004) *Understanding and Managing Tourism*. Frenchs Forest: Pearson Education Australia.

Williams, C. and Buswell, J. (2003) *Service Quality in Leisure and Tourism*. CABI: Wallingford.

Useful Websites

International Organization for Standardization: www.iso.org

12 Public Sector Involvement in Tourism

The use of travelling is to regulate imagination by reality, and instead of thinking how things may be, to see them as they are. (Samuel Johnson, in Piozzi, 1786: 305)

Police outside Central Park, New York

Source: Valérie Svobodová

Learning Outcomes

After reading this chapter you will understand:

- how the public sector can be involved in tourism
- the differences between and characteristics of different levels of government involvement in tourism: from international to local
- the role of the public sector in managing, controlling, improving, promoting and branding destinations
- how the public sector can play a role in crisis planning and management in the face of different types of crises that can affect the tourist industry.

Introduction

Throughout this book, the complex structure of tourism has been emphasised – its fragmentation between generating and destination regions, its range of diverse suppliers and stakeholders, and its potential positive or negative economic, environmental and socio-cultural impacts within destinations. This complexity has created a role for public sector involvement in tourism at international, national, regional and local levels.

The public sector undertakes a broad range of roles in tourism and the extent of their involvement varies between countries. In this chapter we consider the tourism roles of the public sector, the activities of public sector agencies, and how public sector involvement differs at various geographical levels. The discussion of public sector involvement at the local level has been written by a specialist in the field, Nancy Stevenson. We end the chapter by discussing the role of the public sector in managing tourism throughout a crisis.

Public Sector Involvement in Tourism

In Chapter 7 we explained that the term public sector refers to central and local government and their administrative departments – organisations that are funded by taxation and corporations that are owned by the state.

Elliott (1997) notes that central governments are highly important to the tourism sector: without them, international tourism would not be possible. They have the power to provide the political stability, security and the legal and financial framework which tourism requires and they provide essential services (e.g. issuing passports) and basic infrastructure (e.g. roads and public transport facilities). Moreover, national governments negotiate and make agreements with other governments about issues such as visas, entry requirements and international transit routes. National governments are indeed often highly visible stakeholders in tourism. There are however a range of other stakeholders in the public sector that may play a role in the provision and management of tourism. This section will look in more detail at the roles the public sector might play on an international and national level.

Types of Government Involvement in Tourism

Governments can be involved in tourism in a variety of ways. There are significant differences between countries with regard to how governmental involvement is shaped, which public institution looks after tourism, where the centre of power is situated (locally, regionally, nationally) and the aspirations and goals countries set for their tourism industry. In some settings these tasks are performed by the (central, regional, local) government itself, whereas in other settings there may be a public agency that operates at arm's length from the government but receives financial support from taxation and is responsible to the government for its performance.

In practice this means that the public authority for tourism can lie with a range of different institutions. Tourism may be a part of the responsibilities of the national (or central) government. In this case, tourism can be part of a range of departments, for example:

- In the UK, it is part of the Department of Culture, Media and Sport.
- In Germany, it is part of the Department of Economy and Technology.
- In France, it is part of the Department of Economy, Finance and Industry.
- In Austria, it is part of the Department of Economy, Family and Youth.
- In Romania, there is a dedicated Ministry of Tourism.

In some countries, there is no part of the central government that looks after tourism – tourism may be the responsibility of regional authorities. In Belgium, for example, the Flemish and Wallonian regional governments can make autonomous tourism decisions. In many countries, however, regional governments cooperate with the national government in the area of tourism by adapting policies that were designed on a national level to their specific region. The same can apply for local governments, who in their turn may implement plans that were formed at a regional level.

Apart from these different levels of government, there are also organisations active in tourism that operate at arm's length from the government but receive financial support from taxation and are responsible to the government for their performance. National Tourist Organisations are an example of this type of institution. They are usually responsible for the practical implementation of the policy objectives that were set by governments through building partnerships or providing business support; for supporting policy making through research; and/or tourism marketing. Similar organisations may exist on the regional and local level – in the UK examples include VisitBritain, Visit England and London and Partners.

Hall (2008) identifies seven broad functions of the public sector:

- Coordination.
- Planning.
- Legislation and regulations.
- Entrepreneurship.
- Promotion.
- Social tourism.
- Protector of the public interest.

We will now consider each of these.

Coordination

The tourism industry can be seen as a complex web of different stakeholders, each of which will have their own roles and objectives. It is often the role of the public sector to bring these stakeholders together and try to develop a shared set of goals. These goals can take different forms: the public sector can, for example, be the main driver behind a new tourism brand for a destination, invest in new infrastructure, or work with private partners to develop a new tourism product. Co-ordination is also important to try and reduce the negative impacts of tourism as much as possible: the government may put laws and regulations in place to support sustainable tourism development, or might consult and represent the local community when they feel tourism has negative social or cultural impacts.

An example of a coordinating activity is local government involvement in a convention bureau. A convention bureau is a not-for-profit organisation that promotes and supports MICE or business tourism development in a destination. Many convention bureaux are partnerships between the public and the private sector – the local, regional or national government usually works together with hotels, attractions, meeting venues and other companies to bring business to the destination in the form of conferences, meetings and exhibitions. A convention bureau may take the form of a membership organisation, whereby a range of businesses will pay a membership fee to support its activities. In return, these businesses will be promoted by the convention bureau. For example, The Perth Convention Bureau markets Western Australia nationally and internationally as a destination for business tourism. The organisation is coordinated by Tourism Western Australia and the City of Perth as public sector partners, but it also has hundreds of industry partners.

Planning

The public sector is involved in the planning process of tourism when they decide which areas of tourism will be developed in the future, how expansions will be achieved, which steps need to be taken to achieve these, and how success will be measured. The result of this planning activity is usually combined in tourism plans, policies or strategies. These are discussed in more detail later in this chapter. Tourism plans can focus on a range of different goals, for example increasing the volume of tourist arrivals or attracting more high-spending tourists, managing tourists more effectively, or dispersing tourists to a new part of the destination.

There are many different forms of tourism plans, but usually they are formulated to be executed over a number of years, normally between five and 10. Some plans are formulated over even longer periods of time: the Kuala Lumpur (Malaysia) tourism plan, for example, is formulated to run for 20 years, from

2000 until 2020. Key objectives of the plan are to make Kuala Lumpur more attractive as a tourism destination and to increase the average length of stay. The city wants to create a distinctive identity to achieve this, based on the promotion of culture and sports, and by creating a tropical garden city and opportunities for eco-tourism (http://www.dbkl.gov.my/). On a local level, planning may include decisions on planning permission to construct new hotels or attractions.

Legislation and Regulations

The public sector has legislative and regulative powers which can influence tourism directly or indirectly. Visa policies, for example, enable or restrict access for foreign visitors to the destination. There are also health and safety regulations, environmental regulations and fiscal laws that affect not only the tourism industry, but also many other industries. These laws and regulations have usually not been set with the tourism industry specifically in mind, but still affect tourism indirectly.

An example of a law or regulation that affects tourism indirectly is the Disability and Equality Act that was introduced in the UK in 2010. The Act aims to prevent the discrimination disabled people may face in many areas of life. It gives individuals with disabilities rights in the areas of education, employment, and access to goods and services, to name but a few. The access to services includes tourist services such as holiday accommodation, tourist attractions, restaurants and transport providers. The Act states that people with disabilities should receive the same level of service as other service users, even if this means the service provider needs to make certain changes especially for them. Examples of these changes can be providing a low desk for wheelchair users, or having at least one copy of a menu available in Braille, or providing adapted rooms in tourist accommodation.

Entrepreneurship

The public sector may also own and operate tourism ventures. For example, museums, art galleries and parks may be operated by a public body, but be part of the tourist attractions within a destination. The Louvre in Paris, the Van Gogh museum in Amsterdam, and the Prado museum in Madrid are all examples of publicly owned attractions. Some of the hotel provision may be state-owned: this is the case for example in China, Spain (Paradores) and Portugal (Pousadas). The public sector may also own parts of the transport infrastructure such as the bus network, rail network or airline. State ownership of transport has reduced as a result of the spread of deregulation (see Chapter 5) since the late 1970s, but some airlines are still wholly state owned (United Arab Airlines) or partially state owned (Singapore Airlines).

The Louvre, Paris

Source: Sandra Charrasse

Stimulation/Promotion

The public sector stimulates tourism development in a variety of ways:

- By providing financial incentives to the private sector such as **tax concessions** or low-interest loans. For example, the government of Argentina offered no-interest loans to tourist businesses to help boost domestic tourism in 2008 in response to the global economic crisis.
- By sponsoring research activities and the compilation of relevant statistics. Commissioning market research is often one of the responsibilities of the public sector.
- Finally, the public sector may also want to play a role in tourism through promoting and branding (see further in this chapter).

Social Tourism

Social tourism refers to initiatives that involve groups in tourism, who would otherwise be excluded because of health or financial reasons. Individuals with a disability or illness, for example, may find it difficult to participate in tourism and individuals on a low income may not have

Tax concessions: Governments may decide to reduce taxes to encourage certain behaviours or actions. For example, when the taxes on buying a house are reduced, this may encourage people who rent to buy their own house

Social tourism: Social tourism refers to tourism initiatives with a strong moral or ethical dimension: their primary aim is to include groups into tourism, who would otherwise be excluded from it

enough discretionary income to pay for a holiday. Many governments in mainland Europe operate schemes that specifically aim to engage these groups in domestic travel. The motive for this may be to support the local economy of a destination, or the belief that participation in tourism is a right that should not be denied to anyone on the basis of income, because of the role tourism can play in personal development.

This role of tourism has been highlighted by the European Economic and Social Committee, who linked social tourism to increased citizenship, well-being, the development of beneficiary and host communities, and improved health and employment (Minnaert et al., 2009).

Public social tourism schemes can take a variety of forms. In several countries of mainland Europe, such as France and Hungary, a holiday voucher scheme is in place that can be used by employers as an incentive for their employees. This tends to take the form of a tax-free savings scheme whereby the employee sets aside a small part of his or her wage, which is then supplemented by the employer and paid out in vouchers. The vouchers are accepted in a range of domestic tourism businesses. Whilst the scheme thus enables people on a low income to travel, it also supports the domestic tourism industry. A disadvantage of the scheme, however, is that people who are unemployed, and often financially unable to travel, cannot access the vouchers since they are not in employment. Other social tourism initiatives can take the form of cooperations between the public and private (and in some cases also social) sectors. The scheme below is an example of this.

 Snapshot 12.1   Tourism in Flanders, Belgium

Flanders is the northern, Dutch-speaking region of Belgium. The central organisation in social tourism provision in Flanders is the Holiday Participation Centre, a publicly funded team within Tourism Flanders, the regional Tourist Board. The Centre liaises between the public, private and social sectors. The private tourism sector plays an important role: accommodation providers and private attractions offer voluntary discounts and reduced tariffs for low-income groups. The Holiday Participation Centre communicates these reduced tariffs to the social sector and the holiday makers, via their website and yearly brochures. The system is designed as a win–win situation for all the parties involved: the private sector gains access to a new target group and free marketing and can use the initiative as part of their corporate social responsibility policy; the social sector gains access to low-cost holiday opportunities; and the public sector can employ a social intervention method, reaching thousands of low-income and socially excluded citizens, at minimal cost. In 2008, almost 73,000 people, most of whom would otherwise have

(Continued)

(Continued)

not been able to enjoy a break away or day trip, used the offer of the Holiday Participation Centre to participate in travel (Tourism Flanders, 2008: 20).

Source: © Courtesy of Ans Brys

Protecting the Public Interest

The public sector has a role in safeguarding the public interest – protecting the public from activity that would be harmful to them. This may mean turning down offers from big investors if these are shown to be environmentally or socially unsustainable. The public sector would also be expected to protect the long-term interest of the community, rather than choosing to support initiatives that would bring only short-term gains. In respect of tourism it is often seen as the task of the government to strive to reduce the negative impacts of tourism on the local community and environment.

In Belfast, Northern Ireland, tourism developments are not granted permission by the local government if the proposed development could be detrimental to:

- The environmental quality of the area or the views.
- The character of the area's built heritage or proven archaeological importance.

- Nature conservation interests or the coast.

- Road traffic volumes or would cause congestion on the road network.

    (www.planningni.gov.uk).

Negative social and environmental impacts are here thus avoided by prohibiting detrimental changes to the built environment. This topic is also discussed in Chapter 10.

Tourism Policy

At the centre of government activity in tourism is tourism policy. Hall and Jenkins (1995; Hall and Page, 2002: 138) highlight that a range of definitions of policy exist, and propose that tourism policy is simply whatever governments decide to do or not to do with regards to tourism. Policies may be introduced when the destination is faced with a specific problem or challenge (e.g. in the case of a crisis, see below), or may be part of a more continuous planning process. A range of stakeholders may be involved in policy making, of which the government will be just one. Several groups of people who feel they will be affected by policy decisions may try to influence policy or put pressure on policy makers. Examples of these groups are the tourism businesses, the host community and their leaders in a destination, and pressure groups such as environmental charities and investors.

Tourism policy can be formulated on different levels. Local tourism policies are usually the most specific as they deal with only one destination in great detail. (The involvement of local governments in tourism will be discussed more fully later in this chapter.) Regional and national policies are often more general and may set guidelines for local policy makers. They have to take into account the differences between destinations and set an overall direction for coherent action. The national tourism policy for Germany for example has to set principles and guidelines that can apply to nature tourism in mountainous areas in the South, urban and cultural tourism in cities like Berlin and Hamburg, business tourism in cities like Hanover and Frankfurt, and sports tourism in Garmisch-Partenkirchen. Because national tourism products are often diverse and complex, national tourism policies tend to have more generalised objectives than local policies. International tourism policies are rare, for the same reason: if coordinating policy objectives for one country is challenging, than this is even more the case for different countries and regions.

One example of an attempt to internationalise tourism policy is the proposed EU tourism policy. This policy was formulated in 2006 and aims to provide growth for European tourism and the creation of more and better jobs. Sustainability, quality management and competitiveness are other objectives. This will be achieved via stronger regulation and policy coordination between different countries. The policy provides general ideas for national governments to adopt in their tourism policies, but is not prescriptive: the EU does not have the power to enforce this on the member states, but instead aims to influence and steer them. The following section will focus more specifically on international government involvement in tourism.

Public Sector Involvement on an International Scale

As tourism is a globalised industry, there is a role for public sector involvement in tourism on an international level. Tourism is affected by the following types of organisations, which represent national and regional governments: international trade organisations, international tourism organisations, international conservation organisations and international political organisations.

International Trade Organisations

International trade organisations regulate trade relationships between different countries. These organisations are neither specialised in nor focused on tourism: they treat tourism simply as one of the services that may be traded between countries.

The World Trade Organisation, or WTO, is the only global organisation dealing with the rules of trade between nations. It allows governments of different countries to come together and discuss trade problems, maintain or remove trade barriers, and generally regulate how the countries will trade together. Most of these rules are set out in agreements or 'commitments': these are signed between countries that open their markets to each other and regulate how open those markets will be, and what the restrictions for trade must cover. For example, it is common for a nation to allow the consumption of goods or services by foreign nationals (e.g. through tourism) more freely than the supply of these services (e.g. by opening a tourism business in another country). Tourism and travel services are one of the service areas the WTO covers. In this area, commitments have been made between 125 WTO members, which is more than any other services sector. This means that there is a high level of liberalisation in tourism in general (www.wto.org).

The OECD, or the Organisation of Economic Co-operation and Development, is a trade organisation that represents 30 (mainly European) countries. It provides a setting where governments can compare policy experiences, seek answers to common problems, identify good practice and coordinate domestic and international policies. The OECD gathers economic and social data and uses these to monitor and forecast trends. In terms of tourism, the OECD provides a policy forum to support the sustainable economic growth of tourism (www.oecd.org).

International Tourism Organisations

International tourism organisations, as opposed to international trade organisations, focus fully on international cooperation for tourism. The most important international tourism organisation is the United Nations World Tourism Organisation (UNWTO).

This is a specialised agency of the United Nations and the leading international organisation in the field of tourism. It provides training, research and policy advice, and promotes responsible and sustainable tourism. It has a membership of 161 countries and territories and there are also 370 affiliate members who represent the private sector, educational bodies, tourism associations and local tourism authorities. In its statutes, the organisation states its aim as 'the promotion and development of tourism with a view to contributing to economic development, international understanding, peace, prosperity, and universal respect for, and observance of, human rights and fundamental freedoms for all without distinction as to race, sex, language or religion' (UNWTO, 2008).

As an agency it represents the industry in the face of global challenges, for example climate change, health scares (such as SARS, bird flu and swine flu), the economic downturn and poverty alleviation. It also makes recommendations to governments regarding these topics to support and develop the tourism industry, with a special focus on supporting tourism in developing countries.

International Conservation Organisations

International conservation organisations have links with tourism via the role of heritage attractions as tourism products. In contrast to international trade or international tourism organisations, they firmly place conservation above economic development. Although international conservation organisations can play an instrumental role in tourism development, it is important not to see their goals as purely tourism-related.

The UNESCO World Heritage Centre (WHC) oversees the implementation of the World Heritage Convention: an agreement made in 1972 setting out the criteria which need to be fulfilled by natural and cultural attractions on the World Heritage list. Countries that have signed the convention can nominate a site for the World Heritage List. The World Heritage Committee then makes the final decision on the application. The sites chosen can apply for funding from the World Heritage Fund. This fund is made up from compulsory contributions from member countries, voluntary contributions and sales of documentation. The money can be used for the provision of experts or the supply of equipment or training. Often the funding is awarded as a low-interest loan. Although the WHC is not a tourism organisation, its activities can have a profound impact on tourism. World Heritage status can increase visitor interest in a destination, or can bring with it a stricter regulation of tourism activity. The WHC provides a Tourism Management Manual for World Heritage Sites on its website and aims to help governments support tourism at these sites with appropriate policies and management tools (http://whc.unesco.org/).

International Political Organisations

International political organisations bring together political representatives from different countries and regions and provide a forum for discussing issues that have effects that cross national boundaries. Tourism is usually only one of these, as are issues of environment, trade, customs, justice and defence.

Within the European Commission, tourism falls under the Directorate General for Enterprise and Industry. The tourism unit focuses on researching tourism in a pan-European context and the development of competitive and sustainable destinations. The development of high quality tourism that is accessible to groups who may otherwise find it hard to participate in tourism is also a priority – for instance for individuals with disabilities or those on a low income.

By being a member of the European Union, countries can boost their tourism revenues. Not only does accession to the EU enhance a country's image and visibility, it can also reduce trade costs because it now operates in a single market. Being part of the EU can also mean that standards of tourism improve as the country has to conform with European legislation. This may be costly, but EU members can in return apply for EU funding. This funding is usually not specifically tourism-related, but can be applied to tourism projects. European Regional Development Funds, for example, support projects that improve the competitiveness and employment levels of a region, through such programmes as knowledge exchange or support for SMEs (small and medium-sized enterprises). The European Fisheries Fund, the European Social Fund and the European Agricultural Fund for Rural Development can also be used for tourism projects, although once again none of these are specifically focused on the tourism industry (http://ec.europa.eu/enterprise/tourism/index_en.htm).

The Organisation of American States (OAS) brings together the 35 independent countries of the Americas as a forum to strengthen cooperation between them. The countries are involved in discussions around topics such as public security, social development, financial and legal affairs, trade, culture, science and education. The tourism role of the OAS focuses mainly on tourism development and competitiveness, with a particular emphasis on the role of tourism for poverty alleviation and nature conservation. The OAS tourism section also provides internationally recognised training certification (www.oas.org).

The Role of the Public Sector at the Local Level _____

Written by Nancy Stevenson, University of Westminster

Local government is elected to make decisions about geographically defined places. Specific roles vary in different countries but are likely to include areas such as education, economic development and regeneration, housing, transport, land use planning, social and cultural services and environmental services. While many local places attract tourists they are often not reliant on tourism as their main economic activity. In places where tourism is perceived to be an important element of the local economy, or where it is considered to adversely affect a local area, local government may engage in activities to manage, control and improve tourism in their areas. However, in many places tourism activity is discretionary at the local level which means that government may or may not choose to engage in tourism management or service provision. Its engagement will depend on a wide range of issues including local political priorities, the importance of tourism to their areas, and the views of local residents.

The Context

The nature of government engagement at the local level will vary and depend upon the wider context or environment. The scope of local government to deliver services, make decisions, and develop and enact policies and projects is prescribed by higher levels of government. In federal systems significant powers will be held at regional level (e.g. Germany and Brazil), whereas in countries with more central power structures (e.g. the UK) more powers will be held at the national level.

When studying local government involvement in tourism it is important to consider the context in which it is developed. Its role will vary depending on a variety of contextual or environmental considerations including:

- The national policy framework.
- The importance of tourism to the national economy.
- How tourism policy is defined and its fit with other policy areas.
- Political considerations such as how power is allocated to decision makers at the local level.
- The approaches that have been taken to policy making in the past and approaches that have been perceived to be successful in other areas.
- Alliances between areas and countries.

Governance and Partnerships

Governance is the term used to describe an approach to delivering policies and services in partnership between different organisations. Governance has arisen due to concerns about the role and effectiveness of the state within a rapidly changing and complex environment and seeks to improve efficiency and effectiveness and to focus government away from direct service provision and toward strategic leadership (Giddens, 1998; Stoker, 2004; Stoker and Wilson, 2004). The debates about governance and developing partnerships at the local level are also tied in with ideas about sustainability and the implications that local people need to be more involved in decision making.

Many people hold the view that if local government works in partnership with other stakeholders it can develop a more effective long-term sustainable vision and deliver better services. Partnership working is seen as a way of:

- Bringing in wider expertise and experience about the local area.
- Making local government more accountable.
- Getting things done more effectively.

Changes associated with governance mean that local government is likely to work closely with partners to manage and plan for tourism.

The Local Level

Jeffries (2001) refers to the local arena as a place where issues and actions have a coherence. He contrasts this with higher levels of government where policy statements or intentions might be very generalised. One advantage of studying government action and involvement at the local level is that our attention is focused on places which are geographically defined and relatively small scale. This means it is often easier to identify the attributes, opportunities and problems associated with tourism in an area and the major stakeholders and the structures and practices for working together to solve problems. It is possible to investigate questions about what happens in practice and also to see how local and regional initiatives are implemented.

Hall's (2008) seven functions of government are outlined earlier in the chapter. At the local level coordination is particularly important in the context of governance, which means that local government is likely to be involved in setting up, participating in and maintaining partnerships. For example, local government might work with partners to coordinate the marketing and promotion of their areas, to develop new conference facilities, or to stage an event. Many of these partnerships will have an entrepreneurial aspect and involve activity to stimulate development in their areas (Stevenson, 2009). Places will compete with one another for a range of resources including private and public sector investment and specific development projects. Local governments have an increasingly important role in mobilising funds. This involves working in and coordinating partnerships to develop projects and make funding bids.

Local governments may also own and operate local resources which will attract tourists such as parks, museums, art galleries, conference centres, shopping centres and hotels (Hall, 1995; Stevenson and Lovatt, 2001). They can coordinate the provision of information to tourists as well, sometimes through the provision of Tourist Information Centres or by developing and delivering Destination Management Systems. The latter can provide much wider information functions in terms of information dissemination and collection, reservations and event management (see Chapter 7 for more detail).

Local planning and policy functions are usually designed to achieve longer-term goals, focusing on a mixture of controlling and stimulating development to create lasting benefits. The planning function is often broad based and developed from a 'strategic vision' about the best way to develop a place. Service delivery around 'place-making' encompasses elements that will attract visitors but are part of a broader objective to attract inward investment and improve people's lives within an area. Some places will have a 'vision' that involves the preparation of a specific tourism plan while in others tourism development objectives will be expressed within broader land use and economic development plans. These may be designed to fit with different activities and uses in an attempt to create places which are vibrant and attractive to residents, visitors and businesses.

Local governments will also often have a regulatory function. For example, they might be responsible for implementing legislation on quality standards in hotels, grading schemes, and inspecting and monitoring bars and restaurants. Local regulations will support and implement the regulatory systems setup at a national and regional level.

Understanding the Role of Government in Managing, Controlling and Improving Supply at the Destination

When setting out to understand the role of government in tourism at the local level it is important to ask a series of questions to find out more about the context within which policies are made and about the nature of tourism policy development and delivery. These might include:

- What is the power structure in the country? Is power centralised or devolved?
- What is the history of government involvement in the management of tourism?
- How is tourism defined and how does it fit with other policy areas?
- How do governments engage in tourism? What do they do? Who do they work with?
- How successful has their involvement been?
- How important is tourism to the area and what are the views of local people and businesses?

Snapshot 12.2 English Local Authorities

Local governments in England have considerable scope to decide whether and how to engage in tourism activities. Local governments' engagement in tourism activity and service provision is discretionary, minimally funded, and usually delivered on the margins of larger service areas. In the absence of a strong lead from national government, the nature and extent of tourism activity are subject to local interpretation. This means that at the local level there will be a wide variety of approaches to tourism. Surveys by Richards (1991) and Stevenson and Lovatt (2001) show that local government is involved in a range of tourism activities. These include direct activities such as the creation of tourism partnerships, marketing and promotion, the provision of visitor information, attraction and event planning, management and development. Indirect activities include infrastructure and service provision that impacts upon visitors and their overall experience. A growing number of tourism activities are carried out by agencies or through partnership arrangements with other governmental and non-governmental organisations. In the 2001 survey, commonly cited examples of the type of service offered in partnership with other organisations included promotional campaigns, marketing and research, developing a tourism product, improving service quality and event organisation (Stevenson and Lovatt, 2001).

Destination Promotion

The public sector is often involved in promotion campaigns for tourism destinations. This involves working with partners to identify target markets, developing campaigns to attract them, and deciding which characteristics of the destination to promote. Promotional campaigns may target domestic or international tourists, leisure or business tourists, different demographic groups, or niche markets. The following paragraphs will discuss the concept of destination image and how image is different from a destination brand. The role of the government in tourism promotion will also be examined. Finally, different forms of promotion, and the role of technology in them, will be discussed.

Destination Image

Promoting tourism destinations has been compared to selling a dream, particularly when it comes to tourists who have not visited the destination before. The collective ideas, impressions, beliefs and conceptions of tourists about a destination are referred to as the destination image. There are many definitions for this concept (for a list, see e.g. Gallarza et al., 2002), which highlights that the concept is very complex and also fluid: it has evolved strongly over time and is still a very prominent research area for tourism scholars.

A person's image of a destination can be positive, negative or neutral, and is not fixed but can change over time. Gunn (1988) explains that images can be formed on two levels: the organic level and the induced level.

The organic image is developed through an individual's everyday assimilation of information, which may include a wide range of mediums, from geography classes in school over mass media to actual visitation. The induced image is formed through the influence of tourism promotions such as advertising (Pike, 2008: 205). Reports of a terrorist attack in the media can give the destination a more negative image in the mind of many tourists. If the destination hosts an internationally acclaimed event, this can make its image more positive. Media coverage, films, word of mouth, books and pictures can all influence the organic destination image. The image of a destination will probably be different before and after the actual visit, and can still change after every subsequent visit. Promotional campaigns aim to either strengthen the positive image of a destination, or turn the negative or neutral image of a destination into a positive one. Via the induced image, campaigns try to reinforce or change the organic image tourists may have already formed in their minds before the campaign.

Destination Branding

The concept of branding is discussed in Chapter 13. By building a brand, a destination's government can send out a clear and uniform message that firmly links the destination to a chosen set of attributes or benefits. Kolb (2006) describes branding as a creative process, involving the formulation of a slogan and designing a symbol or logo. A well designed brand quickly and easily communicates the benefits a tourist will experience from visiting the destination. To reinforce the brand it will need to be integrated into all communications, including brochures, advertisements and billboards.

The role of the public sector in branding a destination is usually one of research, coordination, and, in many cases, funding. The tourist destination is a complex amalgam of different attributes and stakeholders and none of these stakeholders will have complete control over the products. This makes it much more difficult to develop a coherent brand for a destination, than, for example, for a soft drink or washing powder. It is usually the task of government to research which type of brand or promotional activity would be useful, and then to bring the various stakeholders together and develop a campaign that most of them will be in agreement with. In many cases, government will then (completely or partly) fund the design and the implementation of the campaign.

Governments will invest in branding for a range of reasons. One of the advantages of a strong brand is that it can encourage **brand loyalty** and repeat purchases. If tourists have had a positive experience of a destination, an unchanging brand will remind them of this and highlight that that positive experience is still available. Rather than communicating the benefits of a visit to new customers, the role of branding has in this case changed to reminding previous customers of the same benefits. Other advantages are that a clear brand can support internet marketing efforts and bring the different stakeholders in the destination together for long-term planning (Middleton et al., 2009)

> **Brand loyalty:** The commitment by a consumer to purchase the same brand again

Snapshot 12.3   Uniquely Singapore

In 2009, the Singapore Tourism Board launched its 'Uniquely Singapore – 2009 Reasons to Visit Singapore' campaign. This global marketing campaign aimed to show visitors that Singapore could offer quality, unique experiences, and value for money in terms of pricing. The image challenge for Singapore was that many in the West saw it as a sterile business city. For foreign visitors, the campaign included a slogan, a logo, a competition, and a range of price promotions. But the campaign also targeted the host community: it invited Singapore residents to get out and enjoy the tourist attractions, so as to create more buzz and demand. As tourism ambassadors, local residents were asked to encourage their family and friends overseas to visit their city. The campaign was aimed at independent travellers, group travellers and business tourists. It was part of a S$90 million support package by the Singapore Tourism Board, aimed at helping the tourist industry cope with the effects of the global recession. In 2010, the Uniquely Singapore brand was followed by a campaign entitled 'Your Singapore', which again focused on the colourful vibrancy of the city (www.yoursingapore.com; http://www.prweek.com/uk/news/1042860/Image-refresh-Singapore).

Source: © Singapore Tourism Board

Destinations and Crisis Management _____

As discussed in the previous paragraphs, governments have a responsibility in the development, management and marketing of tourism destinations. These responsibilities are severely tested during and in the aftermath of a crisis. In the following sections, different types of crises that can affect the tourism industry are discussed. The role of governments in planning for and responding to crises will also be examined.

Glaesser (2003) and Henderson (2007) researched tourism and crisis management. They identified six forms of crisis that affect tourism:

- Political crises.
- Terrorist attacks.
- Environmental crises.
- Natural disasters.
- Health scares.
- Economic crises.

Political Crises _____

Political crises come in many forms but in general these include civil war, coups d'état, mass arrests, political assassinations, armed attacks, riots, demonstrations and the threat of war with other countries.

Political unrest and instability have a profound impact on demand for and the image of a tourism destination. When tourists perceive a destination as dangerous, many will choose an alternative destination instead. In the case of persistent or violent political crises, governments may advise their citizens against travelling to a destination. The media attention that political crises attract can also induce a negative image of the destination for years to come, even though political stability may have returned.

The former Yugoslavia was a popular tourist destination for Western and Central Europeans. Croatia was one of the popular tourist areas there, because of its long coastline and several historic cities with a rich cultural heritage. Between 1990 and 1995, the war of independence greatly disturbed the tourist influx and the image of the country. In the first year of the war, tourist arrivals decreased by 70 per cent, and nights spent reduced by 80 per cent compared to the previous year. By the end of the war, many accommodation facilities and much of the supporting infrastructure had been destroyed or damaged during the conflict. Some areas of the country, furthest from where the military forces were based, had managed to keep a minimal level of tourist activity. In the years following the war, Croatia slowly rebuilt its positive image and allure for tourists. Even though the country maintained its political stability after 1995, it took 10 years, until 2005, for the number of nights spent by tourists to reach the same level as before the war. The main markets for Croatia are Germany, France, the UK and Slovakia (Perko and Iđaković, 2008).

Terrorism

Terrorism, as a form of political crisis, has affected the tourism industry significantly in recent years, particularly when tourists are the target of an attack. Terrorism is not a new phenomenon: the IRA in Northern Ireland and ETA in the Basque region of Spain are notable examples of organisations that employ terrorist acts to achieve their goals. Nationalism and separatism were conventional motivators for terrorism in the 1970s and 1980s; nowadays, religion plays an important role. Terrorist activities tend not only to affect the destination's appeal to tourists, who may now see it as unsafe and decide to visit other destinations instead, terrorist acts can also instil a sense of fear and mistrust more generally, which in turn might discourage people from travelling at all.

Examples of terrorism are bombings, suicide bombings, violent attacks, threats of violence, hijackings, kidnappings, murders and events and demonstrations that are linked to extremism.

Terrorist attacks in a destination have a profound influence on tourist demand for a destination. For example, the 9/11 attacks on New York in 2001 caused a sharp decline in international arrivals and tourist expenditure in New York, and for some the United States in general was instantly seen as dangerous and unsafe. Air travel into/out of and around the USA suffered sharp declines in passenger numbers because of the tarnished image of aviation. US inbound and outbound tourist numbers went down, and domestic tourism was also badly hit, resulting in job losses and bankruptcies.

However, it has been shown that terrorist acts, especially if these are singular, one-off events, do not affect the tourism industry in the longer term. Tourism in New York was back to pre-2001 levels in 2005. Mintel shows that destinations like Turkey, Spain and Egypt, each of which have been affected by terrorist activity, have seen a general growth in tourist arrivals in recent years (Mintel, 2006).

Environmental Crises

Fragile natural environments, such as coastlines, mountain areas and lakes, are often popular tourism destinations due to their natural resources. These natural environments can come under threat, sometimes because of tourism itself (see Chapter 10 for a full discussion on the environmental impacts of tourism). But other industries, such as agriculture, fishing, mining, transport and logging, can also have a strong detrimental impact on the environmental conditions in the destination. Environmental crises are events that cause widespread environmental damage in a short timescale, and, as opposed to natural disasters, they are usually connected to human activity.

Examples of environmental crises are oil leaks, oils spills, loss of cargo from ships, polluted smoke from industrial fires, nuclear and radiation accidents, gas leaks, waste water spills and sewage leaks.

In March 2009, the Australian state of Queensland, home to what is known as the 'Sunshine Coast', was tainted by an oil spill after a container ship leaked fuel oil in a storm. Thirty-one shipping containers of ammonium nitrate fell overboard, rupturing the ship's fuel tank and causing it to leak. The oil spill contaminated 60km (36 miles) of beaches and threatened the habitats of wildlife such as turtles and pelicans. The area was declared a disaster zone and the beaches were closed to tourists. This not only affected the destinations where the beaches had been closed, but also others in the state of Queensland, because of the worldwide media attention connected to the disaster. The government of Queensland was quick in mounting a clean-up operation and a branding campaign to support suffering businesses (http://www.qld.gov.au/oil-spill/).

Natural Disasters

Many natural locations that are popular with tourists, such as coasts, lakes, riversides and mountains, are at a heightened risk of nature-related disturbances. Some of these can be predicted or occur at particular times of the year, whereas others occur unexpectedly. These disturbances pose a danger to tourists and can cause significant damage to tourism-related infrastructure. Some commentators predict that climate change will increase the likelihood of natural disasters and extreme weather conditions.

Examples of natural disasters are floods, hurricanes, typhoons, earthquakes, blizzards, avalanches, tsunamis, landslides and volcanic eruptions.

On 24 December 2006, dramatic images of a tsunami hitting the shores of South Asia spread around the world. Tsunamis are great displacements of water caused by earthquakes on the sea bed. Large waves form from the epicentre of the earthquake and reach maximum height near coastal areas. Sri Lanka, Thailand, Indonesia and the Maldives were the hardest hit tourism destinations, with much of the coastal tourism infrastructure destroyed. These destinations saw bookings fall: in the rankings of destinations in the affected area, the Maldives was down from first place in 2004 to sixth in 2005 and Thailand fell out of the top 10 (Mintel, 2006). The travel industry in general recovered rapidly after the tsunami, but tourists diverted to other resorts, with, for example, an increased interest in the Caribbean. Even though most areas have since recovered, the speed of recovery is greatly dependent on the level

Presidential Palace in Port au Price, Haiti after the earthquake in 2010

Source: Valerié Svobodová

of damage and the speed and quality of reconstruction of tourist facilities such as hotels and leisure infrastructure.

Health Scares

Travelling can expose tourists to increased health risks due to the standards of hygiene and exposure to unfamiliar infections and diseases at the destination. Tourists are explicitly warned about infectious diseases like malaria, dengue fever, yellow fever and cholera, for example, when they travel to certain destinations, and for a range of destinations immunisation against certain diseases is part of the entry requirements. Tourists who engage in sexual activities or drug use during a trip add to the health risks a holiday can represent. Health scares differ from these risks to travel in the sense that they usually concern previously unknown infections or diseases that spread around the world quickly due to international travel. Due to the media attention that often surrounds these diseases a sense of panic can ensue, and governments may decide to put in place travel restrictions and increased vigilance regarding incoming tourists from affected areas.

Examples of health scares in recent years have been SARS, bird flu, foot and mouth disease, mad cow disease (and its human variant Creutzfeldt-Jakob syndrome), legionnaire's disease and swine flu.

The Case of SARS

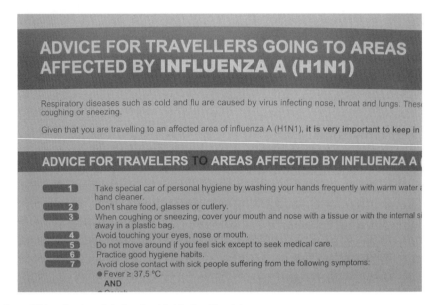

ADVICE FOR TRAVELLERS GOING TO AREAS
AFFECTED BY **INFLUENZA A (H1N1)**

Respiratory diseases such as cold and flu are caused by virus infecting nose, throat and lungs. These coughing or sneezing.

Given that you are travelling to an affected area of influenza A (H1N1), **it is very important to keep in**

ADVICE FOR TRAVELERS TO AREAS AFFECTED BY INFLUENZA A

1. Take special car of personal hygiene by washing your hands frequently with warm water a hand cleaner.
2. Don't share food, glasses or cutlery.
3. When coughing or sneezing, cover your mouth and nose with a tissue or with the internal s away in a plastic bag.
4. Avoid touching your eyes, nose or mouth.
5. Do not move around if you feel sick except to seek medical care.
6. Practice good hygiene habits.
7. Avoid close contact with sick people suffering from the following symptoms:
   ● Fever ≥ 37.5 °C
   AND

Notice at Valencia airport during the bird flu health crisis

Source: Lynn Minnaert

SARS, or Severe Acute Respiratory Syndrome, is a potentially fatal respiratory infection. It was first recorded in the Guangdong province of China in 2002. In 2003, due to international air travel, the disease spread around the world. This outbreak led to the deaths of more than 800 people worldwide. It also severely affected tourism in China, Hong Kong, Singapore and Vietnam, where it was estimated about 3 million people lost their jobs. Tourism arrivals also fell by 70 per cent or more in other Asian tourist markets, even those that were not, or hardly, affected by the disease. McKercher and Chon (2004) link this downturn in the general Asian tourism industry to the warnings issued by many governments and the World Health Organisation not to travel to Asia unless this was strictly necessary. The movements of Asian tourists were also often restricted, through bans, the withholding of visas and quarantines. Because SARS was an unknown virus, many of these measures were put in place as a first reaction to the health crisis, even though it later transpired that the disease could be controlled by asking departing tourists a few questions and conducting a temperature check.

Economic Crises

Seeing that level of income is usually a key determinant in participation in leisure travel, the tourism industry is to a large extent dependent on the buoyancy of the overall economy. Economic improvements often go hand in hand with increases in holiday participation and spending: examples are the fast-growing outbound tourism markets of China, India, Russia and Brazil. By contrast, economic slowdowns and crises tend to negatively affect all expenditure that is seen as non-essential, and tourism is usually seen as discretionary spending.

Examples of economic crises are downturns, slow-downs, recessions, depressions, inflation and devaluations of currency.

The tourism industry is largely dependent on the overall state of the economy, as was proven in 2008 in the aftermath of the global economic downturn. Although, overall, the number of international tourist arrivals worldwide grew by 2 per cent compared to 2007, in the second half of the year growth came to a standstill with the number of international arrivals declining slightly. The strongest declines in arrivals were noted in Europe and Asia. A slowdown in tourism-generating countries in advanced economies was also noted and this started spreading to major emerging markets such as China, India and Brazil at the beginning of 2009. Still, several destinations noted remarkable growth, even in the second half of the year: examples were Honduras, Panama, the Lebanon, Morocco, India, Indonesia and Turkey. Tourism has been described as a resilient economic activity, one that is able to play a key role in economic recovery for many countries and regions (www.unwto.org).

Crisis Planning

It is often said that the best way to handle a crisis is to prevent it from occurring. In a time of crisis which disrupts the usual flow of activities and puts pressure on all the stakeholders involved, it is often not possible to call a meeting, get all the stakeholders around the table and discuss possible responses: a crisis demands a swift and effective response, so this should be planned beforehand. However, considering all the things that can potentially go wrong, it is difficult to plan ahead for every possible scenario. Many crisis plans will therefore remain purposely vague: the exact circumstances of a crisis cannot usually be predicted, but the plan must allow destinations to access a frame of reference when this is needed.

It is important that the crisis plan refers clearly to the responsibilities of the different stakeholders in a crisis. Who will be in charge when a crisis occurs? Who will ensure coordination between different stakeholders? Who will speak with the media? To determine these responsibilities, a planning committee or crisis committee should be formed: this committee can include destination managers, public officials, legal advisers, press officers, representatives from the emergency services, external experts, marketing managers, etc. Once responsibilities have been established, communication channels and hierarchies should be put in place, ensuring that everyone has access to the information that will be needed when the time comes.

When this is in place, a number of scenarios or contingencies can be explored, in what is called a contingency plan, or an emergency plan. These scenarios can go into a much higher level of detail than the generic crisis plan, and will usually focus on crises that are seen as likely to occur in the destination. The aim of the contingency plan is to prepare the destination as fully as possible for a number of contingencies, so that when a crisis occurs, a clear template for the required response will already be in place. It is vital however that the plan is actually used in times of a crisis; even though these plans may be in place, in the panic that ensues after a crisis, they may be ignored when they are most needed. Regular exercises may be one way to prevent this from happening. It is also important that the plan is easy to follow and not overly complex, so that it is not rejected when a crisis occurs (Glaesser, 2003; Henderson, 2007).

Snapshot 12.4   The National Tourism Incident Response Plan for Australia

The National Tourism Incident Response Plan for Australia was developed after international crises like 9/11, the bomb attacks in Bali and London, and SARS had affected the national tourist industry. The plan was developed by the public sector in close collaboration with the private sector and aims to ensure a coherent national response in crisis situations. It contains detailed flowcharts specifying responsibilities and communication flows. A quick response in the case of more serious crises is ensured by the appointment of a Central Incident Management Group: the plan describes which types of individuals should be in this group and what their key responsibilities should be. The Central Incident Management Groups may convene additional committees in charge of communication, policy making, research and monitoring. General strategies are also suggested in the plan to aid recovery after the crisis in the form of action plans, templates and matrices. The National Tourism Incident Response Plan is always active, but there are different levels of activation: from the lowest level, when there is no threat (green), to the highest level (red). In response to the swine flu outbreak of 2009, the activation level was raised to amber (incident response required) (www.ret.gov.au).

Crisis Recovery

When a crisis does occur, the way a destination handles the event can determine how long the negative effects of the crisis will persist and how long the tourist sector will be negatively affected by these. A range of techniques exists for destinations to use in the aftermath of a crisis: these relate to products, price and communication.

In terms of products, it is important that the quality of the tourism facility or service is restored as soon as possible. If there are elements that will endanger a tourist's personal safety, these need to be removed as quickly as possible. When an oil spill has contaminated a beach, for example, and skin contact with the oil constitutes a health risk, then the beach should be closed off and a cleaning programme should be instructed as soon as possible. In the event of substantial damage, restoring this can take considerable time, and the negative effects on the destination's image can last even longer. In this case, Glaesser (2003) suggests a number of short-term strategies based on product diversification to encourage visitation. The destination can, for example, stage an event, such as a concert or festival, attracting the media and diverting attention away from negative connotations. Another strategy, which may be useful for safe destinations in countries that are involved in a political crisis such as a war, may be to focus on domestic and/or regional tourism. These tourists are likely to know the area better and thus are less likely to be put off by the negative reputation the political conflict has caused.

The second area for action is price. Businesses in the destination may offer discounts or promote special offers to attract tourists back to the area. Although price is by all means a significant factor in the decision-making process, price promotions are a risky strategy. Firstly the consumer may get used to the cheaper prices, refusing to pay the higher price when the crisis is nothing but a distant memory. Secondly, the crisis is the reason for the price reduction, so by bringing the price down the tourism providers are also highlighting the reason why the product did not sell.

Communication is the third action area in the aftermath of a crisis. A crisis is likely to attract media attention, with images of the destination in crisis being sent throughout the world in many cases, over which the destination itself has little or no control. These images of negative events may influence the image of the destination, as tourists form ideas or misconceptions about the area as a potential holiday destination. As stated before, the negative image of the destination that is thus formed may outlast the crisis, and live on long after its effects have become unnoticeable. It is therefore important that a destination aims to control the damage done to its reputation as soon as possible. This can be done by providing more positive and hopeful messages to the press, for example, or by commissioning an advertising or promotion campaign. The public sector may also encourage businesses in the destination to communicate directly with their customers, informing them of the situation, and reassuring them that they do not need to cancel or postpone their holiday.

CASE STUDY 12.1

CRISIS MANAGEMENT IN LONDON AFTER THE BOMBING OF 7 JULY 2005

On Thursday 7 July 2005, four suicide bombers struck in central London, killing 52 people and injuring more than 770. The attack targeted the public transport system, with three bombs going off on the metro system, and one on a double-decker bus. The suicide bombers were radicalised Muslims. On 21 July of the same year, a second attempted bomb attack was narrowly prevented. Both events were heavily publicised in the media, and the image of London as an unsafe city was sent around the world.

Whilst the first two quarters of 2005 showed high growth in overseas residents' visits to the UK, growth rates fell sharply after the terrorist attacks. Despite the overall increase in visits to the UK in 2005, visits to London declined by 3.7 per cent in quarter 3 and by 1.2 per cent in quarter 4 when compared with the same period in 2004. These falls compared with large increases of 13 per cent and 10 per cent in visits to the capital in quarters 1 and 2 respectively. Leisure tourism also declined more sharply than business tourism (National Statistics, 2006).

After the attack, London's mantra was 'business as usual'. The London Development Agency, and the local tourist board, Visit London, developed a guide to help tourism through the first few weeks after the crisis. The guide gave advice on communication, pricing and product strategies businesses could use to reduce the negative impacts of the crisis. It also provided legal and financial advice, strategies for dealing with employees, and a list of contacts in relevant public agencies in London and their responsibilities. Below are a number of examples of the guidelines provided:

Websites: We live in an era of instant communication and your customers will use websites to inform themselves. It is important that you review your own website and post some information on there immediately. This can be developed over the next few days but a brief statement reassures customers that you are well prepared.

Be proactive: Review your bookings and identify any that are particularly valuable. Prepare a message for your future bookings in letter, telephone, script and web form. Identify the positive reasons why people should still travel. Contact your customers and tell them that you are looking forward to welcoming them.

Review your offer: In a few days you will have some idea of how badly your business is affected. You will need to act to replace lost customers. In the short term, you will need to offer customers some incentive, and this can be a special offer, some added value, a discounted price, a loyalty bonus, a new feature.

Positive public relations: In the early days of a crisis it is very easy to believe that there is only bad news. The danger is that this will become a self-fulfilling prophecy – the tourism industry 'talks down' London and therefore visitors stay away. Taking a positive approach means being realistic but optimistic. Try to develop a focus on what visitors will be able to enjoy and emphasise the welcome they will receive from Londoners.

(Continued)

(Continued)

Build your relationships: If you receive business from agents, tour operators or incoming handling agents, get in touch with them. They will be able to give you good market intelligence and you can talk to them about what you can do together to encourage customers.

Review marketing campaigns: You will need to check whether any booked advertising is appropriate. You may decide to cancel some advertising because the message is wrong given the circumstances. Hong Kong tourism experienced an example of this. They had booked colour advertising that featured the slogan 'A breath of fresh air', which was due to run at the height of the SARS outbreak when residents were wearing face masks. The cost of cancelling advertising is better than the bad publicity generated by insensitive messages. (LDA, 2005)

Reflective Questions

1 These guidelines place a heavy emphasis on online communication. Why is the internet such an important and useful communication tool in the aftermath of a crisis?
2 Have you ever decided against visiting a destination for safety reasons? What would convince you a destination was safe again after a crisis?

Summary

This chapter has highlighted the complex and varied nature of government involvement in tourism. It was shown that governments are involved in tourism for different reasons and at different levels: locally, regionally, nationally, and even internationally. The roles and responsibilities of governments also vary widely: governments may aim to develop tourism to bring economic benefits to a destination, but at the same time they have to protect the public interest and try to reduce the negative impacts of tourism as much as possible. They play a central role in bringing together a wide range of stakeholders involved in tourism and consult with them to develop policies and regulations. This central role also makes them a key partner in the development, consultation and funding process that underpins tourism promotion and branding.

At a local level, the activities of government are shaped by a range of contextual factors and vary within and between countries. Local governments have a role in creating places which are attractive to people (such as residents, workers and visitors) and they are likely to be involved in bidding for resources for particular projects or events to meet this objective. Local governments are often involved in managing and improving the tourism supply in their areas, however these tourism initiatives are often integrated within broader objectives to improve the image or attractiveness of certain sites.

Finally, it has been shown that at times when a coordinated response from all stakeholders is most crucial, namely in times of crisis, governments play a central role in planning for crises and managing their effects. Crises can take a wide range of forms and are characterised by their unpredictability – however a coordinated response can lead the way to a swift recovery.

 ■ Self-test Questions ■

1 What sort of tourism activities might be undertaken by local government?

2 Why do they undertake these activities?

3 What questions should you ask before trying to understand local government involvement in tourism?

Further Reading

Glaesser, D. (2003) *Crisis Management in the Tourism Industry*. Oxford: Elsevier Butterworth-Heinemann.

Hall, C. (2008) *Tourism Planning: Policies, Processes and Relationships*. Harlow: Prentice Hall.

London Development Agency (LDA) (2005) *Business as Usual*. Available at: http://www.lda.avensc.com/documents/Business_as_Usual_PDF.pdf

Minnaert, L., Maitland, R. and Miller, G. (2009) 'Tourism and social policy: the value of social tourism', *Annals of Tourism Research*, 36(2): 316–334.

Mintel (2006) *Holidays, the Impacts of Terrorism and Natural Disasters*. London: Mintel.

Perko, J. and Iđaković, M. (2008) *Rise and Fall of Croatian Tourism and the Effects of the War of the 90s*. Available at: http://www.forumstat.tourisme. gouv.fr/ftp/ang_S5_5_perko.pdf

Useful Websites

Disability Discrimination Act (2005): http://www.direct.gov.uk/en/ DisabledPeople/RightsAndObligations/DisabilityRights/DG_4001068

European Commission – Supporting European Tourism: ec.europa.eu/enterprise/ tourism/index_en.htm

Organization of American States: www.oas.org

The Organisation for Economic Co-operation and Development: www.oecd.org

World Heritage Convention: whc.unesco.org

UN World Tourism Organization: www.unwto.org

World Trade Organization: www.wto.org

13 Tourism Marketing

Marketing is the art and science of finding, retaining and growing profitable customers. (Kotler et al., 2009: 11)

Signage for tourist services, Imlil, Morocco

Source: Clare Inkson

Learning Outcomes

After reading this chapter you will understand:

- **what marketing is and the challenges of marketing tourism products**
- **common methods for segmenting tourism consumers**
- **how the marketing mix is applied in tourism**
- **the impact of digital technology on tourism marketing.**

Introduction

Marketing is a complex, dynamic, creative and innovative process that seeks to influence consumer behaviour. Advertising is a highly visible part of this process but marketing consists of other important activities too.

The core principle of marketing is that companies and organisations achieve their objectives most successfully by focusing on satisfying customers' needs more effectively than competitors do. In order to do this, information must be collected about:

- Consumers' motivations, needs, expectations and the way they purchase products.
- Which groups of consumers should be targeted as potential customers.
- How products should be designed and how they can be made available for sale to consumers.
- Which prices to charge.
- The best way of communicating with consumers and the most effective messages to provide.
- How to keep customers loyal.

In addition, effective marketing considers the wider external environment as well; that is any changes to political, economic, social and technological conditions, and activities by competitors that may create opportunities or threats and how these will influence demand for the product. Marketing therefore involves a continual process of researching in order to gather evidence on which to make decisions, and researching to monitor the effectiveness of those decisions in order to inform future decision making.

Marketing became widely recognised as a management function and academic discipline in the 1960s and since then our understanding of the principles of marketing theory and practice has evolved considerably. Research into marketing service products, of which tourism is one example, did not develop until the late 1970s and therefore a wider understanding of effective tourism marketing was late to emerge. Since the final decades of the twentieth century, competition between destinations, and between suppliers in the same destination, for the same customer markets has intensified, and individual attraction, accommodation and transport operators, as well as destinations themselves, have had to adopt a marketing approach in order to sustain their success (Middleton et al., 2009).

Marketing is now approached by tourism academics and practitioners as a disciplined business function and has also been adopted by non-commercial tourism organisations, such as museums, art galleries, natural attractions, state-funded transport operators, and destination organisations in order to achieve the objectives on which their funding is dependent.

Tourism marketing has changed rapidly since the 1990s as a result of dramatic transformations in the operating environment. Globalisation and liberalisation in some sectors, particularly air transport, has intensified competition, new tourism markets have emerged as a result of economic developments in Brazil, Russia, India and China, and the internet has revolutionised the way many consumers research and purchase tourism products and services.

In this chapter we consider the principles of tourism marketing and their application in practice through segmentation and the marketing mix. In particular, we focus on the impact of the internet on tourism marketing.

Tourism Marketing

Tourism industries are part of the service sector, for which a particular approach to marketing is necessary.

Services marketing theory evolved in the late 1970s and early 1980s with research by Shostack (1977), Grönroos (1978), Zeithaml (1981) and Lovelock (1983), whom Hoffman et al. (2009: 25) refer to as 'services marketing pioneers', because they proposed that services could not be marketed in the same way as goods.

According to Berry (1980, in Hoffman et al., 2009: 6), goods are 'objects, devices or things, whereas services can be defined as deeds, efforts or performances'. In reality, the distinction between goods and services is not always clear, as the production and sale of objects, devices or things often requires some service elements, for example during the sales process or in after-sales support, while the production and sale of a service like hospitality also requires physical objects as part of the product.

It is useful to consider the distinction between goods and services in the context of ownership: with goods, the customer owns something physical after the purchase, whereas with a service, there is not always any physical evidence after the performance has been provided. For example, a holiday or a business trip requires the temporary use of physical products such as transport, accommodation and attractions, but at the end of the trip, none of these products are owned by the consumer.

Services are distinct from goods because they are characterised by intangibility, heterogeneity, perishability and inseparability. Each of these characteristics is discussed in detail in Chapter 5, so in this section we will consider how they affect tourism marketing.

Intangibility creates difficulties in communicating the benefits of a tourism service to potential consumers and increases the consumer's perceived risk of purchasing the product because they cannot inspect it before reserving, travelling to, and often paying for, the product. For instance, tourist accommodation may be booked and paid for in advance, but the customer does not know for sure that the purchasing decision is the right one for them until they arrive. Tourism marketers need to find ways of assuring potential consumers that the product matches their needs and expectations.

The physical distance between tourism service providers in destinations and their potential consumers in generating regions magnifies this challenge by making it harder to research consumer markets and communicate with them. This is particularly true for SMEs and microbusinesses whose financial resources and level of knowledge and expertise in marketing are likely to be limited, and who may therefore require support from an external body in researching markets and communicating with potential customers. This support role is often provided by a destination tourist organisation, or is achieved through membership of a consortia or becoming a franchisee (see Chapter 5).

Inseparability creates variations between customers in their experience of a **service encounter** because of the consumer's involvement in its production. This causes difficulties in creating consistency in all consumers' experience of a service product and highlights the importance of the individuals providing the service in managing the quality of customers' experience (McCabe, 2008).

> **Service encounter:** Interaction between the customer and the service provider, sometimes called 'the moment of truth'

Inseparability does however create some marketing advantages because it provides opportunities to gather feedback from customers about the quality of their experience, either formally through surveys or interviews, or informally, during any stage of the purchase and consumption process. In addition, inseparability facilitates customisation of the product to the individual needs of each customer, for example through offering upgrades or additional products and services, or allowing customers to select elements of the product, for instance the location of their seat on a flight, or the preferred location of rooms in a hotel.

Perishability creates marketing challenges because of the difficulties in matching supply with demand and ensuring an adequate level of revenue for each unit of capacity before it expires. It is therefore crucial that effective ways to optimise revenue are found. Perishability is exacerbated in tourism by demand variations on a seasonal, daily or hourly basis, that create pressures on producers to earn enough revenue during periods of peak demand to compensate for lower revenues when that demand falls. Tourism marketers use a range of techniques to manage demand and to 'smooth' it by reducing peaks and troughs. The high ratio of fixed to variable costs (see Chapter 5) that is characteristic of tourism products creates opportunities for marketers to use pricing as a tool to smooth demand by selling the same product at different prices depending on the consumer's price sensitivity. Effective marketing ensures that customers who would be prepared to pay higher prices are unable to purchase the product at lower prices.

Heterogeneity creates quality control and service quality management challenges for tourism marketers because of the difficulty in replicating the same experience for all customers and maintaining a consistent quality in all service encounters, either within the same company with different members of staff, or across a number of suppliers within the same destination.

Zeithaml et al. (2006: 355) suggest that 'services marketing is about promises – promises made and promises kept to customers'. The ability of a company to keep these promises through their service performance and service encounters is often the responsibility of individual employees. This crucial role of people in services adds an increased dimension to the services marketing process. This dimension is illustrated by the strategic framework known as the service marketing triangle.

The Services Marketing Triangle

The services marketing triangle identifies three types of marketing – external, internal and interactive, as Figure 31.1 illustrates:

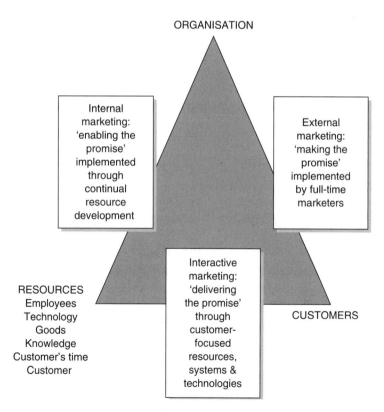

Figure 13.1   The services marketing triangle

Source: adapted from Grönroos (2007: 62). Reproduced with permission of *Australian Marketing Journal* (formerly *Asia-Marketing Journal*).

- *External marketing*: involves the activities that research and communicate the promise to customers, such as the tangible product elements, promotional messages and prices charged, and is often the responsibility of a marketing department.

- *Interactive marketing*: is the process by which services are produced and delivered, and requires the involvement of staff and customers as a result of the inseparability of the services product. Grönroos (2007) proposes that interactive marketing involves all employees and the way in which the physical product, technology and internal systems support the customer-focused service delivery. Therefore interactive marketing involves the whole company and not just the marketing department.

- *Internal marketing*: is the process by which conditions inside the company equip all employees with the skills, knowledge and attitudes necessary to enable the company to keep its promises to customers. The services marketing triangle suggests that the relationship between a company and its employees has a direct impact on the quality of the service product and the customers' perception of the company. Ultimately, in order to satisfy customers, employees themselves must be satisfied. Internal marketing is the process undertaken by an employer to develop good relationships with and between employees throughout an organisation.

Contemporary approaches to marketing recognise the contribution of external, interactive and internal marketing to services' customer satisfaction, and to organisational success; the marketing mix, which we discuss later, has been adapted for services to reflect this. Before we discuss the marketing mix, we consider tourism customers in more detail, and in particular how the total tourism customer market can be broken down to identify groups of customers with common characteristics.

Segmenting the Tourism Market

The customer is at the heart of marketing because marketing strategy and activities are intended to influence customer behaviour, for the benefit of the company or organisation. In order to plan and design marketing activities, the marketer must first identify exactly who their potential customers are.

In tourism, the whole consumer market consists of hundreds of millions of consumers in generating regions around the world, with varying needs, expectations, budgets and buying behaviours. Clearly, tourism suppliers and destinations cannot seek to attract them all as customers, so they need to divide the total market into those sections, or segments, which are most likely to desire and consume their products, and which will enable the company to achieve its strategic objectives.

Each segment will be defined by specific characteristics that are shared by the consumers within that segment. Once a segment is identified as a potential source of customers, it is known as a target market. All marketing activities are then directed towards the target market, or markets if more than one is identified. Kotler et al. (2009) identify segmentation as the identification of measurable criteria to segment the market, detailed profiling of each segment, and a careful assessment of its profitability. After the most desirable segments have been selected, the marketer must decide on the position it would like to be perceived by in the target market relative to its competitors; for example as the best quality, most luxurious, best value, largest, cheapest, most reliable, and so on. Then appropriate marketing mix activities are designed to communicate relevant messages to the target market most effectively.

Market segmentation enables the design and implementation of focused marketing activities to influence and manage the consumer behaviour of each target market and is therefore a key part of the marketing process. However, identifying these segments is a complex activity.

Middleton et al. (2009) identify seven main criteria by which tourism suppliers can segment their markets:

- Purpose of travel.
- Buyer needs, motivations and benefits sought.
- Buyer behaviour/characteristics of product usage.
- Demographic, economic and geographic profiles.
- Geodemographic profile.
- Psychographic profile.
- Price.

These segmentation criteria will vary in complexity and the resources required, and some will be more useful than others. As a result, some criteria will be more widely used. Tourism suppliers will often use several of these criteria simultaneously to identify very focused market segments.

Middleton et al. (2009) stress that effective segmentation requires each segment to be:

- *Discrete*: each segment must be identifiable by specific criteria.
- *Measurable*: the size of the segment must be measurable in order to monitor the effectiveness of marketing activities.
- *Viable*: the revenue generated from each segment will exceed the cost of targeting it in line with financial objectives.
- *Appropriate*: the segment must be compatible with the company's image, products and other segments targeted.
- *Sustainable*: the segment must be compatible with environmental and social objectives, and this is particularly relevant to destination marketing. Middleton et al. (2009) suggest that the sustainability of target segments will be given more importance in the future.

We now consider each of the criteria used to identify target markets.

Purpose of Travel

Purpose of travel is one of the fundamental methods of segmentation in tourism because it influences the needs, expectations, budgets and consumer behaviour of tourists. In broad terms, purpose of travel is divided into leisure or business because usually there are distinct differences in the needs and buyer behaviour of leisure tourists and business tourists. In practice, leisure and business tourism markets are sub-divided further by more specific purposes of travel (Middleton et al., 2009).

The leisure tourism market can be further segmented by purpose, for example: whether the trip is the main holiday, a honeymoon, a short break or day trip, or VFR, as well as by the type of activity that is sought such as skiing, wind-surfing, culture-seeking, sun-seeking, or getting married.

The business tourism market can be segmented further depending on whether the purpose of the trip is for a meeting, incentive, conference or exhibition. In addition, the conference market itself is usually sub-divided further depending on whether the customer is: a company, known as corporate; an association, such as a charity, society or a trade union; a government or public sector organisation; or part of SMERF (social, military, educational, religious and fraternal sectors) (Davidson and Rogers, 2006).

Segmentation by purpose of travel is a useful starting point for segmentation, however it is usually refined using one or more of the other criteria.

Buyer Needs and Benefits Sought

The needs and benefits sought by tourism consumers are intrinsically linked to the motivation to engage in tourism. For example, relaxation may be the need motivating many leisure tourists, but the products they require to achieve this may vary – some might require indulgence and hedonism while others may require a physical, cultural or intellectual challenge; some may want higher standards of comfort than their usual environment provides, while others may be happy with more basic facilities. Business tourists could be motivated by the need to increase sales, develop new contacts or enhance their knowledge, but the products required to achieve this will vary by need, for example many business travellers will prioritise comfort and efficiency in the travel products they choose but some will also require prestige and comfort, while for others, their budget might be a key consideration.

Segmentation using buyer needs and benefits sought is one of the most difficult segmentation criteria to implement because in-depth research is needed to understand the needs, motivations and benefits sought by tourists (Middleton et al., 2009).

Buyer Behaviour/Characteristics of Product Usage

Consumer behaviour helps companies to understand how their products are purchased and consumed and is a common method of market segmentation because the evidence is relatively easy to collect. Middleton et al. (2009) identify the following characteristics of consumer behaviour:

- Frequency of consumption of a product and loyalty to a particular supplier.
- Expenditure per head.
- Lead-in time of the purchase decision.
- Level of flexibility required to alter or cancel reservations.
- Length of stay.
- Party size and composition.
- Sources of information used to research the purchase decision.
- Use of intermediaries.
- Satisfaction levels and desire to repeat the purchase.

Many of these characteristics are identified through market research surveys of samples of customers as well as via database analysis that tracks customer behaviour. Several of the consumer behaviour characteristics are collected by companies as part of the reservations process and are therefore relatively easy to acquire.

Demographic, Economic and Geographic, and Life Cycle Profiles

Demographic, economic and geographic profiles identify market segments on the basis of one or some of the following: age, sex, occupation, income, or place of residence. Life cycle refers to the stage of life of individuals – infancy, childhood, adolescence, single, couple, parenthood, empty nesters – because their behaviour as tourists and their needs will be significantly different at each stage.

This information about consumers is relatively straightforward to identify through consumer surveys. Often, individual tourism operators will collect these data about their customers during the reservations and registration process. Tourism destination organisations research these profiles of tourism consumers from different generating regions, and commercial market research companies conduct regular surveys to gather profiles of tourists.

This form of segmentation facilitates a broad understanding of consumers' needs and levels of disposable income, but by itself does not provide sufficient information for a marketing campaign. It is particularly useful in refining segmentation when combined with other methods.

Geodemographic Profile

Geodemographic profiles integrate census data with postcodes to identify the demographic, economic and lifecycle characteristics of each household in the country, which are then grouped together using a range of characteristics such as family structure, age, life cycle and income. In the UK this profile is known as ACORN (A Classification of Residential Neighbourhoods) (Middleton et al., 2009).

Geodemographic segmentation is particularly useful in identifying potential customers once a target market has been identified because mailing lists with the addresses of consumers that share particular characteristics can be purchased and those consumers can be communicated with directly. Geodemographic segmentation is also used to assess the viability of a new location, for example for a travel agency or a transport operator, by identifying the characteristics of a potential catchment area.

ACORN data can be combined with data from commercial surveys that analyse consumer behaviour, including the consumption of tourism products, to provide a very focused mailing campaign or understanding of a catchment area.

Psychographic Profile and Lifestyle

The psychographic profile of a consumer reveals their attitudes, opinions, and the psychological dimensions of their consumer behaviour, and helps companies to understand why consumers use, or do not use, their products. Collecting information to develop psychographic profiles is complex and expensive but is now facilitated by software that analyses the responses to carefully designed research and identifies groups with common characteristics and consumer behaviour patterns. This helps to understand how companies should position themselves in relation to competitors, the messages they should use in their communications, the look and style of their product, and the development of their brand.

The relationship between attitudes and consumer behaviour creates a profile of an individual's lifestyle – their interests and activities – which facilitates the design of products and marketing communications. This method of segmentation involves detailed marketing research and is usually combined with segmentation by purpose and life cycle. Snapshot 13.1 illustrates this.

Price

Price segmentation identifies consumers on the basis of the price they will pay for a product (Middleton et al., 2009).

The use of variable pricing to reflect the price sensitivity of consumers is a common practice in tourism, but is usually combined with other segmentation criteria such as buyer behaviour and demographic, and economic and lifecycle profiles.

Some segmentation criteria are easier or cheaper to research than others. However, using more criteria should result in more focused and refined target markets and the design of more effective marketing strategies and activities.

National and multinational tourism companies with large marketing budgets are more able to research the buyer needs and psychographic profiles of consumers and therefore will have a distinct marketing advantage over SMEs and microbusinesses. Tourism destination organisations often fill this gap in marketing intelligence by conducting research and identifying relevant market segments: this information is then made available to all suppliers within their destination.

The snapshot below describes the methods of market segmentation used by a destination marketing organisation in south-west England.

Snapshot 13.1   South West Tourism (SWT)

South West Tourism's Market Segmentation

SWT was responsible for creating and promoting a distinct regional identity. Their challenge was to match tourism suppliers with the most appropriate market segments.

In 2003, SWT identified seven main customer bands to the region, based on life-stage and socio-economic profiles:

1   Young, Free and Singles, aged 16–24, with relatively low budgets.
2   DINKS (double income, no kids) and SINKS (single income, no kids) are affluent and aged 25–35.
3–5 Families with either pre-, primary or secondary school aged children.
6   Empty Nesters, aged late 40s to 60s and affluent.
7   Third Agers, aged 70+ and affluent.

Each band varies in terms of length of stay, time of travel, lead-in time, use of the internet to research trips, type of attractions and amenities required, and budget.

SWT then matched the benefits sought by its leisure tourists to the relevant customer bands. They developed 10 clear market segments, including:

(Continued)

(Continued)

- Sheer Indulgence – Seek luxury and pampering. Require luxury accommodation. Activities include cuisine, art galleries, unique shops, spa treatments, golf. Target market: SINKS, DINKS, Empty Nesters, Parents (without their children).
- It's Adventure! – Seek challenges, thrills and new experiences. Activities include surfing, sailing, paragliding, body-boarding. May camp, self-cater or stay in hotels. Target market: Young, Free and Singles, SINKS, DINKS, families with secondary school-aged children.

SWT's promotional campaigns for each segment used images and words that conveyed the experiences on offer.

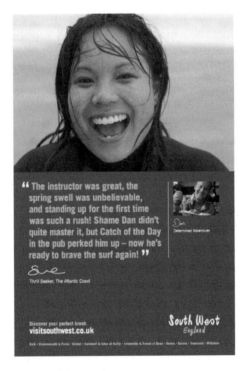

Print advertisement targetting the It's Adventure! segment

Source: Courtesy of South West Tourism Alliance

The snapshot above shows the link between the segmentation of consumer markets using multiple criteria, and the design of focused communications that deliver specific messages about the destination. Communication is one of a range of activities in a process known as the marketing mix.

The Marketing Mix

The marketing mix is a blend of actions taken by marketers to manage and develop demand for their products. Traditionally this mix has consisted of four variables – product, price, place and promotion – originally described by McCarthy in 1960 as the 4Ps framework (McCarthy, 1981, in Middleton et al., 2009: 138). This framework has been adopted widely by marketing academics and practitioners and has since been extended to seven or sometimes eight Ps to reflect services marketing activities.

Holloway (2004: 52) describes the marketing mix as '… one of the most important in marketing – indeed, it can be called the core of all marketing planning'. The way marketing managers adapt and blend the variables develops in response to marketing research into the external environment, the actions of competitors, the needs of the target market, and levels of customer satisfaction. These variables are the only elements that marketing managers can control directly, and the mix is used to create and communicate a **competitive advantage** to, and manage demand from, the target market segments. Control over the marketing mix involves a regular or continuous process of adjustment of the mix in response to research findings.

> **Competitive advantage:** Factors that give a product, a service or a company superiority over its rivals

In the following section we discuss the marketing mix in relation to the services marketing triangle, beginning with external marketing.

External marketing involves the marketing mix variables that make promises to potential customers – product, price, promotion and place.

Product

Product is considered to be the most important of the marketing mix variables. Middleton et al. (2009: 119) state that 'Product decisions, with all their implications for the management of service operations and profitability, influence not only the marketing mix but also a firm's long-term growth strategy and policies for investment and human resources'.

Product forms the foundation of the marketing mix, because decisions about the other Ps will depend on the design and operation of the product. For example, the prices that can be charged, the messages used to promote it to the target market, or the skills of the people required to provide it. Holloway (2004: 129) suggests that if the product does not match the needs and wants of the target market, then decisions about the remaining Ps are immaterial: 'if the product is not what the market wants, no amount of price adjustment, dependable delivery or brilliant promotion will encourage consumers to buy it – or at least, not more than once … '.

The challenge with the tourist product is defining what it is that the consumer is actually purchasing.

We explained earlier that consumers seek particular benefits from their tourism experiences. These benefits aren't tangible products that can be purchased or consumed, but are actually the outcome of the experiences provided through the temporary ownership of physical products; that is, transport, accommodation and attractions.

In order to explore the link between product and benefits, Kotler (1984), following research by Levitt (1981), deconstructed products into three main levels: core, formal and augmented.

The core level – this element of the product is intangible and relates to the benefits that the customer is seeking. For business tourists this may be speed, punctuality, efficient service, comfort and a professional environment, while leisure tourists may seek relaxation, an escape from stress, stronger relationships, a physical challenge, cultural enrichment or fun. Marketing managers must identify the benefits sought from their target markets, develop a product that provides these, communicate this to the target market more effectively than their competitors, and monitor their success in satisfying them. Snapshot 13.1 describes the core level of product sought by each target market.

The formal or tangible level – this part of the product is physical, for example a seat on a plane or a room in a hotel. In the tourism sector there is often great similarity in the formal product level of suppliers competing for the same target market. For instance, airlines operating flights between the same two cities do not vary significantly in the tangible product they offer, nor do two hotels of the same standard in the same destination. Marketing managers must ensure that the quality of the formal product matches the expectations of its target market, but must also find a way to make their own formal products stand out or differentiate themselves from those of their competitors. This differentiation is achieved through the next product level.

The augmented level – this part of the product is key to providing a superior value to that of competitors; that is, the augmented product adds value to the formal product and enables it to be differentiated. The formal product may be augmented by tangible or intangible elements at any stage of the delivery process and adaptations to the augmented product level can be implemented relatively easily. For example, accommodation providers may augment their formal product by providing locally-sourced food for their meals, designer bathroom products, or luxury bedding, and transport operators may augment their product by offering improved entertainment, technology or catering. Some product augmentations may justify higher prices and some may be copied by competitors. Product augmentations can often be customised to the needs of individual consumers; for example, hotels may augment their product for families by offering adjoining rooms, cots, baby listening devices and children's meals. A popular method for augmenting the product in tourism is through branding.

Branding

Branding is the process of developing, communicating and maintaining a particular identity for a supplier, and an image for the consumer (Pike, 2008).

A brand is the image of a company, organisation or destination from the consumer's perspective, who then mentally positions it in relation to its competitors. This image is reinforced through the messages that are communicated about it, and by the consumer's experience of it. Branding has been widely used in goods marketing since the middle of the twentieth century, but it was only during the 1980s that its importance for service marketing was widely recognised (Grönroos, 2007).

Branding involves the blending of tangible and intangible qualities, symbolised by a trademark, which creates and communicates specific value in the minds of the target market, and may allow a higher price to be charged. The target market perceives the brand as superior to competitors, and if their experience of the product confirms this, the market remains loyal to it through repeat purchases. Successful branding helps to overcome the challenges of distance from markets and intangibility that is inherent in tourism products.

The services marketing triangle requires branding to be applied to external, interactive and internal marketing. As tourism usually involves prolonged service delivery processes, for example over several hours on a flight, days in a hotel or weeks on an inclusive tour, it is vital that the added values of the brand are integrated into every service encounter.

Middleton et al. (2009) identify a number of advantages that branding offers to tourism service providers:

- It creates a distinct identity for a supplier or a destination, that helps it to stand out from its competitors.
- It reduces intangibility and the perceived risk for the consumer by creating familiarity and signalling quality and reliability.
- It facilitates market segmentation by attracting some and putting off other market segments.
- The perceived additional value of the product provides some protection from price wars with competitors, and may reduce recovery time after a crisis.
- It may clarify consumers' expectations for employees and destination stakeholders and create greater consistency in service encounters.
- It may encourage customer loyalty, particularly where one supplier provides its product in several locations, for example a hotel chain, an airline, or a tour operator.

Successful branding requires detailed research and costly investment in the development and implementation of a brand identity and image. However, while there are several examples of successful and high profile branding in tourism, for example Disney, Virgin, and Singapore Airlines, in tourism, branding is not restricted to large suppliers with significant financial resources; through franchises and consortia (explained in detail in Chapter 5), SMEs can also exploit the advantages of branding by adopting the brand of a third party, for example Holiday Inn Express or Best Western International.

The concept of branding destinations is relatively new in tourism marketing – it was first included in tourism literature in the late 1990s (Pike, 2008) and is now increasingly used as a tool to communicate the value offered by a destination and to differentiate it from its competitors. A further exploration of destination branding can be found in Chapter 12.

Price

Price is the only element in the marketing mix that directly affects a company or organisation's revenue; all the others represent costs. Price therefore plays a crucial role in determining profitability for commercial enterprises. For public and not-for-profit organisations, price may be used to achieve societal benefits – perhaps through charging high prices to restrict demand to protect or conserve a fragile environment, for example historic or religious sites that introduce high entrance fees to deter some visitors; alternatively, low prices or even free access may be offered to encourage use of the resource by all social groups, for example entrances to museums and galleries whose function is to conserve their resources for the benefit and education of the public.

Pricing in tourism is a complex activity for a number of reasons:

- Detailed information about potential consumers and their willingness to pay, and competitors' pricing decisions, is not easily available.
- There may be a long lead-in time between setting prices and selling the product.
- Demand from international markets may be increased or reduced by exchange rate fluctuations.
- The high fixed to variable cost ratio (see Chapter 5) creates opportunities to sell capacity at different prices to different market segments. This is known as price discrimination and is widely used in the tourism sector.
- Pricing is often used as a tool to manipulate demand and smooth seasonal, daily or hourly variations in that demand by charging higher prices for capacity at peak times, and lower prices at off-peak times. Demand with low price elasticity will pay the higher prices, whereas demand with high price elasticity will be shifted to periods where prices are lower. Price elasticity is explained in Chapter 3.
- Price has a significant role in achieving a competitive advantage in markets with a high elasticity of demand and often results in price-cutting and price wars.

Tourism service providers often use price as a tool to manage demand and many compete on the basis of price. Pricing decisions can be made using one of a range of approaches, as the list below, adapted from Hudson (2008), describes:

- *Cost-plus pricing*: the addition of a fixed percentage mark-up on costs. Does not account for competitors' prices or levels of demand.

- *Value-based pricing*: prices are based on the target market's perceived value of the product. Different segments may perceive different values. Continual monitoring of market perception and satisfaction is required, plus competitors' actions.

- *Competition-based pricing*: prices are set at the same rate as competitors' prices.

- *Differential (or demand-based) pricing*: different prices are charged depending on the consumer's ability to pay. Requires a constant monitoring of demand and amendment of prices. Usually prices will vary according to how far in advance and where reservations are made, and the degree of necessity of the purchase. This approach may be combined with variable pricing.

- *Price skimming*: used for new products. Charging the highest possible price until demand falls, then reducing the price to attract the next segment, and so on.

- *Penetration pricing*: pricing new products below competitors' products in order to gain a market share. However competitors may copy prices and low prices may affect perceptions of quality.

- *Portfolio pricing*: pricing products in the same range differently by including different features e.g. a hotel with standard rooms, executive rooms and suites.

- *Prestige (or premium) pricing*: setting prices high to reflect the exclusivity of the product, e.g. for cabins on the Airbus A380, or rooms in the 7-star Burj Al Arab luxury hotel in Dubai.

- *Variable (or marginal) pricing*: covers the variable costs of the product but not the fixed costs. It assumes that fixed costs are met by charging higher prices to other customers. Marketers must ensure that consumers who would be prepared to pay higher prices are unable to purchase the product at the lower price. This strategy is common in the transport sector, but can be dangerous if the forecasted demand at higher prices is not realised.

- *Price bundling*: combining products at a lower price, e.g. book Friday and Saturday night in a hotel, get Sunday free; free travel insurance with the sale of a package holiday.

- *Discount (sales promotion) pricing*: short-term measures to stimulate demand through price reductions, special offers, early booking discounts. Used to shift excess capacity, improve cash-flow, or undermine competitors.

Place

Place refers to the types of point of sale at which the product is purchased. In tourism this is particularly important because the point of sale of the product is often not the same as the point of production and consumption. For example, in the case of transport, accommodation or a major attraction, the purchase must be made some time in advance of production and consumption, often while the buyer is still in the generating region, and sometimes many

Table 13.1   Tourism distribution channels

Direct – the point of sale is provided by the supplier	Indirect – the point of sale is provided by intermediaries
A ticket office on the site of a visitor attraction or transport operator An airline sales office in the generating region A hotel reservations department, in the hotel or through a reservations office in the generating region Online booking facility via the producer's own website	Wholesalers who sell the product on to the trade or to the consumer Operators who add other elements to the product to create a package or inclusive tour, selling via agencies or direct to the consumer Agencies who are paid a commission for each sale (Each of these types of intermediary is explained in detail in Chapter 6.)

Source: Hudson (2008).

months, or even years, in advance. The importance of effective points of sale in these situations cannot be overestimated.

In tourism, the term place can be confusing, so to avoid confusion, in tourism marketing the 'place' element of the marketing mix is more commonly called 'distribution'.

Different types of points of sale are known as distribution channels. Distribution channels can be direct or indirect as illustrated in Table 13.1.

Some suppliers may use only one channel of distribution, while others, particularly large companies that target a range of market segments, may use multiple channels. The perishability of the tourism product creates a need to secure as many sales in advance of production as possible; this in turn requires selection of the most effective distribution channels and reservations systems to manage and control sales.

Choice of Distribution Channel

The choice of distribution channel is flexible; suppliers can use one channel alone or several types simultaneously. Middleton et al. (2009) stress that the choice of channel is mainly influenced by financial considerations and also stress the importance of careful planning to identify required sales volumes and revenue within a specified time period. The type of distribution channel to use is determined by cost, market coverage, sales volume, buyer behaviour in the target market, and the level of control over sales that is required.

Table 13.2 identifies the main advantages and disadvantages of direct and indirect distribution.

Direct distribution, particularly when the physical, cultural and language differences between suppliers and consumers are large, can be complex and costly, and represent fixed costs paid in advance, increasing the financial risk. Indirect distribution on the other hand is more straightforward, requires less marketing

Table 13.2   The advantages and disadvantages for suppliers of direct and indirect distribution

Advantages of direct distribution	Advantages of using intermediaries
Control over information provided about the product	Much of the cost of promotion is borne by the intermediary
Control over type of customer attracted	Payment of commission to agencies, or discounted rates to wholesalers and operators, represent a variable cost – these are only incurred if a sale is made by the intermediary
Gather detailed information about potential and actual consumers	
Potential closer match between benefits sought by customer and their satisfaction by the producer	Easier access to distant markets using the market knowledge of intermediary
Disadvantages of direct distribution	**Disadvantages of using intermediaries**
Cost of market research	Limited control over information provided about the product
Investment required in facilities to process the sale – development and maintenance of a website, recruitment of more staff in reservations department, establishment of sales outlets in generating region or in the destination	Limited control over type of customer attracted
	Limited control over commitment of intermediary to prioritise supplier's product over competitor's
	No control of service standards in intermediary
Investment in promotion to guide potential customers to the direct points of sales	Unable to gather detailed information about potential consumers, and limited knowledge of actual consumers
These investments represent a fixed cost – they must be paid whether or not a sale is made	Potential mismatch between benefits sought by the customer and their satisfaction by the supplier

effort, and represents a variable cost that will only be paid if the distributor sells a unit of capacity. However, indirect distribution can also be costly: travel agencies usually require a commission of 10–15 per cent, and operators and wholesalers will normally need a reduction on published prices of about 30 per cent.

Distribution and the Internet

> *... the Internet has become the primary channel for consumer access, distribution and direct marketing.* (Middleton et al., 2009: 275)

The internet has revolutionised the distribution of tourism products. Direct distribution from supplier to consumer is more straightforward and less costly online. Suppliers' websites allow consumers to research products, make reservations and pay for them, and receive documentation online. Some tourism sectors, particularly the airline and hotel industries, have embraced the opportunity to distribute their products direct via their own websites, in order to reduce their reliance on travel agencies and avoid paying commission.

The key to successful direct distribution online is making sure that target markets choose to visit the supplier's website, rather than the hundreds or thousands of competitor websites available. This problem is discussed in detail in our section on promotion below, but has actually generated a new form of distribution that is becoming widely used in the tourism sector.

Affiliate Marketing

Affiliates are the online partners of companies who target the same market segments in different sectors, for example, music, clothing and travel. The affiliate's website contains a link to the partner's website, and if a reservation is made through that link, then the affiliate is rewarded either with a flat fee or a commission. This is another form of indirect distribution in which affiliates act in a similar way to travel agencies, although they do not require any facilities, equipment or specialist knowledge. Affiliate marketing is used by all sectors in the tourism industry. Thomson Holidays, part of the TUI Travel group, is a tour operator selling a range of holiday products to the UK outbound market. It uses a specialist agency to promote its affiliate programme and provide online banners, text links and discount codes to be displayed on its affiliate partners' websites. The affiliate then earns between 1 and 4 per cent commission if a viewer clicks through to the Thomson website and subsequently makes a booking within 30 days (Thomson Holidays, 2010).

Promotion

This element of the marketing mix is more commonly referred to as marketing communications, in order to embrace the range of methods used to communicate messages about the value of the product to the target market. Marketing communications have a key role in overcoming the intangible and distant nature of tourism products and in conveying the value that the product or company offers. There are a number of methods available to communicate the benefits of a particular supplier or destination. Often a supplier will blend a number of methods, known as the communications mix, specifically for each target market.

The internet has transformed the communication channels used by consumers, and suppliers have had to respond accordingly. Middleton et al. (2009: 261) suggest that 'the website is now the centre of the marketing communications mix'. The problem for companies, though, is encouraging customers to visit their website amongst the plethora available. Middleton et al. (2009) suggest that the remaining communications activities should focus on attracting customers to the website. We will now explain the main communications methods and their applications in tourism. We should note that the internet has created new opportunities in each form of promotion and, increasingly, the distinction between them is becoming blurred. Methods of communicating include:

- Word of mouth.
- Advertising.
- Public relations (PR).
- Personal selling.
- Sponsorship.

Each of these will now be discussed.

Word of Mouth (WOM) or Customer to Customer (C2C) Communications

WOM or C2C communication is the discussion of a company or organisation between people who appear to have no personal interest in promoting them. The intangibility of tourism services makes C2C communication particularly useful to consumers because it reduces the intangibility of the product and the perceived risk of purchasing it by providing first-hand accounts of the experience. However, the inseparability and heterogeneity features of tourism services create particular challenges for tourism suppliers because of the difficulties in ensuring consistency of quality across all consumers. Positive WOM is of course free good publicity but negative WOM can be very damaging.

The internet has revolutionised WOM communications and increased their importance in the communications mix by providing opportunities for C2C communication. C2C is available online through:

- Social networking sites such as Facebook, Twitter and MySpace, and the travel specific networking site WAYN.
- Online communities of individuals with shared interests, who communicate via wikis, chat rooms, message boards and forums, for example www.travellerspoint. com; www.lonelyplanet.com.
- Blogs – online diaries written by individuals and available for invited users to view. Many blogs are created by travellers to record their experiences, for example www. travelpod.com; www.travelblog.org.
- Review sites where consumers share their experiences of a supplier, with reviews, photographs, and information, for example tripadvisor.com.
- Information sharing sites such as Youtube where film can be posted for worldwide audiences to view.

The snapshot below presents a customer review site that has been created specifically for tourism consumers.

Snapshot 13.2   Tripadvisor

Tripadvisor was set up in 2000 to provide a forum for members to review their travel experiences and share them with site visitors. They now have 18 different review sites that are visited by 50 million monthly viewers (tripadvisor, 2011).

Molesworth Manor B&B Reviews, Little Petherick

 tripadvisor.co.uk

BEST DESTINATIONS OF 2011   GET THE LIST ▶

Molesworth Manor

Little Petherick PL27 7QT, England
+44 1841540292+44 1841540292
E-mail hotelE-mail hotel
Hotel website

Hotel photos (4)

TripAdvisor Popularity Index

#**1**of 1 B&Bs in Little Petherick
44 reviews

Check Rates and Availability

Check-in 20/5/2011   Check-out   Adults 2

Show Prices

- ☑   Booking.com

Free Newsletter

Interested in **Molesworth Manor** and **Little Petherick**?

We'll send you updates with **the latest deals, reviews and articles for Molesworth Manor and Little Petherick** each week.

Enter your email

Sign up

- Save Molesworth Manor
- E-mail this page

What travellers say about Molesworth Manor
- Fresh fruit(5) Full english(4) Breakfast room(3) Daily special(3) Good value(3) Lovely view(3)
- Very comfortable(3) Honesty bar(3)

Reviews you can trust

Write a Review
Filter traveller reviews
Trip type

☑ All reviews (44) ☐ Business reviews (0) ☐ Couples reviews (35) ☐ Family reviews (4) ☐ Friends reviews (0) ☐ Solo travel reviews (0)
Traveller rating

☑ All (44) ☐ Excellent (37) ☐ Very good (3) ☐ Average (1) ☐ Poor (3) ☐ Terrible (0)

Reproduced with permission from tripadvisor 2011

Tripadvisor webpage for Molesworth Manor

Source: © Reproduced with permission from Tripadvisor and Molesworth Manor 2011

(Continued)

(Continued)

Tripadvisor's stated mission is to 'Help people around the world plan and have the perfect trip'. They do this by allowing non-members to read reviews of tourism products before making reservations themselves. Reviewers rate their experience on a scale from 'excellent' to 'terrible' and provide descriptions and photos. In the event of a poor review, proprietors can post replies with explanations and descriptions of remedial action.

Molesworth Manor, a family-run 13 room hotel in south-west England, has 43 reviews on tripadvisor; it's average rating is 'excellent'. Geoff and Jess French, the proprietors, consider tripadvisor to be a valuable marketing tool that communicates positive messages about their hotel to a very wide audience that they could not reach independently. They monitor their reviews regularly to identify the strengths and weaknesses of their product, and consider that the majority of their new customers check their tripadvisor rating before making a booking.

Advertising

Advertising is the paid-for promotion of products to large audiences (Hudson, 2008) and includes print adverts in newspapers and magazines, television, cinema and radio advertising, and billboard advertising.

The key point about advertising is that it must be positioned in places where the target market is most likely to see or hear it. For example, a cruise line promoting a new ship or cruise itinerary may advertise in trade newspapers read by travel agents, and operators organising clubbing holidays for young adults may advertise in magazines, on radio stations and on advertising slots on TV programmes whose audience is predominantly made up of that market. The internet offers particular advantages for targeted advertising through pay-per-click adverts.

Pay-per-click is display advertising on the internet through pop-ups and banners on websites that target the same customers. The adverts encourage potential customers to click through to the advertiser's website and the advertiser pays for each click. For instance, accommodation wholesalers and car hire companies may advertise on airline websites and hotels may advertise on search engine results pages when their destination's name is searched. Ski holiday operators might advertise on the websites of ski equipment and clothing brands. Many social media websites and online community websites wikis, reviews and blogs, allow targeted pay-per-click adverts based on the profile of users. For instance, tour operators specialising in activity holidays may advertise on community websites and blog pages for surfing, sailing or diving enthusiasts.

Pay-per-click advertising is important, particularly for tourism SMEs, for a number of reasons:

- Payment is required only when a potential customer clicks through to the website, compared to traditional media advertising where payment is made regardless of the number of people who may see it.

- Expenditure is controlled through setting a pay-per-click budget, allowing a quota of advert displays based on the financial resources of the company.

- Action is immediate because the advert is displayed when the potential customer is actively seeking information, rather than requiring them to remember the advert and take action at another time.

- The customer can be tracked from enquiry to booking, which provides valuable information about consumer behaviour.

- Advertising is targeted more accurately at potential consumers who are seeking related information.

Search Engine Optimisation (SEO) is the process by which a company's listing on search engine results pages is manipulated. When an internet user searches for information using a search engine such as Google or Yahoo, they type in keywords; if those keywords match the content of a website, that website will be listed. The greater the match, the higher up the list the website will appear. Website design and content is therefore crucial in manipulating the website's position on search engine results pages. Specialist agencies offer SEO services and also handle pay per click advertising spend.

Public Relations (PR)

> ... *the aim of marketing PR is to obtain favourable publicity for an organisation and its products in the media.* (Middleton et al., 2009: 306)

PR is the acquisition of media coverage that is not directly paid for. PR activities include press releases, press conferences, feature stories in travel magazines or supplements, familiarisation (fam) trips for journalists and intermediaries, event sponsorship, celebrity visits, exhibiting at trade or consumer travel exhibitions, product placement in films or TV programmes, and maintaining an image library for the media to use.

A major advantage of PR, particularly in tourism, is that the information is usually perceived to be coming from an impartial third party and therefore has greater credibility than advertising (Middleton et al., 2009). However, there is some risk here as the business, organisation or destination has no control over what is actually shown or said.

PR is a communication method widely used by national or regional tourism organisations to influence perceptions of their destination and to bring small suppliers and potential customers together. Familiarisation trips to destinations are organised by tourism organisations for carefully selected journalists who will then write a feature story about the trip, or for trade intermediaries in order to train them on destinations and products.

PR is a crucial tool in the event of a crisis involving tourists or destinations, to manage the negative publicity generated by the media. Through a carefully managed relationship with the press, using press releases, press conferences and media site visits, it is possible to influence the way a crisis is portrayed by the media, and its subsequent impact on the image of the destination or supplier, as well as on future demand.

Personal Selling

Personal selling is the use of personalised communication with potential consumers to maintain relationships, gather marketing intelligence, provide sales support and generate sales (Hudson, 2008).

Personal selling is important in tourism as it helps to reduce the intangibility of the product, but can be difficult because suppliers are located some distance away from their potential consumers. Tourism destination organisations play an important role in creating opportunities for suppliers within their destination to use personal selling as a communications tool. In tourism personal selling is implemented through:

- Exhibiting at a trade or consumer travel exhibition, for example 'ITB' in Berlin or 'Destinations' in London: Tourism destination organisations sell space on their stands to small companies who would otherwise be unable to exhibit.
- Employing sales managers or account managers to liaise with travel trade intermediaries or corporate customers and maintain a relationship with them.
- Workshops organised by tourism destination organisations for producers and trade intermediaries to meet face-to-face, either at the destination or in the generating region.
- Telephone or face-to-face contact with customers via sales offices or sales desks.
- Postal or email communications.

The internet has created new opportunities for remote personal selling through RSS feeds, and subscriptions to companies' social media sites, enabling companies to send updates on products and prices to subscribers. It is also common for individual tourism companies, organisations and destinations to have their own sites on social media to which interested individuals can subscribe to find out about product developments, special offers and company news. Large companies employ staff to monitor and manage social media campaigns by maintaining relationships with bloggers, answering questions, responding to negative WOM on review sites, and updating social media sites. For example, large companies from all of the tourism industries have Facebook and MySpace pages, use Twitter to make short announcements, and upload promotional material onto YouTube.

Tourism suppliers have a range of communication options available to them. The choice of method, and its content, should be determined by knowledge of the methods that reach the target market most effectively. In addition, the success of each method used should be carefully measured to inform any future decisions about marketing communications.

In reality, often the choice of method and the ability to measure its effectiveness are constrained by cost considerations. Large companies that invest huge sums in advertising will employ specialist agencies to design campaigns, test proposed messages using focus groups, and use marketing research agencies to measure the effectiveness of campaigns through surveys. Smaller companies, public sector and not-for-profit suppliers are usually unable to approach their marketing communications in the same way, but they benefit from the communications mix used by tourism destination organisations to promote the destination in which they are located. Where communication budgets are limited, marketers must be creative and innovative in using the communications mix to attract the attention of their target markets. The case study below describes a communications campaign mix implemented by a regional tourist organisation in Australia.

CASE STUDY 13.1

TOURISM QUEENSLAND'S COMMUNICATION CAMPAIGN – THE BEST JOB IN THE WORLD

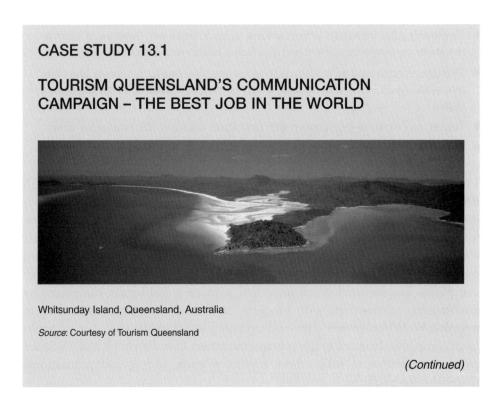

Whitsunday Island, Queensland, Australia

Source: Courtesy of Tourism Queensland

(Continued)

(Continued)

In 2009, Tourism Queensland (TQ) launched an innovative and ground-breaking interactive communications campaign to raise awareness in global experience seekers in eight international markets of the 100+ islands in Queensland.

Attractions include beautiful beaches, rainforests, coral reefs and wildlife, and experiences include snorkelling, diving, kayaking, sailing and walking. To create a distinct identity, TQ branded the region 'Islands of the Great Barrier Reef' and developed a communications campaign embracing digital marketing technology using social media, viral campaigning, and user-generated content.

TQ sought to increase global awareness of the islands through a competition, with one prize of 'The Best Job in the World'. The job was Island Caretaker and the winner would write a weekly blog about the islands. They would live in a three-bedroomed villa with pool on Hamilton Island for six months, with a salary of AU$150,000.

The campaign was launched with small classified print adverts on newspaper recruitment pages in target market regions and online recruitment websites. The adverts presented the location as 'Islands of the Great Barrier Reef, Queensland, Australia', and directed interested readers to the website www.islandreefjob.com, which featured stunning images of the islands showing the attractions and activities there.

Applicants had to submit a 60-second video presentation explaining why they should win. Visitors to the website could watch the videos and vote for applicants. The applicant with the most votes would be interviewed, along with 10 applicants chosen by the judges.

The campaign was supported by a presence on YouTube, MySpace, Twitter and Facebook, by banner advertising on websites, and through regular press releases updating TV and print media about the progress of the competition.

In the first weekend after the campaign launched the website received 200,000 hits, with 25,000 in one hour alone. Publicity for the islands gained momentum through viral messages as friends spread the details via email and social media networks. The caretaker job became a news item on major TV news networks such as CNN, BBC and ABC, and articles were written in magazines and newspapers globally. Internet discussion groups, bulletin boards and blogs were also set up by potential applicants, as well as a website to share ideas and tips.

Almost 35,000 applicants from 197 countries applied, and the winner was a 34-year-old British man.

TQ estimates that the campaign generated media coverage worth AU$400 million and reached an audience of 3 billion globally.

The campaign won six awards at the Cannes Lions International Advertising Festival in 2009 and has been voted 8th in the top 50 PR stunts of all time.

TQ capitalised on increased awareness of the islands by setting up a competition for families to win a holiday there, 'The Best Experience in the World', issuing regular press releases about the winner's activities and publishing his blog on the TQ website. They arrange regular fam trips for intermediaries from the eight target markets, to train them on the attractions of holidays there.

Source: Tourism Queensland (2009).

(Continued)

(Continued)

Reflective Questions

1 Which elements of the communications mix were blended in TQ's campaign?
2 What advantages did TQ's approach offer that could not have been achieved through traditional print, radio and TV advertising alone?

During the 1990s, Kotler suggested that the 4Ps framework could reflect a more consumer-focused approach if it were expressed as the 4Cs (Kotler and Armstrong, 1999):

- *Product* becomes *Customer value*, defined as the benefits sought, the perceived quality of experience, and the value for money compared to that of competitors.
- *Price* becomes *Cost,* as consumers compare the cost to them against competitors' customer value.
- *Promotion* becomes *Communication* and includes all forms of contact between service supplier and consumer.
- *Place* becomes *Convenience* and includes all forms of consumer access to organise the purchase or use of the service.

Kotler's interpretation of the marketing variables as 4Cs is useful because it clarifies the meaning of each variable in a services marketing context. However, it has not been widely adopted by marketing academics and practitioners; the 4P framework remains in use because it simplifies the concept of the marketing mix and has allowed other variables to be integrated with it.

The Extended Marketing Mix for Services – Interactive and Internal Marketing

The 4Ps framework discussed above is applicable to both goods and services. However, the distinct characteristics of services and the services marketing triangle create a need for more variables. In addition to the 4Ps, Booms and Bitner (1981) added three more marketing mix variables that are used in services marketing:

- People.
- Processes.
- Physical evidence.

Goeldner (2000, in Fyall and Garrod, 2005) proposed that partnership be added to the extended marketing mix for tourism because of the growing importance of collaboration between suppliers, although this has not been widely adopted yet.

We now consider people, processes and physical evidence.

People

The characteristics of inseparability and heterogeneity and the services marketing triangle demonstrate the importance of the role of people in the delivery and consumption of the tourism experience. Usually this marketing mix variable is interpreted as employees who interact with customers. However, from the tourist's perspective, there are two other groups of people that influence the quality of their experience – other customers consuming the product at the same time and the local community with whom the customer may come into considerable contact.

Employees

Holloway (2004: 54) describes employees as 'an integral part' of the service experience and highlights the importance of the quality of personal service provided. Frontline employees have direct contact with customers and their behaviour, appearance and service skills will affect the customer's perception of the company or organisation. They also interact with customers in situations that can sometimes be very stressful, for example at peak times with long queues, in the event of a delay or technical problem, or when customers are dissatisfied and complaining. The personalities of employees, their motivations and attitudes to their work, and the level of support and recompense provided to them will ultimately influence the quality of service they provide.

The services marketing triangle suggests that there is a direct link between employee satisfaction and customer satisfaction. Therefore the recruitment and training processes that a company or organisation implements, the benefits and support provided, and the way in which employees are managed, will influence the quality of service experienced by the customer, at all stages of the service delivery. Internal marketing is used to manage the relationship between employer and employee.

Other Customers Consuming the Experience at the Same Time

Other customers consuming the product at the same time have the potential to enhance or reduce the quality of each customer's experience of the tourism product.

Middleton et al. (2009) stress the importance of effective market segmentation in achieving compatibility between customers. This should ensure that all customers within the target market seek the same benefits and share some characteristics. This in turn will facilitate the selection of customers whose behaviour and attitudes are compatible and will contribute towards their harmonious integration during the consumption of the product.

However, when more than one segment is targeted, the potential for conflict between them can be high if the benefits sought are different. Marketing managers must ensure, through the design and operation of a product, that incompatible segments do not interact. This emphasises the importance of layout and design in facilitating the separation of segments with different needs. The snapshot below illustrates how Disney Cruise Lines manage the different market segments on board.

 ## Snapshot 13.3   Disney Cruise Lines

Disney operates cruises in the Bahamas, Caribbean, Mexican Riviera, Europe and Alaska. They own a Bahamian island, Castaway Cay, at which all Bahamian and Caribbean cruises call.

Disney promises that their cruises are 'dreams', 'magic', 'enchantment' and 'paradise', and targets the family and couples markets. To deliver these promises for each passenger, Disney augments the formal cruise product carefully. Customer segments are carefully managed to deliver 'paradise' to those with varying expectations.

On board facilities, activities, catering and entertainment are tailored for adults, teenagers, and children:

- Adults have an exclusive pool, spa, fitness centre, restaurant, pub, piano bar and nightclub, and group activities like wine tasting and cooking classes.
- Teenagers have a private lounge with activities and a nightclub.
- Children have a customised deck with supervised splash pools, games, age appropriate play areas, entertainment, Disney characters, and organised childcare from morning to midnight.

Families dine together in a different restaurant each night. Their servers are the same each night to encourage familiarity with the individual needs of each group. Castaway Cay is zoned as Serenity Bay for adults only, a family beach, a teenagers' activity area, and a supervised kids/play area.

Source: Disney Cruise Lines (2010)

The Local Community

The third group of people that tourists will interact with during their tourism experience is the host community. Often, the nature of this interaction will be commercial; that is, a situation where the tourist is being served by a member of the local community, perhaps in a shop or restaurant. Less frequently, the interaction may be non-commercial, where the tourist shares facilities with local people, engages in conversation with them, or seeks assistance from them. Contemporary definitions of marketing include the host community as stakeholders who should benefit from the marketing process, but the attitude of the local community to tourism can also positively or negatively affect the tourism consumer's experience and perception of the destination. Destination marketing organisations can affect this through involving local communities in decision making, keeping them informed of the benefits of tourism, and ensuring that the negative impacts of tourism are reduced. For example, in Jamaica, TV advertising was used to remind the host community of the importance of tourism to the country's economy and a training programme for all workers who come into contact with tourists, for example taxi drivers and craft sellers, was introduced to equip them with the skills required to provide good service to tourists.

Physical Evidence

Physical evidence refers to the environments in which service encounters occur. This environment may be on the service company's premises, or in the customer's own environment during the research and reservation stage. Bitner (1992, cited in Hoffman et al., 2009: 371) describes this environment as the 'servicescape', and stresses its role in managing the service process because its design influences customer and employee behaviour.

This element of the marketing mix is particularly important in tourism because it communicates information about the intangible elements of the product such as type, style, quality and atmosphere at the enquiry, reservation and confirmation, as well as the consumption stages. Middleton et al. (2009) suggest that physical evidence is particularly important at the point of sale and to reduce post-purchase anxiety, for example in the form of brochures and documentation, and through the display of products on websites. Consistency of physical evidence at each stage of the service delivery process is essential because it is used to create expectations and differentiate the product from those of competitors, reinforce a brand image, and encourage desirable behaviour amongst consumers.

Kotler et al. (2004) define physical evidence as the atmosphere that is perceived by the customer, and several tourism marketing academics (Holloway, 2004; Hudson, 2008; Middleton et al., 2009) describe this atmosphere in relation to five senses: sight, sound, scent, touch and taste. Hudson (2008) identifies common elements of physical evidence (see Table 13.3).

Table 13.3 The servicescape

Servicescape facility exterior	Servicescape facility interior	Other tangibles
exterior design	layout	uniforms
landscape	equipment	business cards
signage	signage	stationery
lighting	scent	website
background noise	air temperature	invoices
	interior design	brochures
	lighting	
	background noise	

Source: adapted from Hudson (2008: 151).

The servicescape allows the target market to appraise the product before the purchase decision is made and during consumption. In other words, it communicates the value of the product. Physical evidence can also be used to deliver some elements of the augmented product. For example, a relaxed atmosphere in a holiday hotel may be communicated through soft background music at a low volume in public areas, subdued lighting, soft furnishings, the scent of fresh flowers and a casual style of staff uniform.

Physical evidence is also used to facilitate the service process by providing cues or instructions to consumers. Hoffman et al. (2009: 267) use airports as an example where signage and information announcements move the traveller 'through the service encounter' by directing passengers to the check-in, baggage drop, security, shopping and catering services, and the boarding gate.

Process

The simultaneous production and consumption of services emphasises the process of service delivery. Inseparability and heterogeneity make service encounters hard to control and unsatisfactory 'moments of truth' will affect customer satisfaction and loyalty and the image of the company. The management of the service delivery process is therefore particularly important in delivering service quality, in customer satisfaction and retention, and in positive WOM promotion. Some tourism service providers attempt to manage each service encounter through standardising the process.

Standardised Service Processes

One approach to managing service quality is to standardise the service process through the use of scripts and automation.

In tourism, many service encounters are remote. For example, many airports and hotels have automated check-in facilities, many attractions and destinations provide recorded information systems, and many suppliers interact with customers via websites to provide availability advice, confirm reservations, and send documentation.

An alternative or complementary way of standardising service encounters is to script the process. Scripted processes determine the sequence of actions, words and equipment to ensure consistent, satisfactory service encounters. Service encounters by telephone can be scripted to some extent, through standard introduction and closing statements that all employees use for every customer. Short and uncomplicated face-to-face encounters can also be scripted, for example in food and beverage services or on-site ticket sales for an attraction, and tour guides can to some degree script their presentation.

Scripted interactions need to be understood by customers and physical evidence is used to provide cues, for example a single queuing system for a ride at a theme park, or signage in a restaurant advising customers they should wait to be seated.

Standardisation of the service process may reduce the problem of heterogeneity and increase the likelihood of customer satisfaction, however it also reduces the service provider's ability to respond to customers' individual needs and requests (Hoffman et al., 2009). In complex service encounters that require a service provider to have a clear understanding of the customer's needs, for example with a travel agency, an operator or a tourism destination organisation, scripted processes are not appropriate.

Service Blueprints

Shostack (1977) proposed blueprinting service operations through a formal flowchart illustrating the service system and clarifying the roles of those involved in delivering the service. Service blueprints identify:

- All service encounters between the customer and service provider.
- The activities of all participants.
- The activities that are visible to the customer, and support activities that take place behind the scenes.
- The time allowed for each activity, plus the targets to be met.
- The stage in the process where customers are required to wait the longest.
- Stages in the process where visible moments of truth are vulnerable to service failure.
- Physical evidence of the quality of service.

The resulting blueprint allows companies to calculate productivity targets for employees and specifies exactly how the service delivery process should take place. Middleton et al. (2009) suggest that the blueprint approach is most appropriate for multi-site operators using standardised processes for large daily volumes of service encounters. However, they also suggest that smaller companies and organisations could consider the principles of blueprinting as a guide to improving service quality and customer satisfaction.

Process then has a crucial role in delivering customer satisfaction, creating customer loyalty and opportunities for positive word-of-mouth promotion. But at the same time, it also has the potential to deliver customer dissatisfaction, prevent repeat business, and encourage negative word-of-mouth communication.

An integral part of the process variable is the ability to recover from service errors. Grönroos (2007: 131) suggests that a service recovery system should focus on three areas: 'monitoring processes to identify problems, solving problems effectively, and learning from problems and the recovery process'. Following Zemke's research into service recovery (1992, cited in Grönroos, 2007: 131), Grönroos proposes that in the event of a service error, customers expect an apology, empathy, compensation, value-added extras and reliable information about the service recovery. The snapshot below illustrates how service quality recovery is implemented at an airport.

Snapshot 13.4   London Gatwick Airport (LGW)

In 2003, Gatwick's then owner, BAA, introduced a service guarantee to airlines operating at LGW. This Service Quality Rebate Scheme sets strict targets for service performance; if targets are not met, airlines will receive a fee rebate.

The scheme identifies key service process points that affect service quality for airlines and passengers:

- The availability of passenger sensitive equipment (lifts, escalators, moving walkways), baggage reclaim belts, runway capacity and airfield equipment (stands, piers, jetties, power supplies).
- Security queuing times.
- Passenger perceptions of the airport (seat availability in lounges, cleanliness, ease of wayfinding, flight information).

The on-going Quality of Service Monitor Survey measures passenger perceptions of LGW and the airport's own data measure equipment availability. Scores are calculated and published each month. If individual criteria targets are not met, airlines will receive a rebate. The maximum rebate is 7 per cent of airport charges, which equates to £17million a year. In 2008, a rebate of £69,659 was given each month from April to September because the target for direct passenger access between aircraft and terminal building was not met.

The scheme also incentivises improved service quality by rewarding the airport with bonuses if targets are exceeded.

Source: Gatwick Airport (2010).

The extended marketing mix highlights the role of a whole company, and all employees, processes and systems, in delivering customer satisfaction.

Grönroos (2007) suggests that interactive and internal marketing require a new approach to marketing that must extend beyond the marketing department and involve a company-wide focus on customer satisfaction and developing long-term relationships with customers. He proposes that while marketing is considered to be the function of specialists, rather than an approach that permeates throughout an organisation, service organisations will struggle to remain competitive.

Some authors suggest that these three new variables are actually part of product and promotion and there does indeed seem to be some overlap between them. However, Middleton et al. (2009) suggest that these additional three Ps are particularly relevant to tourism services marketing.

High levels of contact between tourism service providers and consumers, sometimes over several days or weeks, emphasise the role of people; the complex, multi-stage service delivery, often in different locations, requires a focus on the service process; and the inseparability of production and consumption and the intangibility of the benefits of the tourism service require particular attention to be paid to physical evidence.

Grönroos (2007) points out that these three additional Ps are usually the responsibility of departments other than the marketing department. For example, where 'people' refers to staff, recruitment and selection is often conducted by human resources (HR) functions. The 'process' of service delivery is usually the responsibility of operating departments such as reservations, check-in, food and beverage, and baggage handling, while decisions about physical evidence may be made by interior designers or operating departments. This implies that elements of services marketing are not directly controlled by the marketing department and highlights the role of the whole company in achieving effective marketing. Grönroos stresses Gummesson's (1987, cited in Grönroos, 2007: 280) view of employees outside the marketing department as 'part-time marketers' because of their role in the interactive and internal marketing stages of services marketing.

Summary

We have seen that tourism marketing is a complex task. The characteristics of tourism services create particular challenges in identifying, anticipating, and satisfying customer needs. The services marketing triangle concept, and the 7Ps framework, are particularly useful in understanding how these challenges can be overcome.

Large tourism corporations have extensive marketing resources while SMEs are more dependent on the marketing research and promotion carried out by tourism destination organisations. These organisations have a vital role in creating a clear identity for the varied attractions and amenities that exist within most destinations and play a key part in assisting and supplementing the marketing efforts of individual suppliers.

The emergence of the internet during the last decade of the twentieth century has transformed the marketing process and in particular has created new opportunities for tourism SMEs and microbusinesses, however the principles of marketing remain the same.

This chapter has been intended as an introduction to marketing concepts and their application in tourism; the scale of the topic precludes a comprehensive discussion of these in one chapter alone. There are, however, a number of textbooks devoted to tourism marketing and it is recommended that these are consulted for a broader and more detailed discussion of tourism marketing.

 ■ Self-test Questions

1 Consider a travel product that you have purchased – can you identify its core, formal, and augmented product levels?

2 Using the main segmentation criteria, describe yourself as a consumer purchasing your most recent tourism experience.

3 Why is the extended marketing mix relevant to tourism?

Further Reading

Fyall, A., Kozak, M., Andreu, L., Gnoth, J. and Lebe, S.S. (2009) *Marketing Innovations for Sustainable Tourism*. Oxford: Goodfellow.

Hudson, S. (2008) *Tourism and Hospitality Marketing*. London: Sage.

Kotler, P., Bowen, J.T. and Makens, J.C. (2009) *Marketing for Hospitality and Tourism*. New Jersey: Pearson.

Middleton, V., Fyall, A., Morgan, M. with Ranchhod, A. (2009) *Marketing in Travel and Tourism*. Oxford: Butterworth-Heinemann.

Pike, S. (2008) *Destination Marketing: An Integrated Marketing Communications Approach*. Oxford: Butterworth-Heinemann.

Rogers, T. and Davidson, R. (2006) *Marketing Destinations and Venues for Conferences, Conventions and Business Events*. Oxford: Butterworth-Heinemann.

Useful Websites

Best Job in the World: www.islandreefjob.com

VisitBritain market profiles: www.visitbritain.org/insightsandstatistics/markets/index.aspx

14 Tourism and the Future

The tourism industry offers flexibility, choice and involvement in one of the largest and fastest growing industries in the world. There are more tourism courses available than ever before at different levels, and more people are realising that tourism is an industry they can see themselves working in for years to come. (Reily Collins, 2004b: v)

University of Westminster Graduates

Source: Courtesy of The University of Westminster and Jo Mieszkowski, photographer

Learning Outcomes

After reading this chapter you will understand:

- **the role of scenario planning in thinking about the future of tourism**
- **how scenarios are written, and what the advantages and disadvantages are of scenarios**
- **a number of potential directions in which the tourism of the future could develop**
- **how to approach planning your own future within tourism**
- **the types of employers, roles and skills required in tourism employment.**

Introduction

Our book has provided a detailed introduction to tourism, tourists, destinations, suppliers and impacts, and given you an understanding of the industries that make up tourism, their influence on each other and how they influence the destinations that attract tourists. We hope that, after reading the previous chapters, we have inspired you to find out more about how tourism demand and destinations are likely to develop in the future, and the opportunities that exist for you within that future. This final chapter is divided along two lines – the future of tourism and your future in tourism.

The future of tourism is of great importance to planners, decision makers and managers in the tourism sector, so what does the future hold for tourism? Will more people travel because of growing prosperity in a number of recently developed countries, such as India, China and Brazil? How will the earth cope with the environmental consequences of this increased demand for tourism? How will we travel when the earth's fossil fuel reserves have been depleted? Questions like these affect tourists, destinations and tourism suppliers alike. They are not easily answered: 'The future is, for the most part, not only unknown: it is unknowable. The decision maker's dilemma, therefore, is how best to commit to a course of action in the absence of knowledge about the future' (Ralston and Wilson, 2006: 3). The first section of this chapter discusses scenarios and scenario planning as a potential way to deal with the insecurities of the future, and how to be prepared for the different courses this future may take.

Your future in tourism focuses on the importance of planning your career and the types of employment opportunities that are available in tourism. The section is intended as an introduction to encourage you to begin considering your career aspirations; detailed information can be found in the texts listed as further reading at the end of the chapter.

Scenario Planning

The word 'scenario' can be used in a range of different ways. In the world of theatre and film, it refers to a storyline. In a military context, it refers to a detailed contingency plan for different eventualities. Planners and managers use the term in a future-oriented sense, to describe a possible view of the future that allows them to make decisions (Ringland, 2002). Scenario planning is thus a disciplined method for imagining possible futures in detail (Schoemaker, 1995), whereby various possibilities are explored for the opportunities and threats they pose for a business. The following sections define what scenarios are, explore why they are used and how they can be developed, and discuss what their benefits and limitations are.

What are Scenarios?

There is no single definition for what scenarios are. Instead, different researchers have defined the phenomenon in different ways (see Table 14.1).

Table 14.1 Definitions of scenarios

An internally consistent view of what the future might turn out to be (Porter, in Lindgren and Bandholt, 2003: 21)

A tool for ordering one's perceptions about alternative future environments in which one's decision might be played out right (Schwartz, in Lindgren and Bandholt, 2003: 21)

A scenario tells a story of how various elements might interact under certain conditions (Schoemaker, 1995: 26)

That part of strategic planning which relates to the tools and technologies for managing the uncertainties of the future (Ringland, in Lindgren and Bandholt, 2003: 21)

Scenarios are possible views of the world, providing a context in which managers can make decisions (Ringland, 2002: 2)

Scenarios are a descriptive narrative of plausible alternative projections of a specific part of the future (Fahey, 2003: 7)

Ralston and Wilson (2006) argue that all scenarios have the following characteristics:

- They have a *narrative* nature: they have a plot and a storyline, and provide rich detail. Some scenarios are accompanied by quantitative data, such as graphs and tables.

- They are *plural*: because the future is uncertain, one must consider not just one, but a set of alternative scenarios.

- They are *holistic*: they investigate different elements that together build a complete picture. From this perspective they are different from trend analysis, where one trend is usually investigated at a time.

Scenarios are thus more than forecasts, in the sense of relatively unsurprising projections of the present. In the traditional sense of the word, forecasts require relatively stable conditions and are constructed over relatively short timeframes. Neither are scenarios visions of a desired future, a 'best-case scenario' (Lindgren and Bandholt, 2003).

The origins of scenario planning can be traced back to 1950s military planning. Herman Kahn and his associates at the RAND Corporation adapted the meaning and method of theatrical scenarios to war planning. Kahn used scenarios to represent alternative futures, for example he developed four scenarios of how nuclear war might erupt between the US and the Soviet Union (Millett, 2003).

The method was later adapted to new environments. The energy and petrochemical company Shell has used scenario planning since the early 1970s as part of a process for generating and evaluating its strategic options. The company, which is still considered a corporate champion of scenarios today, has been consistently better in its oil forecasts than its competitors (Schoemaker, 1995: 25). In recent decades scenario planning has become an established method, adopted by most major companies and consultancy firms (Lindgren and Bandhold, 2003).

Developing Scenarios

Scenario planning attempts to compensate for two common errors in decision making – under-prediction and over-prediction of change. Under-prediction is the most common error of the two: most people and organisations find it difficult to imagine a future that is very different from the present. A hundred years ago it would have been difficult to predict a world with technologies such as jet planes, the internet and mobile phones. Yet there are also people who tend to over-predict, expecting levels of change that fail to materialise: space travel for example is not yet common, and there is not yet a cure for AIDS. Scenario planning allows managers to steer a middle course between under- and over-prediction (Schoemaker, 1995: 27).

When developing scenarios, we combine the things we think we know about the future with elements about which we are not certain. Some assumptions can be made about the future with relative certainty: we know, for example, that the world population is growing, and that in many developed countries the average age of the population is rising. We also know that new technologies are replacing previous approaches: the popularity of digital music, for example, has reduced the number of CDs that are sold, and the number of tourists booking their holiday online instead of at a travel agency is rising.

Many aspects of the future however are still unknown: they are forces that may move in different directions and have significant implications for companies and destinations (Fahey, 2003). The results of elections are one example: if the green party, for instance, became a significant partner in government, this would probably lead to increased taxation on polluting activities such as air transport. Oil prices are another example: these are often influenced by political relations between different countries. Rises in oil prices lead to increases in the prices of a range of products and services, from groceries to transport. Higher prices often result in a reduced demand for products, and as many transport providers in tourism (such as airlines and cruise liners) are heavily dependent on oil, this can have a far-reaching effect on their level of business.

When we combine the two elements above – the things we think we know about the future, and a few key uncertainties – we can develop a range of futures. This is usually done via a set of workshops with representatives from different parts of the company or organisation. The further ahead we look, and the more complex the situations we try to predict, the more numerous the options become – hence we need to prepare for not one, but multiple possible futures. At the same time, we cannot explore every possible future. We need to reduce the complexity here in order to handle it. The number of scenarios that are developed can vary widely, and depend on the number of certain trends and uncertainties that are relevant to the organisation.

Aims

Scenarios can be developed with several purposes in mind. Fahey (2003) discusses three types of aims:

- Scenarios can foster preparedness. That is, they can allow managers to anticipate a range of potential futures, and to get ready for them before they occur. For example, tourism businesses may use scenarios to consider the consequences of a potential rise in the number of elderly tourists, seeing that this is a population group that is growing in many Western countries.

- Scenarios also allow managers and planners to consider what they would do if each future were to materialise. In the case of the scenario above, the company could consider the products and services that would be popular with elderly tourists, and the changes the company would have to make to meet their needs.

- Finally, scenarios can allow managers and planners to develop a new understanding of the present. Although scenario planning is mainly focused on the future, by analysing what this future may look like, the current strengths and weaknesses of the organisation or destination may become apparent. Thinking about the future in a detailed way can also lead to the challenging of tacit beliefs and assumptions in the organisation. We have already explained that organisations often underestimate the changes the future will bring – scenario planning can be a tool to challenge this belief. By thinking in detail about a future with more elderly tourists, the company may challenge existing opinions about the level of accessibility that is needed or the type of new products that should be developed.

Benefits and Limitations

Scenarios can be powerful instruments for the future planning of an organisation or destination, and bring a number of benefits:

- They are *easily memorable* and *compatible* with how the human brain works. Because of their narrative format (stories with images), scenarios can be visualised, which often means they are more believable, so that they force the mind to think differently about the future.

- The format of scenarios *reduces complexity* and is *communicative*. Scenarios are easy to discuss, because they reduce the amount of uncertainty to a manageable level. They also provide the organisation with a common language to discuss the future (Lindgren and Bandhold, 2003).

- Scenario planning requires different teams within the organisation to think together about the future, and can thus encourage *teambuilding*. Developing the scenarios themselves can be a learning process, and allow the participants to build links with other persons in the organisation, so that decision making becomes more integrated (Millett, 2003).

Scenario building equally has a number of limitations. Lindgren and Bandhold (2003) name the following:

- *Uncertainty in conclusions*: scenario planning does not give one single answer about the future. Decision makers who are looking for 'the' answer to their questions about the future may find it a speculative and demanding process. Scenario planning also requires a holistic look at the future, whereas traditionally managers are taught to divide challenges into different smaller parts, and find solutions for each part separately – as such scenario planning may feel counter-intuitive.

- *Soft methods and soft answers*: although some scenarios include statistics, models and figures, the narrative basis of the scenarios makes them a qualitative rather than a quantitative method. Qualitative methods look for relations, motivations and interactions, whereas quantitative methods look for numerical answers. Many businesses are rather numbers-oriented, and thinking about problems in a more qualitative way may be challenging and new.

- *Time consuming*: developing scenarios in workshops with representatives from different teams in the organisation is a time-consuming process, and the coordination of the project requires specialist knowledge.

Scenarios for the Tourism of the Future

In 2009, the Forum for the Future (FF) developed scenarios for what tourism could look like in 2023. The report was prompted by a KPMG study the year before about the effects of climate change on business: this study found that tourism was one of the six sectors in the 'danger zone', least prepared for the effects of climate change (KPMG, 2008). Tourism companies like ABTA, British Airways, the cruise company Carnival UK, Co-operative Travel, the Travel Foundation, Thomas Cook and TUI travel shared their views on the future of tourism, and this led to four scenarios. The scenarios focus on two variables: whether the economy, politics, technology and energy costs combine to encourage or restrict overseas travel; and whether the appeal of overseas destinations and consumers' sensitivity to the environmental impacts of travel make tourism more or less attractive (FF, 2009: 5).

The scenarios were further informed by trends we can be fairly certain about as well as uncertainties. The fairly certain trends were:

- *Impacts of climate change*: these could manifest themselves as hurricanes, rising sea levels, forest fires, heat waves and more extreme weather.

- *Drought and water scarcity*: by 2025, 1.8 billion people are expected to be living in countries or regions where water scarcity is a major problem.

- *Growth in visitor numbers*: because the world population is expected to grow, and because the middle classes in China and India are expected to have greater travel needs, the number of tourists is expected to rise.

- *Rising cost of resources*: population growth will lead to increased competition and higher costs for resources like food, building materials and energy.

- *An ageing Western population*: the older age group will grow significantly in many Western countries due to higher life expectancies. However, there is a degree of uncertainty about how affordable travel will be for this group.

- *Political instability, regional conflicts and terrorism*: these are expected to increase due to growing populations, dwindling resources and climate change (FF, 2009).

There are also many uncertainties about the future, however – for example:

- Will people change their travel behaviour out of environmental concerns?
- How will legislation affect travel?
- How expensive will energy (e.g. oil) be?
- How strong will Western economies be?
- Will new technologies, such as green fuels, be successful?
- How active will older people be?
- How will new economies, like China, India and Brazil, develop?
- How attractive and welcoming will new destinations be?

CASE STUDY 14.1

FOUR PROPOSED FUTURE TOURISM SCENARIOS

We will now examine how each of the four proposed scenarios will affect a hypothetical family in 2023. The Jones family lives on the outskirts of London. The dad, Mark, works as the manager of a car dealership, while the mum, Jessica, is a part-time medical secretary. They have two children, Adam (10) and Holly (5). What will their travel behaviour look like in the future?

(Continued)

(Continued)

Source: © Ans Brys

Scenario 1: Boom and Bust

Mark Jones is having a good day: it's only Tuesday and already he has sold three new, cell-powered cars this week. Head office is going to be pleased and there may well be a nice bonus coming his way soon! The UK economy is booming and the Jones family are benefiting from the positive economic climate: the family finances are healthy and Mark's flexible work hours allow the family to spend lots of quality time together. Mark and Jessica love travelling and they take the children with them wherever they go – air travel is affordable, and this year the family has already had a beach break in Australia, a week at the carnival in Rio, and a skiing trip to Hungary. The next trip they would like to take is to the United States, on one of the new cruise ships that can transport up to 7,000 passengers. They are like floating cities!

Transport networks have expanded massively and the world is now the Jones' oyster. They can take a high speed train from London to Barcelona, or fly from their local airport to all five continents. New technologies have reduced the negative environmental impacts of flying to some extent: engines are now more efficient and tourists can pick airlines that fly on 'green fuel' – even though this is often more expensive.

The disadvantage of this booming tourism sector however is that some destinations have become very overcrowded. Last year the Jones family visited Rome, and the city was so crowded that it was at times hard to enjoy attractions like the Coliseum and the Pantheon. Luckily these attractions offered tourists special 3D glasses that filter out other visitors and hide the degradation of tourism to the buildings. Mark has thought long and hard about a destination where he can take the family, and where

(Continued)

(Continued)

the crowds will be less dense – so next year Antarctica may be the destination of choice. They need to go quickly before tourism spoils that country too! Or if they win the lottery, they could go on one of the new space tours ... Now that certainly would make the neighbours jealous.

Some of Mark and Jessica's friends have commented that the travel lifestyle they lead is not responsible – other industries have had to cut carbon emissions to support the growth of tourism. Mark and Jessica are not sure if what they do is fair ... but for now they enjoy flying around the world every few months.

Scenario 2: Divided Disquiet

Jessica Jones is in a bad mood. The holiday she had booked for her family to Kenya has been cancelled at short notice, due to political unrest in the area. The news reporters said that the same reasons are yet again underlying the unrest: the population of the region has grown dramatically over the last 20 years, and there is just not enough water and food for everyone. The Jones family had visited Kenya five years ago, and had found it overcrowded – but at least it was less overcrowded than many other destinations, like those in the Mediterranean area. The pollution and over-development there had now become so bad that the Joneses, like many other families, did not want to go back there any more.

Cancelled holidays were a reoccurring problem for Jessica. Last year she had wanted to take the family to the Maldives, but due to rising sea levels the island they were booked to visit was evacuated, and the inhabitants were relocated to India. Two years ago, when they visited Morocco, they were told that due to water shortages in the area they may not be able to go. Luckily, though, the tour operator imported the necessary water in a special tanker ship and the holiday went ahead.

So this year the family are again facing the cancellation of their holiday – Jessica considered her friends' advice to buy one of those 'virtual windows' with the holiday budget instead. These windows allow you to experience any destination in the world in your own living room – she would be able to have lunch with her sister in Atlanta without having to leave the house. Many people were saying tourism was dead, and that it had been a costly mistake of the past, partly responsible for the environmental problems the world was experiencing. Were they right?

Jessica had one last option. Doomsday Tours Ltd offered trips to sites that would soon be ruined forever, such as the Himalayas and Patagonia. Jessica knew it was not the ethical choice: tour operators like these kept developing destinations, regardless of the damage it did. But if she did not book this trip, Holly and Adam would perhaps never get to see these amazing places ... She decided to sleep on it, and ask Mark's opinion later.

Scenario 3: Price and Privilege

It is a very special year for the Jones family. After years of carefully saving up, Mark and Jessica are finally able to take the children to the United States. Jessica's sister lives in Atlanta, but because travel is so expensive, Holly and Adam have never met

(Continued)

(Continued)

their cousins. This was one of the main reasons why the Jones family received a travel permit – competition for these is fierce, and tourists have to compete against each other to show they are deserving.

Mark and Jessica often think back fondly of when they first met, in 2005, when flying was cheap and they visited foreign destinations several times per year. However, since the cost of oil has risen by 1000 per cent, flying is only affordable for the rich. Jessica used to work for a low-cost airline then – none of them exist now though, and all the staff were made redundant.

Luckily for the Jones family, however, the extensive European train network has several hub stations in London. A few years ago they visited Poland by train – it was an enjoyable journey, and due to the latest technological developments it was relatively fast and comfortable.

Mark is a key campaigner in the 'Right to Fly' movement, that campaigns for government support and inclusive legislation to ensure everyone can fly at least once. Mark recognises the severity of climate change, but considers travel to be a key human desire. So far the government has not yet responded to the demands of 'Right to Fly', but with a growing membership base, the lobbying power of the organisation is increasing.

In the celebrity magazines Jessica reads, there are sometimes reports of the rich and famous who travel to exclusive tropical islands. Jessica often wonders if Holly and Adam will ever be able to experience places like these, and she sometimes asks herself if a different approach to fossil fuels 20 years earlier could have kept travel more inclusive.

Scenario 4: Carbon Clampdown

Jessica has just come back from an afternoon of volunteering at the local care home, and is calculating the carbon credits her volunteering role has earned her so far. Since personal carbon allowances were introduced, the family can do with this credit boost: Mark commutes to work by car, and that takes a big bite out of their carbon allowance as a family. The Jones family are saving up carbon emissions for a trip to Atlanta, where Jessica's sister lives. Usually Jessica is rather opposed to travel via air, because of the impact it has on the environment, but she wants Adam and Holly to get to know their aunt and cousins, so she is making an exception. The airlines will surely appreciate the business: since personal carbon allowances were introduced they have experienced a large drop in profits.

Usually the Jones family holidays in the UK – they went to Devon last year, and visited the Lake District the year before. In Devon they stayed in an all-inclusive resort that offered lots of activities for when the weather was not so good. In the Lake District they went camping – the kids had a wonderful time! The UK is one of the most carbon-neutral places in the world, and the Jones family like to do their bit to keep it that way.

When Adam and Holly are older, Mark and Jessica hope they will join the Global Peace Corps: an organisation that allows young people to travel around the world to

(Continued)

help in humanitarian projects. It's a way to see the planet without ruining it. Holly and Adam have learnt about ecology from a very young age, and for them making green decisions is second nature. Mark and Jessica sometimes think back to how wasteful the tourism sector used to be 20 years ago, and are ashamed of the way they once acted. They are pleased that government regulation has stepped up to the challenge – it took some getting used to but they are convinced a greener planet is worth it in the end.

Reflective Questions

1   How do you think each of the scenarios above would affect the following businesses:

- An airline?
- A cross-European rail operator?
- A destination in the Mediterranean that is heavily dependent on tourism?

2   Which scenario, if any, is in your opinion most likely to happen? Can you think of other options?

The sample scenarios above can help us imagine what the future of tourism will look like – but what about your own future in tourism ? The final section of this book considers career opportunities in tourism.

Your Future in Tourism

Reily Collins (2004a) describes the scope of career opportunities in tourism as 'staggering' because of the different types of industries that create, distribute and market tourism products, the involvement of the public, private and voluntary sectors, and the geographic location of tourism organisations and businesses in generating and destination regions. Career opportunities in tourism are provided by a wide variety of industries and in innumerable locations globally. In short, the career opportunities available are vast; it is important that you understand what these are, and how they can help you to achieve your professional goals. We begin by considering the importance of career planning.

Career Planning

Career planning is also known as career management and is an element of personal development planning (PDP). The principle underlying each of these is that individuals can proactively influence their career to reflect their personal goals, interests and aspirations.

Before we consider the role of planning, though, it is useful to define the term career. Arnold (1997: 16) defines it as ' ... the sequence of employment-related positions, roles, activities and experiences encountered by a person'. This definition avoids interpreting 'career' as an occupation within one industry, or relating it to promotion. Instead, it sees a career as the personal experiences of an individual over time and shows how an individual's roles, responsibilities, skills and interests have changed and evolved. Careers can be influenced by leisure activities, education, domestic tasks and family responsibilities, through the development of new skills and exposure to new experiences. In short, a career is an individual's journey through employment, entrepreneurship or self-employment; it does not necessarily involve promotion to higher levels, and is not confined to one occupation or industry.

Career planning is a structured process that requires you to identify your long-term goals, targets or objectives, plan the most effective route to achieving them, and monitor the success of your plan, making adjustments where necessary (Povey and Oriade, 2009). In other words, you need to clearly define the position and role that you aspire to, your 'dream job', and then plan the steps necessary to acquire the skills, knowledge and experience to progress to that position. Educational qualifications play an important part in this plan, and so too do activities and experiences that demonstrate broader skills and interests; in tourism, a passion for travel or a love of meeting and interacting with new people is a pre-requisite for many roles, and can be demonstrated through leisure activities.

This proactive approach to career planning centres on the individual and stresses the control that you have over your career success. Povey and Oriade (2009) suggest that career development in tourism is largely self-directed, meaning that you must take charge of your employment opportunities; therefore you must play a key role in directing your career development. Career planning should not start when you are actively seeking your first permanent full-time position, it should be put in place long beforehand to allow you to prepare for securing employment in positions that will contribute to your long-term vision. Povey and Oriade (2009) identify the main elements of the career planning process as:

- *Self-knowledge*: an accurate evaluation of your own skills, attitudes, values, interests, strengths and weaknesses.

- *Aspiration and expectations*: identifying realistic long-term career goals based on your ability, skills and formal educational achievements.

- *Planning for success*: your goals must be specific, measurable, achievable, realistic and timed (SMART) in order to monitor your success in achieving them, and may relate to income, responsibility or experiences.

- *Mobility*: moving between jobs in order to develop the skills, knowledge and experience to progress towards your career goals. This mobility can be achieved through moving between different occupations, to higher levels in the same occupation, and between different industries or different geographical locations.

- *Employer's role*: supporting and facilitating your career development through training programmes and continuing professional development (CPD) opportunities.

Career planning therefore involves reflecting on your own abilities and aspirations, setting realistic goals, and identifying the skills and abilities you will need, as well as a pathway to your goal through carefully selecting occupations and employers. The career planning process will be on-going throughout your studying and working life, and will include educational achievements as well as skills developed more broadly through work experiences, recreational activities and through community participation. In the UK the Quality Assurance Agency for Higher Education (QAA) requires universities to include elements of career planning as part of PDP on all undergraduate courses, in order to equip students with the skills to understand their abilities, evaluate their performance, and plan and manage their educational, personal and professional development (Cottrell, 2010).

Cottrell (2010) suggests that the kinds of jobs sought by many graduates require a number of skills and qualities that develop over time and demand close support and clear planning; for instance, people skills, self-management, problem solving and project work. People 1st (2010) identify the main skills required for managerial positions as:

- *Organisation skills*: the ability to prioritise tasks, manage deadlines and monitor several tasks.

- *People management*: recruiting, training and motivating staff, and having knowledge of some traditional personnel functions like employment law.

- *Budget management*: daily financial management and long-term financial planning.

- *Strategic management and planning*: identifying long-term goals and developing plans to attain them.

- *Managing the customer experience*: understanding and enhancing service quality.

- *Delegation skills*: distributing tasks and projects to staff.

- *Communication skills*: the ability to liaise with people at all levels, to write accurately, to negotiate, to be able to react appropriately under pressure.

Increasingly, academic tourism programmes are designed to develop and practise these skills.

Tourism Education

There are many opportunities to gain educational qualifications in tourism, ranging from vocational diplomas for ages 14–16, to degrees and postgraduate studies. Some individuals will use education as a starting point for their tourism career development, while others may obtain qualifications after gaining industry experience (Povey and Oriade, 2009). Postgraduate qualifications are not essential, but for individuals with industry experience, a postgraduate qualification can develop the skills required to progress to higher levels (Prospects, 2011).

Educational programmes provide an opportunity to develop skills that are not easily acquired during employment. For example, a degree in tourism supplies you with a broad range of transferable skills as well as an in-depth understanding of tourism and tourists, suppliers, intermediaries and impacts and the principles of their effective management. The multi-disciplinary nature of tourism degree programmes also develops strong business management and communication skills which are equally transferable to other career areas.

Tourism undergraduates acquire and practise skills in leadership, problem-solving, ICT, research, written and verbal communication, presentation, critical analysis, teamwork, organisation, and the ability to work under pressure to deadlines. Degree programmes are structured to enable you to specialise in particular areas of tourism as you progress each year; for example in business or events tourism, aviation, or sustainability, in line with your career aspirations and goals, and the final year dissertation gives you the opportunity for in-depth analysis of a tourism topic of your choice that particularly interests you. Many universities also offer modules in entrepreneurship and languages (Prospects, 2011).

Tourism degree programmes provide many opportunities for students to meet tourism practitioners and find out more about their roles and responsibilities, and to network and build up contacts through guest lecturers, site visits and field trips. Work placements or internships also allow for valuable industry experience; many tourism employers will advertise placements on their websites and through university careers services. Students can also be proactive by approaching companies speculatively (Prospects, 2011).

Some large tourism employers run management programmes specifically for graduates; successful applicants are fast-tracked into management positions via these programmes. The snapshot below describes the TUI International Management Trainee Programme.

Snapshot 14.1 TUI International Management Trainee Programme

The TUI Travel PLC International Management Trainee Programme is open to outstanding graduates from around the world and will give you amazing exposure within the world's leading travel company.

(Continued)

(Continued)

Once on board you'll have the choice of a variety of assignments throughout our business. All of them will help develop your skills and experience over the course of the 18-month programme.

What you can look forward to:

- An exciting mix of day-to-day business and project work – enjoy what you do!
- 3-month or 4-month assignments across different businesses.
- Exceptional experience of all aspects of our organisation, sharing our passion to make travel experiences special.
- Working with senior managers in different locations across the world.
- Targeted personal development through training opportunities and development workshops.
- Feedback on your performance and potential.
- Competitive salary – in addition to support with rented accommodation and expenses associated with international assignments.
- Being part of a winning team – share your ideas, bring our vision to life, and celebrate success with us.

TUI management trainee

Source: Courtesy of TUI Travel Plc

What we're looking for:

- A good degree (or equivalent) from a university or business school.
- Fluency in two languages (one must be English).
- International experience (work experience, internship or study).
- An innovative, entrepreneurial, motivated and professional approach.
- Excellent customer focus and communication skills.
- The flexibility to be internationally mobile.

(Continued)

(Continued)

What you'll need:

- 2:1 degree and a minimum of 280 UCAS points.
- At least 6 months' work experience dealing with customers.
- Customer obsession.
- Boundless enthusiasm.
- Passion for travel.
- Commercial awareness.
- An adventurous spirit.

Source: Courtesy of TUI Travel PLC.

This snapshot shows the importance not only of education but also of relevant work experience and the particular personal attributes that can be demonstrated through leisure and volunteering activities. Career planning helps you to identify valuable work experience opportunities and to understand how your activities outside education and work can demonstrate a broader range of skills and personal qualities.

A number of sources of advice are available to guide your career planning and find out about career opportunities.

Career Planning Support

Career planning support is provided by careers services, through practical experience and networking.

Careers services available in schools, colleges and universities provide specialist advice about career planning and development and employment opportunities. They provide guidance on writing effective CVs and application letters and also arrange regular employer events to provide industry-specific information and recruitment. Many employers advertise their vacancies and graduate recruitment through university careers services. They also advertise part-time and temporary jobs which can be used to expand your industry exposure and provide valuable experience.

There are many opportunities in tourism to supplement your academic development with practical experience, helping you to understand the areas that interest you most and how your skills match practitioner roles, and to test your enjoyment of different tourism industries. The seasonal and part-time nature of many tourism jobs provides students with the opportunity to work part-time during term-time or to take temporary full-time jobs during the long vacations, building up their experience as practitioners. Work experience acquired in hotels, bars, restaurants, tourist attractions, tourist information centres and so on is useful in demonstrating the ability to work successfully in customer-facing roles or in customer-focused organisations and to demonstrate a passion for travel.

Networking is a key part of career development (Arnold, 1997; Littleford et al., 2004). Networking involves establishing links and developing relationships with people with whom you share a common interest. Each new contact expands your network and links your network to theirs. Professional networks develop relationships with others and provide potential sources for sharing advice, guidance or business opportunities in the future. Networks can be a valuable source of information, provide support, and facilitate your career development. A professional network can be started quite simply by establishing links with colleagues, fellow students, teachers and lecturers, forming a base to which further contacts can be added as your career develops.

In tourism there are many different types of networking opportunities. Trade exhibitions such as World Travel Market and IMEX bring destination organisations, accommodation, transport and attraction suppliers and intermediaries together to showcase products and trends, enabling you to learn about and meet suppliers and potential employers. Membership of professional associations such as the Tourism Society, the Institute of Travel and Tourism, and Meeting Planners International (MPI) provides learning opportunities through seminar programmes and conferences, and access to social events that will facilitate networking opportunities. Many professional associations also offer student membership, allowing you to begin establishing your network and develop relationships before entering the job market. Professional networking websites such as www.linkedin.com are growing in popularity as a means of keeping in touch and extending networks.

Littleford et al. (2004) suggest that there are a number of basic principles that affect the success of networking, including:

- Recording, storing and updating contacts systematically.
- Keeping in touch and being aware of new opportunities.
- Maintaining relationships by informing contacts of the outcome of their help.
- Creating a positive impression so that contacts have confidence in you.

In addition to academic qualifications and work experience, other activities also provide evidence of skills, attitudes and personal attributes, for instance membership of societies, volunteering activities, family responsibilities, sport, leadership roles, and so on. The self-knowledge stage of the career planning process helps you to identify the skills and attributes developed by your broader experiences and the skills that still need to be developed.

To summarise, your potential to achieve your personal goals through a career in tourism requires you to identify your vision, evaluate your achievements and performance, and plan to develop the required skills and experience. We will now consider the types of employers and common roles within tourism.

Tourism Employers

As we have seen throughout this book, tourism includes a number of distinct industries, and this diversity is reflected in employment. Employers in tourism come from a range of industries as Table 14.2 shows.

Table 14.2   Tourism employers

Accommodation sector	Hotels – providers of serviced accommodation from budget standard to luxury
	Holiday centres – self-catering accommodation with leisure and entertainment facilities on one site
	Youth backpacker hostels – shared budget accommodation
	Self-catering accommodation – providers of villas, apartments, cottages
Passenger transport sector and cruise companies	Scheduled and charter coach companies, airlines, rail operators, ferry operators, car rental companies
	River and ocean voyage providers
Events sector	Suppliers of venues for conferences, conventions, exhibitions, sport, cultural and music events
	Owners of events
Visitor attractions sector	Leisure parks, theme parks, museums, art galleries, historic attractions, zoos, aquariums, sightseeing tours, activity courses
Travel services sector	Intermediaries that organise and reserve business and leisure travel products – travel agencies, online travel retailers, foreign exchange providers, tour operators, MICE operators, wholesalers, travel ticketing
Tourist services	Organisations that provide marketing, development, and policy support for inbound and domestic tourism – national tourism organisations, regional and local tourism bodies, local government, tourist information centres, tourism partnerships, convention and visitor bureaux

Source: adapted from People 1st (2010).

While it is possible to specialise and progress within one particular industry, many of the skills required in tourism are transferable and it is possible to develop your career through roles with employers in different tourism industries.

Employer Size

Progression opportunities and recruitment practices often differ substantially between large and small employers, and you should consider this when planning your career development.

Large employers are usually defined as organisations with more than 250 staff. There are many large tourism employers, some with thousands of employees, and often with operations in many locations, and they provide a wide range of career opportunities. It is possible to have an international career with the major tourism employers, through roles with one employer in different countries. Large companies are usually structured into departments based on a specialist function, for example marketing, finance, human resources, and sales and reservations, as well as operations relevant to their industry, and they often recruit specialist staff for each department (Prospects, 2011). Individual departments are usually structured using a hierarchy of responsibilities from entry level, for which few qualifications or little experience are necessary, through to manager and director level, and there are often career progression opportunities within the same organisation.

Large companies often use complex and lengthy recruitment processes, led by their human resources department. They may advertise their vacancies on their own website or at recruitment fairs, and use a variety of testing and assessment tools, over a number of stages, to recruit the best staff. For instance, successful online applications may be followed by a telephone interview and then attendance at an assessment centre where skills and competencies are tested through in-depth group and individual exercises (Prospects, 2011). Many large tourism employers, particularly in the hotel and travel organisers' industries, run graduate training programmes to fast-track carefully selected graduates into management roles.

Tourism SMEs are less likely to have a formal human resources department, and recruitment may be conducted by individual managers or supervisors, or by the owner/general manager. SMEs are unlikely to use complex and lengthy recruitment procedures, and will often advertise their vacancies through the local or trade press, university careers service bulletins, local graduate vacancy listings, and through word of mouth (Prospects, 2011). SME employers often offer the advantage of opportunities to become involved in all aspects of the business, and to have close working contacts with colleagues in all roles and at all levels. Small organisations are also less likely to formally provide specialist functions such as finance, marketing, and so on, and therefore it is possible to gain a close involvement in all areas and wide experience quite quickly.

Tourism also offers many opportunities for self-employment; the Tourism Alliance estimates that approximately 130,000 UK tourism employees are self-employed (Prospects, 2011), for example as tour guides, consultants, home-based travel agencies and business start-ups. There are a growing number of consultants engaged in policy development and research on behalf of tourism companies and organisations. To become established as a consultant, in-depth sector specific knowledge is required, usually gained by professional experience or through research-based knowledge. Graduates who become consultants usually have previous tourism or related experience and a relevant postgraduate qualification (Prospects, 2011).

There are a number of occupations in tourism that are also found in other sectors, for example business functions like marketing, human resources management, finance and IT; practitioners have specific skills and knowledge that are transferable between sectors. There are also 'core' occupations that are unique to a specific industry and are not found in other sectors, for example tour guides, travel agents and event organisers. Tourism employers usually require a combination of core and general business functions, although this will vary depending on the size of the organisation, as we explained above.

Tourism Occupations

Tourism occupations are often described by their proximity to the customer – that is, whether they are customer facing roles, or back office roles.

Tourism is 'inseparable', meaning that the customer is inevitably present when the tourism product or service is produced, and by necessity this frequently involves a face-to-face, telephone or email interaction between staff and customers. Customer facing roles in tourism are varied and include:

- Reservations staff who interact with customers via phone or email, or in person.
- Front desk employees in accommodation, attraction or transport providers, or tourist information services.
- Operations employees such as aircraft cabin crew, coach drivers, food and beverage employees, resort representatives and tour guides, housekeeping staff.
- Sales staff such as travel agents and account managers of hotel, attraction or transport providers or MICE operators and destination organisations.

Many customer facing staff will have a high degree of personal contact with customers and will therefore require a high level of interpersonal skills. Some roles will be unsupervised and individual employees will have complete responsibility for the quality of a customer's experience, for example tour guides, tour leaders, sales consultants and account managers.

Customer contact jobs often require a complex range of skills, which Baum (2006) calls 'the skills bundle':

- Technical or professional skills that may require formal training and qualifications, for example the use of specific computer systems such as Galileo or Sabre or tour guiding qualifications.
- General skills such as fluency in other languages, verbal and written communication skills, organisation and administrative skills and IT expertise.

- Personality traits that facilitate the ability to work in conditions that can often be stressful and demanding.
- Interpersonal skills in order to interact effectively with consumers, clients, suppliers and colleagues.

The work of customer contact employees is often described as emotional labour because of the requirement for employees to transmit positive feelings as part of their job, whether contact with consumers is face-to-face or by telephone (Hoffman and Bateson, 2001). Emotional labour involves demonstrating qualities such as friendliness, sincerity, courtesy and reliability, consistently to all customers, who will often be strangers, for the duration of the hours of employment. Cultural and linguistic differences between employees and customers may make this more challenging, and so too will the attitude of the customer, and the occurrence of stressful incidents such as delays, complaints or overbookings. The ability to use emotional skills is an essential part of a customer contact role and cannot easily be taught in the same way that technical skills can be; consequently many tourism employers will prioritise personality and attitude rather than technical skills in their recruitment process (Baum, 2006).

The breadth of tourism employment creates a range of types of interaction between consumers and frontline staff, which will require different levels of technical and personal skills. Mills and Margulies (in Schlesinger and Heskett, 1991) categorise role types in customer contact tourism employment as follows:

- *Maintenance interactive*: short interactions with customers that involve limited complexity, for example food and beverage service, ticket desk, housekeeping staff, information desk.
- *Task interactive*: short interactions that involve quite technical tasks requiring accuracy, for example flight tickets, check-in for a flight or hotel, hotel or holiday reservations.
- *Personal interactive*: long interactions that involve clarifying and fulfilling the customer's needs, for example MICE sales and operations, event planning, customer account management, travel agency selling holidays, tour guide, resort representative.

The required skills, qualifications, level of education, personality and attitude of staff will vary depending on the type of interaction involved.

There are a number of occupations within tourism that do not involve direct contact with customers but are essential for the daily operation and long-term success of the organisation. These can be identified as functional roles such as finance, marketing, human resources and IT, or operational roles such as security, contracting, housekeeping, scheduling, ticketing, and so on, depending on the nature of the industry.

Large companies with multiple sites will usually establish corporate offices from which key business functions for the whole organisation will be provided.

For example, IHG has corporate and regional offices throughout the world that provide functional specialists such as finance and business support, strategy, sales and marketing, brand management, corporate communications and PR, procurement, IT and HR to all of their hotels within the region (IHG, 2011b)

The snapshot below describes the career to date of a recent tourism graduate in a functional role.

Snapshot 14.2   The Career Development of a UK Tourism Graduate

Shai Joyram

Source: Shai Joyram

(Continued)

(Continued)

Shai graduated from the University of Westminster in 2003 with a 2:1 degree in Tourism and Planning. She is now Human Resources (HR) Manager at the 5-star Baglioni Hotel, London, with responsibility for HR strategy, policy and practice for 120 employees. She describes her career as follows

'At university, I loved studying Urban Tourism and Tourism Hospitality, and I also worked in a travel agency and in retail customer service. After graduating, my first job was with Hilton Hotels in London as HR Administrator. I took advantage of all CPD opportunities and was promoted to HR Officer. I then began studying for an MA in Human Resources.

'While studying, I was appointed to lead HR at the Bentley Kempinski Hotel, London, and later moved to my current role at Baglioni Hotels. I love my job as it combines my passion for hospitality with my expertise in HR.

'My advice is to research potential employers thoroughly, prioritising those with a commitment to CPD. Long-term goals are valuable, but knowing which steps to take to achieve them is equally important. Looking back, certainly my work experience helped, together with my industry contacts. The graduate market is fiercely competitive, and such experiences differentiate you. Moreover, being able to demonstrate your ability to apply the skills and knowledge acquired during previous work, education and leisure experiences provides a strong advantage'.

This section on your future in tourism has provided a brief introduction to career planning and to potential roles in tourism. Detailed guidance is available in texts listed at the end of this chapter.

We hope this book will encourage you to find out more about this varied, growing and exciting sector, and we wish you a rewarding career in tourism.

 ■ Self-test Questions ■

1 Consider your long-term vision – imagine yourself in 10 or 20 years' time – where would you like to be living, what level of workload and stress would be desirable, would you be working alone or in a team, would you be in command, how much recognition would you like for your work, how important will a high salary be?

2 Having considered the range of industries and sectors that comprise tourism, which ones particularly interest and inspire you?

3 Identify relevant trade and professional associations, events, exhibitions and publications for your chosen industries and sectors, and explore your potential membership or attendance.

Further Reading

Burns, J.B. and McInerney, J.A. (2010) *Career Opportunities in Travel and Hospitality*. New York: Infobase Publishing.

Cottrell, S. (2010) *Skills for Success: The Personal Development Planning Handbook*. Basingstoke: Palgrave Macmillan.

Lindgren, M. and Bandhold, H. (2003) *Scenario Planning: The Link between Future and Strategy*. Basingstoke: Palgrave Macmillan.

Useful Websites

IMEX: www.imex-frankfurt.com
Institute of Travel and Tourism: www.itt.co.uk
Meeting Professionals International: www.mpiweb.org
Prospects – graduate careers website: www.prospects.co.uk
The Tourism Society: www.tourismsociety.org
World Travel Market: www.wtmlondon.com

Bibliography

ABTA (2010) *Protecting your Travel Arrangements.* http://www.abta.com/consumer-services/protecting_your_travel_arrangements

Accor (2010) *Brand Portfolio.* www.accor.com/en/brand-portfolio.html

AEG Ogden (2011) *About Us.* http://www.aegogden.com/aegogden/about.asp

Agarwal, S. and Shaw, G. (eds) (2007) *Managing coastal tourism resorts – a global perspective (Aspects of Tourism).* Bristol: Channel View Publications

Albrow, M. (2004) 'Travelling beyond local cultures', in F. Lechner and J. Boli (eds), *The Globalisation Reader.* Malden: Blackwell

Amadeus (2007) *Commission cuts –opportunities and best practices for travel agencies* http://www.amadeus.com/travelagencies/documents/travelagencies/White%20Paper_ForWebUse.pdf

American Express Travel (2011) *About American Express.* www.americanexpress.com

Ap, J. (1992) 'Residents' perceptions on tourism impacts', *Annals of Tourism Research* 19(4): 665–690

Aramberri, J. (2005) 'How global is tourism?', in J. Aramberri and R. Butler (eds), *Tourism Development: Issues for a Vulnerable Industry.* Bristol: Channel View Publications

Arduin, J. and Ni, J.(2005) 'French TGV network development', *Japan Railway and Transport Review* 40: 22–28

Arnold, J (1997) *Managing Careers into the 21st Century.* London: Paul Chapman Publishing Ltd

Ashley, C., Roe, D. and Goodwin, H. (2001) *Pro-Poor Tourism Strategies: Making Tourism Work For The Poor.* London: Overseas Development Institute

Ashworth, G. (2003) 'Urban tourism: still an imbalance in attention?', in C. Cooper (ed.), *Classic Reviews in Tourism.* Bristol: Channel View Publications. pp. 143–162

Association of Leading Visitor Attractions (ALVA) (2010) *Visits UK Leading Visitor Attractions 2009.* www. alva.org.uk

Augustyn, M.M and Knowles, T. (2000) 'Performance of tourism partnerships: a focus on York', *Tourism Management* 21: 341–351

Australian Bureau of Statistics (2009) *Tourism Satellite Account.* Canberra: Australian Bureau of Statistics

Backman, K., Backman, S., Uysal, M. and Sunshine, K. (1995) 'Event tourism: an examination of motivations and activities', *Festival Management and Event Tourism* 3(1): 15–24

Baggini, J. (2008) *Welcome to Everytown*. London: Granta Books

Bagwell, P.S. (1974) *The Transport Revolution from 1770*. London: BT Batsford Ltd

Bain, C. and Wilson, N. (2004) *Lonely Planet: Malta and Gozo*. London: Lonely Planet

Baranowski, S. (2007) 'Common ground: linking transport and tourism', *Journal of Transport History* 28(1): 120–124

Barbaza, Y. (1970) 'Trois types d'intervention du tourisme dans l'organsiation de l'espace littoral' *Annales de Géographie* 434, 446–469

Barker, M. (2004) *Crime and Sports Event Tourism*. Bristol: Channel View Publications

Barnes, B. (2011) 'Disney report 54% rise in profit', *New York Times* 8 February. http://www.nytimes.com/2011/02/09/business/media/09disney.html

Barrett, J. (1958) 'The seaside resort towns of England and Wales'. Unpublished PhD thesis. London: University of London

Barton, S. (2005) *Working Class Organisations and Popular Tourism 1840–1970*. Manchester: Manchester University Press

Bateson, J. (1995) *Managing Services Marketing*. Orlando: The Dryden Press.

Baum, T. (2006) *Human Resource Management for Tourism, Hospitality and Leisure: An International Perspective*. Andover: Thomson, UK

Baum, T. and Lundtorp, S. (2001) *Seasonality in Tourism*, Advances in Tourism Research Series. Oxford: Pergamon

Beard, J. and Ragheb, M. (1983) 'Measuring leisure motivation', *Journal of Leisure Research* 15: 219–228

Beaver, A. (2002) *A Dictionary of Travel and Tourism Terminology*. Wallingford: CABI Publishing

Becken, S. and Hay, J.E. (2007) *Tourism and Climate Change: Risks and Opportunities*. Bristol: Channel View Publications

Beech, J. and Chadwick, S. (eds) (2006) *The Business of Tourism Management*. Harlow: Pearson Education

Beeton, S. (2006) *Community Development through Tourism*. Collingwood: Landlinks Press

Begg, D., Fisher, S. and Dornbush, R. (1994) *Economics*. London: Mc-Graw-Hill Book Company

Beirman, D. (2003) *Restoring Tourism Destinations in Crisis*. Wallingford: CABI Publishing

Benavides, D. (2002) 'Overcoming poverty in developing countries through self-sustainable international tourism', in B. Rauschelbach, A. Schäfer and B. Steck B. (eds), *Co-operating for Sustainable Tourism, Proceedings of the Forum International at the Reisepavillion 2002*. Heidelberg: Kasparek Verlag

Berry, L.L. (1980) 'Services marketing is different', *Business Magazine* (May–June 1980) pp. 24–29

Beynon, J. and Dunkerley, D. (eds) (2000) *Globalisation: The Reader*. London: Athlone Press

Bhutan Country Strategy Paper (2007) ec.europa.eu/external_relations/bhutan/csp/07_13_en.pdf

Bishop, E. (1968), *Questions of Travel*. New York: Farrar, Strauss and Giroux

Bisson, J (1986) *À l'Origine du Tourisme aux îles Baleares: Vocation Touristique ou Receptivité du Milieu d'Accueuil?* Paper presented at the meeting of the IGU Commission of the Geography of Tourism and Leisure, Palma de Mallorca (mimeo)

Bitner, M.J. (1990) 'Evaluating service encounters: the effects of physical surroundings and employee responses' *Journal of Marketing,* April: 42–50

Black, M. (1995) *In the Twilight Zone: Child Workers in the Hotel, Tourism and Catering Industry*. Geneva: International Labour Organisation

Blewitt, J. (2008) *Understanding Sustainable Development*. London: Earthscan

Boer, A., Thomas, R. and Webster, M. (1997) *Small Business Management: A Resource-based Approach for the Hospitality and Tourism Industries.* London: Cassell

Boissevain, J. (ed.) (1996) *Coping with Tourists: European Reactions to Mass Tourism.* Providence: Berghahn Books

Bolwell, D. and Weinz, W. (2008) *Reducing Poverty through Tourism* (working document). Geneva: International Labour Organisation

Bongar, B., Brown, L., Beutler, E. and Zimbardo, P. (2007) *Psychology of Terrorism.* New York: Oxford University Press US

Boniface, B. and Cooper, C. (2005) *Worldwide Destinations Casebook.* Oxford: Butterworth-Heinemann

Boniface, B. and Cooper, C. (2009) *Worldwide Destinations: The Geography of Travel and Tourism.* London: Elsevier

Booms, B.H. and Bitner, M.J. (1981) 'Marketing strategies and organisation structures for service firms', in J. Donnelly and W.R. George (eds), *Marketing of Services.* pp. 47–51 Chicago:American Marketing Association

Borman, E. (2004) 'Health tourism: where healthcare, ethics and the state collide', *British Medical Journal* 328: 60–61

Bornhorst, T., Ritchie, J.R.B. and Sheehan, L. (2010) 'Determinants of tourism success for DMOs and destinations: an empirical examination of stakeholders' perspectives', *Tourism Management* 31(5): 572–589

Bournemouth Tourism (2010) *BTMB.* http://www.bournemouth.co.uk/site/business/btmb

Bowdin, G., Allen, J., O'Toole, W., Harris, R. and McDonnell, I. (2006) *Events Management.* London: Elsevier

Bowen, D. and Clarke J. (2009) *Contemporary Tourist Behaviour: Yourself and Others as Tourists.* Wallingford: CABI

Bradford Council (2002) *Tourism Strategy.* Bradford: Bradford Council

Bramwell, B. and Lane, B. (eds) (2000) *Tourism Collaboration and Partnerships: Politics, Practice and Sustainability.* Bristol: Channel View Publications

Brenner, C. and Aguilar, A.G. (2002) 'Luxury tourism and regional economic development in Mexico', *The Professional Geographer* 54 (4): 500–520

British Postal Museum and Archive (2005) *The Mail Coach Service.* Postal Heritage Trust

Bromley, D. (1990) *Behavioural Gerontology: Central Issues in the Psychology of Ageing.* Hoboken: John Wiley & Sons

Buckley, M. (1994) *The Structure of Business.* Harlow: Longman

Buhalis, D. (2000) 'Marketing the competitive destination of the future', *Tourism Management* 21: 97–116

Buhalis, D. (2001) 'Tourism distribution channels: practices and processes', in D. Buhalis and E. Laws (eds), *Tourism Distribution Channels: Practices, Issues, and Transformations.* London: Continuum, pp. 7–33

Buhalis, D. (2003) *eTourism Information Technology for Strategic Tourism Management.* Harlow: Prentice-Hall

Buhalis, D. and Kaldis, K. (2008) 'eEnabled internet distribution for small and medium sized hotels: the case of Athens', *Tourism Recreation Research* 33(1): 67–81.

Buhalis, D. and Laws, E. (eds) (2001) *Tourism Distribution Channels: Practices, Issues, and Transformations.* London: Continuum

Buhalis, D. and Licata, M.C. (2002) 'The future eTourism intermediaries', *Tourism Management* 23(3): 207–220

Burns, C. (2008) *Quotable Quote,* in *GWAHS Newsletter,* October/November. New South Wales: GWAHS

Burns, P. (1998) 'Tourism in Russia: background and structure', *Tourism Management* 19(6): 555–565

Business Traveller (2009) 'BA to drop Gatwick–New York route', *Business Traveller,* 29 May. www.businesstraveller.com

Butler, R. (1980) 'The Concept of a Tourist Area Cycle of Evolution', *The Canadian Geographer* 24 (1): 5–12

Butler, R. (1993) 'Pre and post impact assessment of tourism developments', in D. Pearce and R. Butler (eds), *Tourism Research: Critiques and Challenges*. London: Routledge

Butler, R. (2001) 'Seasonality in tourism: issues and implications', in T. Baum and S. Lundtorp (eds), *Seasonality in Tourism*. Oxford: Pergamon. pp. 5–22

Butler, R. (ed.) (2006a) *The Tourism Area Life Cycle, Vol 1 Applications and Modifications*. Bristol: Channel View Publications

Butler, R. (ed.) (2006b) *The Tourism Area Life Cycle, Vol 2 Conceptual and Theoretical Issues*. Bristol: Channel View Publications

Butler, R. (2006c) 'The Concept of a Tourist Area Life Cycle of Evolution: Implications for Management of Resources', in R. Butler (ed.), *The Tourism Area Life Cycle, Vol 1 Applications and Modifications*. Bristol: Channel View Publications, Chapter 1

CAA (2009) *The CAA's ATOL Scheme*. http://www.caa.co.uk/docs/33/ATOL_Fact_Sheet.pdf

Cabezas, A. (2008) 'Tropical blues: tourism and social exclusion in the Dominican Republic', *Latin American Perspectives* 160(35–3): 21–36

Cahill, K., Marion, J. and Lawson, S. (2008) 'Exploring visitor acceptability for hardening trails to sustain visitation and minimise impacts', *Journal of Sustainable Tourism* 16(2): 232–245

Carlson Wagonlit Travel (2011) *Corporate Brochure*. http://www.carlsonwagonlit.com/export/sites/cwt/en/global/our_company/corporate-brochure.pdf

Carmona, M., de Magalhães, C. and Hammond, L. (2008) *Public Space, the Management Dimension*. Oxford: Routledge

Carr, M. (1997) *New Patterns: Process and Change in Human Geography*, Surrey: Nelson

Cartwright, R. and Baird, C. (1999) *The Development and Growth of the Cruise Industry*. Oxford: Butterworth-Heinemann

Casson, L. (1974) *Travel in the Ancient World*. London: George Allen and Unwin Ltd

Causevic, S. (2010) 'Tourism which erases borders: an introspection into Bosnia and Herzegovina', in O. Moufakkir and I. Kelly (eds), *Tourism, Progress and Peace*. Wallingford: CABI

Ceballos-Lascuráin, H. (1996) *Tourism, Ecotourism and Protected Areas*. Gland: IUCN

CESD (Center for Ecotourism and Sustainable Development) (2006) *Cruise Tourism in Belize Perceptions of Economic, Social and Environmental Impact*. CESD.

Chartered Institute of Marketing (2009) *Marketing and the 7Ps: A brief Summary of Marketing and How it Works*. Maidenhead: CIM Insights

China Outbound Tourism Research Institute (COTRI) (2008) *China Outbound on the Road*. www.china-outbound.com

Christaller, W. (1963) Some considerations of tourism location in Europe: the peripheral regions – underdeveloped countries – recreation areas *Regional Science Association Papers* XII, Lund Congress 95–105

Civil Aviation Authority (2010) *Learn about ATOL* http://www.caa.co.uk/default.aspx?catid=1080&pagetype=90

Clarke, J. and Critcher, C. (1985) *The Devil Makes Work: Leisure in Capitalist Britain*. London: Macmillan

Clegg, J. (2008) 'Brits holiday more than other Europeans', 4 June. www.ttglive.co.uk

Clift, S. and Forrest, S. (1999) 'Gay men and tourism: destinations and holiday motivations', *Tourism Management* 20: 615–625

Clover, C. (2007) 'Eathlog: A Spanish Tragedy', *The Telegraph,* 3 May. http://www.telegraph.co.uk/earth/earthcomment/charlesclover/3292364/Earthlog.html

Coccossis, H. and Mexa, A. (2004) *The Challenge of Tourism Carrying Capacity Assessment.* Farnham: Ashgate Publishing

Cohen, E. (1972) 'Toward a sociology of international tourism', *Social Research* 39(1): 164–189

Cohen, E. (1979) 'A phenomenology of tourist experiences', *Sociology* 13: 179–201

Cohen, E (1984) 'The sociology of tourism: approaches, issues and findings', *Annual Review of Sociology* 10: 373–392

Cohen, S. (2010), 'Reconceptualising lifestyle travellers: contemporary 'drifters', in K. Hannam and A. Diekmann (eds), *Beyond Backpacker Tourism: Mobilities and Experiences.* Bristol: Channel View Publications

Cole, S. (2008) *Tourism, Culture and Development: Hopes, Dreams and Realities in East-Indonesia.* Bristol: Channel View Publications

Cole, V. and Sinclair A. (2002) 'Measuring the ecological footprint of a Himalayan tourist centre', *Mountain Research and Development* 22(2): 132–141

Connolly, P. and McGing, G. (2007) 'High performance work practices and competitive advantage in the Irish hospitality sector', *International Journal of Contemporary Hospitality Management* 19(3): 201–210

Continental Airlines (2009) *2008 Annual Report to Stockholders.* http://phx.corporate-ir.net/External.File?item=UGFyZW50SUQ9NjQ0OTl8Q2hpbGGRJRD0tMXxUeXBlPTM=&t=1

Convention Industry Council (2003) *APEX Industry Glossary* http://glossary.convention industry.org

Cooper, C. (1997) 'The technique of interpretation', in S. Medlik (ed.), *Managing Tourism.* Oxford: Butterworth-Heinemann

Cooper, C. (ed.) (2003) *Classic Reviews in Tourism.* Bristol: Channel View Publications

Cooper, C. and Hall, M.C. (2008) *Contemporary Tourism: An International Approach.* Oxford: Butterworth-Heinemann.

Cooper C., Fletcher J., Fyall A., Gilbert D. and Wanhill S. (2008) *Tourism Principles and Practice*, Harlow: Pearson Education

Cottrell, S. (2010) *Skills for Success: The Personal Development Planning Handbook.* Basingstoke: Palgrave Macmillan

Crompton, J.L. (1979) 'Motivations for pleasure vacation', *Annals of Tourism Research* 6(4): 408–424

Cunill, O.M. (2006) *The Growth Strategies of Hotel Chains: Best Business Practices by Leading Companies.* Binghampton, NY: Haworth

Daby, D. (2003) 'Effects of seagrass bed removal for tourism purposes in a Mauritian bay', *Environmental Pollution* 125: 313–324

Dann, G. (1977) 'Anomie, ego-enhancement and tourism', *Annals of Tourism Research* 4(4): 184–194

Davidson, R. (2001) 'Distribution channel analysis for business travel', in D. Buhalis and E. Laws (eds), *Tourism Distribution Channels: Practices, Issues, and Transformations.* London: Continuum. pp. 73–87

Davidson, R. and Cope, B. (2003) *Business Travel: Conferences, Incentive Travel, Exhibitions, Corporate Hospitality and Corporate Travel.* Harlow: Pearson

Davidson, R. and Maitland, R. (1997) *Tourism Destinations.* London: Hodder and Stoughton

Davidson, R. and Rogers, T. (2006) *Marketing Destinations and Venues for Conferences, Conventions and Business Events.* Oxford: Butterworth-Heinemann

Davidson, T.L. (2005) 'What are travel and tourism – are they really an industry?', in W.F. Theobald (ed.), *Global Tourism.* Burlington, MA: Elsevier, pp. 25–32

Dawes, J. and Rowley, J. (1996) 'The waiting experience: towards service quality in the leisure industry', *International Journal of Contemporary Hospitality Management*, 8(1): 16–21

Dawson, S. (2007) 'Working Class Consumers and the Campaign for Holidays with Pay', *Twentieth-Century British History,* 18: 277–305

De Botton, A. (2002) *The Art of Travel*. London: Penguin

De Bruyn P., Bain K.,Vankatraman, N. and Joshi, S. (2008) *Frommer's India*. Hoboken, NJ: Wiley Publishing

Delaney-Smith, P. (1987) 'The tour operator – new and maturing business', in A. Hodgson (ed.), *The Travel and Tourism Industry*. Oxford: Butterworth-Heinemann. pp. 94–106

Department for Transport (DfT) (2003) *The Future of Air Transport*. London: The Stationery Office

Dilts, J.C. and Prough, G.E. (1991) 'Travel agent perceptions and responses in a deregulated travel environment', *Journal of Travel Research* 29: 37–42

Disney Cruise Lines (2010) *Disney Cruise Line*. http://disneycruise.disney.go.com/

Doganis, R. (1991) *Flying off Course: The Economics of International Airlines*. London: Harper Collins Academic

Doganis, R. (2009) *Flying Off Course Airline Economics and Marketing Airlines*. London: Routledge

Dollar, D. and Kraay, A. (2004) 'Growth is good for the poor', in F. Lechner and J. Boli (eds), *The Globalisation Reader*. Malden: Blackwell

Donaghy, G. (2007) 'Convention centres: is the model evolving?' *MICE International* May–June: 71–72

Douglas, N. and Douglas, N. (2004) *The Cruise Experience*. Sydney: Pearson

Doxey, G. (1975) 'A causation theory of visitor-resident irritants: methodology and research inferences in the impact of tourism', *Sixth Annual Conference Proceedings of the Travel Research Association*. (September): 195–198

Dredge, D. (2006) 'Policy networks and the local organisation of tourism', *Tourism Management* 27(2): 269–280

Dresner, S. (2008) *The Principles of Sustainability*. London: Earthscan

Drummond, S. and Yeoman, I. (eds) (2001) *Quality Issues in Heritage Visitor Attractions*. Oxford: Butterworth-Heinemann,

Durbarry, R. and Sinclair, M.T. (2002) *The Price Sensitivity of Tourism Demand in Malta: A Report for the Malta Tourism Authority*. The Christel DeHaan Tourism and Travel Research Institute, Nottingham University Business School

Duval, D. (2003) 'When hosts become guests: return visits and diasporic identities in a Commonwealth Eastern Caribbean community', *Current Issues in Tourism* 6(4): 267–308

Duval, D. (2007) *Tourism and Transport, Modes, Networks and Flows*. Bristol: Channel View

Easyjet (2010) *2010 annual report* http://2010annualreport.easyjet.com/easyjet-at-a-glance.asp

Economist (2001) *Globalisation*. London: Profile Books

Ecorys (2009) *Study on the Competitiveness of the EU Tourism Industry – with Specific Focus on the Accommodation and Tour Operator and Travel Agent Industries*. Rotterdam: Ecorys SCS Group

Egger, G. (2007) 'Personal carbon trading: a potential "stealth intervention" for obesity reduction?', *Medical Journal of Australia* 187(3): 185–187

Elliott, J. (1997) *Tourism: Politics and Public Sector Management*. London: Routledge

Euromonitor (1988) *The World Package Holidays Market 1980*–1995. London: Euromonitor Publications

Euromonitor (2006) *Travel and Tourism in Albania*. London: Euromonitor Publications

Euromonitor (2010) *Global Hotels Lagging but Not Lost*. London: Euromonitor Publications

Euromonitor International (2008) *Travel and Tourism Country Reports*. London: Euromonitor Publications

Euromonitor International (2010) *State of the Global Hotel Industry*. London: Euromonitor Publications

European Commission (2005) *The New SME definition User Guide and Model Declaration.* Enterprise and Industry Publications

European Commission (2007) *Case No: COMP/M 4600-TUI/First Choice* 04/06/2007. Luxembourg: Office for Official Publications of the European Communities

Eurostat (2008) *Panorama on Tourism.* Luxembourg: Eurostat

Facebook (2011) *Statistics.* http://www.facebook.com/press/info.php?statistics

Fahey, L. (2003) 'How corporations learn from scenarios', in R. Randall (ed.), *Integrate Scenario Learning with Decision Making.* Bradford: Emerald Group

Faulkner, B. and Tideswell, C. (1997) 'A framework for monitoring community impacts of tourism', *Journal of Sustainable Tourism* 5(1): 3–28

Federation of Tour Operators (FTO) (2009) *Advance Planning.* http://www.fto.co.uk//operators-factfile/advanced-planning/

Font, X. and Buckley, R. (2001) *Tourism Ecolabelling: Certification and Promotion of Sustainable Management.* Wallingford: CABI

Ford, R. (2008) 'Chasing MICE and fellow travellers: a history of the convention and visitor bureau industry', *Journal of Management History* 14(2): 128–143

Forsyth, P (2008) 'Tourism and aviation policy', in A. Graham, A. Papatheodorou and P. Forsyth (eds), *Aviation and Tourism: Implications for Leisure Travel.* Hampshire: Ashgate Publishing Ltd. pp. 73–85

Forum for the Future (FF) (2009) *Tourism 2023.* London: Forum for the Future

France, L. (ed.) (1999) *An Earthscan Reader in Sustainable Tourism.* London: Earthscan

Frechtling, D. (1999) 'The tourism satellite account: foundations, progress and issues', *Tourism Management* 20: 163–170

Frechtling, D. (2001) *Forecasting Tourism Demand: Methods and Strategies.* Oxford: Butterworth-Heinemann

Friends of the Earth (2000) *From Planes to Trains: Realising the Potential from Shifting Short-haul Flights to Rail.* London: Friends of the Earth.

Fuentes, A. (2006) 'Human culture and monkey behavior: assessing the contexts of potential pathogen transmission between macaques and humans', *American Journal of Primatology* 68: 880–896

Fyall, A. and Garrod, B (2005) *Tourism Marketing A Collaborative Approach.* Bristol: Channel View Publications

Fyall, A., Garrod, B., Leask, A. and Wanhill, S. (2008) *Managing Visitor Attractions: New Directions.* Oxford: Butterworth-Heinemann

Gale, T. (2006) 'Mass tourism businesses: tour operators', in J. Beech and S. Chadwick (eds), *The Business of Tourism Management.* Harlow: Pearson Education. pp. 399–413

Gallarza, M., Saura, I. and Garcia, H. (2002) 'Destination image: towards a conceptual framework', *Annals of Tourism Research* 29(1): 56–78

Garcia-Altes, A. (2005) 'The development of health tourism services', *Annals of Tourism Research* 32(1): 262–266

Garrod, B. (2008) 'Managing visitor impacts', in A. Fyall, B. Garrod, A. Leask and S. Wanhill (eds), *Managing Visitor Attractions: New Directions.* Oxford: Butterworth-Heinemann

Gartrell, R. (1994) *Strategic partnerships: Destination marketing for convention and visitor bureaux.* Dubuque: Kendall/Hunt Publishing Co, pp. 230–232

Gatwick Airport (2010) *Service Quality Rebate Scheme.* http://www.gatwickairport.com/business/performance/rebate-scheme/

Getz, D. (2007) *Event Studies: Theory, Research and Policy for Planned Events.* Oxford: Butterworth-Heinemann

Giddens, A. (1998) *The Third Way: The Renewal of Social Democracy.* Cambridge: Polity Press

Gilbert, D. (1954) *'The need for countries to differentiate their tourist product and how to do so'.* Seminar papers for Ministers of Tourism and Directors of National Tourist Organisations – Tourism Managing for Results, November, University of Surrey

Gilbert, D. (1991) 'An examination of the consumer decision process related to tourism'. in C. Cooper (ed.), *Progress in Tourism, Recreation and Hospitality Management, Vol. 3.* London: Belhaven

Gilbert, E.W. (1939) 'The growth of inland and seaside health resorts in England', *Scottish Geographical Magazine* 55: 16–35

Gill, R. (2010) '*UK visits abroad fall by 15%*', ttglive.co.uk, 13 July.

Gladstone, D. (2005) *From Pilgrimage to Package Tour: Travel and Tourism in the Third World.* London: Routledge

Glaesser, D. (2003) *Crisis Management in the Tourism Industry.* Oxford: Elsevier Butterworth-Heinemann

Glastonbury Festival (2011) *History.* www.glastonburyfestivals.co.uk/history

Godfrey, K. and Clarke, J. (2000) *The Tourism Development Handbook: A Practical Approach to Planning and Marketing.* London: Thomson Learning

Goeldner, C.R., Ritchie, J.R.B. and MCIntosh, R.W. (2000) *Tourism: Principles, Practices, Philosophies.* Chichester: John Wiley and Sons

Gomez-Ibanez, J.A. and de Rus, G. (eds) (2006) *Competition in the Railway Industry: An International Comparative Analysis.* Cheltenham: Edward Elgar

Gooroochurn, N. and Sinclair, T. (2005) 'Economics of tourism taxation: evidence from Mauritius', *Annals of Tourism Research* 32(2): 478–498

Gormsen, E. (1997) 'The impact of tourism on coastal areas', *Geojournal* 42(1): 39–54

Government of India (2007) *Incredible India: The Global Healthcare Destination.* Delhi: Ministry of Tourism

Government of Jamaica (2009) *Team Jamaica* (Tourism Product Development Co. Ltd). www.tpdco.orgll

Graham, A. and Dennis, N. (2009) 'The impact of low cost airline operations to Malta', *Journal of Air Transport Management* 15(4): 149–150

Graham, A. Papatheodorou, A. and Forsyth, P. (eds) (2008) *Aviation and Tourism – Implications for Leisure Travel.* Hampshire: Ashgate

Graham, M. (2009) 'Different models in different spaces or liberalized optimizations? competitive strategies among budget air carriers', *Journal of Transport Geography* 17(4): 306–316

Grant, D. and Mason, S. (2007) *Holiday Law: The Law Relating to Travel and Tourism.* London: Sweet and Maxwell

Gray, C. (2009) 'Which way for ATOL reform?', *Travel Trade Gazette UK and Ireland,* 17 September

Grönroos, C. (1978) 'A service-orientated approach to marketing of services', *European Journal of Marketing* 12(8): 588–601

Grönroos, C. (2007) *Service Management and Marketing: Customer Management in Service Competition.* Chichester: Wiley and Sons

Gummesson, E. (1987) 'Marketing revisited: the crucial role of the part-time marketer', *European Journal of Marketing* 25(2): 60–67

Gummesson, E. (2008) *Total Relationship Marketing: Rethinking Marketing Management: from 4Pss to 30Rs.* London:Butterworth-Heinemann

Gunn, C. (1972) *Vacationscape: Designing Tourist Regions.* Austin: University of Texas

Gunn, C. (1988) *Vacationscape: Designing Tourist Regions.* Austin, TX: University of Texas

Gunn, C. and Var, T. (2002) *Tourism Planning.* New York: Routledge

Gupta, V. (1999) 'Sustainable tourism: learning from Indian religious traditions', *International Journal of Contemporary Hospitality Management* 11(2/3): 91–95

Hall, C.M. (2006) 'Introduction' in R. Butler (ed.), *The Tourism Area Life Cycle, Vol 2 Conceptual and Theoretical Issues.* Bristol: Channel View Publications, pp. xv–xix

Hall, C. (2008) *Tourism Planning: Policies, Processes and Relationships*. Harlow: Prentice-Hall

Hall, C. and Jenkins, J. (1995) *Tourism and Public Policy*. London: Routledge

Hall, D., Kirkpatrick, I. and Mitchell, M. (eds) (2005) *Rural Tourism and Sustainable Business*. Bristol: Channel View Publications

Hall, M. and Page, S. (2002) *The Geography of Tourism and Recreation: Environment, Place and Space*. Abingdon: Routledge

Hanlon, P. (1996) *Global Airlines Competition in a Transnational Industry*. Oxford: Butterworth-Heinemann

Hanlon, P. (2007) *Global Airlines Competition in a Transnational Industry*, 3rd edn. Oxford: Butterworth-Heinemann

Harrington, D. and Lenehan, T. (1998) *Managing Quality in Tourism, Theory and Practice*. Dublin: Oak Tree Press

Harriott, V., Davis, D. and Banks, S. (1997) 'Recreational diving and its impact in marine protected areas in Eastern Australia', *Ambio* 26(3): 173–179

Harris, R., Griffin, T. and Williams, P. (2002) *Sustainable Tourism: A Global Perspective*. Oxford: Butterworth-Heinemann

Hasler, H. and Ott, J. (2008) 'Diving down the reefs? Intense diving tourism threatens the reefs of the Northern Red Sea', *Marine Pollution Bulletin* 56: 1788–1794

Haven-Tang, C. and Jones, E. (2005) 'The heterodoxey of tourism SMEs in E. Jones and Haven-Tang (eds), *Tourism SMES: Service Quality and Destination Competitiveness*. Wallingford: CABI, pp. 337–356

Hawkins, D.E. and Ritchie, J.R.B. (eds) (1991) *World Travel and Tourism Review: Indicators, Trends and Forecasts, Vol. 1*. Wallingford: CABI

Hazel, N. (2004) 'Holidays for children and families in need: an exploration of the research and policy context for social tourism in the UK', *Children and Society* 19: 225–236

Henderson, J. (2006) 'Tourism in Dubai: Overcoming barriers to tourism development', *International Journal of Tourism Research* 8: 87–99

Henderson, J. (2007) *Tourism Crises: Causes, Consequences and Management*. Oxford: Elsevier Butterworth-Heinemann

Heskett, J., Earl Sasser, Jr, W. and Schlesinger, L. (1997) *The Service Profit Chain: How Leading Companies Link Profit and Growth to Loyalty, Satisfaction and Value*. New York: The Free Press

Higginbottom, K. (2004) *Wildlife Tourism: Impacts, Management and Planning*. Altona: Common Ground

Higgins-Desbiolles, F. (2006a) 'Reconciliation tourism: on crossing bridges and changing ferries', in P. Burns and M. Novelli (eds), *Tourism and Social Identities*. Oxford: Elsevier

Higgins-Desbiolles, F. (2006b) 'More than an "industry": the forgotten power of tourism as a social force', *Tourism Management* 27: 1192–1208

Hilling, D. (1996) *Transport and Developing Countries*. London: Routledge

HM Revenue and Customs (2010) *Notice 550 Air Passenger Duty August 2010* http://customs.hmrc.gov.uk/channelsPortalWebApp/channelsPortalWebApp.portal?_nfpb=true&_pageLabel=pageExcise_ShowContent&id=HMCE_CL_000505&propertyType=document

HM Treasury (2006) *Pre-Budget Report*. London: HM Treasury

Hodgson, A. (ed.) (1987) *The Travel and Tourism Industry: Strategies for the future*. Oxford: Butterworth-Heinemann

Hoffman, K.D. and Bateson, J.E.G. (2001) *Essentials of Services Marketing: Concepts, Strategies and Cases*. Ohio: South-western

Hoffman, K.D. and Bateson, J.E.G. (2006) *Essentials of Services Marketing: Concepts, Strategies and Cases*. Ohio: South-western

Hoffman, K.D. Bateson, J., Wood, E. and Kenyon, A. (2009) *Services Marketing, Concepts, Strategies and Cases*. London: Cengage Learning

Holden, A. (2003) 'In need of new environmental ethics for tourism?', *Annals of Tourism Research* 30(1): 94–108

Holden, A. (2005) *Tourism Studies and the Social Sciences*. London and New York: Routledge

Holden, A. (2008) *Environment and Tourism*. London and New York: Routledge

Holloway, J.C. (1985) *The Business of Tourism*. Harlow: Prentice-Hall

Holloway, J.C. (1998) *The Business of Tourism*. Harlow: Prentice-Hall

Holloway, J.C. (2004) *Marketing for Tourism*. Harlow: Prentice-Hall

Holloway, J.C. (2006) *The Business of Tourism*. Harlow: Prentice-Hall

Holloway, J.C., Humphreys, C. and Davison, R. (2009) *The Business of Tourism*. Harlow: Prentice-Hall

Hope, C. and Klemm, M. (2001) 'Tourism in difficult areas revisited: the case of Bradford', *Tourism Management* 22(6): 629–635

Horner, S. and Swarbrooke, J. (1996) *Marketing Tourism Hospitality and Leisure in Europe*. London: Thomson

Horner, S. and Swarbrooke, J. (2004) *International Cases in Tourism Management*. Oxford: Butterworth-Heinemann

House, J. (1954) 'Geographical aspects of coastal holiday resorts'. Unpublished PhD thesis. Durham: Kings College

Howie, F. (2003) *Managing the Tourist Destination*. London: Thomson Learning

Hudman, L. and Jackson, R. (2002) *Geography of Travel and Tourism*. Florence: Cengage Learning

Hudson, S. (2008) *Tourism and Hospitality Marketing*. London: Sage

Hughes, H. (2002) 'Marketing gay tourism in Manchester: new market for urban tourism or destruction of "gay space"?', *Journal of Vacation Marketing* 9(2): 152–163

Hughes, J.C. and Rog, E. (2006) 'Talent management: a strategy for improving employee recruitment, retention and engagement within hospitality organisations', *International Journal of Contemporary Hospitality Management* 20: 743–757

Hughes, M. (2008) 'An open passenger market beckons', *Railway Gazette International* 19 February.

Humphreys, C. (2006) 'Mass tourism businesses 2: travel agents', in J. Beech and S. Chadwick (eds), *The Business of Tourism Management*. Harlow: Pearson Education. pp. 415–439

Hunter, C. (1997) 'Sustainable tourism as an adaptive paradigm', *Annals of Tourism Research* 24(4): 850–867

Hunter, C. (2004) 'On the need to reconceptualise sustainable tourism development', in S. Williams (ed.), *Tourism: Critical Concepts in the Social Sciences*. London: Taylor & Francis

Hunziker, W, and Krapf, K (1942) *Grundriss der Allgemeinen Fremdenverkehrslehre*. Zurich: Polygraphischer

IATA (2009) *IATA Agency Programme*. http://www.iata.org/pressroom/facts_figures/fact_sheets/Pages/agency.aspx

IATA (2011) 'Scheduled passenger – kilometres flown', *WATS*, 54th edition. http://www.iata.org/ps/publications/Pages/wats-passenger-km.aspx

IHG (2011a) *Hotel and Room Stats, March 2011*. http://www.ihgplc.com/files/pdf/factsheets/factsheet_worldstats.pdf

IHG (2011b) *About Us: Overview*. http://www.ihgplc.com/index.asp?pageid=16

IMO (2009) *Second IMO GHG Study 2009*. London: International Maritime Organization (IMO)

Inglis, F. (2000) *The Delicious History of the Holiday*. London: Routledge

Inkpen, G. (1998) *Information Technology for Travel and Tourism*. Harlow: Longman

Inskeep, E. (1991) *Tourism Planning: An Integrated and Sustainable Development Approach*. New York: Van Nostrand Reinhold

International Labour Organisation (ILO) (2001) *Human Resources Development, Employment and Globalisation in the Hotel, Catering and Tourism Sector.* Geneva: International Labour Office

International Labour Organisation (ILO) (2010) *Working Conditions Laws Report 2010.* Geneva: ILO. www.ilo.org/travail

Ioannides, D. (2003) 'The economics of tourism in host communities', in S. Singh, J. Dallen and K. Ross (eds), *Tourism in Destination Communities.* Wallingford: CABI

IUOTO (1963) *Conference on International Travel and Tourism.* Geneva: UN

Jafari, J. (1977) 'Editor's page' *Annals of Tourism Research* 5. Supplement 1, 6–11

Jafari, J. (2003) *Encyclopedia of Tourism.* London: Routledge

Jago, E. and Deery, M. (2002) 'The role of human resource practices in achieving quality enhancement and cost reduction: an investigation of volunteer use in tourism organisations', *International Journal of Contemporary Hospitality Management* 14(5): 229–236

James, L. (2006) *The Middle Class: A History.* London: Little, Brown

Japan Travel Bureau (2011) *About Us.* www.jtbuk.com

Jeffries, D. (2001) *Governments and Tourism.* London: Reed

Jones, E. and Haven-Tang, C. (2005) *Tourism SMEs: Service Quality and Destination Competitiveness.* Wallingford: CABI

Kasiev, M. (1971) 'Health protection and the social security of workers in the USSR', *International Social Security Review* 24(2): 274–283

Keyser, H. (2002) *Tourism Development.* Oxford: Oxford University Press

Kimes, S. (2000) 'Yield management: an overview', in A. Ingold, McMahon-Beatty' U. and Yeoman, I. (Eds), *Yield Management: Strategies for the Service Industries.* London: Cassell

Klein, A.R. (2002) *Cruise Ship Blues.* Gabriola Island, BC: New Society Publishers

Knowles, R., Shaw, J. and Docherty, I. (eds) (2008) *Transport Geographies: Mobilities, Flows and Spaces.* Oxford: Blackwell Publishing

Knowles, T. (1996) *Corporate Strategy for Hospitality.* Harlow: Longman.

Kolb, B. (2006) *Tourism Marketing for Cities and Towns: Using Branding and Events to Attract Tourists.* Burlington: Butterworth-Heinemann

Kotler, P. and Armstrong, G. (1999) *Principles of Marketing.* New York: Pearson US Imports

Kotler, P., Bowen, J.T. and Makens, J.C. (2009) *Marketing for Hospitality and Tourism.* Pearson: New Jersey

Kotler, P., Haider, D.H. and Rein, I. (1993) *Marketing Places: Attracting Investment, Industry and Tourism to Cities, States and Nations.* New York: Free Press

Kotler, P., Wong, V., Saunders, J. and Armstrong, G. (2004) *Principles of Marketing: European Edition.* New York: Prentice-Hall

KPMG (2008) *Climate Changes your Business.* New York: KPMG International. www.kpmg.com

Krippendorf, J. (1984) *The Holiday Makers: Understanding the Impact of Leisure and Travel.* Oxford: Butterworth-Heinemann

Kuniyal, J., Jain, A. and Shannigrahi, A. (2003) 'Solid waste management in Indian Himalayan tourists' treks: a case study in and around the Valley of Flowers and Hemkund Sahib', *Waste Management* 23: 807–816

Kuo, I. (2002) 'The effectiveness of environmental interpretation at resource-sensitive tourism destinations', *International Journal of Tourism Research* 4(2): 87–101

Kuoni Travel Group (2011) *Online Annual Report 2010.* www.kuoni.com

Kweka, J., Morrissey, O. and Blake, A. (2003) 'The economic potential of tourism in Tanzania, *Journal of International Development* 15: 335–351

Lagiewski, R.M. (2006) 'The application of the TALC Model: a literature survey', in R. Butler (ed.), *The Tourism Area Life Cycle, Vol 1 Applications and Modifications.* Bristol: Channel View Publications, pp. 27– 50

Lake Macquarie Tourism (2010) *Everything to Know about Lake Macquarie Tourism.* http://www.lakemacquarietourism.com.au/

Lane, B. (1994) 'Sustainable rural tourism strategies: a tool for development and conservation', *Journal of Sustainable Tourism* 2: 102–111

Lane, B. (2005) 'Sustainable rural tourism strategies: a tool for development and conservation', *RIAT Interamerican Journal of Environment and Tourism* 1(1): 12–18

Langer, G. (1996) 'Traffic noise and hotel profits – is there a relationship?', *Tourism Management* 17(4): 295–305

Lapunzina, A. (2005) *Architecture of Spain.* Santa Barbara: Greenwood Publishing Group

Laurance, W. (2007) 'A new initiative to use carbon trading for tropical forest conservation', *Biotropica*, 39(1): 20–24

Law, C. (1996) *Tourism in Major Cities.* London: International Thomson Business Press

Law, C. (2003) *Urban Tourism: The Visitor Economy and the Growth of Large Cities.* London: Continuum

Law, R. (2009) 'Disintermediation of hotel reservations: the perception of different groups of online buyers in Hong Kong', *International Journal of Contemporary Hospitality Management* 21(6): 766–772

Law, R., Leung, K. and Wong, J. (2004) 'The impact of the internet on travel agencies', *International Journal of Contemporary Hospitality Management* 16(2): 101–107

Laws, E. (1995) *Tourist Destination Management, Issues Analysis and Policies.* London: Routledge

Laws, E. (1997) *Managing Packaged Tourism: Relationships, Responsibilities and Service Quality in the Inclusive Holiday Industry.* London: Thomson

Laws, E. (2000) 'Perspectives on pricing decision in the inclusive holiday industry', in A. Ingold, U. McMahon-Beatty and I. Yeoman (eds), *Yield Management: Strategies for the Service Industries.* London: Cassell

Laws, E. (2001) 'Distribution channel analysis for leisure travel', in D. Buhalis and E. Laws (eds), *Tourism Distribution Channels: Practices, Issues, and Transformations.* London: Continuum. pp. 53–73

Laws, E., Prideaux B. and Chon K. (2007) *Crisis Management in Tourism.* Wallingford: CABI

Leask, A. (2008) 'The nature and role of visitor attractions', in A. Fyall, B. Garrod, A. Leask and S. Wanhill (eds), *Managing Visitor Attractions: New Directions.* Oxford: Butterworth-Heinemann. pp. 3–16

Lechner, F. and Boli, J. (2004) *The Globalisation Reader*, 2nd edn. Malden: Blackwell

Lee-Ross, D. (2005) 'Perceived job characteristics and internal work motivation: an exploratory cross-cultural analysis of the motivational antecedents of hotel workers in Mauritius and Australia', *Journal of Management Development* 24: 253–266

Leiper, N. (1979) 'The framework of tourism: towards a definition of tourism, tourist and the tourist industry', *Annals of Tourism Research* 6(4): 390–407

Leiper, N. (1990a) 'Tourist attraction systems', *Annals of Tourism Research* 17: 367–384

Leiper, N. (1990b) 'The partial industrialisation of tourism', *Annals of Tourism Research* 17: 600–605

Leslie, D. (2001) 'Urban regeneration and Glasgow's galleries with particular reference to The Burrell Collection', in G. Richards (ed.), *Cultural Attractions and European Tourism.* Wallingford: CABI

Levitt, T. (1981) 'Marketing intangible products and product intangibles' *Harvard Business Review* May/June: 37–44

Li, L. (2007) 'On the road: China on holiday', *The Economic Observer Online*, 26 September. www.eeo.com.cn/ens/Industry/2007/09/26/84236.html

Lindgren, M. and Bandhold, H. (2003) *Scenario Planning: The Link between Future and Strategy.* Basingstoke: Palgrave Macmillan

Lindsey, P., Alexander, R.L., Frank, G., Mathieson A. and Romanach S. (2006) 'Potential of trophy hunting to create incentives for wildlife conservation in Africa where alternative wildlife-based land uses may not be viable', *Animal Conservation* 9: 283–291

Litteljohn, D. and Baxter, I. (2006) 'The structure of the tourism and travel industry', in J. Beech and S. Chadwick (eds), *The Business of Tourism* Management. Harlow: Pearson Education, pp. 21–39

Littleford, D., Halstead, J. and Mulraine, C. (2004) *Career Skills: Opening Doors into the Job Market.* Basingstoke: Palgrave Macmillan

London Development Agency (LDA) (2005) *Business as Usual.* http://www.lda.avensc.com/documents/Business_as_Usual_PDF.pdf

London Development Agency (2009) *London Tourism Action Plan 2009-13* www.lda.gov.uk/Documents/London_Tourism_Action_Plan_2009-13_6537.pdf

Lopez, E. and Garcia, F. (2006) 'Agro-tourism, sustainable tourism and ultraperipheral areas: the case of the Canary Islands', *Pasos* 4(1): 85–97

Lovelock, C.H. (1983) 'Classifying services to gain strategic marketing insights', *Journal of Marketing* Summer: 9–20

Lubbe, B. (2005) 'A new revenue model for travel intermediaries in South-Africa: the negotiated approach', *Journal of Retailing and Consumer Services* 12(6): 385–396

Lück, M. (2008) *The Encyclopaedia of Tourism and Recreation in Marine Environments.* Wallingford: CABI

Lumsdon, L. (1997) *Tourism Marketing.* London: International Thomson Business Press

Lumsdon, L. and Page, S.J. (eds) (2004) *Tourism and Transport Issues: An Agenda for the New Millennium.* Oxford: Elsevier

MacCannell, D. (1999) *The Tourist: A New Theory of the Leisure Class.* London: University of California Press

MacKinnon, D., Pirie, G. and Gather, M. (2008) 'Transport and economic development', in R. Knowles, J. Shaw and I. Docherty (eds), *Transport Geographies: Mobilities, Flows and Spaces.* Oxford: Blackwell Publishing. pp. 10–29

Macleod, D. (2004) *Tourism, Globalisation and Cultural Change: An Island Community Perspective.* Bristol: Channel View

Mair, J. (2006) 'Eco-tourism: a sustainable trade?', Available online at http://news.bbc.co.uk/1/hi/sci/tech/6179901.stm

Mak, J. (2004) *Tourism and the Economy: Understanding the Economics of Tourism.* Honolulu: University of Hawaii Press

Maslow, A. (1954) *Motivation and Personality.* New York: HarperCollins

Mason, P. (2008) *Tourism Impacts, Planning and Management.* London: Elsevier

Mathieson, G. and Wall A. (1982) *Tourism: Economic, Physical and Social Impacts.* London: Longman

Matley, I. (1976) *The Geography of International Tourism.* Commission on College Geography, Association of American Geographers, Washington, DC

Mayhew, L. (1987) 'The travel agent – rise or fall?', in A. Hodgson (ed.) *The Travel and Tourism Industry: Strategies for the Future.* Oxford: Butterworth Heinnemann. pp. 49–73

McCabe, S. (2008) *Marketing Communications in Tourism and Hospitality.* Oxford: Butterworth-Heinemann

McCabe, V., Poole, B., Weeks, P. and Leiper, N. (2000) *The Business and Management of Conventions.* Jacaranda: Wiley Australia

McCarthy, E.J. (1981) *Basic Marketing: A Managerial Approach.* New York: Irwin

McIntosh, R., Goeldner, C. and Ritchie, J. (1995) *Tourism Principles, Practices and Philosophies.* New York: John Wiley

McKercher, B. and Chon, K. (2004) 'The over-reaction to SARS and the collapse of Asian tourism', *Annals of Tourism Research* 31(3): 716–719

McLean, F. (1997) *Marketing the Museum.* Abingdon: Routledge

Mercer (2009) *Employee Statutory and Public Holiday Entitlements – Global Comparisons* 13 October. http://uk.mercer.com/press-releases/1360620

Meuller, H. and Kaufmann, E. (2001) 'Wellness tourism: market analysis of a special health tourism segment', *Journal of Vacation Marketing* 7(1): 5–17

Micklethwait, J. and Wooldridge, A. (2004) 'The hidden promise: liberty renewed', in F. Lechner and J. Boli (eds), *The Globalisation Reader*. Malden: Blackewell

Middleton, V. and Clark, J. (2001) *Marketing for Travel and Tourism*. Burlington: Butterworth-Heinemann

Middleton, V., Fyall, A., Morgan, M. with Ranchhod, A. (2009) *Marketing in Travel and Tourism*. Oxford: Butterworth-Heinemann

Mihalič, T. (2002) 'Tourism and economic development issues', in R. Sharpley and D. Tefler (eds), *Tourism and Development: Concepts and Issues*. Bristol: Channel View Publications

Miles, S.J. and Mangold, G. (2004) 'A conceptualisation of the employee branding process', *Journal of Relationship Marketing* 3(2/3): 65–87

Miles, S.J. and Mangold, G. (2005) 'Positioning South West Airlines through employee branding', *Business Horizons* 48: 535–545

Millett, S. (2003) 'The future of scenarios: challenges and opportunities', in R. Randall (ed.), *Integrate Scenario Learning with Decision Making*. Bradford: Emerald Group

Mills, P.K. and Margulies, N. (1980) 'Toward a core typology of service organisations', *Academy of Management Review* 5 (2): 255–265

Milner, L., Collins, J., Tashibana, R. and Hiser, R. (2000) 'The Japanese vacation visitor to Alaska', *Journal of Travel and Tourism Marketing* 9(1–2): 43–56

Minnaert, L., Maitland, R. and Miller, G. (2009) 'Tourism and social policy: the value of social tourism', *Annals of Tourism Research* 36(2): 316–334

Minnaert, L., Quinn, B., Griffen, K. and Stacey, J. (2010) 'Social tourism for low-income groups: benefits in a UK and Irish context', in S. Cole and N. Morgan (eds), *Tourism and Inequality*. Wallingford: CABI

Mintel (2005a) *World's Leading Outbound Markets*. London: Mintel

Mintel (2005b) 'The Hotel Industry' *Travel and Tourism Intelligence*. June

Mintel (2006) *Holidays: The Impacts of Terrorism and Natural Disasters*. London: Mintel

Mintel (2007) 'Saudi Arabia', *Travel and Tourism*, November

Mintel (2008) 'India', *Travel and Tourism*, February

Miossec, J.M. (1977) 'Un modele de l'espace touristique', *L'Espace Geographique* 6 (1): 41–48

Mook, D. (1996) *Motivation: The Organization of Action*, 2nd edn. New York: W.W. Norton & Company

Moscardo, G. and Ballantyne, R. (2008) 'Interpretation and attractions', in A. Fyall, B. Garrod, A. Leask and S. Wanhill (eds), *Managing Visitor Attractions: New Directions*. Oxford: Butterworth-Heinemann

Moutinho, L. (1987) 'Consumer behaviour in tourism', *European Journal of Marketing* 21(10): 3–44.

Mowforth, M. and Munt, I. (2003) *Tourism and Sustainability: Development and New Tourism in the Third World*. Oxford: Routledge

Mowforth, M. and Munt, I. (2008) *Tourism and Sustainability: Development, Globalisation and New Tourism in the Third World*. Abingdon: Routledge

Munier, N. (2005) *Introduction to Sustainability: Road to a Better Future*. Dordrecht: Springer

National Statistics (2006) *Travel Trends: A Report on the 2005 International Passenger Survey*. London: Office for National Statistics

Noronha, R. (1976) *Review of the Sociological Literature on Tourism*. New York: World Bank

Noronha, R. (1977) *Social and Cultural Dimensions of Tourism: A Review of the Literature in English*. Washington, DC: World Bank

Nyiri, P. (2006) *Scenic Spots: Chinese Tourism, the State, and Cultural Authority*. Seattle: University of Washington Press

O'Connor, J. (2000) 'The big squeeze: tourism concern', *Focus* 36: 4–5.

OECD (2002) *National Tourism Policy Review of Japan*. Paris: OECD

OECD (2008a) *Measuring the Role of Tourism in OECD economies: The OECD Manual on Tourism Satellite Accounts and Employment*. Paris: OECD

OECD (2008b) *Tourism in OECD Countries 2008: Trends and Policies*. Paris: OECD

Office for National Statistics (ONS) (2010) *Travel Trends*. http://www.statistics.gov.uk/downloads/theme_transport/travel-trends-2010.pdf

Ogilvie, F.W. (1933) *The Tourism Movement*. London: Staples Press

Orams, M. (2002) 'Feeding wildlife as a tourism attraction: a review of issues and impacts', *Tourism Management* 23: 281–293

Oxfam (2004) 'Growth with equity is good for the poor', in F. Lechner and J. Boli (eds), *The Globalisation Reader*. Malden: Blackwell

Page, S. and Getz, D. (1997) *The Business of Rural Tourism: International Perspectives*. London: International Thomson Business Press

Page, S. and Hall, C. (2003) *Managing Urban Tourism*. Harlow: Prentice-Hall

Page, S.J. (2005) *Transport and Tourism: Global Perspectives*. Harlow: Pearson

Page, S.J. and Connell J. (2006) *Tourism: A Modern Synthesis*. London: Thomson

Parrinello, G. (1993) 'Motivation and anticipation in post-industrial tourism', *Annals of Tourism Research* 20: 232–248

Pearce, D. (1978) 'Tourist development: two processes' *Travel Research Journal*, 43–51

Pearce, D. (1989) *Tourist Development*. Harlow: Longman

Pearce, D.G. and Butler, R.W. (eds) (1999) *Contemporary Issues in Tourism Development*. London: Routledge

Pearce, P. (1997) 'Towards the better management of tourist queues', in S. Medlik (ed.), *Managing Tourism*. Oxford: Butterworth-Heinemann

Pearce, P. (2005) *Tourist Behaviour: Themes and Conceptual Schemes*. Bristol: Channel View Publications

Pearce, P. and Lee, U. (2005) 'Developing the travel career approach to tourist motivation', *Journal of Travel Research* 43: 226–237

Pearson, M.N. (1996) *Pilgrimage to Mecca: The Indian Experience 1500–1800*. New Jersey: Marcus Wiener Publishers

Pender, L. (2001) *Travel Trade and Transport: An Introduction*. London: Continuum

People 1st (2009) *Industry Profile*. www.people1st.co.uk

People 1st (2010) *Skills Priority Paper for the Hospitality, Leisure, Travel and Tourism Sector, 2010*, 22 December

Perko, J. and Idaković, M. (2008) *Rise and Fall of Croatian Tourism and the Effects of the War of the 90s*. (Statistical Yearbook of the Republic of Croatia). Zagreb: Croatian Bureau of Statistics

Phuket Tourism (2010) *Phuket, Pangnga, Krabi Tourism Club Welcome to Greater Phuket, Thailand*. http://www.phukettourism.org/about/index.html

Pike, S. (2008) *Destination Marketing: An Integrated Marketing Communications Approach*. Oxford: Butterworth-Heinemann

Pimlott, J.A.R. (1947) *The Englishman's Holiday*. London: Faber

Piozzi, H. (1786) *Anecdotes of the late Samuel Johnson*. http://books.google.com/books?id=tcIIAAAAQAAJ&printsec=frontcover&source=gbs_ge_summary_r&cad=0#v=onepage&q&f=false

Piznam, A. and Mansfield, Y. (1999) *Consumer Behaviour in Travel and Tourism*. Philadelphia: Haworth Press

PKF Consulting (2011) *London Hotel Performance 2007–2009*. http://www.pkf.co.uk/pkf/publications/hotel_britain_2011&goto=4

Plog, S.C. (1972) 'Why Destination Areas Rise and Fall in Popularity'. Paper presented at the Southern California Chapter of the Travel Research Bureau, 10 October

Plog, S.C. (1974) "Why destination areas rise and fall in popularity', *Cornell Hotel and Restaurant Administration Quarterly* 14 (4): 55–58

Plog, S.C. (1991) *Leisure Travel: Making it a Growth Market … Again!* New York: John Wiley & Sons

Plog, S.C. (2004) *Leisure Travel: A Marketing Handbook.* Upper Saddle River, NJ: Pearson Education

Poon, A. (1993) *Tourism, Technology and Competitive Strategies.* Wallingford: CABI

Povey, G. and Oriade, A. (2009) 'Career development skills and strategies in the travel industry', in P. Robinson (ed.), *Operations Management in the Travel Industry.* Wallingford: CABI

Powder Blue Ltd (2010) *About the Area.* http://www.laplagnet.com/about-the-area/la-plagne-and-paradiski.htm

Prideaux, B. (2000) 'The resort development spectrum: a new approach to modelling resort development', *Tourism Management* 21: 225–240

Pritchard, A., Morgan, N., Sedgly, D. and Jenkins, A. (1998) 'Reaching out to the gay tourist: opportunities and threats in an emerging market segment', *Tourism Management* 19(3): 273–282

Prospects (2011) *Tourism Overview.* http://www.prospects.ac.uk/industries_tourism_overview.htmerview

Proust, M. (1923) *La Prisonnière.* Paris: Grasset

Prytherch, D. and Huntoon, L. (2005) 'Entrepreneurial regionalist planning in a rescaled Spain: the cases of Bilboa and Valencia', *GeoJournal*, 62: 41–50

Ralston, B. and Wilson, I. (2006) *The Scenario-Planning Handbook.* Mason: Thomson/South-Western

Reily Collins, V. (2004a) *Working in Tourism: the UK, Europe and Beyond for Seasonal and Permanent Staff.* Oxford: Vacation Work Publications

Reily Collins, V. (2004b) *Careers and Jobs in Travel and Tourism.* London: Kogan Page.

Reisinger, Y. (2009), *International Tourism: Cultures and Behaviour.* Oxford: Butterworth-Heinemann

Renshaw, M.B. (1992) *The Travel Agent.* Sunderland: Business Education Publisher

Rhoades, D. (2003) *Evolution of International Aviation: Phoenix Rising.* Hampshire: Ashgate

Richards, D. and Smith M. (2002) *Governance and Public Policy in the UK.* Oxford: Oxford University Press

Richards G. (1991) *The UK LA Tourism Survey 1991.* London: Center for Leisure and Tourism Studies; and Plymouth: British Association of Tourism Officers

Richards, G. (ed.) (2001) *Cultural Attractions and European Tourism.* Wallingford: CABI

Richardson, J. and Fluker M. (2004) *Understanding and Managing Tourism.* Frenchs Forest: Pearson Education Australia

Riley, M. (1996) *Human Resource Management in the Hospitality and Tourism Industry.* Oxford: Butterworth-Heineman

Ringland, F. (2002) *Scenarios in Business.* Chichester: John Wiley & Sons

Ritchie, J.R.B. and Crouch, G. (2003) *The Competitive Destination: A Sustainable Tourism Perspective.* Wallingford: CABI

Roberts, K. (1999) *Leisure in Contemporary Society.* Wallingford: CABI

Robinson, P. (ed) (2009) *Operations Management in the Travel Industry.* Wallingford: CABI

Robinson, P., Wales, D. and Dickson, G. (2010) *Events Management.* Wallingford: CABI

Rogers, C. (1990) 'Responses of coral reefs and reef organisms to sedimentation', *Marine Ecology Progress Series*, 62: 185–202

Rogers, P., Jalal, K. and Boyd, J. (2008) *An Introduction to Sustainable Development.* London: Earthscan

Rosenbaum, M. and Wong, I. (2008) 'When tourists desire an artificial culture: The Bali Syndrome in Hawaii', in A. Woodside and D. Martin (eds.), *Tourism Management.* Wallingford: CABI

Royal Borough of Windsor and Maidenhead (2008) *Our Vision for 2012 and Beyond.* http://www.windsor.gov.uk/ebrochure/

Ryan, C. (ed.) (1997) *The Tourist Experience: A New Introduction.* London: Cassell

Ryan, C. (2003) *Recreational Tourism: Demand and Impacts.* Bristol: Channel View

Schoemaker, P. (1995) 'Scenario planning: a tool for strategic thinking', *Sloan Management Review* 36(2): 25–40

Science Museum (2004) *Crystal Palace and the Great Exhibition.* http://www.makingthemodernworld.org

SDG (2009) *Potential for Modal Shift from Air to Rail for UK Aviation*, September, Steer, Davies, Geave for Committee on Climate Change. www.ccc.org.uk

Selin, S. (1999) 'Developing a typology of sustainable tourism partnerships', *Journal of Sustainable Tourism*, 7(3 and 4): 260–273

Sen, A. (2004) 'How to judge globalism', in F. Lechner and J. Boli (eds), *The Globalisation Reader.* Malden: Blackwell

Shackley, M. (1998) *Visitor Management: Case Studies from World Heritage Sites.* Oxford: Butterworth-Heinemann

Sharpley, R. and Sharpley, J. (1997) *Rural Tourism: An Introduction.* London: International Thomson Business Press

Sharpley, R. and Sundaram, P. (2005) 'Tourism, a sacred journey? The case of Ashram tourism, India', *International Journal of Tourism Research*, 7: 161–171

Sharpley, R. and Telfer, D. (eds) (2002) *Tourism and Development: Concepts and Issues.* Bristol: Channel View Publications

Shaw, S. (2007) *Airline Marketing and Management.* Hampshire: Ashgate Publishing

Sheldon, J. (1997) *Tourism Information Technology.* Wallingford: CABI

Shostack, G.L. (1977) 'Breaking free from product marketing', *Journal of Marketing* 41 (April): 73–80

Shostack, G.L. (1987) 'Service positioning through structural change', *Journal of Marketing* 51 (1): 34–43

Shoval, N. and Isaacson, M. (2010) *Tourist Mobility and Advanced Tracking Technologies.* London: Routledge

Smith, M. (2007) *Tourism, Culture and Regeneration.* Wallingford: CABI

Smith, V.L. (1977) *Hosts and Guests: The Anthropology of Tourism.* Philadelphia: University of Pennsylvania Press

Smith Travel Research (2011) *Glossary: A Guide to our Terminology.* http://www.strglobal.com/Resources/Glossary.aspx

Sodhi, J. (1999) *A Study of Bundi School of Painting (from the Collection of the National Museum, New Delhi).* New Delhi: Abhinav Publications

South African Tourism (2011) *Highlights of Tourism's Performance in 2010.* www.southafrica.net/research

Stansfield, C.A. (1978) 'Atlantic City and the resort cycle: background to the legalisation of gambling', *Annals of Tourism Research* 5 (2): 238–251

Stansfeld, S. and Matheson, M. (2003) 'Noise pollution: non-auditory effects on health', *British Medical Bulletin* 68(1): 243–257

Star Alliance (2011) *About.* http://www.staralliance.com/en/about/

Starkie, D. (2008) *Aviation Markets: Studies in Competition and Regulatory Reform.* Hampshire: Ashgate Publishing

Statistics Canada (2008) *Government Revenue Attributable to Tourism, 2007*. Ottawa: Statistics

Stevenson, N. (2009) 'The ebbs and flows of tourism policy making', in R. Thomas (ed.), *Managing Regional Tourism: A Case Study of Yorkshire, England*. Ilkley: Great Northern Press

Stevenson, N. and Lovatt, S. (2001) *The Role of English Local Authorities in Tourism Survey 2000*, University of Westminster Research Report

Stoker, G. (2004) *Transforming Local Governance: From Thatcherism to New Labour*. London and New York: Palgrave Macmillan

Stoker, G. and Wilson, D. (2004) *British Local Government into the 21st Century*. London and New York: Palgrave Macmillan

Swarbrooke, J. (1999) *Sustainable Tourism Management*. Wallingford: CABI

Swarbrooke, J. and Horner, S. (2001) *Business Travel and Tourism*. Oxford: Butterworth-Heinemann

Swarbrooke, J. and Horner, S. (2007) *Consumer Behaviour in Tourism*. Burlington: Butterworth-Heinemann

Swinglehurst, E. (1974) *The Romantic Journey: The Story of Thomas Cook and Victorian Travel*. London: Pica

Terry, F. (ed.) (2004) *Turning the Corner? A Reader in Contemporary Transport Policy*. Oxford: Blackwell

Tesone, D. (ed.) (2008) *Handbook of Hospitality Human Resources Management*. Oxford: Butterworth-Heinemann

Theobald, W.F. (ed.) (2005a) *Global Tourism*, 3rd edn. Burlington, MA: Elsevier-Science

Theobald, W.F. (2005b) 'The meaning, scope and measurement of travel and tourism', in W.F. Theobald (ed.), *Global Tourism*, 3rd edn. Burlington, MA: Elsevier-Science. pp. 3–24

Thomas Cook Group PLC (2008) *Thomas Cook History*. http://www.thomascook.com/about-us/Thomas-cook-history

Thomas Cook Group PLC (2009) *Business Segments and Brands* http://www.thomascookgroup.com/segments

Thomas Cook Group PLC (2011) *Annual Reports and Accounts 2010*. http://www.thomascookgroup.com

Thomson Holidays (2010) *Thomson Affiliate Programme* http://www.thomson.co.uk/affiliates.html

Thurot, J.M. (1973) *Le Tourisme Tropicale Balneaire: Le modele Caraibe et ses Extensions*. Thesis, Centre d'Etudes du Tourisme, Aix-en-Provence

Times Online (2007) 'Briton challenges Kenya tourism scam', 21 June. http://www.timesonline.co.uk/tol/travel/news/article1962885.ece

Tobgay, S. (2008) 'Overview of tourism in Bhutan and how it fits into the general development plans of Bhutan', *Insight: Notes from the Field* 3. www.recoftc.org

Tourism Council of Bhutan (2008) *Bhutan Tourism Monitor, Annual Report 2008*. Thimpu: Tourism Council of Bhutan

Tourism Flanders (2008) *Holidays Are For Everyone: Research into the Effects and the Importance of Holidays for People living in Poverty*. Brussels: Tourism Flanders

Tourism Queensland (2009) 'Best job in the world'. www.islandreefjob.com

Tourism Strategy Group New Zealand (2010), New Zealand Tourism Forecasting Methodology 2010-2016, Available online: http://www.tourismresearch.govt.nz/Documents/Forecasts%20Summary/Forecasts2010-2016/NZ%20Tourism%20Forecasting%20Methodology%202010.pdf

Tourism Thailand (2010) *Phuket* http://www.tourismthailand.org/uk/where-to-go/city-guide/destination/phuket/

Travel Compensation Fund (2010) *Our role* http://www.tcf.org.au/Our_Role.asp?Page=Our_Role

Travel Foundation (2007) *Maasai Village Tours.* http://www.thetravelfoundation.org.uk/index.php?id=112

Travel Trade Gazette (2008) 'XL collapse hits 285,000 customers', 12 September

Travel Weekly (2008) 'XL Failure: the outlook for the travel industry', 18 September

Tribal Voice Communications (2010) *Developing and Marketing a Sustainable Maasai Village Tourism Experience in Kenya.* http://www.tribal-voice.co.uk/TVC2/PDFS/TVC%20Maasai_Project_Final_Report_1.pdf

Tribe, J. (2005) *The Economics of Leisure, Recreation and Tourism.* Oxford: Elsevier

Tripadvisor (2011) *About TripAdvisor Media Group.* http://www.tripadvisor.co.uk/pages/about_us.html

Trofimyuk, N.A. (1977) 'Social insurance and the trade unions in the USSR', *International Social Security Review*, 30(1): 52–58

TUI Travel PLC (2011) *Fact Sheet.* http://www.tuitravelplc.com/tui/uploads/dlibrary/documents/TUITravelPLC_FactSheet_February2011.pdf

Twain, M. (1986 [1869]) *The Innocents Abroad.* New York: Hippocrene Books

Twigg-Flessner, C. (2003) *Consumer Product Guarantees.* Aldershot: Ashgate Publishing

Twitter (2011) *Twitter is the Best Way to Discover What's New in Your World.* http://twitter.com/about

UFI (2008) *Report on UFI Member Exhibitions and Venue Activity.* www.ufi.org

UIC (Union of International Railways) (2009) *Railways and the Environment: Building on the Railways' Environmental Strengths*, January, Community of European Railways and Infrastructure Companies, Brussels

UN (2010) *International Recommendations for Tourism Statistics 2010*, Department of Economic and Social Affairs Statistics Division Studies in Methods, Series M No 83/Rev 1, New York

UNEP (2008) *Climate Change and Tourism: Responding to Global Challenges.* Paris: UNEP

Uniglobe (2011) *About Uniglobe Travel.* http://www.uniglobetravel.com/site/viewhome.asp?aid=7530&sit=211&vty=ARTICLE&tid=8294&sessionid=

United Nations (1983) *Report of the World Commission on Environment and Development: Our Common Future. Transmitted to the General Assembly as an Annex to document A/42/427 – Development and International Co-operation: Environment.* Oxford: Oxford University Press

United Nations (1994) *Recommendations on Tourism Statistics,* Department for Economic and Social Information and Policy Analysis, Statistical Division, Series M, No 83, United Nations, New York, p. 77

United Nations (2010) *International Recommendations for Tourism Statistics 2010 (IRTS)* Department of Economic and Social Affairs Statistics Division. Studies in Methods Series M, No 83/Rev 1, New York

UNWTO (2008) *Statutes of the World Tourism Organisation.* Madrid: UNWTO

UNWTO (2010a) *Why Tourism: Tourism an Economic and Social Phenomenon.* http://unwto.org/en/about/tourism

UNWTO (2010b) *UNWTO Tourism: Highlights Edition 2010.* Madrid: UNWTO

UNWTO (2010c) http://www.unwto.org/statistics/bali/tsa_data.pdf.

Urry, J. (2002) *The Tourist Gaze.* London: Sage

USVIBER (2010) *USVI Occupancy rates 2007, 2008, 2009 YTD.* http://www.usviber.org/H09.pdf

USTOA (2010) *Consumer Assistance.* http://www.ustoa.com/2009/ConsumerAssistance.cfm

Uthoff, D. (1997) 'Out of the tin crisis into the tourism boom: the transition of the tropical island of Phuket by international tourism', *Applied Geography and Development*

Vallen, J.J. and Levinson, C. (1989) 'The new Soviet tourism', *Cornell Hotel and Restaurant Quarterly*, 29(4): 72–79

Vancouver Convention Centre (2011) *About Us*. http://www.vancouverconventioncentre.com/about-us/fast-facts/

Vanhove, N. (2005) *The Economics of Tourism Destinations*. Oxford: Elsevier

Virgin Atlantic (2011) *Codeshare Flights*. http://www.virgin-atlantic.com/en/gb/customer-relations/customer_charter/codeshareflights.jsp

VisitBritain (2006a) 'Issue of the month – tourism satellite accounts', *Foresight*, January

VisitBritain (2006b) 'Issue of the month – Britian's international tourism balance of payments deficit', *Foresight*, September

VisitBritain (2010a) *The UK Tourist – Statistics 2009*.

VisitBritain (2010b) *The Economic Contribution of the Visitor Economy – UK and the Nations*, June

VisitBritain (2010c) *China Market and Trade Profile: Updated 2010*. http://www.visitbritain.org

Visit London (2010) *Event Organisers*. http://business.visitlondon.com/choose_london/entertainment

Wahab, S. and Cooper, C. (2001) *Tourism in the Age of Globalisation*. London: Routledge

Waitt, G. and Markwell, K. (2006) *Gay Tourism: Culture and Context*. Binghampton: The Haworth Hospitality Press

Wall, G. and Mathieson, A. (2006) *Tourism: Change, Impacts and Opportunities*. Harlow: Pearson Education

Wanhill, S. (2008) 'Interpreting the development of the visitor attraction product', in A. Fyall, B. Garrod, A. Leask and S. Wanhill (eds), *Managing Visitor Attractions: New Directions*. Oxford: Butterworth-Heinemann. pp. 16–37

Weaver, D. (2006) *Sustainable Tourism*. Oxford: Elsevier Butterworth-Heinemann

Weiss, T. (2004) 'Tourism in America before World War II', *Journal of Economic History* 64(2): 289–327

Wheeller, B. (1991) 'Tourism's troubled times: responsible tourism is not the answer', *Tourism Management* 12(2): 91–96

Williams, A. and Zelinsky, W. (1970) 'On some patterns in international tourist flows', *Economic Geography* 46 (4): 549–567

Williams, C. and Buswell, J. (2003) *Service Quality in Leisure and Tourism*. Wallingford: CABI

Witt, S. and Witt, C. (1992) *Modelling and Forecasting Demand in Tourism*. London: Academic Press.

Witt, S. and Witt, C. (1995) 'Forecasting tourism demand: a review of empirical research', *International Journal of Forecasting* 11: 447–475

Wolfe, R.I. (1952) 'Wasaga Beach – the divorce from the geographic environment', *The Canadian Geographer* 2: 57–66

World Tourism Organisation (1991) *International Conference on Travel and Tourism Statistics: Ottawa (Canada), 24–28 June 1991 Resolutions*. Madrid: World Tourism Organisation, p. 4

World Tourism Organisation (1996) *International Tourism Overview*. Madrid: UNWTO

World Travel and Tourism Council (2010) *Welcome to WTTC*. http://www.wttc.org

Worthington, I. and Britton, C. (2006) *The Business Environment*. Harlow: Pearson Education Limited

Wuest, B. (2001) 'Service quality and dimensions pertinent to tourism, hospitality and leisure services', in J. Kandampully, C. Mok and B. Sparks (eds), *Service Quality Management in Hospitality, Tourism and Leisure*. Binhampton: Hayworth Hospitality Press

Wunder, S. (1999) *Promoting Forest Conservation through Ecotourism Income? A Case Study from the Ecuadorian Amazon Region*. CIFOR Occasional Paper, 21, Centre for International Forestry Research, Jakarta

Yale, P. (1995) *The Business of Tour Operations*. Harlow: Longman

Yokeno, N. (1968) 'La localisation de l'industrie touristique – application de l'analyse de Thunen-Weber', *Les cahiers du Tourisme Serie C,* No 9, Aix en Provence

Young, W.B. and Montgomery, R.J. (1998) 'Crisis management and its impact on destination marketing: a guide for convention and visitors bureaus' *Journal of Convention and Exhibition Management*, 1: 3–18

YouTube (2011) *Statistics*. http://www.youtube.com/t/press_statistics

Zeithaml, V.A. (1981) 'How consumer evaluation processes differ between goods and services', *Marketing of Services* (J. Donnelly and W.R. George eds). Chicago: American Marketing Association

Zeithaml, V.A., Bitner, M. and Gremler, D. (2006) *Services Marketing: Integrating Customer Focus across the Firm*. New York: McGraw-Hill International

Zemke, R. (1992) 'Supporting service recovery: attributes for excelling at solving customers' problems', in Sheuing E.E., Gummesson, E. and Little, C.H. (eds), *Selected Papers from the Second Quality in Services (QUIS 2) Conference*. New York: St John's University and ISQA, International Service Quality Association, pp. 41–46

Zhang, G. (2003) 'China's tourism since 1978: policies, experiences and lessons learned', in Lew, A. Yu, I. Ap, J. and Zhang, G. (eds), *Tourism in China* Binghampton, New York: Haworth Hospitality Press, pp. 13–34

Zhang, H.Q. and Morrison, A. (2007) 'How can the small to medium sized travel agents stay competitive in China's travel service sector?', *International Journal of Contemporary Hospitality Management* 19(4): 275–285

Index